THE ILLUSTRATED ENCYCLOPEDIA OF KNIVES DAGGERS & BAYONETS

THE ILLUSTRATED ENCYCLOPEDIA OF

KNIVES DAGGERS & BAYONETS

AN AUTHORITATIVE HISTORY AND VISUAL DIRECTORY OF SHARP-EDGED WEAPONS AND BLADES FROM AROUND THE WORLD, WITH MORE THAN 700 OUTSTANDING PHOTOGRAPHS

DR TOBIAS CAPWELL

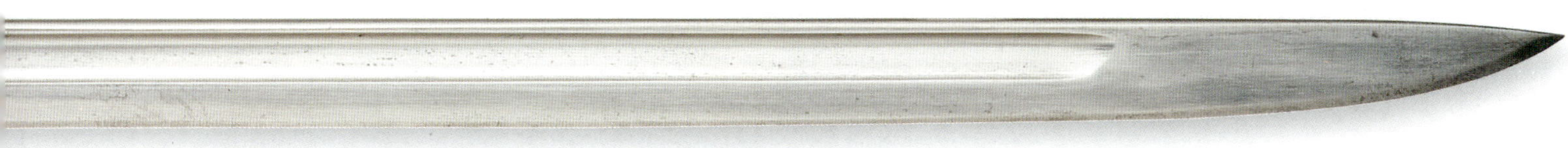

HH

This is a special edition produced for
66 Books Ltd,
Unit 2, Eastman Way,
Hemel Hempstead, HP2 7DU.

Publisher: Joanna Lorenz
Editorial Director: Helen Sudell
Project Editors: Sarah Doughty and Hazel Songhurst
Assistant Editor: Cynthia McCollum
Contributing authors: Jonathan Barrett, Peter Smithurst, Frederick Stephens
Photography: Gary Ombler (Armouries) and David Cummings (Berman)
Designer: Alistair Plumb
Art Director: Lisa McCormick
Production Controller: Ben Worley

With special thanks to the Royal Armouries, Leeds in England and the Berman Museum of World History, Alabama in the United States. Also grateful thanks for the assistance of Hermann Historica Auctioneers, Munich and Wallis & Wallis auctioneers, Lewes, England.

A CIP catalogue record for this book is available from the British Library.

PUBLISHER'S NOTE

Although the information in this reference book is believed to be accurate and true at the time of going to press, neither the authors nor the publisher can accept any legal responsibility or liability for any errors or omissions that may have been made.

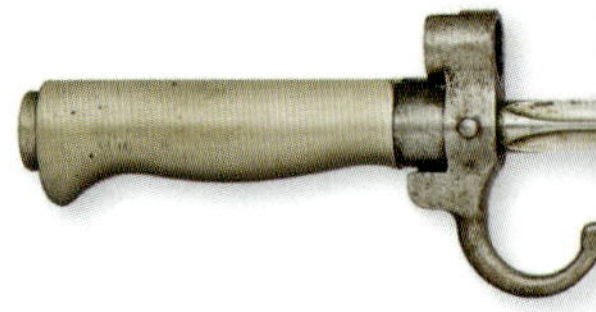

Contents

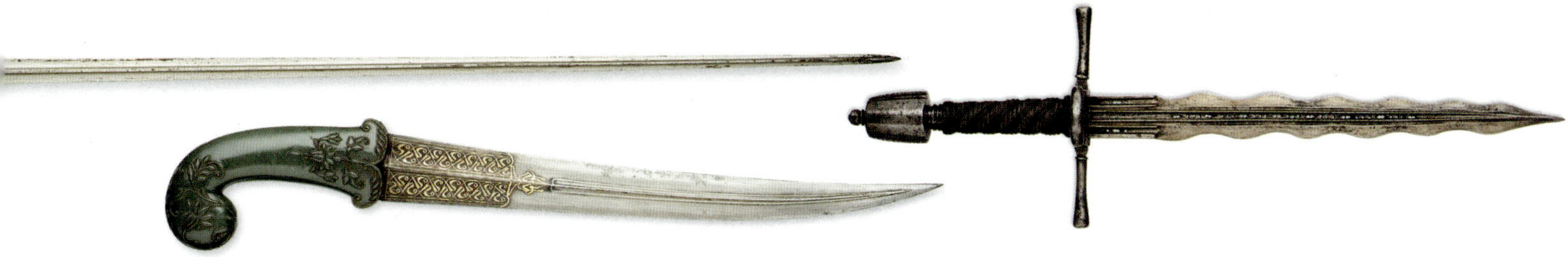

Introduction

From the sharp flints with which primitive humans defended themselves to the carbon-steel bayonets carried by modern soldiers, the fighting knife's history is a complex tale of technical ingenuity, artistic virtuosity and brutal violence. Like its larger cousin the sword, this lethal edged weapon expressed the wealth and taste of its owner. But it was also a vital last resort – easy to carry, quick to draw and always at the fighting man's side.

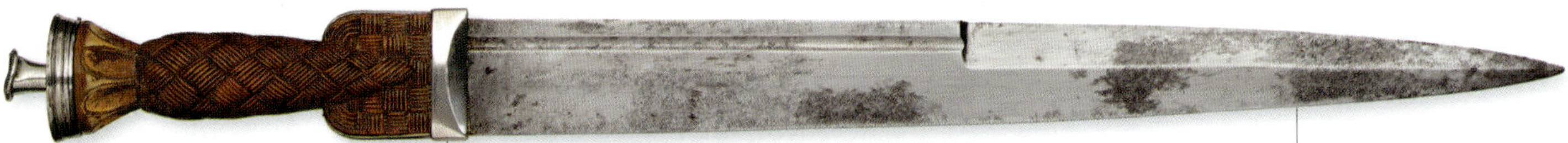

ABOVE Highland dress dirk, Scottish, *c.*1868. The word "dirk" is usually applied to the long fighting knife of the Scottish Highlanders – of which this is a late example – and to certain classes of military dress dagger.

Early daggers and fighting knives

Our story begins well over a million years ago. The earliest sharpened tools were fashioned by knapping flints into sharp shapes. Around 8,000 years ago, copper was first worked in Asia. Four millennia later, alloyed metals were developed. Bronze remained the mainstay of technology until iron became available 2,000 years later. Iron was being produced in large quantities by Roman times, when soldiers were armed with the feared pugio dagger and gladius sword. Just as iconic was the single-edged scramasax of central European peoples.

Medieval and Renaissance daggers

The daggers of the first medieval knights were probably similar to small Viking and Saxon handsaxes. Like the knight's sword, these daggers acquired cruciform hilts and often double-edged blades. As armour became more effective, more specialized medieval daggers evolved to defeat it. New hilt types gave a better grip, while blades were narrowed into sharp triangular or square-sectioned spikes.

From before the 11th until after the 16th century, the dagger was an essential battlefield weapon. It was also carried in civilian life for self-defence because, until the 16th century, swords were not worn with everyday dress. When the long, heavy-bladed civilian

RIGHT King Henry VIII (1491–1547) is portrayed in this portrait by Holbein wearing a gilded dagger as part of his courtly dress. The dagger was an essential fashion accessory for medieval and Renaissance men.

RIGHT Soldiers of the Brazilian army, 1830s. Socket bayonets such as the one carried here quickly found their way into all modern armies throughout the world following their introduction in the 18th century.

rapier came into fashion, the dagger became its parrying aid. But by the early 1600s sword blades were lighter and could be used rapidly to attack and defend. The parrying dagger was discarded, and daggers declined as fashion accessories. Characteristic forms were worn only in certain rural areas, like the long dirks in the Scottish Highlands and the western Mediterranean.

Bayonets from the 17th to the 21st century

Just as the dagger was falling out of favour, it found a new role: the dagger became the bayonet.

The earliest Bayonne daggers were probably not bayonets at all but rather ordinary daggers made in southwestern France. In order to transform a musket into a spear for close-quarters combat, soldiers started jamming daggers into the muzzles of weapons. The plug bayonet was born – a short-lived design, since it was impossible to fire the weapon with the bayonet in place. This was replaced by the socket bayonet, which became the standard issue.

Mechanized warfare in the 19th century meant that fighting forces became more diversified. One consequence was more varieties of bayonet, including unwieldy sword bayonets that, though impractical, remained in use through the 1800s. By the 20th century bayonets had begun to revert to their dagger-like origins; most soldiers now carry some form of knife bayonet, which is both an all-purpose tool and a weapon.

Daggers in Asia and Africa

In Africa fighting knives and daggers assumed exotic, uniquely creative forms. Although important as weapons, many were also status symbols and forms of currency. Turning east, we encounter the dagger culture of the Middle East, where the Arab jambiya remains an essential part of formal male dress, and features in celebrations. We continue into Persia, which produced very skilled bladesmiths, masters of the art of "watered" or wootz steel. Fine Persian daggers are often superlative jewellery objects, rivalled only by the work of the Mughals from northern India.

In the Far East, the Japanese produced the fabulous tanto and aikuchi, smaller companions of the fabled katana sword of the samurai. Finally, our journey ends in the South Pacific with the Indonesian kris, prized by European collectors since the 17th century, purported to have magical powers, and still felt to embody the spirit of the region.

The directory

The directory follows the evolution of these small but deadly weapons from ancient beginnings as sharpened rocks to the very latest blades of hardened steel. The directory is intended as a reasonably complete visual catalogue of all edged weapons shorter than a sword, although this is sometimes a difficult distinction to make. Examples are discussed in detail with unusual features highlighted, and all are organized by origin, date and style.

BELOW Ottoman Turkish knife, 17th century. The finest Persian and Turkish daggers were usually forged of watered steel – giving strength and elasticity to the blade – and fitted with jade, ivory or crystal hilts.

This section traces the fascinating history of the fighting blade through to the 21st century.

A history of knives, daggers and bayonets

From the earliest sharpened flints of prehistory to the survival knives and hardened steel bayonets of modern combat, these edged weapons have helped to shape human history. Used by ancient warriors, medieval knights and soldiers of the American Civil War and the two World Wars, they are symbols of power, survival and progress.

TOP British Elcho sword bayonet, *c.*1872.

MIDDLE TOP American push dagger, *c.*1870.

MIDDLE BOTTOM Balkan Ottoman bichaq, mid-19th century.

BOTTOM Indian chilanum dagger, late 18th century.

The earliest knives

The first weapons invented by humans were made out of the materials that they could pick up off the ground or extract from the bodies of the animals they killed for food. They shaped and sharpened wood, horn and bone for many different uses. They could throw rocks and use them to deal lethal blows. The right sorts of rocks could also be fashioned into extremely sharp cutting tools.

LEFT This late Neolithic flint knife (*c.*2000BC) was found in Jutland, Denmark. Flint flakes have been carefully and skilfully removed to form the sharp blade and tapered grip.

Compared with the most ancient edged implements, the fighting knife and dagger are fairly recent advances. The ancestors of modern humans first began to fashion sharpened objects out of stone about a million years ago. But these early cutting devices were made with a number of utilitarian purposes in mind. Perhaps they could have been used in a fight if the need arose, but there is no evidence to suggest that this was their primary function. Instead, these sharpened stones were mainly used for shaping wooden tools, butchering animals and scraping hides clean before making them into clothes.

The first weapons

The earliest stone tools were not very effective weapons because they were small and did not increase the reach of the user. Neither could they be used to stab, for most had no significant points. The hand axes in use up until around 35,000BC were roughly teardrop-shaped, with a rudimentary point, but these cannot be considered stabbing weapons. As weapons, these axes could have had no more specialist usefulness than any other naturally sharp rock.

For a hand weapon to be considered a fighting knife or dagger, it must increase or alter the user's reach to some advantageous extent, and it must provide the ability to stab. Cutting is in many cases another useful property, but it is secondary in the case of weapons under about 20cm (8in) in length. Stone is a very brittle and weighty material, and could not be used to create weapons with long cutting edges. A stone sword would have been excessively heavy and broken at the first blow. Nonetheless towards the end of the Middle Stone Age (*c.*50,000 years ago), early humans, aided by good stone-working techniques, were able to make short, sharply pointed stabbing knives.

BELOW The design of this Native American antler knife has changed little in 4000 years.

BOTTOM A Bronze Age knife, carved in bone, copies the form of copper knives of the time.

ABOVE This group of flint knives of the late Stone Age and Bronze Age shows a degree of variety but also key similarities. The blades must remain short and stout, or they would simply break.

Stone and metal weapons

The use of stone knives did not end suddenly with the discovery of metals around 3500BC. Indeed, most of the finest surviving stone knives and daggers were made as recently as 2000 years into the Bronze Age (*c.*3500–*c.*700BC). In some places, metal knives seem to have influenced the form of stone ones; for example, stone daggers found in Scandinavia dating from around 1600BC appear to be direct copies of their metal counterparts. This is probably because early metalworking was well under way around the Mediterranean long before it appeared in northern Europe. Metal daggers from the south may have found their way north, where their forms were copied using local materials. The height of this period of technological crossover, roughly 1800–1500BC, is often referred to as the "Dagger Period" because knives and daggers were clearly enormously popular during this time.

Flint knapping

The process by which a hard stone, such as flint, quartzite or obsidian (a vitreous acid volcanic rock) is reduced to a specific shape for use as a tool or weapon is called flint knapping. Along with the ability to make fire, flint knapping was one of the first great technological advances in human prehistory. The simplest knapping technique is called "direct percussion". The piece of stone is struck with another rock or bit of wood to break smaller pieces off and gradually bring it into the desired shape.

This technique worked well when making simple clubs and hand axes, but it was not precise enough to make something as delicate as a knife blade. In order to avoid breaking the emerging tool itself during the knapping process, early humans developed a more controlled technique called "pressure flaking". The pressure flaker would refine the rough form of the stone by applying careful pressure with a pointed piece of antler. This process could be used to chip tiny fragments of stone away, gradually bringing the object into whatever precise shape was desired. A well-made pressure-flaked knife is a thing of real beauty. The flaking scars are sometimes arranged with impressive forethought in flowing rows. In other cases the main body of the blade is ground and polished smooth, while the edges retain a contrasting fluted and serrated finish.

Stones suitable for knapping are found in a variety of colours in Europe and the Middle East, and it is clear that many of these appealed to Stone Age toolmakers. Flint occurs in many tints, ranging from a very light yellow through rich amber to dark brown and black. Quartzite appears in black tints, as well as in red, green and white.

RIGHT Striking the piece of flint would quickly break it. Instead, careful pressure is applied to remove one tiny fragment at a time.

The "Dagger Period" 1800–1500BC

Archaeological finds in Scandinavia have given us a good impression of how the best stone knives and daggers developed. The earliest examples from the Dagger Period have long, narrow blades and are roughly diamond-shaped in profile. One half of the diamond functioned as the grip or handle but was not as finely worked as the other end, the blade, which had precise pressure-flaked edges and a passable point.

ABOVE Found in Hindsgarl, Denmark, these flint daggers (*c.*1700BC) are typical of "Dagger Period" flint-work. The grips have imitation stitching to mimic the leather-bound handles of metal daggers of this period.

ABOVE This detail of a giant statue of a pharaoh, *c.*1260BC, at the Amun Temple in Luxor, Egypt, shows a decorated dagger thrust into a belt. The grip is formed by two sculpted heads depicting the sun-god Ra.

The handle end on later examples gradually loses its taper, becoming more straight-sided, while the cross-section is rounder for a more comfortable grip. Finally, the butt of the handle becomes flared to improve the grip even further. The fully-fledged dagger of this period, in addition to the well-formed grip and butt, generally displays a graceful, leaf-shaped blade that has been cunningly strengthened by broadening and thickening only where necessary.

Flint knives in ancient Egypt

The ancient Egyptians also continued to make flint knives well into the Bronze Age. They served as the Egyptian warrior's sidearms long before any form of sword was known, and they continued to be used into the New Kingdom Period (*c.*1567–*c.*1085BC), by which time metal daggers were well known.

The earliest Egyptian flint knives date from the Early Dynastic Period (*c.*3100–*c.*2780BC). These weapons are easily recognizable by their broad, curved blades. On some examples the flaking pattern has been left over the whole surface of the blade, while others have been polished smooth. Grips were made of wood, horn or bone, and glued firmly in place. On rich examples this handle was sometimes covered with gold foil or carved with battle scenes. Shorter versions, at less than 30cm (12in) in length, were probably serviceable as fighting weapons, but the longer ones, 38cm (15in) or even longer, would have been quite fragile and may only have been used for ritual purposes.

Most of the Later Dynastic (*c.*715–*c.*332 BC) and New Kingdom daggers were short, double-edged stabbing weapons, with simple hilts (handles), made of some organic material. New Kingdom daggers tend to be longer and narrower than older forms. Sometimes the grips also have a central rib or swelling.

Flint knives of pre-conquest America

The indigenous cultures of the Americas lived almost universally without metal tools and weapons until the first continuous contacts with Europeans in the 15th and 16th centuries AD. Before then, even in areas where the working of certain metals, primarily gold, was very advanced, tools and weapons remained entirely non-metallic. The ancient tribes inhabiting the present-day West Indies took advantage of the extremely hard woods found in the tropical lowlands to fashion clubs, swords and daggers, while obsidian was a common material used by the Aztecs of Mexico to fashion knives and daggers as well as the blades of their fierce-looking *macuauhuitl* sword-clubs. One chronicler of the Spanish Conquest of Mexico (1519–21) wrote that a native flint knife could cut "like a Toledo knife" – a reference to blades from the Spanish city, renowned for their high quality.

The end of the Stone Age

Stone was the best weapons material to which prehistoric humans had access. It was hard and dense, which meant that it could be given an extremely sharp edge. Even today, obsidian blades are used by optic surgeons because they are much sharper than any steel scalpels. But it was a very difficult material to work with and could only be made to assume a very restricted group of shapes. A stone blade, once broken, could never be repaired or recycled. These limitations led weapon makers to adopt a new material – metal.

ABOVE This striking flint knife blade is one of a number inlaid with stone of a contrasting colour. Found at Tenochtitlan in Mexico, the Aztec capital city, it dates from the Postclassic Period (*c.*AD1325–1521).

BELOW Ritual Egyptian knives of this type were the largest flint weapons ever made. This particular example, now missing its handle, dates from around 3000BC.

Copper, bronze and iron

The discovery of metalworking immeasurably improved the ability of early humans to construct edged weapons. Metal was flexible, much less brittle and more versatile than stone. It could be melted and cast into a huge variety of forms. When broken, it was possible to melt a metal weapon down and reform it. By the Bronze Age (*c.*3500–*c.*700BC), people were constructing more practical metallic fighting knives and daggers.

The first metal to be used for tools and weapons was copper. Small deposits of pure copper, which required no smelting (ore extraction) before working, were found in Mesopotamia, India, Egypt and North America. Copper weapons were being made in the Middle East as early as 6500BC, and in India by perhaps 6000BC. Pure copper weapons may have first been produced in North America by 5500BC, although the best evidence indicates a more recent date.

Between around 3000BC and 500BC, the "Old Copper Complex" people of the Great Lakes region of North America (Michigan and Wisconsin in the United States, and Ontario in Canada) were taking advantage of the pure copper nuggets found in that area to make knives and spearheads. These activities, along with later instances of copper working among native peoples along the northwest coast, remained the only examples of entirely indigenous metalwork practised by North American Indians until the arrival of Europeans in the 15th century AD.

The discovery of smelting

Naturally occurring pure metals were very scarce elsewhere and it was the invention of smelting that advanced the development of metalworking. The vast majority of the Earth's metals are contained within rock in the form of ore. Smelting is the process by which careful heating produces a chemical reaction that separates the metal from the surrounding materials. Once early humans had mastered this process, their access to metals increased beyond measure. As a result, the rapid evolution of metal-edged weapons began.

ABOVE This 19th-century illustration is copied from an ancient Egyptian bas-relief depicting a metalworker forging a spear. The knowledge of smelting led the Egyptians and other ancient peoples to discover bronze.

Weapons made from copper

Copper is a resilient but very soft metal. Those who made copper weapons had to develop blade shapes that were structurally suited to the material, otherwise

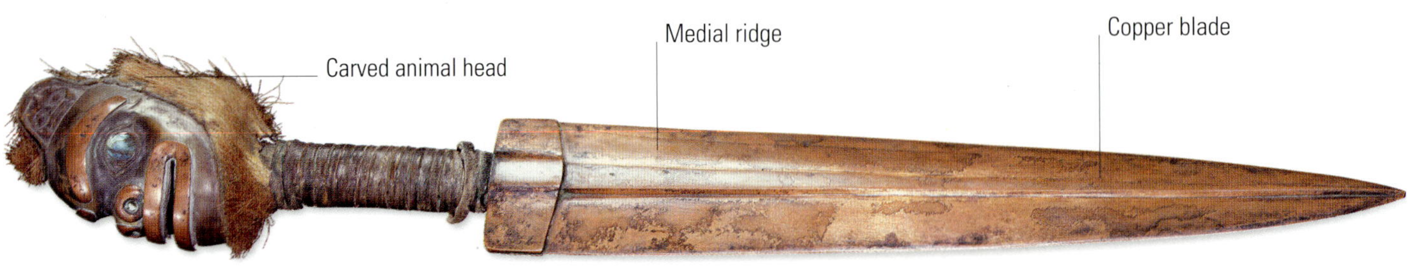

BELOW Certain American Indian tribes have produced copper weapons for thousands of years. This 19th-century dagger, made by the Tlingit of southeastern Alaska and western Canada, has a copper blade.

a weapon would simply bend, crumple or collapse when it struck a blow. Daggers were undoubtedly the earliest metal-edged weapons made for fighting, simply because the softness of the material meant that a copper weapon had to be short and very broad. It was also necessary for a copper blade to be quite thick to give it some degree of stiffness. However, an increase in thickness produced an exponential (rather than proportionate) increase in weight, therefore a longer weapon such as a sword was out of the question. The earliest copper daggers had short, stout blades with a triangular outline that to some extent compensated for the softness of the metal. They were either cast in a mould or cut out and hammered into shape.

Early copper daggers were generally composed of a blade and a separate hilt of some hard organic material. Many excavated Mesopotamian graves of the Early Dynastic Period (*c.*2900–2330BC) have been found to include copper daggers of this type. Hilts were usually riveted to the wide base of the blade, although some surviving examples show no signs of rivets and so were presumably glued in place. A better answer appeared in the form of the tang; the base of the blade was drawn out again into a short, narrow rod, which could then be inserted into the hilt section.

Another key development in the design of early edged weapons was the medial ridge, or rib, cast into both sides of a blade using a two-piece mould. With a thick central spine, the rest of a blade could be made thinner and lighter. Its length and width could be increased, producing a more effective stabbing weapon. Daggers with these stiff medial ridges proliferated throughout the Middle East. The medial ridge was a pivotal development in the evolution of blade forms and remained an essential design element from the Bronze Age to the present day.

ABOVE The form of the latest metal weapons was copied in other materials. This Persian dagger of 1300–1200BC is not bronze but carved wood. The thick medial ridge or spine is designed to stiffen the blade.

BELOW The copper blade of this well-used Bronze Age knife, found in the River Thames in London, has been sharpened many times, grinding it down until only a small stub remains. The grip is a reconstruction.

BELOW The usual form of bronze daggers was short and wide at the hilt to ensure strength. This example, dating from 2300–1800BC and found in Neuheiligen in Germany, also retains its metal hilt.

ABOVE An exceptional number of Early Bronze Age weapons have been found at the site of the ancient Persian city of Luristan. This group includes wide-bladed cutting knives and narrow stabbing daggers.

The introduction of bronze

Just as copper blades represented a great leap forward from the flint implements of prehistoric times, so too the discovery of bronze drove pure copper weapons into obsolescence. Bronze is an alloy, a mixture of two metals – copper and tin. A recipe for a good weapon was around nine parts bronze and one part tin, although exact proportions were at first hard to achieve. Bronze is harder than copper, resulting in stronger weapons that could take and hold a sharp edge better. Bronze blades could be made narrower and longer than copper ones.

Bronze flowed better than copper into moulds, which increased the possibilities for more elaborate and intricate designs. Hilts began to be cast in one piece with the blade, eliminating the weak point of a riveted joint between hilt and blade. Some of the earliest bronze daggers were made around 2500BC in the Sumerian city of Ur in Mesopotamia. These weapons have strong, ribbed blades and thick tangs. Early Bronze Age (*c.*3200–*c.*2800BC) daggers from Luristan (or Lorestan), an area in the west of modern Iran, were cast in one piece with recesses in the grip to take plates of wood or bone, the earliest known examples of grip "scales". These would later become some of the most common methods of grip construction in knife and dagger making throughout the world.

RIGHT This beautiful dagger hilt, made in Mycenae in around 1600BC, is decorated with inlaid lapis lazuli, crystal and gold. Two dragon heads form the guard.

Mycenaean bronze daggers

Knowledge of bronze and bronze working moved gradually west from the Middle East through the Mediterranean and north into Europe, and by around 1600BC most of the peoples populating central and northern Europe were familiar

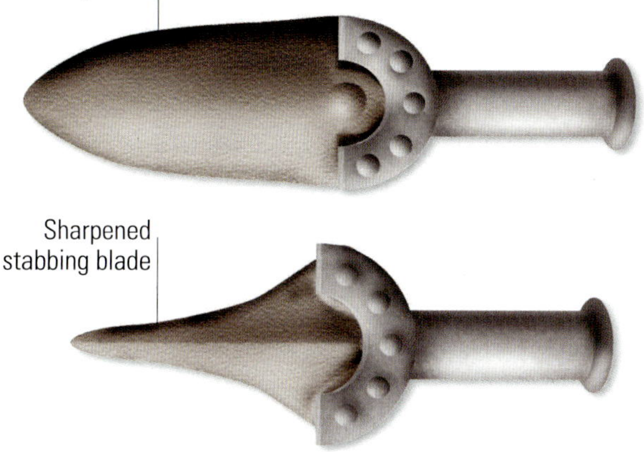

ABOVE A number of the surviving Mycenaean dagger blades carry superb inlaid decoration in gold, silver and niello (a black metal alloy). This blade features a lively hunting scene.

RIGHT After many sharpenings, what was once a wide-bladed, cutting knife could be transformed into a stout bronze needle, its sharpness making it an excellent stabbing weapon.

with it. In Greece, the bronze daggers of Mycenae (*c.*1600–1100BC) are particularly notable, not only because of the skill involved in their basic construction – the fine tapering blades once bearing handles of horn or ivory held in place with gold-capped rivets – but also for their exquisite decoration in gold and silver. Some exhibit well-studied depictions of marine life, while others bear hunting or battle scenes. These themes appealed to the warlike, seafaring Mycenaeans, who dominated the Aegean world by force from around 1400BC, during and after the collapse of the Minoan civilization (*c.*3400–*c.*1100BC). They also may have destroyed the city of Troy around 1180BC, thus forming the basis for the later Greek myth.

The knife becomes the dagger

By 1600BC, characteristic northern European bronze daggers were beginning to appear. One early form, typical of finds dating from around 1500–1450BC in the Rhône Valley, Gaul (present-day France), consisted of a short triangular blade with a rounded base onto which was riveted a hilt with a semicircular guard (protective plate), cylindrical grip and flat, circular butt (end). Metal hilts of this form, cast in one piece, quickly spread throughout France and across to Italy and other parts of central Europe.

Before the Middle Bronze Age (*c.*2800–*c.*1100BC) there is little point in discussing the differences between a dagger and any other sort of knife. But as people gained mastery over bronze, which allowed them to diversify the styles and specific uses of weapons, clear differences began to appear. Simple bronze knives typical of the Middle Bronze Age in western Europe (*c.*1500–*c.*1100BC) have a wide cutting blade and usually a rounded tip – an all-purpose tool. But the cutting edges of a bronze blade had to be continually sharpened. Although it was harder than copper, bronze still could only hold an edge for a short period before use dulled it again. Constant sharpening, during which the edges were ground down using a whetstone, gradually narrowed the width of a knife, and after many sharpenings its size was much reduced and its shape dramatically altered; it became little more than a sharply tapered spike.

A knife's usefulness as a cutting tool over time was thus negligible, but undoubtedly humans soon discovered that such a tool could still be very effective when used exclusively as a stabbing weapon. It was not long before new weapons were being purposefully cast in this acutely pointed shape. During this period in history, dagger and knife became distinct from each other. The dagger was being used purely as a killing tool, almost exclusively for stabbing overarm or thrusting underarm, while a fighting knife remained more general in its applications. Of course, distinctions of this kind gloss over the huge grey areas that always exist between types, and so the present differentiation is meant only as a guiding generalization.

ABOVE This is a typical Hallstatt dagger, which is made of iron and dates from around 750–450BC. The dagger's blade is well formed for both cutting and thrusting actions.

The Hallstatt culture (*c.*1200–500BC)

Hallstatt is a small lakeside town in Austria, southeast of Salzburg. In 1846 an enormous ancient cemetery was discovered there, and excavations carried out during the second half of the 19th century uncovered over 1,000 individual graves. The character of the material possessions found in the graves was very distinctive, being the earliest appearance of what is today often termed the "Celtic" style – organic, flowing forms that expressed the culture's close affinity with, and religious devotion to, the natural world. Objects of this style have since been found throughout Europe, and are collectively referred to as being part of the Hallstatt culture.

The Hallstatt culture dominated most of Europe, in the east over most of what is now Austria, the Czech Republic, Slovakia, Slovenia, Croatia, Romania and Hungary, and in the west across Switzerland and parts of Italy, France and Germany. Its influence also extended to Spain and the British Isles. The culture is especially important because it forms a bridge between the Late Bronze Age (*c.*1100–800BC) and the earliest use of iron in Europe from around 800BC.

The dagger as a work of art

Until around 800BC, Hallstatt dagger blades were made of bronze, and indeed, bronze weapons continued to be used long after iron was well known throughout Europe. Hallstatt daggers are often exquisite works of art as well as weapons, having long, double-edged and multi-ridged blades. The hilts, usually made of bronze but sometimes covered in gold, were more intricate in their design than anything seen previously. The grips, rather than being just a simple cylinder, were gracefully tapered above and below a central swelling, in anticipation of the later Spanish and Roman versions of this design. Pommels (weights at the end of the hilt) took distinct forms. Some were of a flattened oval shape, usually fully pierced with designs. Others bore two intricate wheel-like structures on either side of a central block. Perhaps the most famous Hallstatt hilt was the so-called "antennae" type, the pommel being constructed of two upward-curving arms. Hallstatt daggers were also remarkable in that they were among the first European edged weapons to be made of a new material introduced from Asia – iron.

LEFT These two dagger hilts from northern Austria are excellent examples of the best Hallstatt craftsmanship. Their upward-curving pommel arms are distinguished by complex decorative forms.

LEFT This very fine Hallstatt dagger was found in a tomb dated to the 6th century BC. The "antennae" pommel has complete wheels on either side. It was discovered with its gold-plated scabbard or sheath.

The coming of iron

Grave finds show that the Hallstatt peoples also had contact with Asia Minor – the origin of the earliest discovered iron weapons – from around 1000BC. It is believed that the first iron smelting began in Anatolia, eastern Turkey, about 1500BC. Initially the Hittites, who ruled this region (*c.*1900–700BC), guarded their discovery because of the great technological advantage that it gave them, but they could not restrict its proliferation for very long. Conquest and seafaring traders brought iron to the Biblical Middle East around 1000BC – the Bible mentions that Goliath carried a dagger of iron into battle – and trade across the Mediterranean brought iron to Greece and Italy by 700BC. The Hallstatt culture, being closely linked to these areas as well as directly to Asia Minor, therefore had multiple sources of iron at its disposal, and it is not at all surprising that the culture's later phases quickly brought the general use of iron to Europe.

The La Tène culture (*c.*500–0BC)

By around 400BC a different Celtic culture was taking over most of the areas previously dominated by the Hallstatt culture. Named after the area of the eastern end of Lake Neuchâtel in Switzerland where the first group of its objects were found, the La Tène culture represents the bulk of what modern people regard as Celtic. The weapons of this group of peoples usually display fantastic imagination and technical skill, their designs growing out of observations of the natural world that have been elaborated into a realm of wild abstraction, full of curving, twisting forms.

Most La Tène knives and daggers have blades of iron or steel, although the hilts were still often constructed of bronze. The double-edged daggers of the Hallstatt culture gave way to an increasing preference for broad, single-edged knives. A few double-edged daggers from the La Tène culture are known, and often these exhibit a development of the Hallstatt "antennae" hilt in which the horns of the pommel and guard have been made thicker and given spherical terminals; combined with an added spherical form at the base of the grip between the arms of the pommel, this gives the hilt a distinct anthropomorphic appearance: a small human figure in a spread-eagle position. The figure's head is also sometimes given realistic facial features.

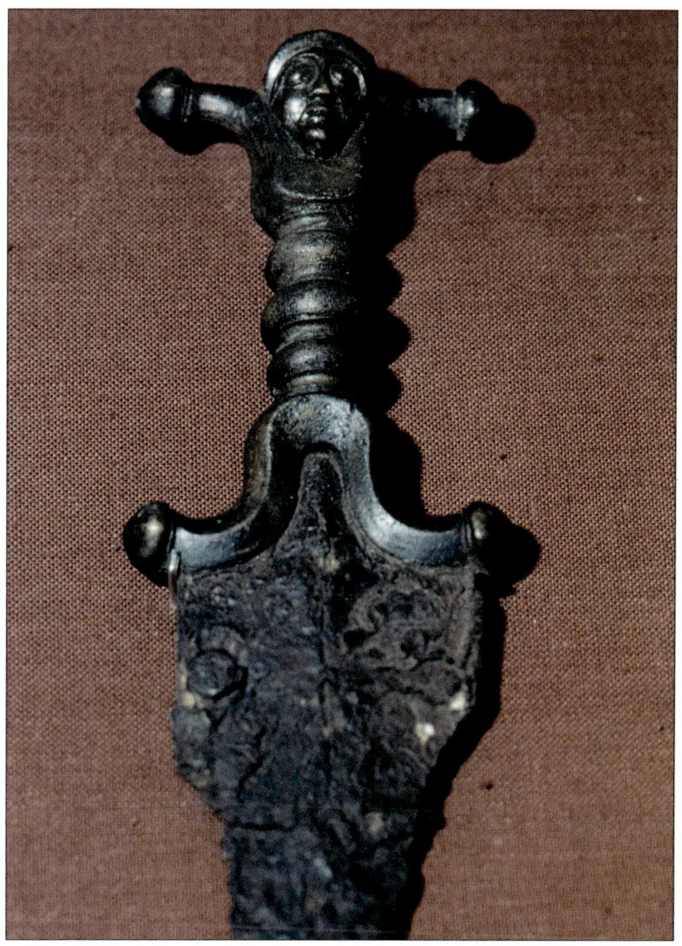

RIGHT This is an excellent example of the classic La Tène hilt of anthropomorphic form, depicting a stylized human figure. Hilts of this type are found on both daggers and swords.

Daggers of the Iron Age

The use of the dagger was not as common in the Iron Age (*c.*1400–*c.*500BC) as it had been throughout the preceding Bronze Age. Unlike their Minoan and Mycenaean ancestors, the warriors of Classical Greece (510–323BC) appear never to have employed the dagger as a military weapon, relying instead on the spear and sword. But in Italy, three vibrant cultures, the Villanovans, the Etruscans and the Romans, each developed forms of the dagger.

Bronze continued to be employed in the making of arms and armour throughout much of the Iron Age. Good-quality bronze was a harder metal than the earliest forms of iron, and it remained the preferred weapons material for a very long time. Iron was more easily sourced and therefore cheaper than the copper used to make bronze, and it had the potential to be forged into sharper- and harder-edged weapons. But the first iron-smelting processes were difficult and not very successful.

ABOVE A series of bronze Etruscan daggers found at Castione Marchesi in Italy. All display the typical steeply tapered blades, semi-circular guards and cylindrical grips that were common to this culture.

Early iron smelting

Metalworkers in the ancient world generally extracted copper metal from ore in furnaces designed to reach temperatures of between 700 and 900 degrees Celsius. It might have been possible to achieve the chemical reactions required to reduce iron from ore at 700 or 800 degrees, but the metal produced remained full of a glass-like substance called slag. This had to be liquefied to separate it from the iron, but this part of the process required a temperature of 1,200 degrees and so was beyond the technology of the time. Iron with a high slag content was brittle and inflexible, and therefore inferior to bronze. Only after metalworkers developed more advanced smelting processes, which could reach the higher temperatures, did they render bronze obsolete and turn to iron as the main raw material used to create weapons.

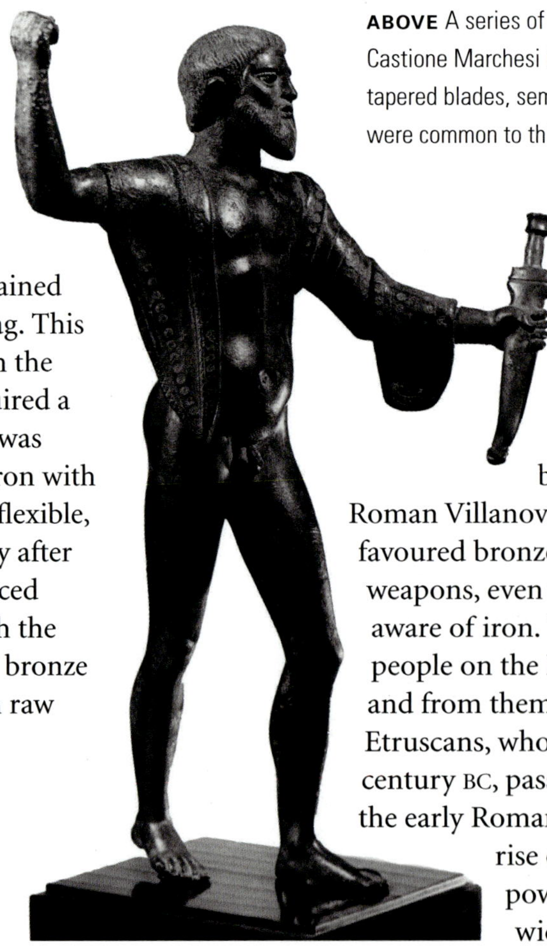

RIGHT An Etruscan image of the war-god Mars. The Etruscans probably invested symbolic significance in their weapons – this dagger stands for masculinity and military might.

The Villanovans (*c.*1100–*c.*700BC) and Etruscans (*c.*800–*c.*100BC)

These technological difficulties meant that most daggers continued to be made of bronze, even after iron had been introduced. In Italy, the pre-Roman Villanovan and Etruscan cultures both favoured bronze as the material for edged weapons, even though they were both well aware of iron. The Villanovans were the first people on the Italian peninsula to work iron, and from them the technology passed to the Etruscans, who were dominant by the 8th century BC, passing from them to their enemies, the early Romans. However it was only with the rise of Rome as the supreme military power that iron came into widespread use.

ABOVE This beautiful Villanovan dagger and scabbard, dating from the 6th–3rd century BC, is a good example of how the use of bronze continued well into the Iron Age.

Villanovan and Etruscan daggers are known in three main forms. Most have leaf-shaped blades although some have straight blades that taper sharply in the last third of their length and end in a thickened stabbing point. Others are triangular, with a consistent degree of taper from hilt to point. All three types include multiple ribs down their length.

The blade usually extended into a tang section at its base, onto which fitted a grip of stone, wood or bone. Some grips had "antennae pommels", which are a sign of Celtic influence, while others had simple T-shaped or disk pommels.

By the late 7th century BC the Etruscans had developed into the strongest military power on the Italian peninsula. They moved south over the River Tiber, taking many towns including Rome. The Etruscans retained their hold on southern Italy until 509BC, when the Romans rebelled and declared themselves a republic.

The Romans (800BC–AD410)

For over 1,000 years Rome maintained the fiercest, most disciplined and well-organized war machine in history. It adapted quickly to changes in enemy equipment and tactics, and often embraced them. Foreign innovations that were appropriated by the Romans included mail armour, armoured cavalry, the legendary *gladius*, or short sword, and the *pugio*, or dagger.

The Roman dagger appears to have been of Spanish origin. Examples from Numantia (in north-central Spain) dating from the 4th and 3rd centuries BC are virtually identical to daggers in the later years of the Roman Republic (509–27BC). However, it seems that the dagger was not immediately adopted by the Roman Army. It is not mentioned at all by Polybius (*c*.200–*c*.118BC), the Greek historian who described with great attention to detail the army of the Roman Republic. Initially the Romans seem to have thought of the dagger as a sort of trophy – an item of prestige that lent a certain military muscularity to a man's appearance. Perhaps a dagger pointed him out as someone who had fought for the Roman Republic in the wars abroad.

RIGHT Most of the earliest evidence for the pugio daggers adopted by the Romans comes from the Iberian Peninsula. This Iberian relief, from the 3rd century BC, shows a man armed with a dagger of pugio form.

FAR RIGHT This classic leaf-bladed Roman pugio blade with raised midrib dates from the 1st century AD. It is a well-designed weapon suitable for both slashing and thrusting attacks.

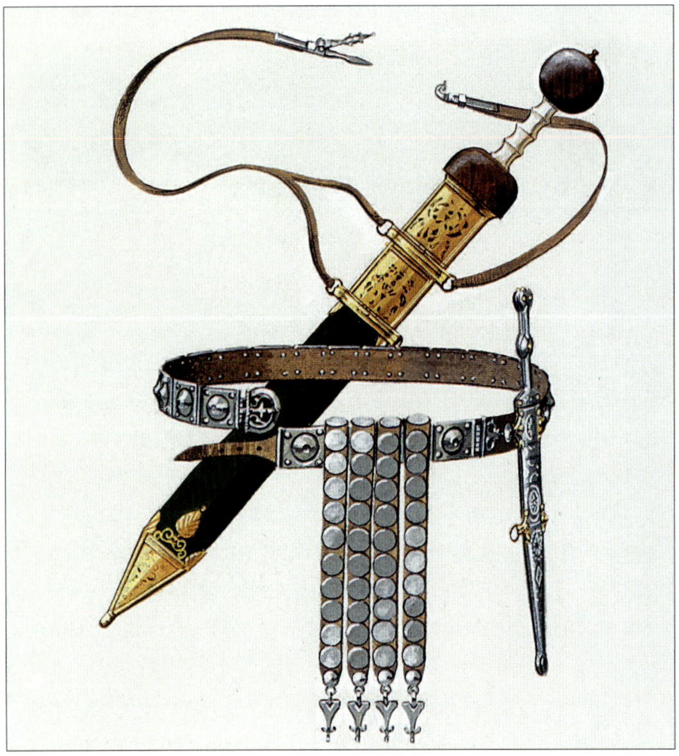

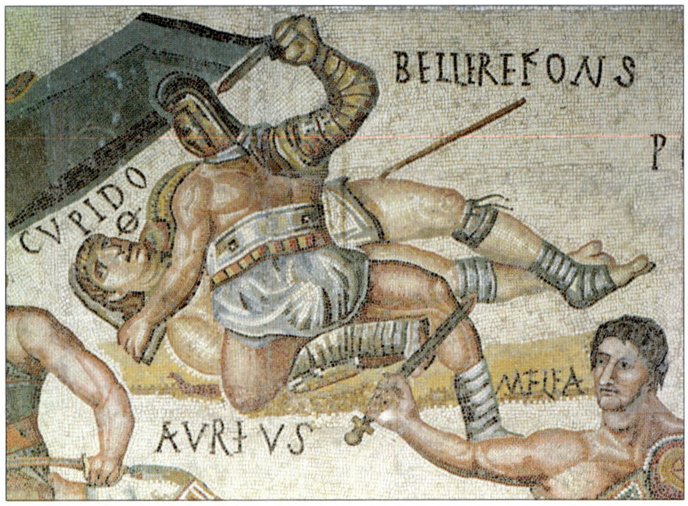

ABOVE The pugio was used in battle, for self-defence and also in the gladiatorial arena. This mosaic of around AD320 shows a gladiator pinning another to the ground while preparing to kill him with the dagger.

LEFT By the 1st century AD the pugio was part of a legionary's basic equipment, worn on the left of a belt that also held the plated *cingulum*.

The legionary pugio

The dagger became a standard part of Roman legionary equipment around the time of Christ. It was taken up as a complement to the sword, worn on the left side of the belt from which also hung the *cingulum*, or girdle. The sword was worn on the right side, suspended from a separate belt. Roman soldiers are frequently depicted armed in this way on tombstones and memorials, as well as in other forms of sculpture.

The pugio had a reasonably wide, waisted blade between 15–35cm (5.9–13.7in) in length. The point was frequently elongated to optimize its use for stabbing, while a strong midrib running down the length of the blade gave it additional strength and rigidity. The hand was protected by a simple guard riveted through the base of the blade, the arms of which sometimes extended a short distance beyond the edges of the blade, although many examples simply sit flush with the base. The pugio handle is very distinctive, having a circular swelling at its mid-point. Early pommels tend to be round, while later types usually have a flattened base or are even crescent-shaped. Generally, the pugio hilt was made in two halves – sometimes in bone or ivory but usually in bronze or iron – that sandwiched either side of the tang and were held in place by rivets through the guard, grip swelling and pommel. Although most pugio hilts were plain, high-status pieces were sometimes inlaid with precious metals.

The decline of the pugio

The legionary pugio dagger seems to have disappeared from use by Roman legionaries around AD200 or possibly earlier. Trajan's Column in Rome – completed AD113 to commemorate the Dacian campaigns of AD101–2 and AD104–6 – one of our most important sources for the appearance of Roman legionaries in the early 2nd century AD, does not include even one dagger.

For whatever reason, the legionary pugio was discarded. A cruder form of this dagger continued to be used by auxiliary troops, soldiers from the Roman Empire's various outer territories. One spectacular find at Künzing, Bavaria, of the stock of a military workshop buried in the 3rd century AD, included 59 dagger blades and 29 sheaths. This indicates that the legionary pugio continued to be used as a military weapon long after it had been abandoned by the legions.

LEFT This Roman pugio, from southern Europe and made in the 1st century AD, retains its iron grip scales decorated with incised grooves and riveted to the blade tang.

The assassination of Julius Caesar, 44BC

In 44BC, Gaius Julius Caesar was the most powerful man in Rome. A great general, he had just been appointed dictator, although Rome was not yet an empire. The granting of absolute power to Julius Caesar was a key step in Rome's transition from a republican to an imperial state. Some members of the Roman senate opposed the slide into dictatorship, and a plot formed to assassinate Caesar.

On 15 March 44BC, Caesar went to a meeting at the request of the Senate to read a petition they wished to put to him. But the petition was a trick, conceived by the assassins, who called themselves "Liberators", to draw him into their trap. As he read the document one of the assassins drew his dagger and struck at Caesar's neck, but managed only to wound him slightly. The rest of the group (some accounts say up to 60 assailants) then attacked, stabbing their victim over and over, in the face, chest, shoulders and sides. Caesar tried to escape, but he stumbled and went down. The attackers continued their frenzied assault, which became so frantic that they accidentally stabbed each other as well as their victim. Caesar eventually died, his body covered in up to 35 stab wounds.

Roman coins commemorating the murder show the head of Brutus on one face and the assassins' daggers on the other: the pugio soon became the Roman legionary's constant companion.

LEFT Caesar's murder was commemorated on Roman coins of *c.*42BC that feature the profile head of Marcus Junius Brutus, leader of the conspiracy, on one side and pugios on the reverse.

BELOW The assassination in the Senate is here recreated by the German historical artist Heinrich Füger (1751-1818).

The Saxon fighting knife

The disintegration of the Roman Empire in the 5th century AD did not at first result in changes in weapons design and manufacture. The Empire's fragments initially tried to retain the trappings of imperial power, but it could not last. The old military structures gave way to much more variegated, clannish warrior cultures founded on personal loyalty and individual prowess. This social change was reflected in the design of weapons.

ABOVE Found in the River Thames, this fine sax blade bears a unique inscription of the complete Anglo-Saxon runic alphabet and also the name of its maker or owner, Beagnoth.

The collapse of Roman dominion in Europe led to many peoples between the 4th and 8th centuries AD (often called the "Migration Period") relocating in search of new prosperity and more fertile lands. Germanic tribes moved north from central Europe, while Scandinavian peoples struck west into Britain, Iceland, Greenland and North America.

The sax

Many Germanic tribes took advantage of the Romans' departure from Britain. While raids into Britain had begun before Roman withdrawal in AD410, they increased dramatically afterwards. These invaders were generically referred to as "Saxons" even though their origins were diverse. Some seized parts of eastern Britain by force, while others allied themselves with the resident Romano-British peoples. Saxon warriors prized the sword above all weapons, but they also became known for a very distinctive fighting knife – the scramasax, seax or sax.

It has long been thought that the term "Saxon" expressed a characteristic preference for the "sax" as a weapon. Its use was not, however, limited to Britain. The earliest known Scandinavian sax dates from about 300BC, and its shape is much the same as those found in a bog at Vimose, on the Danish island of Funen, over six centuries later. In the Early Medieval Period (*c.*AD500–*c.*AD1100) the sax was the commonest sidearm of Saxons, Franks and Vikings, later examples having been found in Norway, Sweden, Denmark and mainland Europe.

Types of sax and their uses

The sax was a broad-bladed, single-edged fighting knife, the blade having a strong back and a wedge-shaped cross-section. Its length varied enormously. Smaller examples, almost "pen-knife" types, have blades as short as 7.5cm (3in) long, while the biggest sword versions are

LEFT Among the weapons found in France in a Merovingian grave of the third quarter of the 5th century AD was this early example of a sax, made of iron and with a finely decorated hilt.

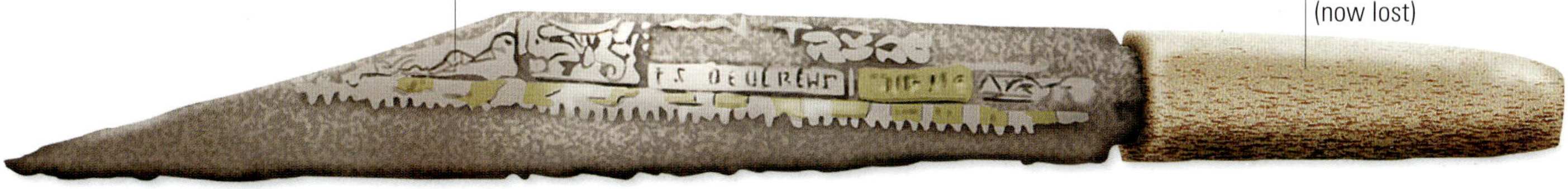

upwards of 76cm (30in) long. This very large form was called a langseax by the Viking spearmen who favoured it, while the average size, usually with a blade around 15cm (6in) long, was called a handseax. The blade was tapered sharply down its last third, and on the back only the cutting edge remained straight or slightly curved. There was no hand guard and only a simple grip of wood or bone. Sax blades could be very ornate, inlaid with copper, bronze and silver. Sometimes the name of the owner or maker was also inlaid, highlighting how important the sax was both as a prized weapon and as a signed work of art.

Although the sax may look more like a utilitarian, all-purpose knife, it was mainly a weapon for close-quarters combat. While the sword is the weapon most celebrated in early medieval literature, the sax makes several notable appearances. *The Tale of Thorstein Rod-Stroke* describes two men dying from fatal stab wounds dealt with a sax, while one of the most dramatic battlefield episodes occurred at the Battle of Bravoll around AD700, a contest for the Swedish throne between old King Harald War-Tooth and his nephew Sigurd. With most of his royal guard and champions dead or dying, King Harald charged his enemies with a sax in each hand, slaying many men before his skull was smashed by an axe-wielding foe.

Despite the sax's prominence in early medieval culture, the respect accorded fighting knives was minimal compared to the sword and spear. Even the Vikings could belittle the smaller forms of sax. In the Icelandic *Saga of Weapon's Fjord*, the warrior Geitir observes that "he with a little sax must try and try again".

ABOVE Found at Sittingbourne in England, this sax blade is ornately decorated with copper alloy and silver. One side carries the inscription "Sigebereht owns me", while the other reads "Biorhtelm made me".

Links between the sax and dagger

However popular the fighting knife was with individual warriors during the Migration Period and Early Middle Ages, its use was entirely a matter of personal preference. The dagger had not been a mandatory military requirement since it had ceased to be standard issue in the Roman Army. But the Franks under Charlemagne brought back many Roman ideas and regulations, including strict discipline and the use of armoured cavalry. In AD805, five years after being crowned with the title of "Emperor of the Romans", Charlemagne issued an edict that required all of his cavalry to be armed with a mail coat, sword, spear, shield and dagger.

Little is known about the transition from the later saxes of the 11th century to the "knightly" daggers of the 13th and 14th centuries. Many Anglo-Saxons at the Battle of Hastings in 1066 probably carried long saxes, while their Norman enemies, themselves descended from the Vikings, may have been armed with smaller sax-like knives in addition to their swords and spears. Indeed, the sax may not have fallen out of fashion at all; knives looking very much like the sax were still being made in England during the 1400s.

BELOW These two excavated sax blades give a good impression of the more typical proportions of these famous weapons. Found in central Europe, they probably date from the 6th–8th centuries AD.

Medieval daggers

The Medieval Period (*c.*1100–*c.*1450) was the age of the knight and of chivalry. The culture of the mounted warrior changed how combat was conducted and led to a reconsideration of how weapons were used. Knights initially thought the dagger to be unimportant, but by the 14th century it had become an essential part of their equipment. Dagger types evolved and multiplied. Their new significance applied on the battlefield as well as in civilian life.

The use of the dagger had remained a matter of personal preference since its requirement by the Roman legions had been dropped in the 2nd century AD. All manner of knives were no doubt carried by fighting men, but there were no specific regulations or accepted practice. The AD805 edict of the Holy Roman Emperor Charlemagne that all imperial cavalrymen should carry the dagger was significant, but several hundred years would pass before Charlemagne's lead was followed.

The unworthy dagger

During the 12th and 13th centuries, daggers do not seem to have been thought worthy of much notice. Since Roman times, the respected weapons of the elite warrior were the spear and the sword. Daggers rarely appear on the funerary monuments of knights of this period, nor do we find dagger combat depicted in art until around 1250. Perhaps because it was advocated only as a last resort when all other weapons were broken or lost, the dagger does not seem to have interested artists until the middle of the 13th century.

The dagger in the 12th century sometimes carried derogatory associations. Usually called a cultellus or coustel, it was commonly connected with criminals; *coustiller* and *cultellarius* were both terms used to refer to thieves, thugs and bandits. A statute of 1152 issued by the Count of Toulouse in France refers to "evil men, called coustillers, who cause havoc with their daggers after nightfall".

BELOW This detail from a 13th-century manuscript version of the Old Testament shows men armed in the style of the time. One of the central figures can be seen stabbing his enemy with a short dagger.

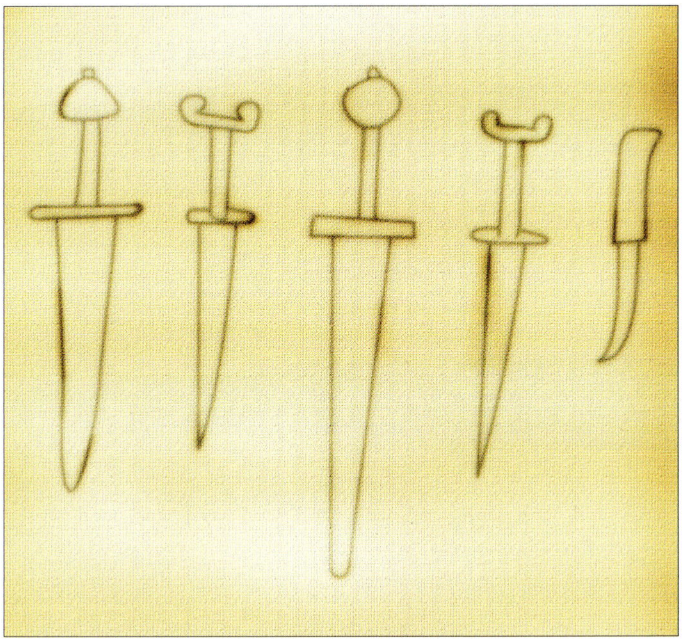

LEFT This illustration, after an 11th-century Italian manuscript, shows the medieval distinction between the two main dagger types: the wide-bladed cutting daggers and the narrow stabbing daggers.

Miséricorde

The word *miséricorde*, meaning mercy or pity, began to be used in the mid-13th century to refer to the dagger wielded by knights. It is commonly thought that the word association comes from the use of the dagger for the mercy killing of wounded men on the battlefield. In fact, it's more likely that it derives from the dagger's effectiveness in compelling an overthrown knight to surrender – with a request for mercy – to avoid being slain in single combat.

ABOVE This 15th-century manuscript detail shows an armoured warrior preparing to either accept his enemy's surrender or finish the fight with a deadly downward dagger blow.

Cutting daggers and stabbing daggers

Despite its wicked reputation, the dagger evolved quickly during the 13th and 14th centuries. By 1300 it was a standard part of the knight's armament, along with the lance, sword and axe or mace. Some daggers remained closely related to knives intended for general use. But others became removed from anything resembling an all-purpose blade, being instead dedicated exclusively to killing people.

Distinctions were clearly being made by the beginning of the 14th century. An inventory of the weapons belonging to Raoul de Nesle, Constable of France, taken after he was killed in 1302, employs specific terminology for two sorts of dagger. The broader-bladed daggers, those resembling utilitarian knives, are called coutiaus à tailler, or cutting daggers. These are distinguished from the coutiaus à pointe, or stabbing daggers.

A number of daggers from this period survive, and they clearly illustrate both types. The cutting daggers are frequently single-edged, with a strong back, the point tapering on the sharp side only, much like a kitchen knife. Stabbing daggers are much longer, narrower and very sharply tapered. By 1375, some forms of stabbing dagger could hardly be considered edged weapons at all; their blades, having no cutting edges, are little more than reinforced spikes of hardened steel for punching through muscle and bone. With enough force behind them, these blades, like giant awls, could probably also pierce the padded textile, mail and light plate armour of the time.

As blade forms multiplied, so did the forms of dagger hilt. Grouped according to the hilt form, there were four primary types of dagger in common use during the Medieval Period.

TOP Although their cross guard construction was simple, many medieval daggers have sculpted pommels and guards. This 15th-century cross-hilt dagger has a pommel and guard of copper alloy cast into ornate forms.

ABOVE Certain medieval daggers such as this 14th-century English cross-hilt example bear some resemblance to the earlier Hallstatt types, having comparable "antennae" pommels.

Cross-hilt daggers

The first daggers to be generally adopted in the 12th and 13th centuries had simple cross hilts, like diminutive swords. These are often called "quillon" daggers, although this is a post-medieval term (referring to the arms of the cross guard, the bar across the hilt).

Most early cross-hilt daggers have a short cross guard, drooping downwards towards the blade, and a crescent-shaped pommel. Some pommels are in fact more suggestive of a pair of horns, very like the Bronze Age "antennae" and "anthropomorphic" daggers of the Hallstatt and La Tène cultures described earlier.

While medieval cross-hilt daggers with "antennae" pommels seem to have gone out of fashion around 1350, versions with the crescent-shaped pommel continued to be popular into the 15th century; a related group of daggers also exhibit pommels wherein the crescent horns have been brought together to form a fully enclosed ring. Cross-hilt daggers also appear after 1350 with pommels shaped like stars, shields or mushrooms. Polygonal and wheel-type pommels were also common. Richer examples were sometimes decorated with the heraldic arms of the owner, in paint, enamel, gold and silver.

Cross-hilt daggers in art are shown being used both overarm, held with the blade projecting downwards from the base of the fist, and underarm with the blade projecting upwards. But as the 14th century progressed, the exclusive practice of overarm, blade-downwards fighting techniques dominated, and this was reflected in the development of dagger hilts. Some daggers are difficult to hold in any position other than blade-downwards. Well-made weapons often express how they "wish" to be used when handled, and it is certainly the case that many medieval daggers feel natural and comfortable when held with the blade downwards, but become remarkably awkward when reversed.

The baselard

This dagger was developed in the late 13th century for civilian as well as military use. Especially popular in Italy, but also found in English art of the 14th century, the baselard may have originated in Switzerland, in the city of Basel. An English song dating from the early 15th century neatly expresses how widespread the baselard had become by that time:

There is no man worth a leak,
Be he sturdy, be he meek
But he bear a baselard.

The baselard is recognized by its distinctive hilt, which is again reminiscent of the Hallstatt culture. Baselard hilts are usually shaped like a capital "I" or an upended "H", the bottom cross piece often being wider than the one that forms the guard. The tang is cut to the shape of the whole hilt and sandwiched between plates usually of wood, and the whole assembly is then riveted together. Baselard blades could be either single-

The overarm blow

Humans and many of the great apes instinctively employ the overarm blow struck with the base of the fist. In humans this in-built attack pattern is commonly observed in young children who, when sufficiently annoyed, almost always employ what is sometimes called "the beating movement", striking their source of frustration with elbow bent and arm raised at the shoulder, the fist or open hand then being brought down with great force.

Overarm stabbing blows with a downward-pointing blade can be much more powerful than an underarm thrust. Medieval dagger fighting adopted this instinctive defensive movement and combined it with a weapon well suited to that mode of attack. When used correctly by an expert martial artist such as a knight, who learned his fighting skills as a child and perfected them over many years of constant practice, such a technique became horrifyingly effective. Fought at close range, dagger combat would almost without question lead to serious or fatal injury. As one 15th-century German fight master wrote in his manual on martial arts: "Now we come to the dagger; God help us all!"

ABOVE This French medieval illustration of a disagreement shows daggers drawn in *The Argument*, from a late 15th-century copy of *The Book of Good Morals* by Jacques le Grant.

ABOVE The I-shaped baselard hilt is seen clearly in these examples. The English type on the left has a long cut-and-thrust blade. The broad-bladed European dagger is an earlier design.

or double-edged, and were generally quite broad. They could also be quite long, more like short swords. The longer forms, however, were not as common as the shorter ones, tending to be more exclusively Swiss.

When worn by warriors, baselards were slung on the right hip, but in civilian life they were usually worn centrally below the waist. From this position the dagger could be swiftly drawn. This method of wearing the dagger could never have avoided the inevitable associations with the erect male genitalia, and from the fashion of wearing the dagger over the groin developed one of the most famous of all European dagger types.

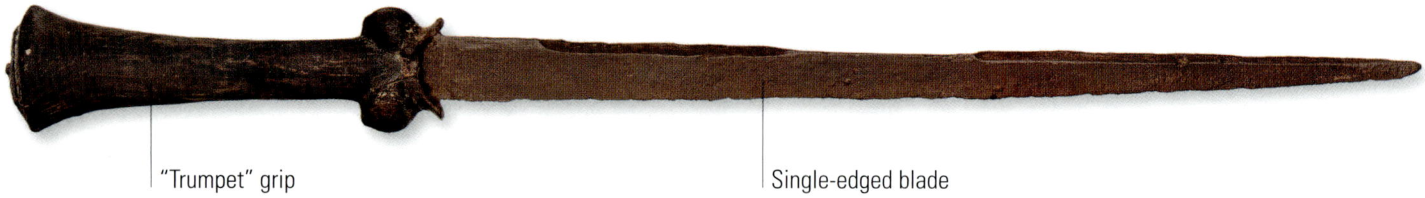

TOP This English ballock dagger, dating from the 15th century, is an early example of the slightly less phallic "trumpet" type, which remained common in the early 16th century.

ABOVE Earlier rondel daggers such as this 14th-century English weapon often have rondels that are reasonably thick; they are frequently made of wood sandwiched between metal disks.

The ballock dagger

Medieval culture was full of phallic imagery and it was flaunted rather than hidden. The ballock dagger, which appeared around 1300, was the logical development of the fashion for centrally slung weapons. The hilt was carved out of a single piece of wood and shaped to resemble an erect penis and testicles, with a bulbous pommel and a rounded lobe on either side of the blade in place of the guard. Some examples are very lifelike while others are more stylized.

Despite the apparently unavoidable inspiration for this dagger's distinctive form, the selective interpretation of the Middle Ages propagated in the 19th century casts a long shadow. The Victorians prudishly renamed these weapons "kidney" daggers, a ridiculous denial of the obvious but one that has survived in usage until very recently.

An important variation of the classic ballock hilt appeared in the 15th century. Here, rather than being surmounted by a bulbous head, the grip flared out almost like a trumpet. The flat-top surface of this flared end was usually capped with a metal disk-shaped plate, often engraved with geometric or vegetal designs. This form never replaced the earlier type, but rather they coexisted well into the 16th century.

The form of blades attached to these hilts varied enormously. The most usual form is triangular in cross-section and tapers consistently from base to point. By the late 14th century, other versions had evolved with square-sectioned tips, to strengthen them for stabbing. Double-edged blades were also fitted to the hilts, although these could never be as wide at the base as those found on baselards, for example; the ballock hilt always required a comparatively narrow blade.

LEFT This detail from *The National Law Codes of Magnus Eriksson* (c.1450) shows the enactment of a violent crime. The distinctive hilt of a ballock dagger can be seen protruding from the victim's chest.

The rondel dagger

It is difficult to be sure when the fourth medieval form of dagger, the rondel dagger, first appeared but it was common by 1350; it may have been known since about 1300. The hilt comprised a grip situated between two disk-shaped "rondels". These gave good protection to the hand while also acting as stops to prevent the hand slipping when a downward stabbing blow was struck. Its use spread over an exceptionally large area, including all of western, central and northern Europe, and even stretching into Poland, and lasted until the mid-16th century.

At first only the guard of rondel-type daggers was disk-shaped, the pommel being polygonal or rounded. But the pommel was soon replaced by another rondel, and the true rondel dagger rapidly assumed an almost universal status as the favourite dagger of knights and men-at-arms. Usually the rondels were strictly circular, although some were faceted, fluted or cusped. The blades tended to be double-edged at first, of flattened diamond section, sometimes even having a central fuller (shallow weight-reducing groove).

After 1400 the rondel dagger evolved considerably. The rondels were made in a number of different ways. Sometimes they were made of wood faced with metal, although more often they were made solely of steel, iron or copper alloy. By the middle of the 15th century, some of the more ornate daggers had rondels built up of multiple disks of different materials – white and yellow metal, but also horn, wood and bone. When smoothed and polished, the edges of these rondels displayed very attractive, multicoloured strata. Sometimes the layering was enhanced with octagonal or hexagonal rather than circular layers.

Rondel dagger grips were constructed in both of the usual ways. Either the tang was made narrow so that it could pass down the centre of the length of the grip to be hammered over on top of the pommel, or it was kept wide and filed into the desired grip shape, with the grip made in two halves, then being riveted onto it on either side.

The basic shape was cylindrical, often widening slightly in the middle and tapering down at either end. Many grip shapes were never more ornate than this simple form. The grip could also be decorated. The more elaborate examples, in particular, tend to be carved or embellished in some way.

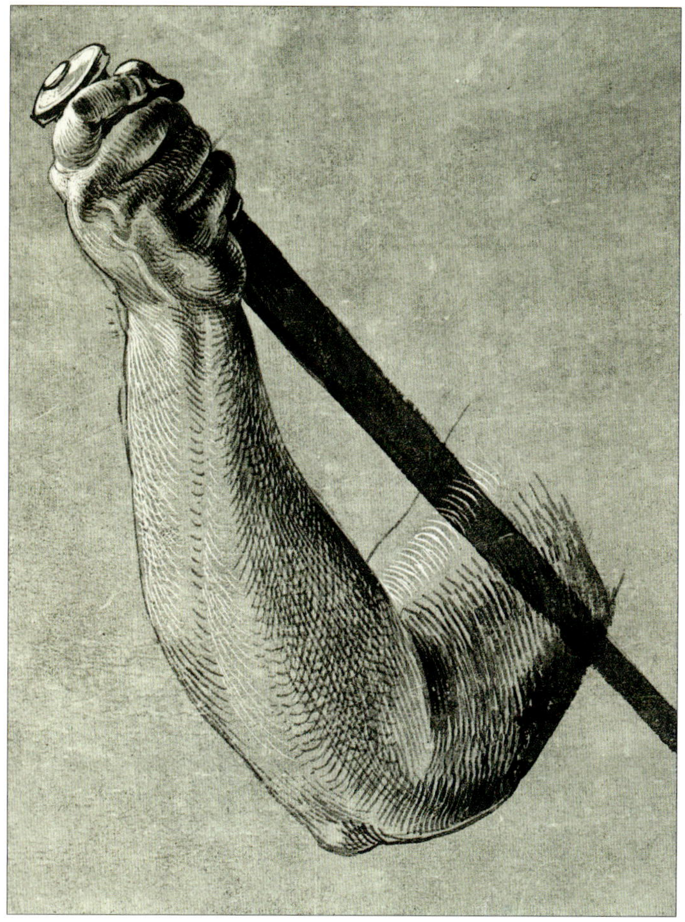

ABOVE This sketch by the German artist Albrecht Dürer is a study of a hand grasping a rondel dagger in the action of plunging it into the chest. It was made in preparation for his painting *The Suicide of Lucretia*, 1518.

Spiral carving was particularly fashionable. The finest examples were made entirely of metal, engraved with intricate designs. Only fragments of these more ornate, knightly rondel daggers survive, although they are depicted frequently on funerary effigies, complete with their exquisitely tooled scabbards. Such elaborate decorated weapons were obvious status symbols.

BELOW Some rondel daggers were extremely ornate. This fragment is all that remains of a once stunning English 15th-century weapon, probably that of a knight. The hilt was entirely fire-gilt (gilded with a heated mix of gold and mercury) and incised with geometric patterns.

Daggers of the Renaissance

Each of the medieval dagger types remained in use throughout the 16th and into the 17th century. Some remained largely unchanged, while others evolved according to more restricted regional fashions. Although in the 16th century the Renaissance dagger was still an important military weapon, it was becoming more common in everyday life and was just as likely to be drawn in a royal palace or urban back alley as on the battlefield.

The 1500s were the golden age of the dagger in Europe. During this century aristocratic fashions in clothes and behaviour became more decadent and extravagant. Nobles dripped with jewels and precious stones, their clothing intricately constructed using many different materials. Individuality had become much more important than it ever had been before, and rich people were anxious to express themselves as individuals through material display. With fine clothes went fine weapons, and the dagger was ever-present, not just as a tool and a weapon but now also as an indispensable fashion accessory.

LEFT Renaissance daggers were often glamorous fashion accessories, as shown by this south German cross-hilt dagger with a curved blade and hilt with gold, gemstones and cameos.

ABOVE The dagger was the constant companion of the Renaissance nobleman. Hans Holbein's 1534 portrait of Charles de Solier, the French envoy at the court of Henry VIII, shows the lord with a fine gilded dagger.

The assassin's choice

The dagger had been a weapon favoured by assassins since ancient times because its small size made it easy to hide. If discovered its presence could be easily explained, since a knife was routinely carried by most people. During the Renaissance, assassination became more common, particularly in the ruthless political environment of the time. Many rulers and statesmen fell under plunging dagger blades.

One case, which occurred in 1537, was that of Alessandro de' Medici, Duke of Florence, who was lured away from his bodyguards by the temptation of a sexual encounter with the beautiful sister of Lorenzino de' Medici ("Bad Lorenzino"), a distant cousin. Once alone, Alessandro was ambushed and stabbed to death by Lorenzino, who later claimed that he had killed Alessandro for the sake of the Florentine Republic, comparing his deed to Brutus' murder of Julius Caesar. Lorenzino was himself stabbed to death in Venice a year later.

RIGHT A number of Renaissance rulers met a grisly end on the point of an assassin's dagger. In 1589 King Henry III of France was stabbed to death by a Dominican friar, who was then killed by the royal guard.

The landsknecht daggers

The modern term "landsknecht" dagger actually refers to three quite different forms, and is somewhat misleading in any case. The Landsknechts were predominantly German, Swiss and Flemish mercenaries who took part in almost every military campaign of the 16th century and were famous for their flamboyant "puffed and slashed" clothing.

Only the first type of so-called landsknecht dagger can be directly associated with these fierce professional soldiers. Both the two-handed great sword and smaller arming sword, or katzbalger, of the Landsknecht have a characteristic form of guard – the long arms are bent into a nearly circular S-shape. This first class of landsknecht dagger has a guard similarly formed, and its pommel also takes the same flaring form found on surviving katzbalgers. The blade is usually double-edged and tapered evenly from guard to point.

Unlike the first type, there is no stylistic similarity between the second type and the other characteristic landsknecht weapons familiar from pictorial representations. It may be an offshoot of the rondel dagger. One of its defining features is a grip that flares, trumpet-like, towards the pommel, the end of which is covered either with a flat metal disk or a domed plate. The guard is usually formed of a small plate cut into three lobes (rounded projections), which bend down towards the blade like drooping leaves. The length of the scabbard is divided by groups of two or three rings, wider than the scabbard itself. On finer examples, some or all of the rings are repeatedly sawn vertically, giving the scabbard an appearance in keeping with the elaborate puffed and slashed clothing of the time.

The third type of dagger in this group is essentially a type of cross-hilt dagger. It is also one of the earliest forms to carry a side ring, placed centrally on the outside of the guard to give added protection to the knuckles. This type is also called a Saxon dagger, as many of them were made in eastern parts of the German Empire. The pommels of these Saxon daggers are usually pear-shaped or conical and often capped with a silver plate. Both this plate and the guard are frequently engraved with floral designs, and the grip is wrapped with fine twisted wire. Saxon dagger scabbards often have silver mounts engraved to match the pommel cap (decorative covering) and guard.

ABOVE This landsknecht dagger's distinctive hilt matches the short and two-handed swords favoured by these renowned mercenaries. Only a very few of these daggers survive today.

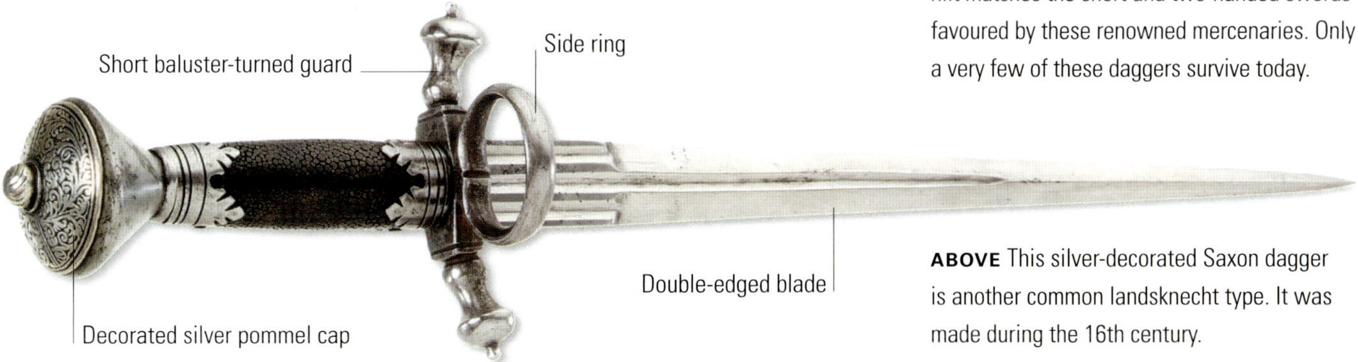

ABOVE This silver-decorated Saxon dagger is another common landsknecht type. It was made during the 16th century.

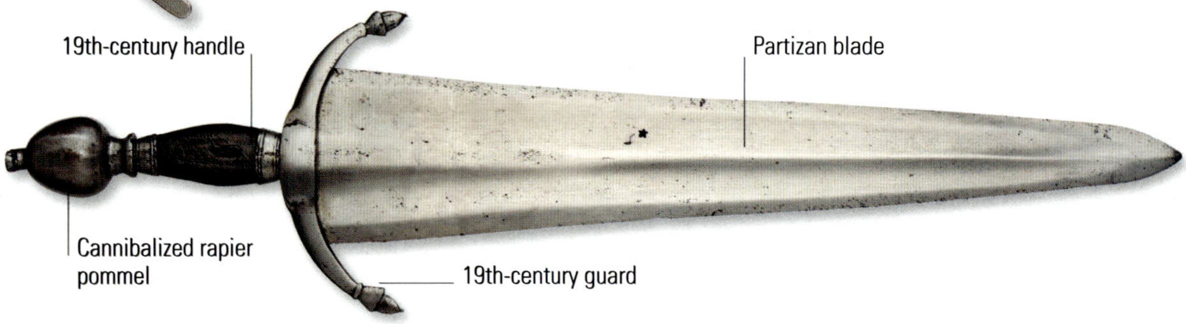

TOP Small cinquedeas are easily classified as daggers, but many have blade lengths closer to short swords. They make effective concussive cut-and-thrust weapons, unlike practically all forms of dagger.

ABOVE Because of their close associations with the Renaissance, cinquedeas were often copied in the 19th century. This fake was built using a staff weapon blade and various other sword hilt parts.

The cinquedea

This type of large Italian dagger is often thought to have gained its name because its extreme width at the guard is about as wide as a man's hand. Since the Italian for "five fingers" is *cinque diti*, this is not an entirely unreasonable assumption. But it is probably not correct. An early 17th-century definition of a cinquedea refers to a Venetian dagger that was five fingers long, not five fingers wide, and the term itself appears not to have been in use earlier than the late 16th century, some time after the supposed cinquedea fell out of fashion. Despite the fact that the use of the term is probably not consistent with the weapon's original historical context, roughly 1450–1520, its present meaning is now universally understood.

The cinquedea was a weapon of high status. The double-edged blade, very wide at the guard, tapered steeply to the point, took the form of a long isosceles triangle and was forged with a series of ridges running down the length of the blade. Two parallel ridges were normally located near the point, these increasing to three in the middle of the blade, with a final set of four at the base. By 1500, cinquedea blades were being elaborately decorated with etched Neo-classical designs or scenes from ancient Greco-Roman myths, as well as with fire gilding and even heat blueing (the application of controlled heat).

RIGHT The cinquedea may have been based on weapons of the ancient world such as this Bronze Age Etruscan dagger. Renaissance artists drew much inspiration from ancient Greek and Roman art.

The cinquedea hilt was just as distinctive as its blade. The guard was formed into a graceful arch, the arms curving downwards towards the blade, and was often drawn to a point in the centre. Because of the extreme width of the base of the blade, only the tips of the arms extended beyond its edges. The guard was also often etched with twisting vines or foliated scrolls. The ergonomic grip, usually plated with bone or ivory, was scooped out on either side to produce recesses for the fingers on both sides of a central swelling. The tubular rivets holding the ivory or bone plates to the tang were generally filled in with inserts beautifully pierced with geometric designs. The rounded pommel, made in one piece with the grip, was usually covered with a piece of gilded metal.

It is tempting to suggest that the cinquedea was just one of the many products of the infatuation with classical art and culture that characterized the Renaissance Period. The cinquedea certainly resembles some types of wide-bladed Bronze Age dagger. Perhaps the Italian dagger is a direct emulation by Renaissance smiths of an ancient design.

RIGHT Ear daggers appear in several Renaissance portraits, including this one of King Edward VI of England (1537–1553).

The ear dagger

Daggers of eared form may have appeared as early as the 14th century, but their greatest period of popularity occurred during the first half of the 16th century. The ear dagger probably originated in Spain, a result of the influence of Islamic design on the tastes of the Iberian nobility. Eared daggers were being made in Persia during the Bronze Age, and the design remained popular for both sword and dagger hilts throughout the Middle East, or "Levant" as the region was called by Renaissance Europeans. Indeed, the ear dagger was referred to in Italy as *alla Levantina*, a term that clearly demonstrates the perceived origin of the design.

The ears of the hilt are usually formed as extensions of the very thick tang, which have been hammered out to create the disk-shaped "ears" diverging at sharp angles from the bottom of the grip. The ears were generally faced with plates of ivory, horn or bone. The grip is generally quite narrow, with a slight central swelling. While the earliest ear daggers appear to have had guards not unlike those on rondel daggers, by the 16th century the guard had shrunk to little more than a small anvil or block-shaped spacer, which was plated with the same organic material as the grip and ears.

Ear-dagger blades are invariably double-edged, one edge often beginning lower on the ricasso (the flattened square of blade near the guard) than the other, producing an odd but pleasing offset effect. Some also have specially thickened stabbing points. The ricasso, exposed sides of the tang and area between the ears are sometimes damascened (woven) in gold. One of the most famous makers of ear daggers was Diego de Çaias, a Spanish maker of high-quality weapons in the 1530s and 1540s who was patronized by Francis I of France and Henry VIII of England.

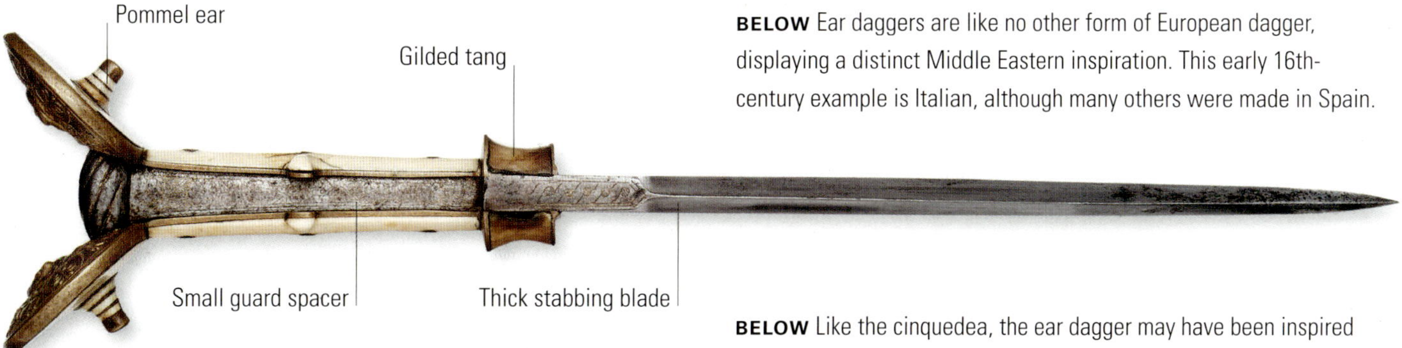

BELOW Ear daggers are like no other form of European dagger, displaying a distinct Middle Eastern inspiration. This early 16th-century example is Italian, although many others were made in Spain.

BELOW Like the cinquedea, the ear dagger may have been inspired by a Classical weapon. This bronze dagger from Luristan dates from *c.*1200BC, but displays exactly the same sort of "ears".

ABOVE Despite the fact that the production of rondel daggers seems to have declined quickly after 1500, older weapons such as this late-medieval example, would have remained in use for much longer.

Medieval daggers of the 16th century

In addition to the ear dagger, other forms of dagger that had developed during the Middle Ages continued to be made throughout the 16th century. The most common types, prevalent throughout Europe, were cross-hilt daggers. Smaller versions continued to be carried for general last-ditch self-defence by both armoured warriors and by civilians, while larger forms had begun to be incorporated into the latest fencing styles by the middle of the century. Ballock daggers also continued to be made in both of their distinctive forms. The grips were still made primarily in wood, although ivory and even agate examples are known. Later ballock dagger blades tend to be very narrow and double-edged, although in some cases they are little more than four-sided spikes.

Rondel daggers, so ubiquitous during the 14th and 15th centuries, seem to have quickly fallen out of favour in the 16th century, either evolving into new forms such as certain of the landsknecht dagger types, or disappearing altogether.

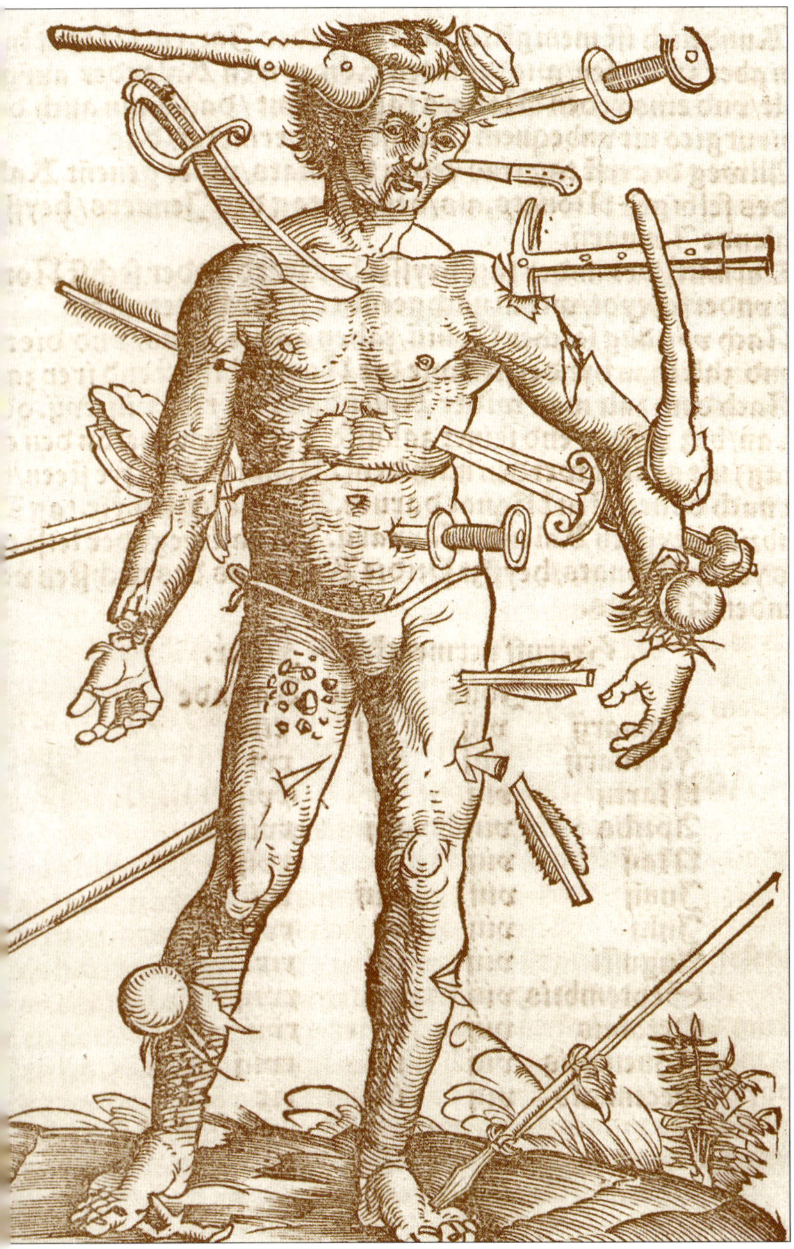

LEFT The "wound man" figure illustrated common injuries in Renaissance surgical texts. This German version from 1528 includes rondel dagger and knife stab wounds to the abdomen, face and head.

"Swiss" and "Holbein" daggers

Another medieval dagger that developed into a new and distinct form was the baselard. The essential form of what became the 16th-century "Swiss" dagger appeared in the last 20 years or so of the 15th century, when the I-shaped hilt of the baselard developed inward-curving arms, strengthened with metal sleeves, at either end of the grip. The blade of the short-sword type of "Swiss" baselard was shortened to dagger length, but unusually retained its greater width and displayed a slight leaf shape. Apart from a single fuller, "Swiss" dagger blades were left entirely plain. Unlike the earlier baselard, on which the arms of the hilt were formed by the tang over which were laid plates of wood, the hilt of the 16th-century "Swiss" dagger was carved from a single

RIGHT In addition to the T-shaped hilt and ornate scabbard, the typical "Swiss" dagger also included a byknife and awl. Decorated to match the scabbard, these fitted into special sleeves in the outer side.

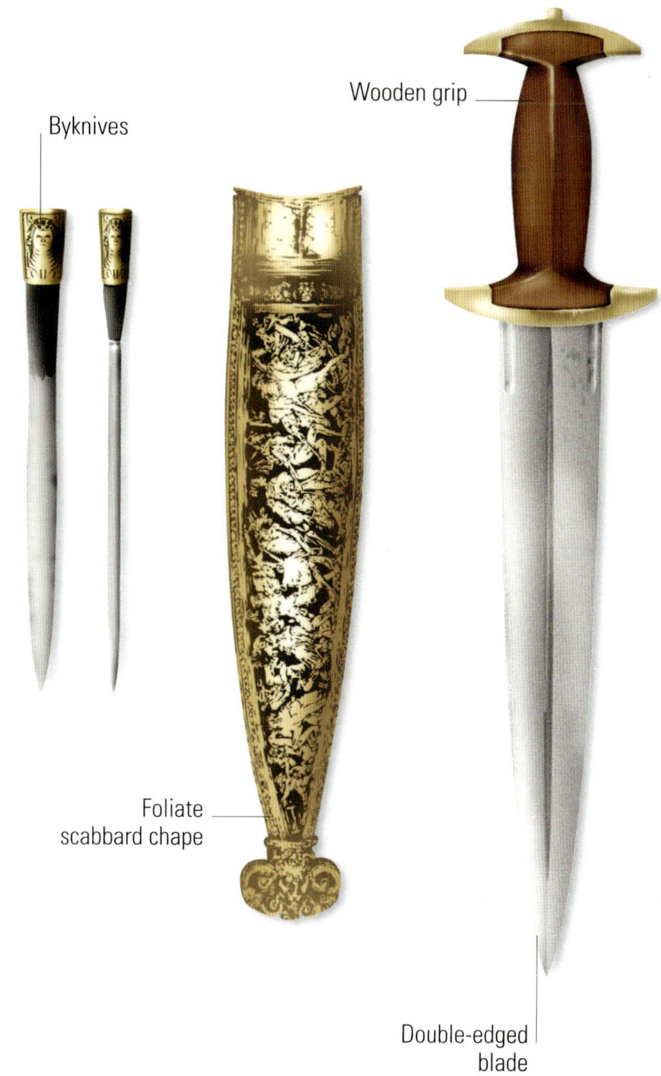

piece of hardwood, the sides of the grip were faceted and the centre was drilled out for the insertion of the narrow tang.

"Swiss" daggers are perhaps most famous for their very elaborate scabbards. The earliest examples were made of wood covered in leather, with a simple metal locket (fitting at the mouth of the scabbard) and chape (fitting at the tip of the scabbard). But after 1510, the metal mounts developed rapidly until the whole front of the scabbard was covered in silver or gilt. This decorative metal sleeve was cast with elaborate, pierced designs in relief, which were often engraved as well to add an additional level of detail.

A number of famous Swiss artists created designs for the decoration of these dagger sleeves, including Urs Graf, Heinrich Aldegrever and Hans Holbein the Younger. These designs usually involved Biblical or mythological scenes. One of Holbein's designs, for which the original drawings survive, depicted the Dance of Death, a popular allegory that expressed the universal nature of death. Death is portrayed as a re-animated skeleton, which dances with people from all levels of society. This design became so common that these weapons are often called "Holbein" daggers.

ABOVE AND BELOW A number of Renaissance artists drew designs for fine weapons.These illustrations from a book on historical dress and decorations, published in 1843, show 16th-century ornamental weapon designs by Hans Holbein.

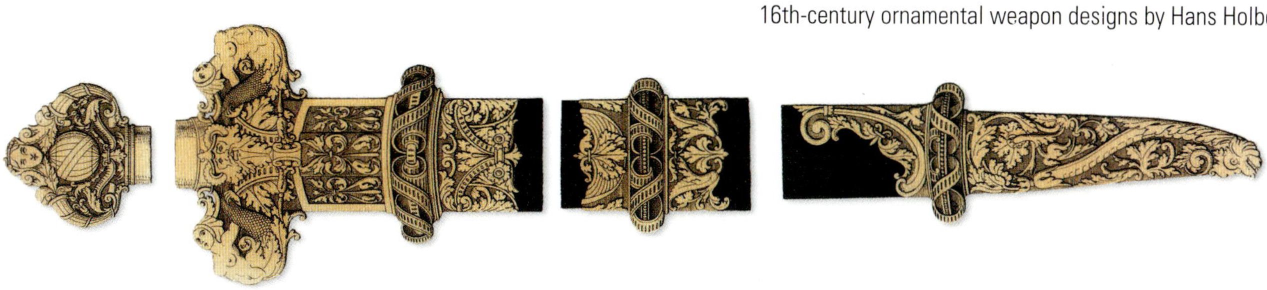

Daggers for the Renaissance duel

The dagger forms had diversified in the 14th and 15th centuries, but the fighting methods that employed them had not changed very much by the 1500s – these same basic rondel, ballock and cross-hilted weapons continued to be drawn as a last resort on the battlefield and in daily life. But the new Renaissance fashion for civilian swordmanship also led to new more specialized daggers, intended to be used exclusively as "defencing" weapons.

Renaissance society was strongly influenced by the rise of a new non-noble class who, despite their lack of aristocratic status, were often wealthy and upwardly mobile. Now it was not just the nobility who could afford luxuries such as fine clothes and weapons. The middle class was just as likely as the aristocracy (if not more so) to want to follow the latest fashions and to have the means to do so. They quickly appropriated a number of the traditional status symbols that in the past had always been exclusive to the nobility.

ABOVE Once the art of fighting with the rapier and dagger had become fashionable, weapons makers began producing fine sets with matching decoration. This exceptional Italian set, made in *c.*1600, features sumptuous inlaid and relief ornament.

LEFT The expensively decorated rapier and dagger set was an integral part of a gentleman's rich attire, as can be seen in Nicolas Neufchatel's portrait of Hieronimus Koler (1528–1573).

The sword enters civilian life

One of the most important new symbols of social status adopted by the *nouveau riche* was the sword. In the Medieval Period the sword had been a knightly weapon; it was expensive and its use required many years of dedicated practice. More importantly, the use of the sword in dealing with personal grievances – through trial by combat – was a right restricted to the nobility. By the mid-16th century, most non-noble gentlemen had adopted the sword as a sign of their own economic "nobility". More importantly, they began to wear it at all times. This was a new development; before the 16th century the sword

was never worn with civilian dress except when travelling. This change in the acceptance of weapons in society was observed by the 16th-century chronicler Claude Haton, leading him to write, of the year 1555: "There is no mother's son at this time who did not carry a sword or a dagger."

ABOVE The weapons in legal judicial duels were often the sword and shield, as in this trial by combat fought in Paris in 1547. For impromptu, illegal combats the inconvenient shield was supplanted by the dagger.

BELOW Sometimes there is more to a rapier and dagger set than meets the eye. This unique set, by Tobias Reichel of Dresden, *c.*1610, includes tiny timepieces hidden in the pommels.

The duel

These new civilian swords brought with them a perceived right to address personal grievances and disagreements through violence; with weapons close to hand they were more easily drawn in anger, and quickly became a first reaction rather than a last resort. But the autonomous right to settle personal disputes with violence was a right restricted to the aristocracy. This made it a luxury that the middle class wanted. The ancient practice of judicial combat was seized upon by fashionable society and twisted into the private duel, fought anywhere and at any time, often for the most trivial reasons.

Duelling quickly became a craze. Hundreds and then thousands of men were killed each year during the second half of the 16th century, all in supposed "affairs of honour". These disputes could be caused by a verbal slight, physical altercation or even an insulting glance. Sir Walter Raleigh – the famous Elizabethan explorer who established one of the earliest American colonies at Roanoke Island in what is today North Carolina – wrote earnestly that "to give the lie deserves no less than stabbin". It was this brutal subculture that led to a number of key innovations in the design and use of edged weapons.

ABOVE Key targets in rapier and dagger combat were the face and throat. A skilled swordsman could parry and attack at the same time, as shown in this early 17th-century manual by Jacques Callot (*c.*1592–1635).

Combat with rapier and dagger

Once the sword was introduced into this new civilian fighting environment, it began to change. Plate armour was not worn in daily life, and so swords began to be designed especially to take on vulnerable but quicker opponents. The use of the thrust became much more important, and sword blades became longer and longer, as the control of distance and the ability to kill an enemy without getting too close became central to civilian fighting styles. By the second half of the 16th century, the civilian sword had evolved into something entirely unlike its military counterpart. The blade was much longer, narrower and thickened down its spine so that it was as ridged as possible, and the hilt – which now had to protect the unarmoured hand – had a number of additional sweeping bars and ring guards added to it. This non-military sword was called *espada ropera* in Spanish, "sword of the robe", or a sword to be worn with civilian clothing. The French called it *épée rapière*, which in turn became the English "rapier".

We tend these days to think of the rapier as a feather-light weapon, the "flashing blade" of the swashbuckling heroes of the silver screen. But this is not really true. Because of their very great length – which often exceeded 1m (3.3ft) or more – and their thickened spines, most rapiers were actually very blade-heavy and somewhat ungainly in the hand.

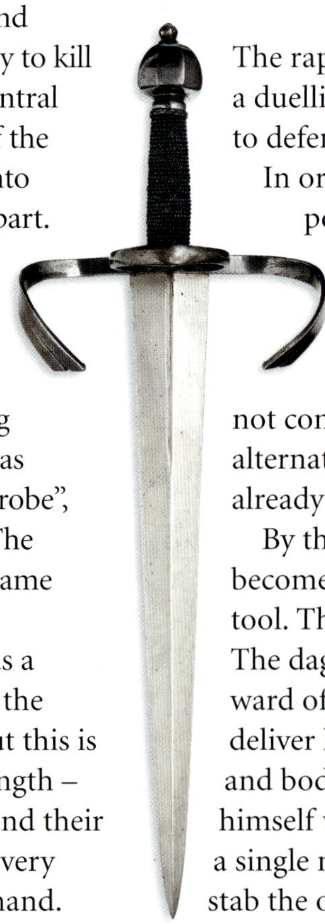

BELOW Some fencing daggers had special features, such as the long down-curving guards of this Saxon dagger dating to about 1610.

The rapier was an excellent attacking weapon, but a duellist had difficulty bringing it back quickly to defend his body with a parry or blocking move.

In order to attack and defend as rapidly as possible, the civilian duellist required a companion weapon. The most common was the shield, which allowed the fighter to defend himself with his left arm while attacking with his right. But shields were not convenient to carry around in daily life. An alternative was found in a weapon that people were already carrying around with them – the dagger.

By the middle of the 16th century, the dagger had become an indispensable self-defence, or "fencing", tool. The art of rapier and dagger fighting was born. The dagger was held in the left hand and used to ward off incoming attacks, leaving the rapier free to deliver lethal thrusts to the opponent's face, throat and body. The most skilled swordsman could defend himself with the dagger and attack with the rapier in a single movement. The dagger could also be used to stab the opponent if he came too close.

The *Duel des Mignons*: the advantages of a dagger

One very famous duel was fought in Paris on 27 April 1578, during the reign of Henry III (*r.*1574–89). The *mignons* (French for "favourites") were a group of obsequious young noblemen with whom the French king surrounded himself. They were known for their effeminate manners and dress, long hair and decadent, shallow lifestyle, and they became deeply unpopular with the French people. At the time of the duel, the French Court had become polarized into factions, one side supporting the king and the other side supporting his bitter rival, the Duc de Guise, a lord who enjoyed widespread popularity. The disagreement that formed the basis for the duel was said to have involved certain courtly ladies, although this may have only been a pretext.

The duel was fought between the courtiers Jacques de Quélus, who supported the king, and Charles de Balzac, Baron d'Entragues, a close ally of the Duc de Guise. Each man brought with him two companions, or seconds, and a bloody three-on-three encounter followed. One second on each side was killed outright. D'Entragues' other second died of his wounds the next day, while Quélus' other second survived with a serious head injury. The main combatants were both severely wounded. D'Entragues perhaps could be considered the victor, since he survived. Quélus suffered 19 wounds and took 33 days to die in terrible agony.

Before he died Quélus complained that the duel had been unfair, for while he had fought only with his rapier, d'Entragues had been armed with a dagger as well as his rapier. D'Entragues is said to have responded: "So much the worse for him; he ought not to have been such a fool as to have left his dagger at home."

BELOW The famous *Duel des Mignons* which was fought in Paris on 27 April 1578 during the reign of Henry III, as imagined by the 19th-century historical artist Cesare-Auguste Detti, *c.*1847.

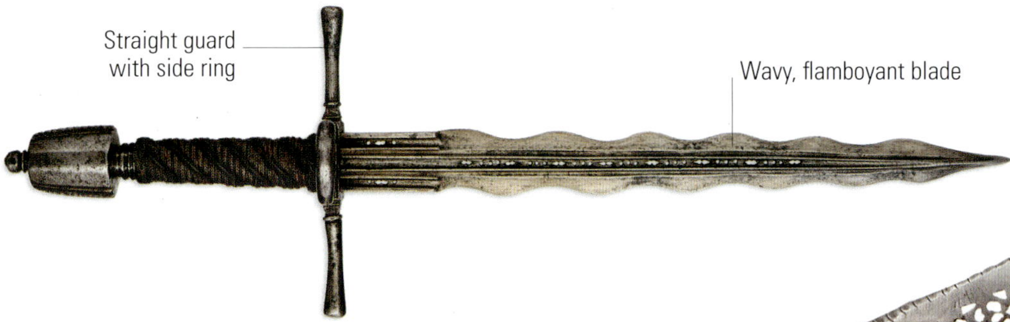

ABOVE This side ring-type parrying dagger features a very fine, wavy blade. The point is also specially strengthened so that it does not bend or break on contact with a harder material such as bone.

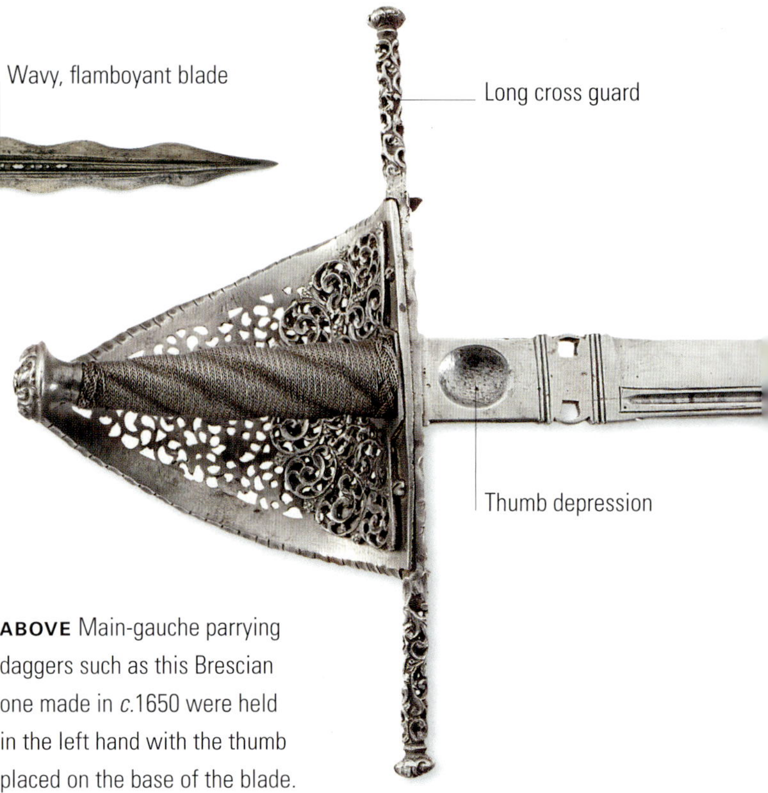

ABOVE Main-gauche parrying daggers such as this Brescian one made in *c.*1650 were held in the left hand with the thumb placed on the base of the blade.

Parrying daggers

Once this new specialist use for daggers had been invented, the weapons themselves changed, becoming better suited to this particular purpose. The cross-hilt dagger was the most suitable type for fencing, since the arms of the guard offered some protection for the hand. To provide even more protection, a simple ring of metal was added to the outside of the guard. The arms of the guard were also lengthened and were often curved down towards the blade. This provided the duellist with the opportunity to ensnare his opponent's blade. If a duellist parried an attack with the lower part of his dagger blade and gave a swift twist of his wrist, his opponent's blade might become trapped between his own blade and one of the arms of the guard. His opponent's weapon might remain ensnared only for a moment, but that moment could afford the duellist the opening he required to strike a killing blow.

Because of the way in which parrying daggers were used in conjunction with the rapier, they are today often called "left-hand daggers". Finer examples were made in sets with matching rapiers; sometimes the mounts and fittings of the sword belt were also decorated in the same way.

The blade of the parrying dagger tended to be somewhat longer than that of most other daggers of the time, generally being 30–45cm (12–18in) long. It was double-edged with a specially thickened ricasso that helped it resist the shock of repeated blows struck against enemy swords. It usually had a strong diamond-shaped cross-section and an even taper from guard to point. The rear side of the ricasso usually had an oval depression shaped into it. When the duellist held his dagger so that the knuckles were protected by the side ring, he would usually place his thumb on the ricasso to strengthen his parrying grip; this depression gave him better purchase on the weapon. Towards the end of the 16th century the blades of parrying daggers became more ornate and more flamboyant. They were often filed with very deep ridges and grooves running down their whole lengths. The troughs between the

LEFT *To the Death: A Sword and Dagger Fight Wherein One Hand Beats Cold Death Aside While The Other Sends It Back.* The full title of this 19th-century imagining of a rapier and dagger combat sums up the style.

ridges were frequently pierced with groups of minuscule round, square or diamond-shaped holes. Cutting deep grooves into the blade, as well as punching large numbers of tiny holes into it, reduced its weight very significantly, and it was a useful way of fine-tuning the balance of the weapon without compromising its strength or rigidity. Some blades were also given wavy edges, producing an impressive and perhaps intimidating visual effect.

ABOVE Later rapiers and main-gauche daggers were also made in matching sets. This handsome pair, the hilts skilfully chiselled, was made by a Neapolitan swordsmith named Antonio Cilenta in the mid-17th century.

Main-gauche daggers

The name of these daggers translates from the French as "left hand". Since the 19th century, English-speaking collectors have, however, used the term to refer specifically to a type of 17th-century parrying dagger that appeared in Spain and Spanish-held parts of the Low Countries and Italy. This weapon is most easily recognized by the curved, usually triangular knuckle guard extending over the hilt, the wide end of which attaches to the guard while the narrow point is affixed to the pommel. The arms of the guard are almost always very long, much longer than those found on any other form of dagger, and usually carry knob-like terminals. Main-gauche dagger pommels normally take the form of a flattened sphere, although some pommels are pear-shaped.

The blades are just as distinctive as the hilts. Some are long, narrow and double-edged, while others are single-edged and wider. The most common blade form, however, is made up of a very wide ricasso, usually pierced with a pair of large holes or sword-catching slots at the top, which then modulates into a narrow, sharply tapered section that forms the main body of the blade. In most cases these upper sections are single-edged along the lower half of their lengths, and double-edged on the top half to the point. The back of the lower section is very often decorated with file-work along the back; similar decoration is also very often found on both edges of the ricasso section.

ABOVE The most distinctive feature of the typical main-gauche dagger is the triangular knuckle guard, which is generally decorated with chiselling as illustrated on this Brescian example, *c.*1650.

17th- and 18th-century daggers

Despite the continuing popularity of combat with both rapier and parrying dagger in Spain and Italy after 1600, the practice suffered a general decline elsewhere in Europe. Swords became lighter, smaller and quicker to deploy, and as methods of fighting with the sword alone became dominant, the dagger quickly fell out of use. Consequently, the wearing of the dagger as a fashion statement also disappeared in most places.

ABOVE Stiletto makers often took advantage of the weapon's all-metal construction to create ornate and unusual hilt forms. This early 17th-century Italian example includes a grip in the form of a standing ape.

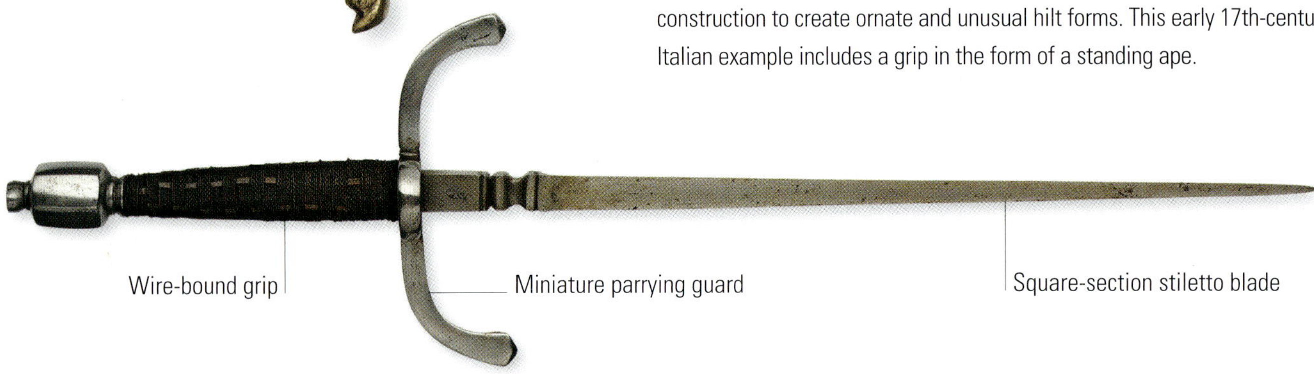

ABOVE The stiletto finds its earliest origins in miniaturized parrying daggers such as this example. They were made as elegant fashion items but never meant to be used in sword fights.

The elegant small sword was adopted throughout Europe almost as soon as it appeared. As well as being a brutally effective duelling weapon, its small size made it easy to carry, and its form was perfectly in tune with the mannered extravagance of the contemporary trends in art, clothing and behaviour. The carrying of daggers began to be seen as conservative or even uncivilized. By the late 17th century, daggers were distinctly out of date, surviving only as a form of localized traditionalism.

The stiletto

In the early 1600s a diminutive form of the ring-hilted parrying dagger appeared. Although it was designed in the same way as its larger cousin, with a straight or dropping cross guard and a side ring, this little weapon was too small to be used for fencing. The blade had been reduced to little more than a three- or four-sided needle of steel, and the stiletto was the result. The typical stiletto, or "stylet", of the 17th century was a very small, all-metal weapon usually measuring 20–23cm (8–9in) long. The rectangular- or triangular-section blade was very narrow, had no cutting edges and tapered to an extremely sharp point. Most of the best surviving examples are Italian and are usually exquisite demonstrations of steel cutting and chiselling. The hilt echoed the pervading fashions in architecture; the arms of the guard, grip and pommel were usually baluster-turned into undulating vase-like or bulbous shapes, and terminated in or incorporated rounded buttons, spheres and ovoid forms; the spaces between them were sometimes faceted, tapered or decorated with foliate designs in relief. Occasionally the grip and/or pommel were sculpted into the shapes of human or animal figures.

One variation was the larger gunner's stiletto. These military weapons had much longer blades, generally measuring 30–50cm (12–20in). The grip was usually

RIGHT In 1628 the commander of the English Army, George Villiers, 1st Duke of Buckingham, was stabbed to death by John Felton, a disgruntled soldier. Felton is shown here brandishing his small dagger.

made of horn, while the steel guard and pommel were often blued or blackened. The most characteristic aspect of the gunner's stiletto was the numbering on the blade. The incremental sequence varies but is most commonly 1, 3, 6, 9, 12, 14, 16, 20, 30, 40, 50, 60, 90, 100, 120. Between each number was engraved a line, which made the blade look something like a ruler.

The numbers represent the most widely used Italian artillery calibres of the time. It is therefore reasonable to assume that these daggers might originally have been designed as tools that artillerymen could use to measure the bore of a cannon, or the diameter of a cannon ball; the number corresponding to the closest line then indicated the correct weight of the ball. However, most of the surviving examples differ in the arrangement of the lines in relation to the numbering, so most would never have worked as instruments for weight calculation. They are therefore purely conventional, probably made for artillerymen as some kind of badge or status symbol. They had an impressive scientific appearance, and that was evidently more highly valued than any genuine functionality.

English cross-hilt daggers

Another of the very few distinctively 17th-century daggers appeared in England during the very early 1600s and remained popular there until at least 1675. The cross hilt of this form was comprised of a rectangular block supporting baluster-turned arms, or quillons, and usually displaying the typical English taste for foliate ornamentation in relief, which on finer examples was sometimes also encrusted in silver. Daggers of this form had no pommel. The hardwood, generally fluted grip simply swelled at the end, echoing the form of earlier ballock daggers.

The narrow blade of the 17th-century English dagger was split into three areas: a short, unsharpened ricasso of rectangular section; a middle cutting area of triangular section having a single sharpened edge, the back being characteristically serrated like a saw; and a reinforced stabbing point of diamond section. The ricasso and mid-section are often etched with heads in profile, scrolling vegetation and mottos, and many examples are also dated.

BELOW English daggers of the 17th century are easily recognized by their characteristic hilts and heavily etched blades, many of which are dated like this example, which is marked 1628.

RIGHT Typical "Mediterranean" dirks such as this one made in the second half of the 18th century in Liguria, northwestern Italy, have very wide bases waisting into narrow tangs.

"Mediterranean" dirks

A third important group of daggers appeared along the north coast of the Mediterranean in the mid-1600s. The weapons, collectively referred to as "Mediterranean" dirks, were actually made in a wide range of sizes and display an extraordinary variety of ornament.

The one-piece handle, made of wood, ivory or horn, is always bored through its centre to accept the narrow tang of the blade; the end is capped with metal, often silver, and the end of the tang peened (hammered) over to secure the blade. The handle in most cases also swells slightly away from the blade. "Mediterranean" dirks almost never have any form of guard. The top of the handle is generally covered with a metal sleeve or protective band at the bottom of the hilt called a ferrule, which modulates upwards into the blade via a short post, called the root of the blade. This is usually turned or faceted in a similar manner to, although stouter than, the balustered forms found on stilettos of the same period.

"Mediterranean" dirks carry either single- or double-edged blades. The single-edged types usually have a deep, unsharpened section called a choil dropping down from the handle in the manner of most kitchen knives. Usually the choil is straight, although in some cases it takes a graceful recurved line. The double-edged Mediterranean blade resembles a broad spearhead, with rounded shoulders at the base. Generally the edges of both types do not taper in straight lines but rather bulge slightly like a very

ABOVE This Native American fighting knife incorporates a European "butcher" knife blade of the 18th or early 19th century, having a straight unsharpened back and curved cutting edge.

Scalping

One practice closely associated with the darker aspects of the frontier experience in North America during the 17th, 18th and 19th centuries was scalping. This brutal exercise in mutilation involved the victim being pinned down to the ground on his or her chest, with one of the attacker's knees or feet placed between the shoulder blades. The head was yanked up by the hair and a deep incision cut all the way around the hairline with a long fighting knife. A swift tug on the handful of hair tore the skin from the skull like a bloody rag.

The scalping of dead enemies was a rare form of trophy-taking in battle among certain Native American tribes before the arrival of Europeans. It had also been practised intermittently in Europe for thousands of years. But it was encouraged on an unprecedented scale in North America after the arrival of European colonists, and was practised by white men as well as native peoples, on living as well as dead victims. In the late 17th century, scalping was endorsed by both sides during the Anglo-French conflicts that played out for nearly 100 years across what is now the United States and Canada. The French began paying for British scalps in the 1680s, and the British reciprocated by offering as much as £100 (about £8,000 today) for French and Indian scalps in the 1690s.

RIGHT This French 18th-century lithograph depicts an Iroquois warrior scalping a bound captive. He is in the process of pulling the scalp off while applying pressure with his right foot.

shallow arch. Most single-edged varieties are also sharpened on the top a few centimetres off the back. Most good examples are decorated at the base of the blade with relief ornament, engraving and piercings.

American "butcher" and "scalping" knives

The fighting knives carried on the North American frontier were quite different from the ornate daggers made in Europe, being plainer, cruder and designed to work well for a much wider range of uses – fighting men and wild animals but also undertaking the daily tasks associated with living in the forests and mountains of the frontier. The large size of these knives can be inferred from descriptions of soldiers joining the American Army in 1775, who, we are told, carried "butcher" or "scalping" knives. Because they were simply made by local craftsmen according to individual preference, they are almost impossible to date precisely, and very little else can be said about them for certain.

Despite these difficulties, it is possible to identify two basic knife forms typically carried by Americans in the 18th century. One was essentially a cross-hilt dagger with a stout double-edged blade, short guard and wooden grip that was simply tapped in place around the tang. The second was single-edged, usually with a slight curve to the back and a shallow choil above the grip. As with contemporary "Mediterranean" dirks, these American weapons looked very much like utilitarian knives, and undoubtedly this similarity led to them being described as "butcher" knives. Given the brutal use to which these knives were put, by all sides in the North American wars, it is an apt description.

Scottish dirks

The 17th century brought with it a rapid decline in the evolution and use of traditional daggers in most parts of Europe. But in a few more isolated areas, the practice of wearing and fighting with the dagger continued unabated. In northern Europe the persistent development of the essentially medieval weapon is most noticeable in Scotland, where, sometime in the 17th century, one of the most iconic daggers of all time appeared.

ABOVE This early 17th-century dudgeon dagger shows clearly its descent from earlier ballock daggers of the 15th and 16th centuries. It retains its cutting edges, but the thick spine makes it primarily a stabbing weapon.

The four important members of the medieval family of daggers experienced quite divergent later histories. The basic cross-hilted dagger multiplied into a number of more specialized forms in the 16th and 17th centuries, including the assorted forms of parrying dagger, stiletto and English dagger of the 1600s. The baselard was transformed into the classic "Swiss" dagger before disappearing by 1600. The rondel dagger, which had been such an essential part of the armoured warrior's arsenal, became scarcer as warfare became modernized and hand-to-hand combat between men-at-arms declined. The last of the great medieval dagger forms, the ballock, died out everywhere in Europe except in Scotland, where it evolved into two important new forms.

The dudgeon dagger

In the first quarter of the 17th century the earlier of the two Scottish derivatives of the medieval ballock dagger appeared in Lowland Scotland. It was generally called a "dagger of dudgeon" or simply "dudgeon dagger". The 17th-century term "dudgeon" referred to the hardwood that was used to fashion the hilt. A single piece of hardwood, most commonly boxwood but also ebony, ivy root and others, was carved into a particular interpretation of the distinctive ballock hilt design. The lobes below the base of the blade were generally quite small and much less bulbous than their medieval forebears, and were often decorated with little copper-alloy or silver rosettes on the top of each lobe. These rosettes were actually washers supporting rivets that held in place a crescent-shaped iron or steel spacer seated on the base of the blade between it and the top of the hilt. The grip swelled towards its top end, but again not in so obvious a

BELOW Dudgeon daggers display very fine etched decoration on their blades, frequently involving scrolling foliage as seen here.

ABOVE This very fine dudgeon dagger in a private collection may have belonged to François Ravaillac, murderer of King Henry IV of France. It is undoubtedly Scottish; the scabbard appears to be later European work.

way as earlier forms of ballock dagger. The grip was usually faceted and bored out for the tang of the blade; the end of the tang, where it protruded from the top of the grip, was generally covered with a metal button.

The long, narrow blade is the most instantly recognizable part of the dudgeon dagger, for despite each of the surviving examples being unique, the blades are all obviously of a type. They taper evenly from base to point and are almost always of a strong diamond (almost square) section, the sides being deeply hollow-ground. Occasionally this shaping is taken to an extreme degree, producing a blade that is essentially flat but which carries a very thick medial ridge. Sometimes the section is varied within zones along the length of the blade; one of these multi-section blades might begin with a typical rectangular-section ricasso, modulating to a hollow-ground diamond-section zone a few centimetres or so up the blade, then giving way to a single-edged area and finally ending with a square-section stabbing point.

Dudgeon dagger blades are always etched with scrolling vines and leafy patterns. Some also carry mottos or invocations. Some are dated, the dates always falling between 1600 and 1625, although it is certain that they were fashionable for a longer period. In 1635 the soldier, politician and writer Sir William Brereton wrote that on a visit to Edinburgh he bought "a dudgeon-hafted dagger ... gilt". All known dudgeon dagger blades are (or were) fire-gilt over their entire surfaces, the gold combining with the etching to give the weapons a very rich appearance.

Several other notable figures in the 17th century owned dudgeon daggers. One is said to have belonged to François Ravaillac (1578–1610), the Catholic zealot who stabbed to death King Henry IV of France (1553–1610). Another was confiscated from Colonel Thomas Blood (1618–1680) after his failed attempt to steal the Crown Jewels of England in 1671.

LEFT This portrait of François Ravaillac commemorates him as the royal assassin of Henry IV. The artist has chosen to depict him grasping a dudgeon dagger with a wavy, flamboyant blade.

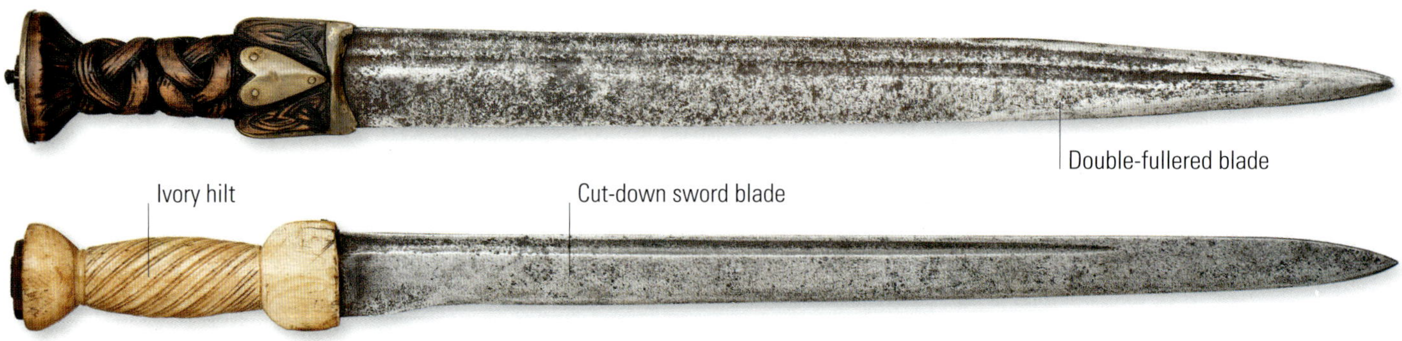

TOP The bogwood hilts of Highland dirks like this one from around 1740 were often decorated with brass plaques or plates. Sometimes the whole hilt would be made of solid brass.

ABOVE This 18th-century dirk is fitted with a less common type of hilt, carved in ivory. Bone was also occasionally used. Here a single piece of ivory has been cut and filed to create a very attractive spiralled grip.

The Highland dirk

The success of the dudgeon dagger kept the ballock dagger alive in Scotland after it had vanished everywhere else in Europe. While the dudgeon dagger was primarily carried in the Lowlands, as well as finding its way to a limited degree to England and the Continent, it may also have made an impression on the Gaelic-speaking Highlanders in the northwest of Scotland. The Highlanders still fought in an essentially medieval way, with swords, round shields and staff weapons. It may not have been long before a few dudgeon daggers fell into the hands of some of the richer clan warriors. Copies were made bigger and longer, better suited to use on the battlefield. By 1650 the Highland dirk had been created.

A number of features connect the Highland dirk and the earlier dudgeon dagger. Highland craftsmen generally used their own type of "dudgeon", namely bogwood, for the construction of the hilt. Bogwood was taken from ancient trees that had been submerged in the local peat bogs for thousands of years. The wood that was used to make dirk hilts, usually oak, was partially fossilized and consequently very hard – perfect for the purpose and easily accessible.

Dirk hilts were also cast in solid brass or, more rarely, carved in bone. They also generally displayed the spacers between blade and hilt observed on the earlier dudgeon daggers, along with a more stylized version of the ballock hilt. The lobes were much subtler, sometimes becoming flattened against the sides of the grip. Only an echo, if anything, of their original inspiration was suggested in the carving of the hilt, which was now covered in intricate knotwork designs. The pommel was flattened and widened into a disk shape, undoubtedly to provide a better grip in battle, and usually covered with a metal cap.

Highland dirk blades could be either single- or double-edged. Single-edged examples tended to be very broad at the ricasso and tapered evenly to a sharp point. The thick back of the single-edged dirk blade was often decorated with file marks or serrations and emphasized

BELOW Decorated dress dirks were produced in large numbers from the 19th century. This silver-mounted example made in Edinburgh in *c.*1900 has a small byknife and fork contained in special scabbard sleeves.

by a fuller running parallel just inside of it. Frequently, the back only extended two thirds of the way towards the point, the last third being double-edged. Other blades were entirely double-edged; indeed it was not uncommon for them to be fashioned out of old or broken sword blades.

Dirk blades were generally very long, some measuring 46cm (18in) or more. Like their medieval ancestors, they were used to stab overarm, with the blade below the fist. When the Highland warrior was fully armed, with his sword in his right hand and his *targe* (shield) in his left, the dirk was sometimes also grasped in the left hand. If enough of the blade extended below the edge of the shield, the dirk could be used offensively in that position, or passed to the right hand if the sword was lost.

After 1750 the Highland dirk began to change, shifting from a traditional weapon used by people living an ancient lifestyle into a somewhat gaudy showpiece. It became a signature badge of the Highland regiments of the British Army and the essential features became exaggerated. The grip began to be studded with small round-headed nails and bulged much more drastically in its midst, taking on an exaggerated thistle shape. In the 19th century the craze for all things Scottish turned the Highland dirk into a parody of itself, the carving of the hilt degenerating into second-rate basketwork, the scabbards set with hulking silver or gilt mounts, and the whole object finished off with large yellow crystals called cairngorms (or more often, glass imitations). This modern version, much removed from the original form, remains a standard part of formal Highland dress.

The sgian dubh (skean dhu)

Another small Scottish knife that should be mentioned at this point, although it is really a 19th-century creation, is the *sgian dubh* (*skean dhu*), or "black knife". Like the later Highland dirk, this very small knife is still worn as part of Highland dress. While this weapon may be a descendant of knives carried by Highland warriors, there are no surviving examples that date from earlier than the 19th century. It is therefore generally thought, probably correctly, that the sgian dubh was a product of the Romantic revival of Highland dress in the 1800s.

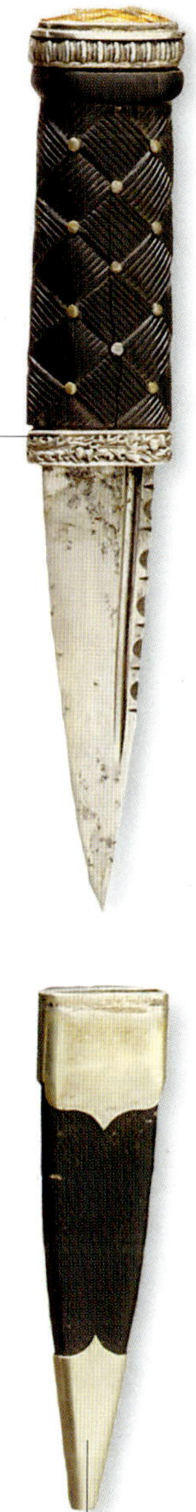

RIGHT The famous sgian dubh may be descended from small knives hidden up the sleeve, but in their well-known form they are entirely modern and cosmetic, as is this early 20th-century Edinburgh-made example.

LEFT The *c.*1870 portrait of John Chisholm of the Clan Chisholm (factions of which fought on both sides at the Battle of Culloden) shows Highland dress complete with the long dirk worn on the right side and the sgian dubh down the right stocking.

17th- and 18th-century bayonets

Early long-guns were one-shot weapons. After firing, they took time to reload. In that time an enemy could rush the shooter to attack him at close-quarters. The shooter could defend himself with an empty musket by swinging it like a club, but this required space to move – an uncommon luxury in pitched battle. The invention of the bayonet made it possible to transform the musket into a short spear, perfect for close combat.

ABOVE This English plug bayonet of the late 17th century shows a very fine inlaid handle. It is fitted with a decorated pommel cap and an ornately wrought cross guard.

It is remarkable that so soon after the enormous technological breakthrough that was the hand-held firearm, men were searching for a way to turn it back into one of humanity's most ancient weapons – a spear. Until the mid-17th century, the spear and the firearm worked together – an army's musketeers were protected by ranks of soldiers armed with long spears called pikes. The pikemen formed a hedge-like defence, which kept the enemy from rushing the musketeers while they reloaded. But this meant that any man with a pike was restricted to an entirely defensive role. This was wasteful and military theorists worked hard to find a way to give the musketeer defensive as well as offensive capabilities. Initial efforts were not very successful. One idea was for the musketeer to unscrew the head of his musket-rest and then insert the long staff into the barrel of his musket, turning it into a spear. But this process was quickly found to be slow and troublesome.

The birth of the bayonet

It is not known when and from whom the inspiration of wedding a knife to the end of a musket first came, but it is likely to have happened in or near Eibar in the Basque province of Guipúzcoa, northwestern Spain. Eibar was an important centre for the production of weapons during the late 16th century, an industry that was also the economic mainstay of many surrounding towns. It is possible that daggers designed for wedging into the muzzles of long-guns were being produced here as early as the 1580s, probably for hunters. Like the soldiers of the time, hunters were armed with single-shot firearms and were in danger of being charged by their wounded prey; they thus had to be protected by another man with a spear. A knife jammed quickly into the barrel of the long-gun allowed a man to hunt alone. It would not be long before the military potential of this invention was realized.

The daggers of Bayonne

This specialized dagger, which would later become universally known as the "bayonet", initially referred to any dagger made in Bayonne in the southwestern corner of France, not far from Eibar. It may have been first employed in battle during the French Wars of Religion (1562–1629). At the Battle of Ivry in 1590, King Henry IV of France is said to have armed his troops with bayonets. Henry himself came from the Basque region where the bayonet was probably developed and at the time of the battle he did not have enough pikemen. The musket-dagger from his native land would have been an excellent solution to this problem. Voltaire (1694–1778), the great French dramatist and satirist, certainly believed that King Henry's men had bayonets at Ivry. In reference to

ABOVE *The Battle of Ivry*, by Peter Paul Rubens, *c.*1628–1630. Henry IV's famous victory on 14 March 1590 over the Catholic League is said to have been the first time the bayonet was deployed as a battlefield weapon.

what turned out to be Henry's great victory, Voltaire in 1723 wrote one of the most evocative descriptions of this new weapon:

United with the musket, the bloody knife
Already for both sides posed a double death.
This weapon which once, to depopulate the earth,
In Bayonne was invented by the demon of war
Mustered simultaneously, those worthy fruits of Hell,
Which are most terrible, the fire and the steel.

The city of Bayonne had also produced edged weapons during the 16th century. The earliest known use of the term "bayonet" describes "a gilded dagger which was given the name Bayonnet". A French-English dictionary of 1611 defines the word as "a kind of small flat pocket dagger… or a great knife to hang at the girdle". Other sources mention daggers "of Bayonne". It seems that these weapons did not differ very greatly from other common types of daggers. Yet once the idea of the bayonet (as it is now understood) had taken off, Bayonne could have become the first manufacturer of the weapon on a large scale. It would not therefore be surprising if such a precise term as "bayonet", a word that lacked an equally unambiguous meaning, were to have gained a more exact use in the application to this newly specialized weapon.

BELOW Musketeers had to be protected when reloading. Here they are marching alongside halberdiers, although pikemen were commonly used to guard them on the battlefield until the introduction of the bayonet.

TOP English bladesmiths initially experimented with curved bayonet blades, such as this one dated 1680, but they were soon abandoned.

ABOVE This slightly later example of an English bayonet, dated 1686, is more typical in form, having a blade that is not dissimilar to the wide spearheads of previous centuries.

Plug bayonets

An important early reference to the military bayonet was made by Jacques de Chastenet (1600–1682), a French commander and native of Bayonne. In a description of the soldiers under his command in 1647, he wrote:

...they had bayonets with handles one foot long, and the blades of the bayonets were as long as the handles, the ends of which were adapted for putting in the barrels of the muskets to defend themselves, when attacked after they had fired.

This passage is not only the first reliable source that places the bayonet in a military context, it is also the first definite use of the term "bayonet" in reference to an edged weapon designed to be inserted into the barrel of a firearm. De Chastenet is discussing what we now call a "plug bayonet", essentially a dagger with a tapered grip that can be jammed firmly into the firing end or muzzle of a musket.

Although undoubtedly an important innovation, the plug bayonet was not without its drawbacks. Once embedded in an enemy, it could be hard to withdraw without it popping out of the barrel, making repeated attacks very difficult. More crucially, the musket could not be fired with the bayonet in place. This weakness of the design had serious consequences. At the Battle of Killiecrankie (1689) the British Army was defeated by the Jacobites, mostly Highland Scots, because their musketeers had to pause to fix bayonets. The Jacobites therefore wisely employed the famous "Highland Charge". After firing the few firearms that they had, the Jacobites rushed downhill into the British line armed with swords and shields. While this tactic meant that the Jacobites received a full barrage of musket fire

BELOW French military scientist Sébastien Le Prestre, Seigneur de Vauban, developed the socket bayonet as a response to the plug bayonet's debilitating drawback of preventing fire while being fixed. His work revolutionized early modern warfare.

as they raced in, those that survived were suddenly amongst their enemies before bayonets could be fixed. At such close range, the swords and shields of the Jacobites outclassed those redcoats who had managed to put their bayonets to use. The British forces were cut to pieces, suffering over 2000 casualties.

The socket bayonet

A number of plug bayonet modifications were considered as ways of getting around the essential firing problem. The "ring bayonet" is often thought to have been one of these modifications, wherein a pair of rings was used to fix the bayonet to the side of the musket barrel. There is, however, no evidence that ring bayonets actually existed beyond the drawing board. Another short-lived idea was the "folding bayonet"– a thin, spear-like projection permanently attached to the barrel, which hinged into place.

The plug bayonet was made obsolete by the invention of the socket bayonet. This new form was composed of a tubular sleeve that fitted over the end of the musket's barrel, to the side of which was welded a bayonet blade. The famous military scientist Sébastien Le Prestre, Seigneur de Vauban (1633–1707), was the most active early developer of the socket bayonet, if not its inventor. In 1687 he wrote that as a result of the adoption of the socket bayonet:

...a soldier with a single weapon would have two of the best in the world in his hand... he could fire and reload very quickly without removing the bayonet. By doing this, there is no doubt that a batallion armed in this way...would be worth at least two of any existing batallions and would be in a position to scorn the pikes and the cavalry of any country...

De Vauban advocated a bayonet blade that was triangular in section, with one flat side facing against the barrel. The earliest socket bayonets had blades

ABOVE King Frederick II of Prussia (1712–1786), called "the Great", was one of the greatest military leaders of all time. This 19th-century lithograph shows him at the head of his army, which bristles with bayonets.

welded directly to the socket, but this was not ideal as slightly bent blades could project into the bullet's path. They also made muzzle loading difficult; a musketeer might accidentally stab himself in the hand while ramming down a charge. To improve the design, the blade was placed on the end of a short arm, or shank, which projected out and away from the line of fire, placing the blade along its own parallel path.

Although a great many slight adjustments to this bayonet concept were to come, the essential idea proved so successful that this remained the standard bayonet form for nearly 200 years. Thus what was really a late 17th-century piece of technology was still in use during World War I, and was even reintroduced by the British Army during World War II.

BELOW Some early socket bayonets such as this 18th-century example had wide blades like the earlier plug versions, but were supported by an L-shaped bracket and socket.

19th-century edged weapons

The Industrial Revolution ushered in the mass production of weapons. Knives and daggers continued to be made by hand but traditional bladesmiths were less essential. The use of fighting knives for personal defence declined dramatically in Europe, but less so in the United States. Mass production made it possible to standardize bayonet manufacture, and millions of duplicates of pattern types were produced for every major world army.

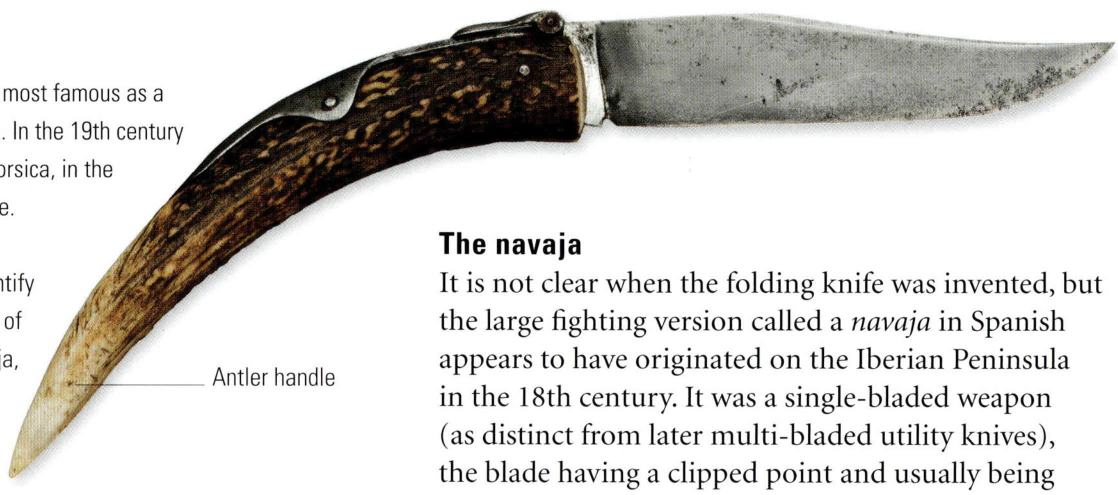

ABOVE The navaja is probably most famous as a Spanish street-fighting weapon. In the 19th century it was also made in Italy and Corsica, in the form of this needle-like example.

RIGHT It is very difficult to identify the exact place of manufacture of other plainer forms of the navaja, like, for example, this simple antler-handled weapon.

In the first half of the 19th century, most European countries were establishing professional police forces charged with keeping the public peace. Law and order became an expected part of everyday civilian life, and personal violence became increasingly unacceptable. The fashion for men to carry knives and daggers as a matter of routine fell away rapidly as the sense of a need for public decorum and civility prevailed in the minds of law-abiding people. An important exception to this general social trend was the recently formed United States of America.

Knives in the United States

In the first half of the 19th century most American men wore knives. The seemingly marked increase in the practice during the 1820s and 1830s, in direct contrast to European developments, was perhaps due to the increasing social discord that later culminated in the American Civil War (1861–65). During these turbulent decades, several key knife-types stood out.

The navaja

It is not clear when the folding knife was invented, but the large fighting version called a *navaja* in Spanish appears to have originated on the Iberian Peninsula in the 18th century. It was a single-bladed weapon (as distinct from later multi-bladed utility knives), the blade having a clipped point and usually being 15–20cm (6–8in) long, although some extended to 30cm (1ft) or even more. The blade was locked open by means of a spring catch. To release it, one usually pulled up on a ring or chain to free the catch and release the blade, which could then be closed again. The narrow grip, which could be straight although most were curved, was usually made up of an iron lining decorated with stag or cow horn. More expensive examples were ornamented with ivory and sometimes even gold.

The navaja was known as the weapon of workers, criminals and sailors. It was made in France, Italy and Corsica as well as Spain. In 1849, a manual on navaja fighting techniques was published in Madrid; it also contained instruction on how to fight with other knives and with scissors.

In North America the navaja is also considered a classic fighting knife, especially in California where no doubt this particular weapon was one of the many legacies of former Spanish rule. The navaja must have been common in the streets of old San Francisco,

ABOVE In 1853 a Hungarian nationalist stabbed the Austrian Emperor Franz Joseph I in the neck as he walked with an aide in Vienna. The Emperor survived and the assassin was executed.

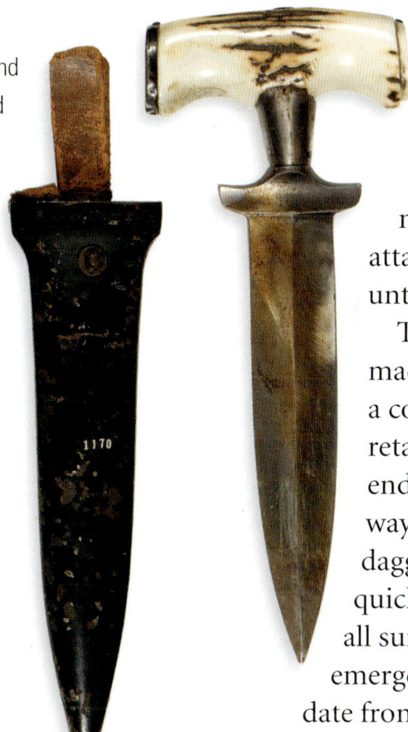

RIGHT The classical 19th-century push dagger was small and designed to be hidden inside the owner's clothing. This good example has a grip of antler and retains its scabbard, which is designed to be worn upside-down for easy access.

which appears to have been an especially violent place in the mid-19th century. One account describes a lawman being stabbed by a judge, although whether or not he used a navaja is not mentioned.

The push dagger

Another classic American weapon of the early 19th century was the push dagger. This deadly little weapon was composed of a stout double-edged blade with a short, round-section tang that terminated in a transverse grip – of bone, horn or wood – giving the dagger an overall T-shape. A man would grip a push dagger in his fist with the blade protruding between the middle and ring fingers, the base of the blade sitting a little less than 2.5cm (1in) above the knuckles. He would strike a blow with a swift punching movement; bystanders might not even be aware that a knife attack had occurred, nor even the victim until he caught sight of his own blood.

The push dagger scabbard was often made to be worn upside-down inside a coat or jacket, having a spring clip to retain the weapon and a hook on the end of the chape for suspension. In this way a man could easily secrete a push dagger about his person and draw it quickly when the need arose. Almost all surviving examples (before their re-emergence in the 20th century) seem to date from before around 1860.

ABOVE This portrait of James Bowie (1793–1836) was probably completed in the late 1820s, around the time he and his brother Rezin were perfecting their famous knife.

ABOVE The 1836 storming of the Alamo mission by Mexican troops. James Bowie died during the battle, purportedly defending himself from his sickbed with firearms and his knife.

The Bowie knife

In 1827 an Arkansas plantation owner named Rezin Pleasant Bowie was attacked by a bull. Rezin tried to stab the bull in the head, but his knife could not pierce the bull's skull. Rezin managed to survive nonetheless, and in his quest for a more reliable knife he had an old file ground down to create a large single-edged knife. The blade was over 23cm (9in) long and 4cm (1.5in) wide, and it was fitted with a cross guard and simple wooden grip. Rezin gave a knife of this form to his brother James, who later that same year was involved in the famous "sandbar fight" at Vidalia, Louisiana, on the Mississippi River. James was shot and stabbed, but still managed to use his brother's knife to disembowel one assailant, wound another and chase off a third. The local press reported the fight, along with details of James Bowie's unusually large knife, and a legend began.

"Jim" Bowie's fame increased in 1829 when he wounded and then spared a man in a knife fight. That episode in itself would perhaps not have proved newsworthy but for the fact that shortly thereafter Bowie was attacked by three associates of his defeated opponent. He apparently decapitated one and disembowelled another. The third fled.

The knife that Jim Bowie used in 1829 was a new version that he had commissioned himself, a modification of his brother Rezin's original idea. The weapon had a longer blade with a clipped point sharpened on both sides. This design became the basis for the traditional Bowie knife, as it is known today.

In 1830 Jim Bowie moved to Texas and became involved in the local rebellion against Mexican rule. After numerous battles, he ended up at the siege of the Alamo in 1836. One hundred and eighty-eight Texans defended this small mission complex against an overwhelming Mexican force. When the Mexicans stormed the mission, the Texans killed at least 200 and wounded another 400 before being wiped out. Bowie was ill in bed during the final assault; nevertheless, he is said to have defended himself with his pistols, a broken rifle and his famous knife before being killed.

After this last battle, it seemed that everyone wanted a Bowie knife, even if nobody could agree on what it was supposed to look like. Clearly it needed to have a

BELOW The English manufacturer James Rodgers & Co produced a number of different types of Bowie knife for the American market in the years immediately before the American Civil War. This Rodgers "medium" includes an antler grip.

ABOVE Sheffield was perhaps the most important foreign producer of Bowie knives in the mid–late 19th century. This silver-handled one is from *c.*1870.

RIGHT Both Union and Confederate armies issued Bowie knives to their soldiers at the start of the American Civil War. This Confederate example came from Selma, Alabama.

big blade and there was a general consensus that it should be single-edged. Soon the name "Bowie knife" was used to refer to any large single-edged knife. They began to be manufactured in Mississippi, Louisiana, Arkansas, Texas, Tennessee and Missouri. The blades were 23–38cm (9–15in) long and generally 4–5cm (1.5–2in) wide. The guards were straight or S-shaped, while grips were usually made of wood or antler. Many Bowie knives were also customized and personalized by their owners in some way.

English cutlery manufacturers quickly realized the potential of this product and began exporting it in large numbers for sale to hunters, trappers, soldiers and others in the harsh environment of the American frontier. As more Bowie knives became available, firms began to compete by producing more elaborate and expensive versions. Mother-of-pearl and turtle-shell grips were mounted on silver hilts, while blades were acid-etched and even blued and gilt. English makers also emblazoned them with jingoistic slogans conceived to appeal to Americans at the time, such as "Death to Traitors" (hinting at rising pre-Civil War tensions), "Death to Abolition" (appealing to the predominant southern demand for the continuation of slavery), and "Equal Rights and Justice for All" (representing the northern stance against slavery).

At the beginning of the American Civil War, the Bowie knife was popular on both sides, the Confederates favouring a version fitted with a D-shaped knuckle guard. This initial popularity in a way mirrored the original passion for the war in both the Union and Confederate States, and just like that enthusiasm, it died out as the conflict became longer and bloodier. By the end of the war both North and South had discarded their fighting knives, and after peace was declared the wearing of knives became distinctly unfashionable. By 1880, the true Bowie knife had disappeared.

LEFT Bowie knives were popular with trappers, mountain men and cowboys. Here the famous gunfighter James Butler "Wild Bill" Hickok (1837–1876) is photographed with two revolvers and a long Bowie knife.

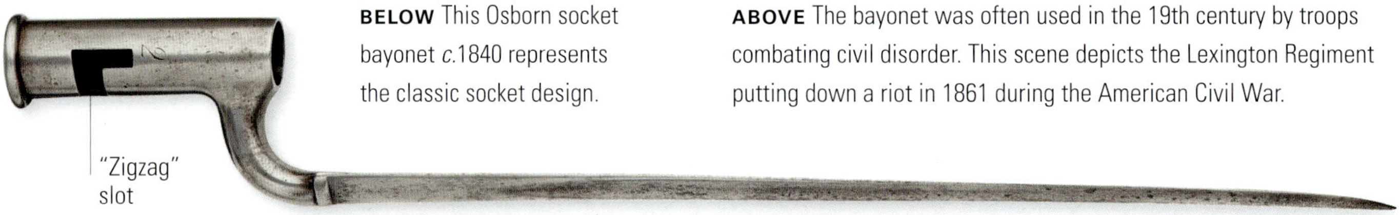

BELOW This Osborn socket bayonet *c.*1840 represents the classic socket design.

ABOVE The bayonet was often used in the 19th century by troops combating civil disorder. This scene depicts the Lexington Regiment putting down a riot in 1861 during the American Civil War.

The socket bayonet

This bayonet remained the primary type issued to the rank-and-file soldier throughout most of the 19th century. While blade forms varied to some extent, the main area of improvement in the 1800s was the method of attachment. In the 18th century the most common method had been a "zigzag" slot in the socket, which engaged with the forward sight and locked with a half turn. This method was not entirely satisfactory. At the battle of Meeanee, during the Indian Sind campaign of 1843, British soldiers encountered problems when their enemies started pulling the bayonets off in combat, requiring them to be tied on more securely with string. British arms manufacturers were meanwhile experimenting with new spring mechanisms to lock the bayonet down more securely.

The spring bayonet

The Hanoverian spring catch came into service in the same year as Meeanee. This little S-shaped catch, fitted to the barrel, engaged a collar on the bayonet and made it more difficult to be dislodged. The locking ring was an even better idea, and was quickly taken up by France and other European countries. The locking ring allowed the sight to seat down into the socket slot through a notch at its join, but then was rotated to lock behind the sight. Britain adopted the locking ring in 1853, when it was fitted to the Enfield rifle bayonet.

The sword bayonet

Late in the 18th century, in Denmark, attempts were made to create two weapons in one when the 1791 cavalry sword was converted into a bayonet by shortening the blade and fitting an attachment mechanism to the side of the weapon. The British married similar long "sword" bayonets to the 1800 Baker and 1837 Brunswick rifles. The French introduced perhaps the most popular sword

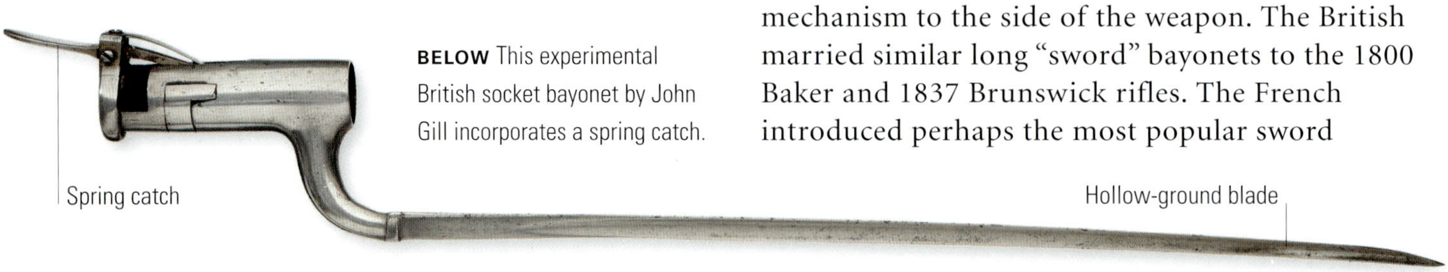

BELOW This experimental British socket bayonet by John Gill incorporates a spring catch.

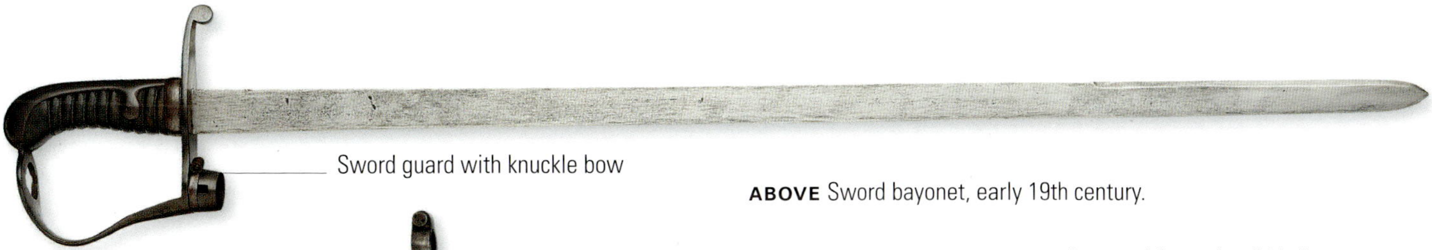

ABOVE Sword bayonet, early 19th century.

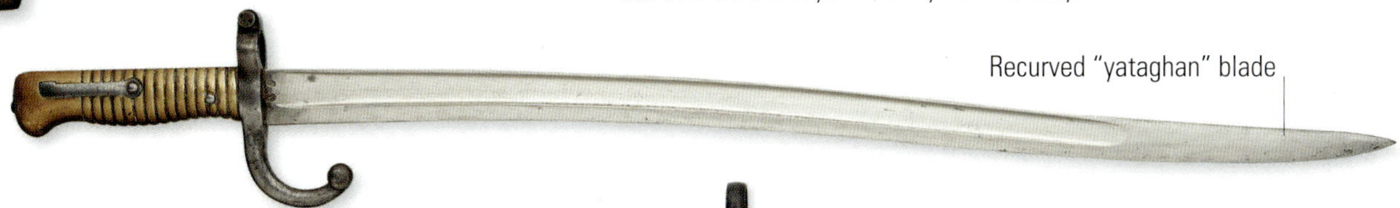

ABOVE Sword bayonet, mid-19th century.

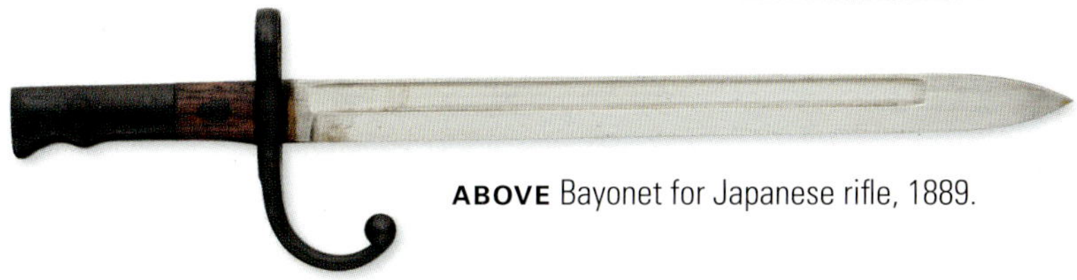

ABOVE Bayonet for Japanese rifle, 1889.

BELOW Elcho sword bayonet for Martini Henry, 1870.

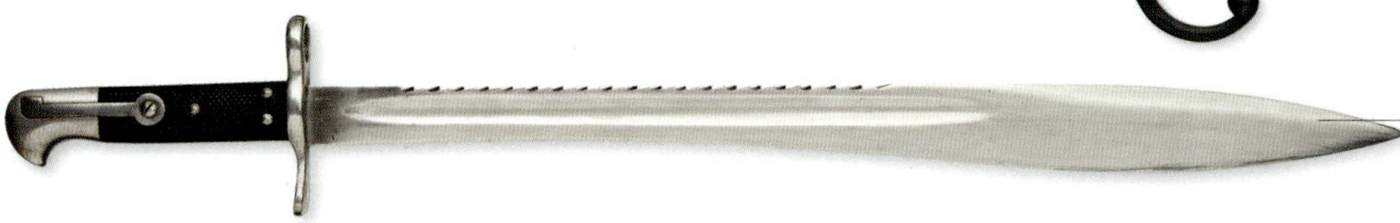

RIGHT Francis Richard Charteris, Lord Elcho, 10th Earl of Wemyss, was a prominent Whig politician, commander of the London Scottish Regiment, and inventor of the Elcho bayonet. He died at the age of 96 in 1914.

bayonet pattern in 1842. It had a brass hilt, simple cross guard, and a beaked pommel. The recurved "yataghan" blade-shape was taken from the famous Turkish sword. It was enormously successful and adopted in Scandinavia, Austria, Britain, the United States and many other countries. The British 1853 and 1856 artillery bayonets were carbon-copies of the French 1842, while in the United States various yataghan-bladed bayonets appeared; these included the 1855 and 1861 (Navy) patterns.

The sword bayonet remained popular until the late 19th century despite being heavy and impractical, and a large number of sword designs proliferated after 1850. Britain took the lead, developing many versions in the ultimately futile search for a multi-use weapon. Cutlass bayonets were issued to the Navy and knuckle-guard types developed for artillerymen. One of the oddest was Lord Elcho's "1870 experimental sword bayonet", which was also a sword, saw and machete. The Elcho suffered from the flaw inherent in all combination weapons – any attempt to design for multiple uses always compromises each of those uses. It was very expensive to manufacture and its heaviness made shooting difficult. Initially rejected, the Elcho was revived in 1895 and saw limited use in the Ashanti campaign of 1895–6.

The long and complicated exercise of developing the sword bayonet was proved to be ultimately futile, being the wrong weapon for a rapidly modernizing battlefield. Artillery and overall firepower superiority were the keys to modern war, and the bayonet was essentially a defensive weapon of last resort. Sword versions were consequently discarded in favour of smaller knife types. In 200 years the bayonet, which had begun its history as a knife jammed into the muzzle, had returned to its roots.

20th-century edged weapons

Advances in firearms technology, and the soldier's increased individual firepower created by the widespread adoption of bolt-action magazine rifles by the early years of the 20th century, reduced the chances of close contact with the enemy. However, bayonets and fighting knives still maintained their place in the soldier's armoury, whether as weapons on the battlefield or ceremonial items on the parade ground.

During the early years of the 20th century, warfare underwent its most dramatic changes since the appearance of the firearm. At sea vast increases in naval firepower meant that battleships now engaged at ranges of miles rather than yards. Boarding parties wielding cutlasses and axes were becoming a distant memory and submarines added a new dimension as stalking assassins. Warfare took to the air, at first tentatively and then in earnest, allowing death to be dealt from above and taking conflict beyond the battlefield to the towns and cities of the enemy. Land warfare also underwent dramatic change. New types of artillery meant that it outranked every other weapon on the battlefield. When joined by the machine gun both had a devastating impact on the way battles were fought. The days of stalemate entrenchment dawned with World War I (1914–18). When the idea emerged of placing artillery and machine guns in armour-plated, fast-moving vehicles, entrenchment gave way to "Blitzkrieg" – lightning war – in World War II (1939–45).

But technology tends to advance faster than the abilities of soldiers to integrate it into new tactics and strategies effectively, especially if they have been tutored in the "old ways". Although long sword bayonets and battlefield derring-do such as cavalry and bayonet charges had been rendered ineffective by the late 19th century, a surprisingly long time had to pass before this equipment and such practices were finally discarded in favour of equipment and tactics more suited to the needs of the tasks in hand.

Bayonets of World War I

Despite the fact that in the late 19th century long sword bayonets had been found to be too cumbersome and awkward to be really effective, most nations retained them as they entered World War I. The old idea of "reach" – the ability to outreach the enemy's rifle with a bayonet attached – persisted. Austro-Hungarian infantrymen were issued with the 1895 Mannlicher 8mm rifle which was fitted with a long sword bayonet. The Turks, carrying the Mauser Gewehr 98 7.65mm rifle, also preferred a very long-bladed bayonet with a cross guard, which had a hook-shaped quillon. Whether used to allow rifles to be stacked together neatly in a tripod arrangement or, as some would believe, to ensnare the enemy's bayonet blade and either break it or deflect the thrust, these bayonets were still far more likely to become snagged on something inconsequential

RIGHT An illustration of a French bayonet charge at Valmy featured on the front page of this French newspaper in 1915.

BELOW The optimistic French bayonet charges of the first half of World War I employed the long needle-bladed Lebel bayonet like this pre-1916 example.

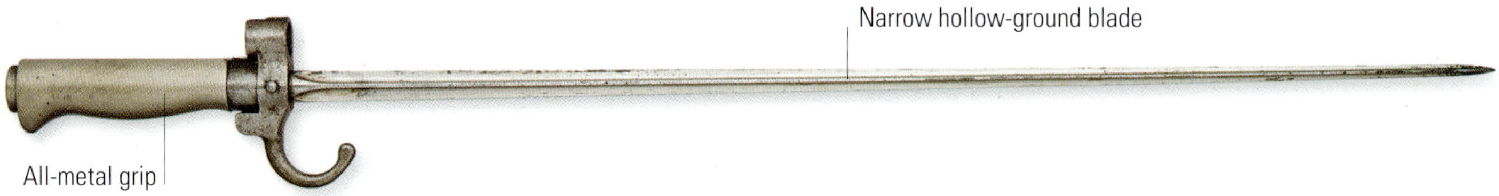

at a crucial moment. The Italian bayonets for the Mannlicher-Carcano and Vetterli-Carcano rifles of the late 19th century which saw service in World War I resembled the British 1907 Pattern.

ABOVE This rare black-and-white photo of the 10th Company of the 9th Russian Guards, taken in 1917, shows the Russian troops armed with old-fashioned socket bayonets.

The British, who had discarded their various long sword bayonets in favour of the shorter knife patterns of 1888 and 1903, returned before World War I to a long-bladed sword bayonet design, the 1907 Pattern, which replaced the 1903 Pattern on their SMLE (Short, Magazine, Lee-Enfield) rifles. The 1907 Pattern, which was equipped with a 43cm (17in) blade, was produced initially with a cross guard featuring a "hook" quillon, reflecting widespread 19th-century fashion. The design was very successful; basically copied from the Japanese Model 1897 Arisaka bayonet, more than 2.5 million were produced in Britain. However, as soldiers found the hooked quillon of this bayonet to be a nuisance, the decision was made to abandon the hook design in 1913 before it had even been used in earnest. The United States of America's Model 1917 was a copy of the British 1914 Pattern bayonet design, itself a modification of the 1907 Pattern but with a longer, straight cross guard.

Another inconvenience of a long bayonet is its weight. Some countries tried to retain the length of the sword bayonet while also avoiding the weight problem. The French developed the long epee bayonet for their 1886 Pattern Lebel rifle, the very narrow blade of which was given a cruciform cross-section to reduce weight even further while at the same time retaining strength. The Russians – perhaps the most poorly equipped major army of the war – went one step further and removed even more weight by abandoning a conventional hilt and using a socket bayonet with a cruciform-sectioned blade on the 1891 Moisin Nagant 7.62mm rifle. This in itself was simply a continuation of tradition, an almost identical form of bayonet being used on the Russian Model 1871 Berdan rifle. In Britain, the contemporary long Model 1895 socket bayonet was designed for the new Lee-Enfield rifle.

BELOW An early British 1907 Pattern complete with hooked quillon. Although the hook was officially declared obsolete in 1913, some still entered World War I in their unmodified state.

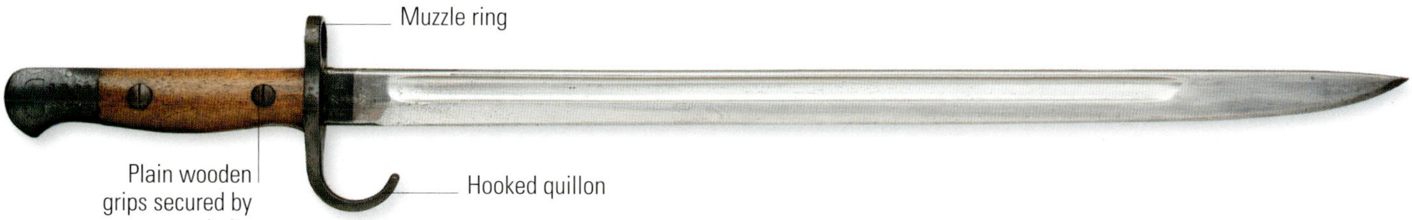

ABOVE This ersatz bayonet of around 1916 was modified to fit the German M88/98 Mauser rifle.

World War I German bayonet forms

Germany had adopted a short "knife" bayonet for the Model 1884 Mauser rifle, and this bayonet continued in use on the Mauser Gewehr Model 1898. The Germans therefore entered the war with a shorter bayonet than those of most of the other protagonists. Even so, the *seitengewehr* (sidearm) bayonet originally designed for the Gewehr 1898 rifle had a blade that was even longer than that of the British 1907 Pattern, and it also saw service. In 1905, Germany found a middle ground in bayonet design with the introduction of the so-called "butcher knife" or "butcher blade" bayonet. The terminology was probably invented by the Allies as part of a propaganda campaign, but the blade certainly had an unusual shape with its increasing width towards the point, reminiscent of the British Elcho of 1871. In various forms this new German bayonet was probably the most widely used during the war. By 1916 Germany was suffering from an increasingly stressed economy and a shortage of raw materials as a result of an Allied naval blockade. In an effort to keep its troops supplied, Germany developed simplified designs and manufacturing techniques. Even old sword blades were cut down and fitted with mounts for Mauser rifles. The Germans also began to recycle captured weapons, and many Belgian, French and Russian bayonets were converted to fit German rifles. These two types of weapon were generally referred to as *ersatz*, or "emergency", bayonets and exist in huge variety.

LEFT British troops, equipped with standard-issue bayonets fitted to their rifles, make fun of Mussolini's characteristic arrogant posture in this portrait of *Il Duce* after the capture of Cyrenaica, Libya, in 1941.

Bayonets of World War II

After World War I, the relevance of the bayonet in modern warfare was frequently questioned. The number of bayonet wounds inflicted in World War I appears to have been minimal. For example, one study showed that of a sample of 200,000 wounds suffered by British soldiers, only 600 were caused by bayonets, while the American forces estimated that only .024 per cent of their injuries were bayonet-related. Even so, bayonets remained a standard part of the infantryman's equipment on both sides during World War II. Some of the types common in World War I remained in use during World War II, the Japanese Arisaka bayonet being one example. But the general trend was towards shorter versions.

The British began to replace their 1907 Pattern with a series of short knife bayonets. Some, like the No 5 bayonet for the Jungle Carbine, had a more or less conventional hilt similar to that of the 1907 Pattern.

RIGHT Propaganda posters such as this American example invariably show idealized soldiers dramatically wielding rifles with fixed bayonets. The bayonet was synonymous with the tough, indomitable "good guy".

Its blade was very different, not only in being much shorter but also in being more akin to that of the fabled Bowie knife. But most of this new series utilized what was in effect a return to the principle of the socket bayonet. The No 4 bayonet for the new No 4 rifle had a cruciform-section blade very similar to that of the French 1886 Lebel but only 20cm (9in) in length. It was fitted to a relatively simple block with a locking device for attachment to the muzzle of the rifle. The rifle muzzle itself had two lugs which engaged with internal slots in the "socket" or muzzle ring of the bayonet. This more or less experimental Mk I bayonet was quickly replaced in 1940 by the Mk II, which had a plain round "spike" or "pig-sticker" blade and was easier and cheaper to manufacture.

This trend continued with the No 7 bayonet. This again had the Bowie-type blade and a complex hilt, which allowed it in one mode to be gripped and used as a knife. The pommel could also be swivelled through 180 degrees, allowing it to act as a socket for fitting to the rifle. Both the No 5 and No 7 bayonets are also characterized by their very large muzzle rings. In the case of the No 5, this allowed the bayonet to accommodate the mouth of the flash hider (the device that masked the firing flash). In the case of the No 7, the "muzzle ring" did not function in that capacity at all. Finally, the No 9 bayonet was produced for the Royal Navy and was a cross between the No 5 and No 4 series in that it had a Bowie blade fitted to a socket.

When the United States entered the war in 1941, most American infantrymen were armed with the pre-World War I 41cm (16in) M1905 Pattern bayonet (later renamed the M1942). But like most other nations, the United States soon recognized the necessity of utilizing a shorter knife pattern, which could also be used as a fighting knife. The M1 bayonet, which had a much shorter 25cm (10in) blade, was introduced in 1943.

ABOVE The popular Japanese 1897 Pattern Arisaka bayonet was copied for the British 1907 design, which was used until the end of World War II.

BELOW The majority of modern bayonet designs focused on multi-use weapons. The 1940 British "pig-sticker" reverted to the other extreme previously inhabited by socket types – it was exclusively a bayonet.

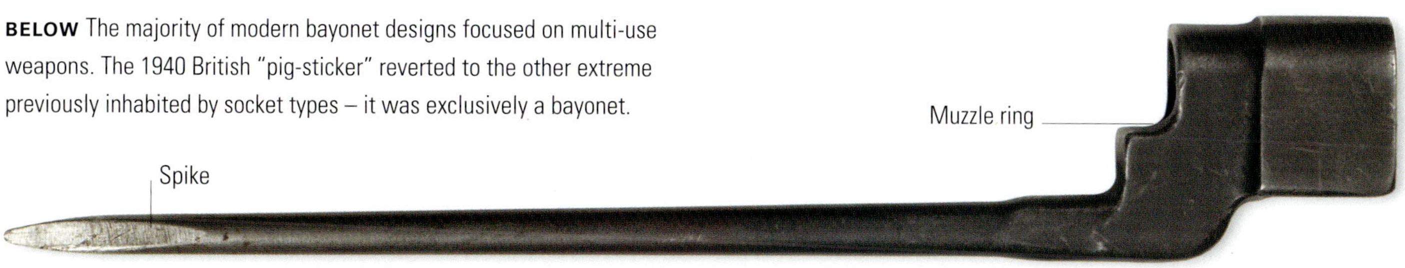

The bayonet in conflict

The effectiveness of the bayonet not only as a hand-to-hand combat weapon but as a psychological weapon was clearly demonstrated during the Battle of the Reichswald Forest in February 1945. At one stage, groups of British and German soldiers were engaged in a bitter firefight as they hid in ditches and holes. With no more than 200m (650ft) between them, the British decided to rush the German line. They fixed bayonets and ran forward. As soon as the British charge began, the Germans ceased fire and raised their hands in surrender. For these modern soldiers, trained to kill from afar and demoralized by many months of continual combat, the threat of "cold steel" was clearly too much. This was the last bayonet charge of the war.

ABOVE Bayonets line the trenches along the Western Front where German soldiers keep guard during World War I.

The fighting knives of World Wars I and II

Above all, World War I was characterized by trench warfare. After an initial advance into Belgium and northern France, the German army was halted by the Allied forces. Both sides "dug in" and fortified their positions with trench systems that extended for hundreds of miles. This stalemate situation led to hand-to-hand fighting on a limited scale. If one side mounted a full-scale assault, rushing en masse across the landmines and barbed wire of "no man's land", any troops who were fortunate enough to get past the enemy machine guns had to be prepared to fight at close quarters in the confined environment of the enemy trench. Here the long-bladed bayonet was of little use, since there was no space to wield it. Trench combat thus necessitated the military reinstatement of the dagger, or fighting knife.

Some early trench knives were simply fashioned from cut-down bayonets, although they were also made from many other objects, including the metal posts that were used to support the barbed-wire defences. As well as their role as close-range combat weapons, trench knives were also useful to small raiding parties sent into enemy territory to take prisoners or gather intelligence, when the ability to kill silently was all-important.

World War I brought the fighting knife officially back to the battlefield after a 200-year absence. Its modern relevance having been acknowledged, the development of the military fighting knife continued throughout the period between the wars.

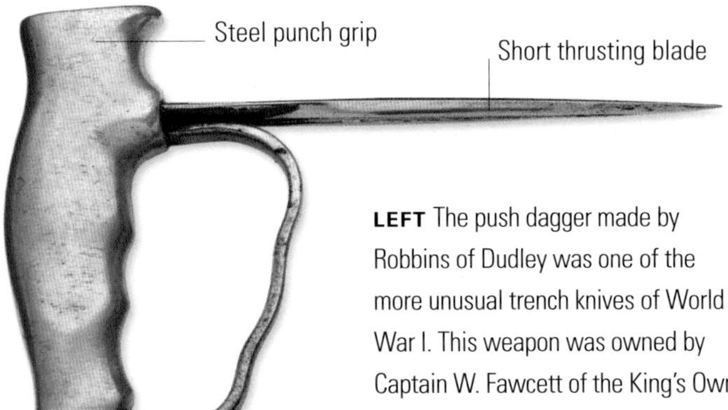

LEFT The push dagger made by Robbins of Dudley was one of the more unusual trench knives of World War I. This weapon was owned by Captain W. Fawcett of the King's Own Royal Lancaster Regiment.

The Mark I trench knife

During the last five months of World War I, the United States made an extensive study of all the diverse forms of trench knife then in use. It rated them on several points, including the blade's weight, length and shape, suitability to be carried while crawling and the probability of the knife being knocked from the hand. The results of these tests led to the development of the Mark I trench knife, which was intended to combine all of the best aspects of the weapons included in the study. The Mark I was composed of a 17cm (7in)

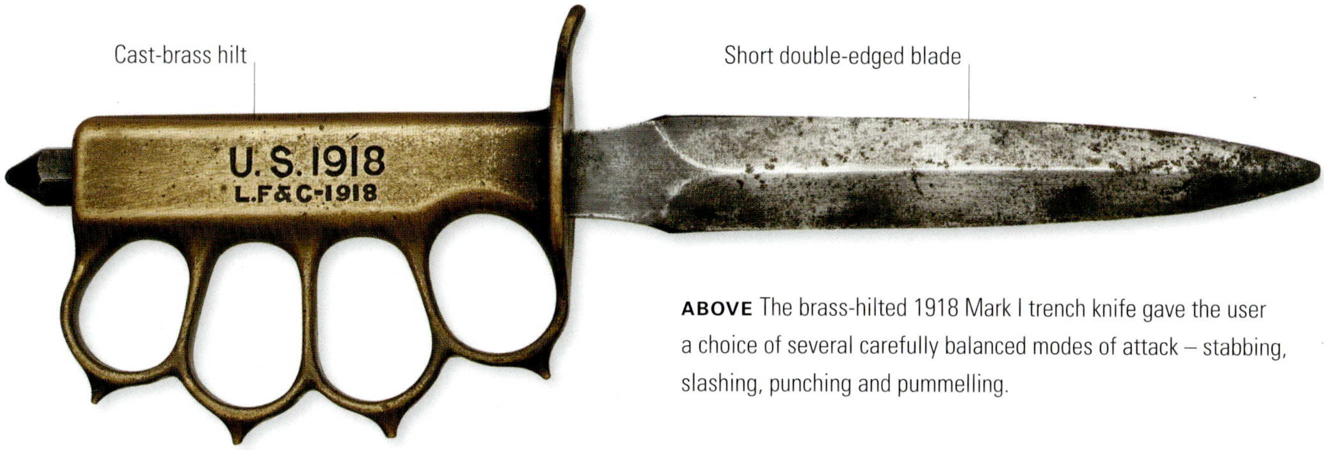

ABOVE The brass-hilted 1918 Mark I trench knife gave the user a choice of several carefully balanced modes of attack – stabbing, slashing, punching and pummelling.

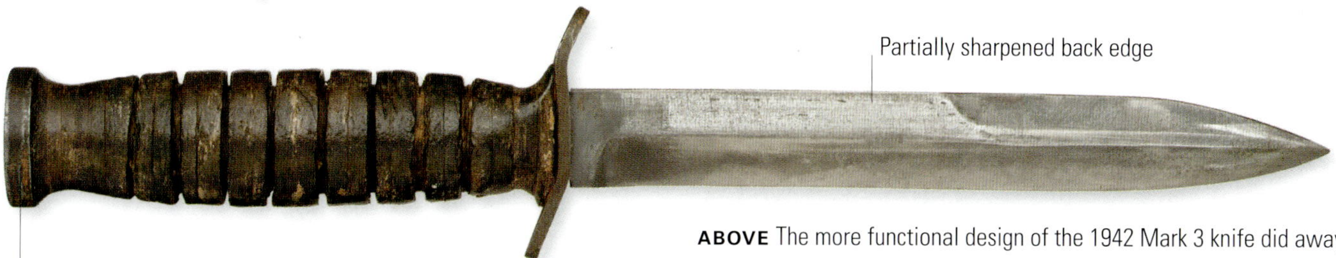

ABOVE The more functional design of the 1942 Mark 3 knife did away with the "knuckleduster" feature, although the solid steel pommel cap could still strike concussive blows.

double-edged blade designed for both cutting and thrusting, and a cast-bronze hilt that incorporated individual loops for the fingers, forming a knuckleduster. It even had a pointed nut on the pommel to secure the hilt and blade together, but which was also able to fracture the skull if used with sufficient force. Although none were manufactured after the 120,000 produced in the United States and France in 1918, this weapon remained in use alongside later knives until it was declared obsolete in January 1945.

The Mark 3 trench knife

When the United States entered the war in 1941, the only fighting knife in the US Army's inventory was the Mark I. A new production run of this model was proposed but then ruled out; the bronze required for the cast hilt was a critical strategic metal, and it was felt that a better design could be found. After several studies, the new knife was designated Mark 3, and was described in the US Army's Catalog of Standard Ordnance Items as "developed to fill the need in modern warfare for hand-to-hand fighting … designed for such shock units as parachute troops and rangers." The knife had a short, straight blade 17cm (7in) long, with a 7cm (3in) "false" edge, and a corrugated grip constructed of compressed leather washers. Some 590,247 Mark 3s were manufactured before production was cancelled in August 1942.

ABOVE A typical patriotic poster of World War I, this one Italian, showing a brave soldier defending his home and loved ones.

ABOVE A Fairbairn-Sykes "commando" knife, *c.*1942. The design of the weapon is remarkably medieval, with a long grip, short cross guard, and diamond-section cut-and-thrust blade.

The FS "commando" knife

In 1940 the British Army formed its first Special Forces unit, the "Commandos", to strike key targets along the Normandy coast of France. The training of this small, elite force was entrusted to Captain William Fairbairn and Captain Eric Sykes. Both had been members of the Shanghai police force, where they had studied martial arts and learned their special skills of armed and unarmed combat, including the ability to use anything at hand, however unlikely, as an effective weapon. They also learnt how to kill silently.

When they took up their new duties, Fairbairn and Sykes discovered the Commandos were armed with a knuckleduster-type knife, the BC41. But Fairbairn and Sykes had their own views on knives and approached the Wilkinson Sword Company, Britain's best-known manufacturer of edged weapons, with an original design. The first shipment of Fairbairn-Sykes (FS) fighting knives arrived in January 1941. The FS knife had a tapering 18cm (7in) double-edged blade, a simple oval cross guard, and a long, slightly bulbous, metal handle. The first pattern of knives had fine cross-hatching to provide a firm grip when the hands were wet, whether with rainwater, seawater or blood. Later models had grips encircled by a series of ribs or grooves. The blades were honed to an edge that would cut paper, and the cross guard was not to prevent an opponent's knife sliding down the blade but to prevent the user's hand from doing the same and suffering serious injury when thrusting with the knife. The knife was made so that the point of balance was on the hilt just behind the cross guard.

The preferred method of carrying the knife was in a sheath sewn to the inside of the left trouser pocket – a pistol was to be carried in the right-hand pocket. But the knife could be worn in many places – on the belt, down the boot or up the sleeve. It could also be sewn to the uniform in any other way that the individual soldier preferred. Many versions of the FS knife were produced, and its design was copied by the Special Forces of other countries; 3,420 were delivered to the US Army in 1943, this version being designated V-42. More British-made FS knives were sold to American soldiers stationed in England before they were deployed to continental Europe or North Africa. The US Marine Corps also adopted the knife for a short period.

LEFT The Fairbairn-Sykes knife could be worn in many different ways. This photograph of a British Commando involved in the raid on Dieppe, taken on 20 August 1942, shows one strapped to the ankle.

The US Navy Mark 2 and the USMC "KA-BAR"

During World War II, the US Navy developed its own fighting knives, primarily for shore personnel near the front line and combat swimmers, or "frogmen". The US Navy Mark 2 Utility Knife was a relation of the Army Mark 3; like it, the Navy Mark 2 had a handle composed of compressed leather washers. The blade was more like that of a small Bowie knife, being nearly 18cm (7in) long with a clipped point. The first combat knife made specifically for the US Marine Corps was identical to the Navy Mark 2 apart from the marks on the blade. Officially called the "fighting-utility knife", it soon became known among Marines as the "KA-BAR", after the trademark of the Union Cutlery Company, which manufactured the earliest versions. By 1943 these knives were in general use, and they remained the US Marine's trusted companion in many subsequent campaigns.

20th-century ceremonial knives

Swords, in both past civilian life and within military forces up to the present day, have been the primary symbol of rank and still have their place on the parade ground and at other ceremonial occasions. In some instances, knives of one form or another have also served a similar function.

The naval dirk worn by the midshipman originally marked him out as a junior officer, and awards of this classic weapon have continued to be made. Similarly, the elaborately adorned dirk of the Scots Guards once served them on the field of conflict and now serves them on parade. The dirk is not only an ongoing part of a military tradition, but also an important part of Highland dress and is still seen on "civilian" occasions such as weddings and other celebrations. The unusual but famous traditional kukri was often worn as part of ceremonial dress by the British Army's Gurkha regiment. The sight of these knives in those same hands created a legendary and formidable combination, sufficient to instil fear in the heart of anyone who might face them in battle.

On a completely different level, the traditional parade uniform of the Boy Scouts' would have been incomplete at one time without the sheath knife. It wasn't, of course, carried as a weapon but as a tool for use in field craft.

ABOVE A Boy Scout in uniform with an unusual sheath knife, with wooden slab grips instead of grips of imitation stag or compressed leather washers.

BELOW Along with the Fairbairn-Sykes commando knife, the US Navy Mark 2, perhaps most famous as the US Marine Corps' KA-BAR, is one of the world's most successful modern combat knives.

ABOVE The Labour Corps dagger was designed to look like the large hatchet-bladed cleaver of a land worker, the wide cutting blade being fitted with an antler grip.

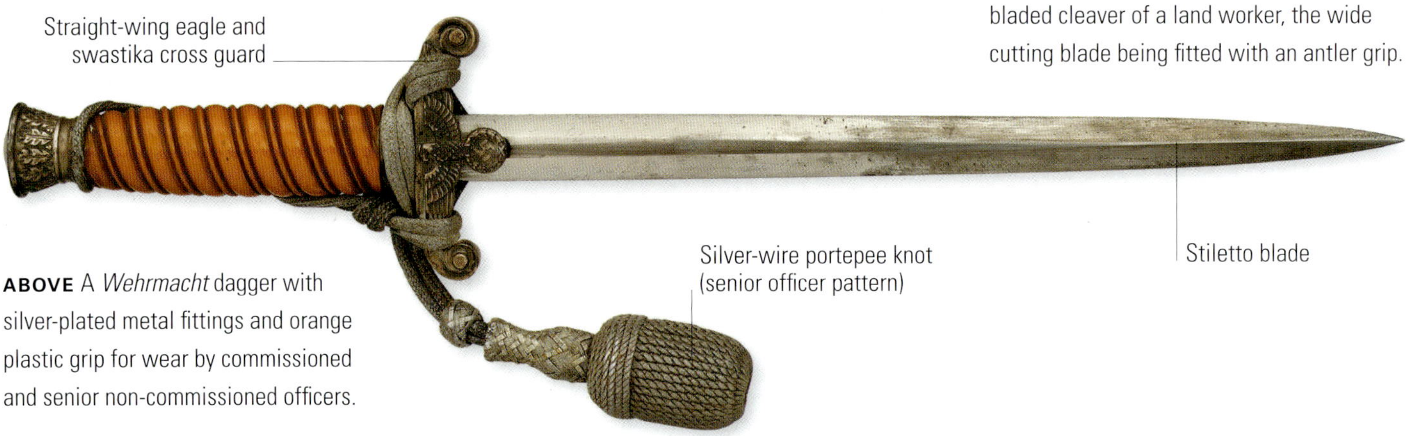

ABOVE A *Wehrmacht* dagger with silver-plated metal fittings and orange plastic grip for wear by commissioned and senior non-commissioned officers.

Daggers of the Third Reich

The concept of the "dress" dagger flourished during the German Third Reich, and an almost boundless variety were created for every branch of the military, quasi-military and even many non-military state organizations. In 1933 a delegation from the sword-making city of Solingen approached Germany's new leader Adolf Hitler with a proposal. It was suggested that the Nazi Party adopt various types of sword and dagger as status and distinguishing symbols for its members. Solingen had been a world-famous centre for the production of fine-edged weapons since the Middle Ages, but defeat in World War I had hit its industry very badly and many of its craftsmen were out of work. Hitler and some of his close associates had embraced and almost resurrected certain aspects of German medieval culture as part of Nazi ideology, and they enthusiastically approved the idea.

The first member of what would become the huge family of Nazi daggers was introduced in 1934 for the *Sturm Abteilung* ("Stormtroopers"), or SA, the Nazi Party's private police force. Solingen craftsmen took as their model the characteristically Germanic "Swiss" or "Holbein" dagger of the 16th century. The design was simplified but the overall form of the I-shaped hilt, with brown grips made of walnut or similar wood, remained unchanged. The broad, spear-pointed blade was etched with the motto *Alles für Deutschland* ("Everything for Germany"). Shortly thereafter, a very

BELOW An off-duty German officer in Paris in 1941, his uniform complete with standard dress dagger.

RIGHT This 1937 photo taken in Nuremberg of Josef Goebbels (left) and Hermann Göring, two of Hitler's closest aides, shows Göring with one of the many forms of Nazi "Holbein"-type dress dagger.

similar dagger was commissioned for the *Schutzstaffel* ("Protective Squadron"), or SS, the Nazis' elite guard. This weapon was almost identical to the SA version, apart from its black hilt and the motto on the blade: *Meine Ehre heißt Treue* ("My Honour is Named Loyalty"). The Army, Airforce and Navy each had their own distinctive daggers, the most distinctive of all, perhaps, being the 1st Pattern *Luftwaffe* ("Airforce") dagger produced in classical "Holbein" style and with a large circular pommel and winged cross guard.

Gradually, nearly every organization of the Nazi Party acquired its own ceremonial knife. They included the Motor Transport Corps, the National Political Education Institute and the Hitler *Jugend* ("Hitler Youth"), an equivalent of the Boy Scout movement but with its main focus on training young minds in Nazi ideology. Dress daggers were also produced for the Postal Protection Service, Waterways Protection Police, Diplomatic Service, the Red Cross and National Forestry Service. Even the Fire Service had parade axes for firemen and daggers for officers.

One of the most distinctive civil service daggers was awarded to the *Reicharbeitsdienst* ("Labour Corps"). Designed to look suitably rustic, the workman-like Labour Corps dagger, often referred to as a "hewer", had a broad chopping blade, staghorn grip and appropriate motto: *Arbeit adelt* ("Labour ennobles"). Special versions of many daggers were also produced for officers and for presentation purposes.

Perhaps one of the rarest presentation daggers is the naval dress dagger awarded by Grand Admiral Erich Raeder, of which only six are thought to exist. It has an elaborately decorated scabbard, a Damascus blade and a 17-diamond swastika in the pommel.

This almost obsessive trend in dagger design by the Third Reich was never copied by other countries. However, many of them adopted ceremonial daggers on a far more limited scale. Until the 1950s, Soviet Russia and many countries under Soviet influence issued such daggers to their army, air force and naval officers. Some South American countries also used them. The Japanese also adopted dress daggers within their military circles. But on the whole this trend has now largely disappeared, and these daggers are preserved only by collectors.

BELOW The SA dagger, manufactured between 1934 and 1945, was perhaps the most common of the many Nazi daggers of "Holbein" form.

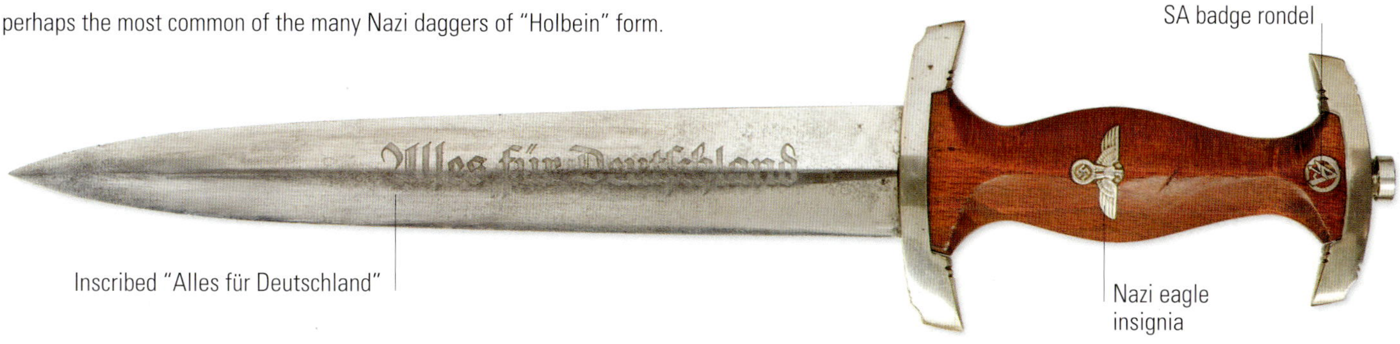

African knives and daggers

As is true of tribal cultures everywhere in the world, the common traditional weapons in Africa were the bow and arrow and the spear. But the native peoples of the African continent also created a profusion of other weapons, including a bewildering multitude of daggers and knives. Despite a generally simple level of technology, the work of African bladesmiths is exceptional in terms of its quality, originality, functionality and design.

Although copper and bronze were commonly worked throughout Africa, iron had been the predominant metal for making weapons since ancient times. Iron ore is found in most parts of Africa – mined but also found close to the surface near rivers or deposited in dry river beds. By the 4th or 3rd century BC, iron was being worked in what is now northwestern Tanzania, northern Nigeria and the Sudan. Excavations of the ancient Nubian city of Meroe, on the east bank of the Nile, north of Khartoum, revealed, along with over 200 pyramids, gigantic slag heaps which testify to very considerable ironworking activities. The context of the excavation site demonstrates that iron was being worked there on an industrial scale by at least the 1st century AD.

In theory, the design of an African edged weapon should be characteristic of, or relate to the specific tribe that created it. However, a well-made weapon was always valuable, a useful trade item or literal form of currency, and so it should not be surprising that the weapons forged by a particular tribe were found in the possession of many of their neighbours. Migration and displacement due to environmental or territorial factors also disseminated distinctive weapons forms over much larger areas.

It is very difficult, therefore, to date particular African weapons precisely or to identify their exact place of origin positively. Weapons studied by early explorers from Europe were usually named after the area where they were found. But this may not have been the land of the tribe who made them. Also, tribal names could be derived from many different things, features in the landscape for example, and one tribe might have more than one name. Yet it is possible to discuss in a general way the areas or cultures that are most closely associated with distinctive knife forms.

Baule knives and daggers

The Baule tribe of the Ivory Coast are famous not only for their wooden figurines and masks but also for their skill in working iron, brass, bronze and gold, and the Baule smith was a skilled weapons maker. The blades of Baule knives and daggers vary considerably in form. Some are long and very wide, being either steeply

LEFT Knives and other edged weapons were collected in Africa by many 19th-century travellers. In this illustration a group of objects collected by Professor Friedrich Ratzel in the Upper Congo, 1898, is shown. The group appears largely to be made up of Ngala, Ngombe and Kuba weapons.

ABOVE This rare 19th-century drawing shows the traditional metalworking processes practised in Africa for hundreds of years, including smelting iron ore in a bloomery and beating a lump of iron, or "bloom".

tapered down the top half or tightly waisted and leaf-shaped. Others are shorter, having a simple, straight shape with a clipped point, not unlike a Japanese dagger or tanto. Another Baule knife form, specifically for ceremonial or ritual purposes, is very wide, curved and sickle-like. Hilts are usually carved of wood, while scabbards are often made of leather exquisitely tooled with geometric patterns or covered with brightly coloured shells.

The knives and daggers of the Azande tribe

Perhaps one of the most martial of all African tribes, the Azande inhabited parts of what is now the Democratic Republic of Congo, southwestern Sudan, and the southeastern end of the Central African Republic. Although technically very militant by traditional standards, the Azande took careful measures to prevent excessive violence in war, which for them was to a great extent symbolic. A battle could be decided by the death or even wounding of an individual opponent, while surrounded and trapped enemies would be allowed to escape, their symbolic defeat having been achieved.

The knives and daggers of the Azande are well made and finely decorated. Ceremonial weapons sometimes have blades of copper, while most practical examples are of iron. Their long leaf blades are designed both for cutting and thrusting, and are generally decorated with tight groups of file-lines or grooves. Sometimes the blades are pierced with large holes or slots. The hilts are often covered with narrow ribbons of copper or bronze, which are either wrapped or plaited around them. Especially valuable knives are sometimes fitted with hilts of elephant ivory, carved with geometric designs.

The Azande traditionally used knives as a form of currency. An Azande dowry, or bridewealth, for example, might be given in the form of a number (usually 40) of dagger blades.

ABOVE Knives and other edged weapons often have purposes other than combat. These elaborate Congolese throwing knives, made of copper, are intended as tributes for Azande leaders from their vassals.

Knives and daggers of the Fang tribe

Living in southern Cameroon, the Gabonese Republic and Equatorial Guinea, the Fang are the creators not only of the remarkable *bieri*, reliquary sculptures that probably had a strong influence on the early development of cubism, but also of the so-called "bird's-head" knife. The concept of this strange, other-worldly weapon may have been inspired by the African horn raven (*Bucorvus caver*). The bird's-head knife is often thought to be a throwing knife, although this is debatable.

The Fang are also known for a long dagger, which is somewhat reminiscent of the Roman gladius, or short sword, having a straight, wide blade. These practical fighting daggers were combined, like the gladius, with a large, square shield, which protected most of the warrior's body while he closed with his enemy and stabbed him with the knife.

LEFT This very long knife, almost a short sword, is typical of Ngala craftsmanship. The large sickle-like blade is decorated with a panel of very dense engraved line ornament; the hilt is composed of a brass-banded wooden grip and a "dumb-bell"-type pommel.

LEFT The sickle knife, or trumbash, is a distinctive feature of Mangbetu material culture. This 19th-century specimen has a fine blade with a prominent medial rib supplemented by secondary ridges and two large decorative holes near the base.

ABOVE The Fang *bieri* or "bird's-head" knife is one of the most striking of all African weapons. The triangular blade cut-out contrasts with its gentle curves, a quality that appealed to Cubist artists, such as Picasso.

The Mangbetu hooked sickle knife

The trumbash, of the Mangbetu in the northwestern corner of the Democratic Republic of Congo is a hooked sickle knife, and easily recognized. The wide blade is formed with a graceful if abrupt right-angle change about halfway along its length. The edges of the blade trace various paths in relation to the centre line, some examples being more angular while others are more rounded and uniformly curved.

Whatever the exact shape, these weapons always possess a singular boldness. The blades are usually ridged in all sorts of highly individual ways, with some ridges being very sharp and narrow, others being wider and flat-topped. Some blades are pierced with pairs of large, round holes, and are sometimes forged with short, knob-like projections at the base of both edges. All of these aspects contribute to a sense of the Mangbetu sickle knife being a piece of abstract art as well as a weapon. The handle is usually carved out of wood or ivory. Many have pommels in the form of a

RIGHT The form of the Kuba ikul attests to this object's role as a peaceful ceremonial object. It is beautifully made and pleasing to the eye, with fluid, flowing lines, but it has been purposely designed to be inconvenient as a weapon.

LEFT This intricately decorated Kuba mask displays the rich artistic culture of this Central African people. The weapons they produce are equally ornate and complex in their design.

large, cylindrical block, sometimes studded with brass nails. The heavy pommel of the trumbash even led to a nonsensical myth that they were dropped on the heads of enemies by warriors hiding in trees. Other grips are carved in the form of a human head and upper body. These, like many Mangbetu figures, are immediately identifiable because of the elongated skulls that they depict; traditionally, Mangbetu babies' heads were bound to induce them to grow into a stretched form that was considered to be eminently attractive.

Knives and daggers of the Kuba

The Kuba kingdom, a pre-colonial state centred near the land south of the Kasai River in Central Africa, was actually a conglomeration of many smaller tribes conquered by the original Kuba or Buschoog ("people of the throwing knife"). Famous as artists obsessed with glorious surface ornament, the Kuba produced extraordinary helmet-like masks, richly patterned textiles and beautiful weapons, the most idiosyncratic of which is the ikul. This very wide, leaf-bladed knife is said to have been introduced by King Shyaam aMbul aNgoong, the founder of the Kuba kingdom, in around 1600. The ikul was an emblem of peace. It is often depicted on Kuba king figures, or *ndop*, which portray the monarch with an ikul in his left hand and an ilwoon, or sword of war, in his right, symbolizing the ruler's dual role as war-leader and peacemaker.

Ikuls are made with blades of iron or copper fitted with grips of wood, often inlaid with brass or copper; to further accentuate their role as symbols of peace, some ikuls are made entirely of carved wood.

Knives of the Ngala and the Ndjembo people

Congolese Ngala knives appear in three main forms. The first is very long, double-edged and curved in a shallow, graceful arc. The second is shorter and wider, the blade often tear-shaped with one or two ridges. The third is almost a form of machete – wide-bladed and long, decorated with ridges, profuse file-lines and cross-hatching. The leading edge is recurved and the trailing edge cut into a series of cuspings, the point forming a stout hook. These knives were often taken to be decapitation implements, but are more likely to have had ceremonial significance. Closely related to the Ngala knife is that of the neighbouring Ndjembo. This is of a similar length but straight until it divides into two long points that curve inwards in a crescent shape.

ABOVE This arm knife or loi boi was made in Chad, probably in the 19th century. Like most arm knives, the simple blade is mounted with a well-carved waisted grip of wood.

ABOVE This Sudanese dagger, which was made around 1900, has a less common curved blade and displays an ergonomic hilt not unlike the European baselard or Indian chilanum.

African arm daggers

The dagger worn on the arm, or loi boi, is a uniquely African weapon popular among various tribes in many different regions of the continent. Generally it is worn in a scabbard attached by means of leather loops or thongs to the inner side of the left forearm, with the blade pointing up towards the elbow and the handle sitting close to the inside of the wrist. From here the arm dagger can be swiftly drawn when needed. Occasionally, it is instead worn on the outside of the upper arm with the blade facing downwards.

Arm daggers are associated with a number of the peoples inhabiting the Sahara and the Sahel – the border country of the Sudan between the northern desert regions and the central tropics. Northern examples are very often fitted with European knife or bayonet blades, or cut-down sword blades.

In northwest Africa the tribe most famous for their use of the arm dagger, or telek, is the Tuareg. Tribes in northern Nigeria, particularly the Nube and the Berom, also make arm daggers in the Tuareg style.

Arm daggers are also very popular among the Hausa of Cameroon. As in most traditional societies, a high-quality dagger for the Hausa reflects the owner's wealth and social status. Hausa daggers are not unlike Swiss daggers of the 15th and 16th centuries – with vaguely I-shaped hilts and wide, straight-sided blades that taper rapidly down the last third of their length to a very sharp stabbing point.

BELOW The Tuareg warriors of northwest Africa carry a variety of weapons but their most distinctive side arm is the telek or arm dagger.

ABOVE The arm dagger is a common traditional weapon in many parts of North Africa. This Sudanese example is reasonably typical, with a simple waisted hilt and arm-thonged scabbard.

African throwing knives

The vast group of African multi-bladed weapons that ethnographers have commonly awarded the term "throwing knives" are unlike any other weapons found anywhere else in the world. Many types do not in fact appear to have been intended for throwing, while others, like the Fang "bird's-head" knife, could be thrown on occasion, though this was probably not its main method of use.

However, some types are without question carefully engineered as lethal aerial blades, which spin through the air like multi-bladed, razor-sharp boomerangs. Indeed, the earliest versions of these unusual weapons may have developed from the very ancient idea of the throwing stick. Emil Torday, an early 20th-century traveller, collector and museum curator, wrote poetically about the use of throwing knives by Kuba warriors:

> *... then all of a sudden, some objects, glittering in the sun as if they were thunderbolts, come whirling with a weird hum through the air. The enemy warriors raise their shields; the shining mystery strikes it, rebounds into the air and continues to the attack; it smites the warrior behind his defence with its cruel blades. A weapon which is capable of killing behind a shield cannot fail to cause a panic ...*

African throwing knives are usually classified into two very general groups: the circular type and the F-type. The former have blades that extend away from the centre of gravity, usually in three directions, while the latter are, to a greater or lesser degree, shaped in the form of the letter "F".

In addition to the Kuba, a great many tribes claim throwing knives as their traditional weapons, including the Azande, Ingessana (Tabi Hills, Sudan), Hutu (Rwanda, Burundi), Bwaka (Central African Republic), Ngbaka (northwest Congo), Masalit (Darfur, Sudan), Sara (Chad) and Nsakara (northeast Congo). The throwing knives of this last tribe are said to be some of the best, with their centre of gravity perfectly placed to produce a good spin. The flight characteristics of Nsakara throwing knives are considered excellent, the slight angling of the blade relative to its plane converting rotational motion into lift, essentially creating a somewhat stable propeller effect which increases the weapon's range and accuracy.

BELOW This Somali throwing knife appears to have been used a number of times, whether it was intended for fighting or not. Three of the blades appear to have been broken off and welded back in place.

Persian and Middle Eastern daggers

Persian daggers from before the 15th century are difficult to identify, as very few of them remain. But from the mid-1400s onwards, a greater number of spectacular pieces have survived. The best 15th-, 16th- and 17th-century examples are signed or have key features that allow them to be more accurately dated and attributed. Some embody distinctive Persian styles, while others represent general fashions throughout the Middle East.

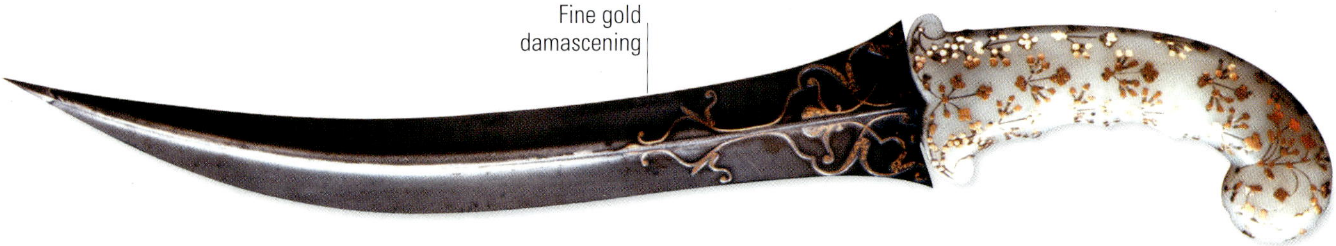

ABOVE An extremely fine Persian dagger from the 17th century mounted with an expensive white jade hilt inlaid with gold.

ABOVE The hilt of this dagger, like the example above, was made in the 1600s in Persia. It is carved from a single piece of almost flawless rock-crystal, a rare material requiring very skilled carving.

For centuries Persia was at the heart of the Islamic world, situated between Turkey and Arabia to the west and Muslim Afghanistan and India to the east. It was a geographical, cultural and military crossroads. The Seljuk Turks ruled Persia from 1037 until the early 13th century, when they lost it to the Khwarezmids, another Turkic people of Mamluk origin. The Shahs of the Khwarezmid Empire in turn had to defend Persia against Genghis Khan, who in 1219 seized key locations along the Silk Road including Samarkand (in modern Uzbekistan) and Otar (a city in what is today Kazakhstan). Subsequently most of Persia became a part of the vast Mongol Empire. Not until 1292 did it return to Muslim rule with the conversion of Ghazan Khan (1271–1304) Persia's Mongol overlord.

Years of conquest and reconquest followed Ghazan's secession from the Chino-Mongol Empire, the borders being continually redrawn by successive invaders, most notably the Turco-Mongol warlord Timur the Lame (1336–1405), who conquered Persia and established the Muslim Timurid Dynasty at the end of the 14th century. The Timurid Emirs ruled Persia for nearly 100 years until the establishment of the Safavid Dynasty in 1500. Under the Safavids, Persia entered its greatest cultural period since the first Islamic conquest in the 7th century.

Weapons production in Persia

Persian weapons were famous throughout the Middle East from ancient times. Samarkand and Isfahan were especially renowned as centres for the production of the finest swords and daggers. Persia was wealthy in the natural resources required for the production of high-quality weapons – iron, silver and gold. A long tradition of the scientific study of metals in the Islamic world led to the development of "watered" steel, fusions of high- and medium-carbon steels that displayed in good measure the two key properties of an excellent blade – hardness and elasticity. The extraordinary silk-like patterns that formed on the surfaces of these blades when etched with acid were a sure sign of their quality.

The problems of identification

Today it is often very difficult to identify daggers, and blades in general, as specifically Persian, partly because so few have survived from earlier times, but mainly because the arms trade operated on a scale far larger and more expansive than Persia itself. Indian blades were imported into Persia, where they might be decorated and assembled into complete weapons by the local craftsmen, while Persian work was also exported, not only back to India but also west into Arabia and Turkey.

Our modern understanding is further hampered by the fact that specialist researchers did not begin the scholarly study of Persian weapons dating from the 15th to 19th centuries until the 1970s. Thus a great deal of basic research is still lacking, and ways of dating daggers in particular, though now much improved, are still very generalized. Indeed, many daggers that bear dated inscriptions remained unread until the late 20th century.

ABOVE Daggers have been made throughout the Islamic world for hundreds of years. This scene of a Yemeni daggersmith's workshop is undoubtedly a sight that has remained largely unchanged in centuries.

The kylin clue

Depictions of the mythical beasts known as kylins appear in art throughout the Middle and Far East. Although exact portrayals vary, the kylin is usually shown as a hooved, dragon-like creature with a scaly body and antlers similar to those of a stag. It is often depicted with its body bathed in fire. It is invariably believed to be a creature sent to punish the sinful, or to protect the good from evil. It is also sometimes considered the pet of divine beings.

Kylins appear on certain early Persian daggers of the 15th century. The specific nature of these appearances, along with dragons and birds, is closely comparable to the decoration on the exquisite leather bindings on Persian manuscripts of the 1400s. Although precise dating of manuscripts of this period is difficult, there seems to be no suggestion that any of them could be later than 1500. It seems likely, therefore, that the presence of such beasts on the hilt of a fine Persian dagger is a good indicator of an early date.

RIGHT The kylin is as iconic in Eastern culture as dragons are in Western medieval and Renaissance art. The horned heads, scales and fiery tails of these Chinese figures are very similar to dragons.

LEFT Some Persian daggers are covered in extraordinary multicoloured decoration. This one includes a hilt mounted with cabochons, highly polished rubies and a scabbard ornamented with gold and enamel.

Dating Persian daggers

Although curved blades have been traditionally preferred throughout the Middle East, many of the best Persian daggers carry straight double-edged blades. Fine Persian blades of the 15th, 16th and 17th centuries are usually decorated with poetic inscriptions. The weapons can be dated through careful examination of the language and type of script used in the inscriptions. Verses in Turkic might lead one to assume that a particular dagger was of Turkish origin. But Turkic was also used by the Safavid Court. In such cases the script itself, rather than the language, might be the most vital clue. Turkic verses sometimes appear on daggers written in fluid *nasta 'liq* script, a style of writing that originated in Persia.

Another important indicator of the date of a fine Persian dagger is the exact character of the background against which the script is set. For example, 15th-century blades tend to have inscriptions set against a plain background, while in the 16th and 17th centuries the backgrounds were usually filled in with flowers, leaves and coiling vines, the density of which seems to increase along with the date of the work.

Decoration and inscriptions

The best daggers produced in Persia and Turkey were usually fitted with hilts carved out of rock-crystal, jade or ivory, or forged of watered steel. Expensive dagger hilts and scabbards were also studded with gems, cabochons often being preferred, perhaps because they resembled drops of blood or water. One poem found on several surviving daggers, in Persian *ruba'i* rhyme, includes a vivid reference to this form of decoration:

Every time that thy dagger talked of vengeance,
It brought the times into confusion by its shedding of blood!
By the elegance and purity of the stones which are on it,
It recalled a willow-leaf covered with dew!

Persian blade inscriptions were usually evocative of, or at least appropriate to the function or character of the dagger, both as a weapon and as a symbol:

I wanted so much to have a gleaming dagger,
That each of my ribs became a dagger.

Stab my breast several times with a dagger,
Open in my heart several doors of delight!

ABOVE Persian noblemen's daggers, though decorative, were also used to settle feuds. This detail from the 14th-century *Jami al-tawarikh*, a history of 13th-century Persia, shows the murder of a nobleman.

Others equate daggers and the wounds they can inflict with women and love:

That oppressive mocker holds in her hand the
dagger of vengeance,
In order to shed men's blood, what more does
she hold in her hand?
Draw the dagger and pull the heart from our breast,
So that thou mayest see our heart among the lovers.

Finally, many inscriptions are much simpler and more straightforward:

Be happy.

The Arabian jambiya

By far the most ubiquitous form of dagger found throughout the Arab world was the jambiya. The name of the weapon is derived from the Persian world *jamb*,

ABOVE The jambiya is still commonly worn in many parts of the Arab world. This young Yemeni man wears his dagger at the waist, tucked into a wide belt as is the usual way in this part of the world.

meaning side. It is often very difficult to distinguish a khanjar from a jambiya and vice versa; indeed, since both terms were used very generally, and meant different things in different parts of the Middle East, as well as in North Africa, India and elsewhere, distinction may be an impossible task. Despite this, writers in English are often tempted to apply general foreign terms to very specific types of weapon, for which they were never intended. The terms *khanjar* and *jambiya* simply mean "dagger". Nevertheless, for the purposes of this book, khanjar is used to refer to the narrower-bladed Indo-Persian daggers which are favoured in the eastern parts of the Muslim world, while jambiya refers in the most generalized terms to the classic "Arabian" dagger that is easily recognized by its wide, steeply curved blade encased in an often highly decorated scabbard that exaggerates the curved form.

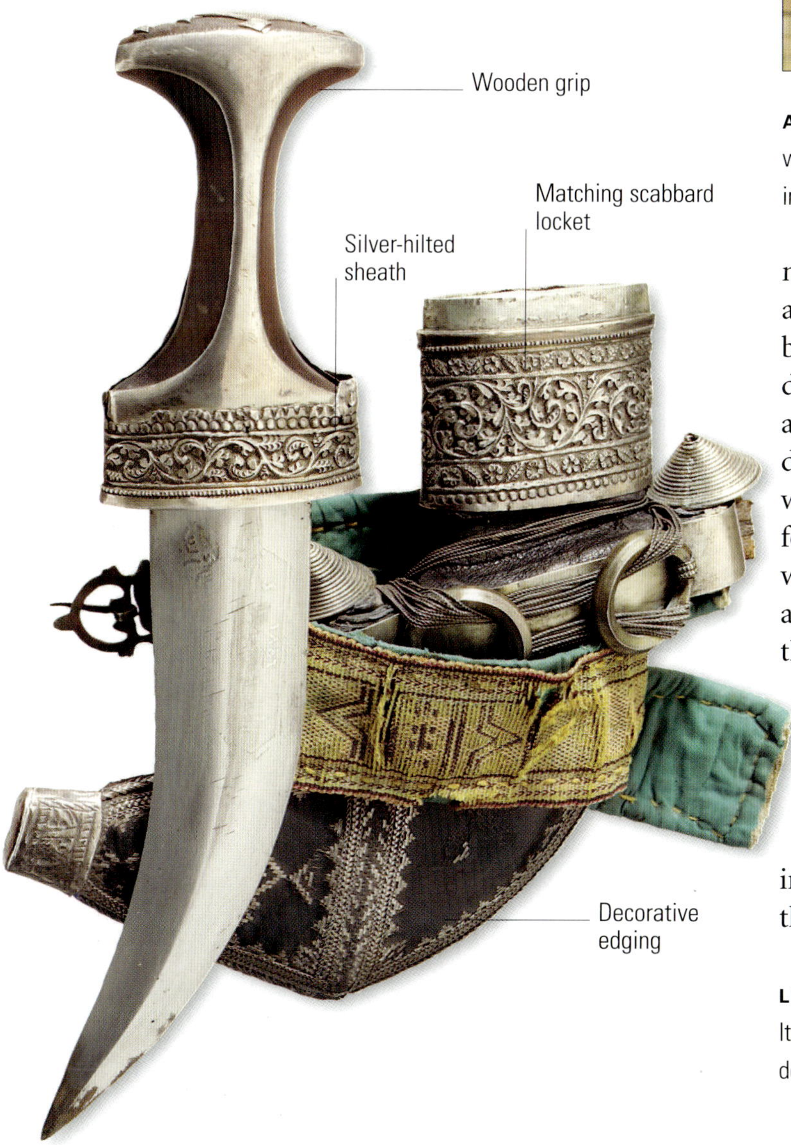

LEFT This good-quality Yemeni jambiya was made in around 1900. It retains its original scabbard and belt, with mounts that have been decorated to match the hilt sheath of the dagger.

ABOVE Jambiyas are still manufactured today in very large numbers throughout the Middle East, and are commonly available from local makers and dealers such as this one in Yemen.

The jambiya blade

The arc of the jambiya blade often begins gradually, just forward of the hilt, but increases rapidly in its sweep closer to the point. The blades are often very wide and stiffened by a very proud medial rib. Scabbards usually exaggerate the curved form even further, the scabbard chape often being brought to a full right angle or even turning back up towards the grip.

While both edges of the jambiya blade were sharpened, the inner edge, much like an amputation knife, was kept especially honed. The blades were said to cut easily through the thickest clothes to the bone. The inner edge was used to slash the throat of an enemy, while the curved design made it possible to stab around the opponent's body to strike his back or kidneys. In 1877 an Englishman named John Fryer Keane visited Mecca and described the jambiya as being excellent for cutting through skin and hair, and also stated that it would cut through a rolled-up sheepskin with a single slash.

The hilt is usually a simple waisted affair, having a flat-topped pommel and similarly formed forward section – without any arms or guard – shaped to fit flush with the locket of the scabbard. Hilts are made of wood, bone, ivory or rhinoceros horn. The jambiya remains an important part of traditional male formal dress in the Middle East, especially in Yemen, Oman and Saudi Arabia. Worn centrally at the waist, the dagger was a prominent fashion statement but was also very quick to draw if the need arose. As jewellery items, jambiya hilts may also be further decorated with gold or silver filagree, amber, coins, coral or semi-precious stones.

Later Persian daggers

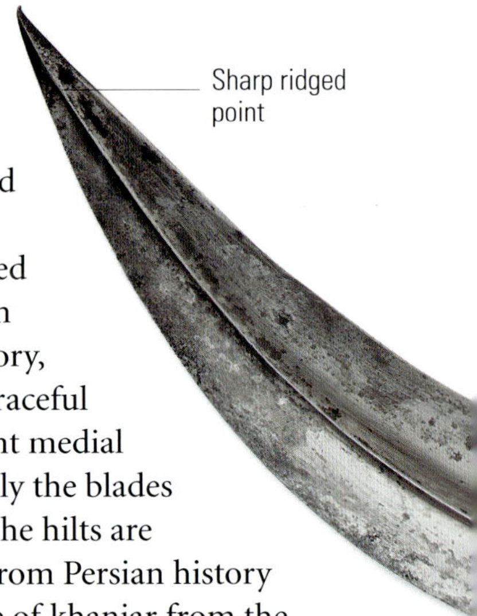

Many of the antique Persian daggers on the market today are khanjars dating from the Qajar Period (1781–1925). Most of these are composed of a hilt shaped like a capital "I", carved from either walrus or elephant ivory, joined to a blade having a graceful curve and either a prominent medial rib or central fuller. Normally the blades are made of watered steel. The hilts are usually carved with scenes from Persian history and mythology. A rarer type of khanjar from the Qajar Period features a hilt and scabbard flamboyantly decorated with multicoloured enamel. The cities of Shiraz and Isfahan were both famous centres of fine enamelling: indeed, Isfahani enamellers are still renowned in modern Iran.

The kard

In addition to the curved jambiya and khanjar designs, straight-bladed daggers were also common throughout Persia, Turkey and the wider Middle East. The two most universal forms were the kard and the peshkabz.

Kard simply means "knife" and this term is still used today to refer to an ordinary kitchen knife. The historical weapon does indeed strongly resemble a cooking knife, having a long, usually single-edged, straight blade and a simple grip. Such a weapon, though primarily intended for fighting, would inevitably be used for other purposes. Timurid miniatures show men cutting dough and slitting the throats of sheep with kards.

Some kards make their primary role as a combat weapon more explicit; the points are sometimes specially thickened and shaped like a modern armour-piercing bullet to strengthen them for

ABOVE Though simple in its basic form, this Persian kard of around 1800 is well decorated, with vine and bead scroll inlay in gold on the blade and handle, which is itself fitted with walrus ivory scales.

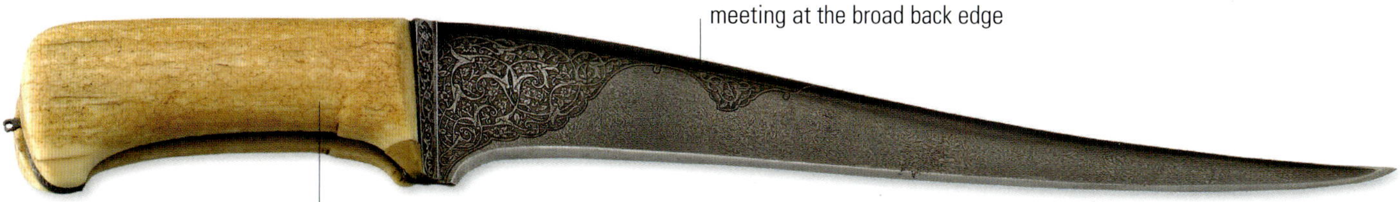

ABOVE This peshkabz, *c.*1800 displays the characteristic recurved blade of the T-shaped cross-section. The blade is forged of fine watered steel and chiselled with intricate arabesque decoration.

ABOVE The carved ivory hilts of Persian khanjars of the Qajar Period are very distinctive. The handles feature very fine carved relief work, and are usually fitted with blades of a high quality.

stabbing. These reinforced points were common enough to warrant their own term; in Persian they are fittingly described as *noke makhruti*, a term meaning "cone-point".

Kard grips were frequently made of walrus ivory, although elephant ivory examples are known. Khan Alam, Persian ambassador to the Mughal Court in India during the early 17th century, gave the Emperor Jahangir a dagger with a handle of a special type of walrus ivory speckled with black crystals ("piebald" ivory). The Great Mughal was very impressed and compared the dagger handle to the swirling pattern of watered steel. Horn was another material commonly used for kard grips, as was steel enamelled or decorated with gold overlay.

The peshkabz

The term *peshkabz* originally described the front of a girdle that Persian men wore while wrestling. The use of the same term to describe a dagger then seems to indicate that a peshkabz was worn centrally, as opposed to the khanjar and the kard, which were tucked to the right and left sides respectively. Of course, multiple knives of these various types were often carried together at the same time

The blade of a peshkabz is easily recognized by its steeply tapered straight or recurved blade, the characteristic feature being its especially thick back. To achieve this thickness while keeping the weight down, the smith would grind down the sides of the blade immediately below the back, so that the back itself could remain 1.5–2mm (.0059–.0078in) wide; the result of this grinding was to give the blade a T-shaped cross-section, rather than the much heavier wedge shape that would otherwise have been the result of the thickening of the back to this extent.

Indian daggers

Daggers from India take many strange and unusual forms. Their variety is a testament to the importance of the elite warrior class for both the Islamic and Hindu traditions. Weapons from the Muslim Mughal Empire, which expanded into northern India in the 16th century, are similar to the Persian weapons from which they are descended, while others, originating in the southern Hindu kingdoms, are unlike anything anywhere else.

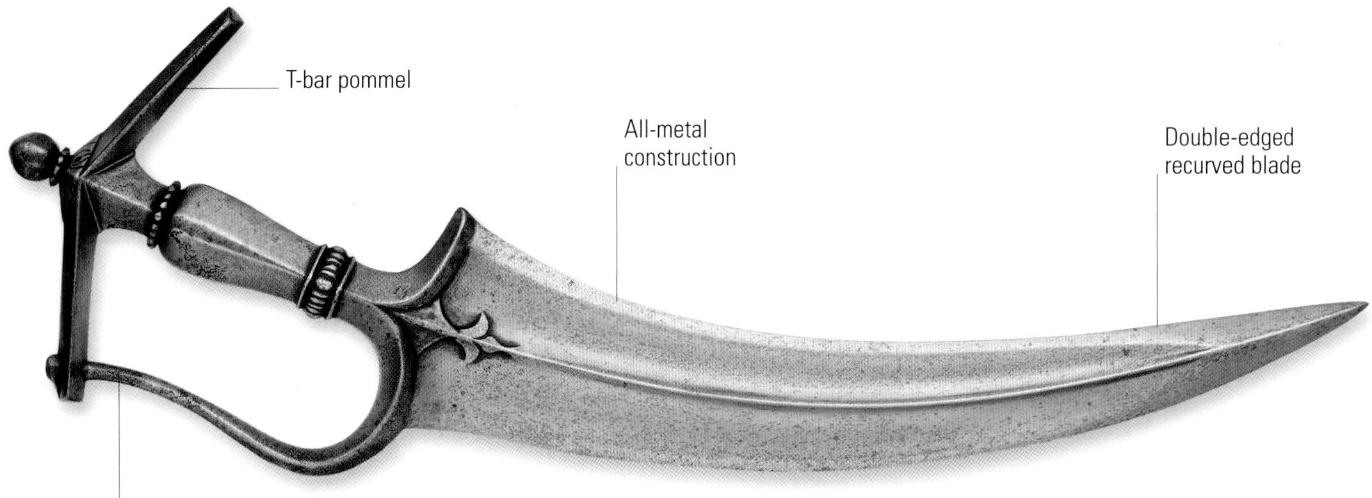

ABOVE This fine all-steel *chilanum*, made in the south of India in the late 18th century, displays all of the usual features of its type – the drooping T-shaped pommel, knuckle-bow and gently curved blade.

India is a vast subcontinent, a place of bewildering variety in art, language and belief. For thousands of years it has been a cultural crossing point, where vast invading empires collided while diverse localized tribes struggled to maintain their lands and unique customs. But even as India's many peoples struggled against each other for territorial and economic supremacy, their many distinctive cultures could not help but influence each other to varying degrees. Thus, for example, did the Muslim Mughals, who were of Persian origin, adopt much from the Hindu and tribal peoples that they conquered in the northern parts of the Indian subcontinent.

The chilanum

One uniquely Indian dagger form is the chilanum. It is characterized by its double-edged recurving blade, usually having a strong central spine and two or more fullers, and by its unusual hilt – the pommel drawn out into a drooping "T", or sometimes curving, frond-like arms. The guard is similarly shaped but with shorter arms, the forward arm often being drawn out to form a knuckle guard. While it has been suggested that the chilanum is Nepalese in origin, it seems to have evolved in the south of India, where it was clearly very common from the 16th century. Sometimes chilanum hilts are carved from hard stone, although most are metal, usually made of steel in one piece with the blade.

Mughal princes were renowned throughout the world for their love of gems and jewels. The finest Mughal chilanums had hilts of pure gold embellished with inlaid precious stones. The chilanum was supposedly introduced to the Mughals by the Rajputs, by way of Emperor Akbar's marriages to Rajput princesses, which brought with them military alliances and a complex intermingling of the Islamic and Hindu cultures. Chilanum blades were invariably of the finest watered steel, and the arms of the guard were worked into plant or animal forms. A famous portrait of Shah Jahan (1592–1666), painted in 1617, shows the Mughal emperor and builder of the Taj Mahal wearing just such a chilanum in his qamarband (waist band).

Wootz steel blades

Some Indian and Persian dagger blades display a beautiful wavy, flowing pattern. This pattern indicates that the blade is made of a high-quality steel generally known today as "wootz". The term perhaps is a derivation or corruption of *ukku*, an old south Indian word for steel.

Possibly as early as the 3rd century BC, centres in south India and Sri Lanka were producing this very high-carbon steel in crucibles; iron and wood charcoal were placed in the crucible, which was heated in a furnace. This produced an iron and carbon alloy – steel. The crucible process causes iron carbide particles to scatter throughout the crystalline structure of the steel. When the steel is tempered through heating and quenching, these particles form into bands. When the steel is lightly etched, by applying a mild acid such as vinegar to its surface, these bands react differently from the steel around them and discolour, producing the extraordinary "watered" pattern. This pattern not only gives the blade an almost magical appearance, it is also a useful indicator of technical quality. This is because patterned blades, having a high carbon content, are very strong and can hold a razor-sharp edge.

RIGHT The mesmerizing patterns of a wootz blade are brought out only when the blade is lightly etched with a weak acid. Over-polishing can easily eradicate the visible pattern.

The khanjarli

An 18th-century variation of the chilanum is the khanjarli. This dagger may be recognized by its wide, mushroom-like pommel, which supplants the chilanum's T-bar but performs very much the same function: to brace the hand against slippage while dealing overarm blows. Khanjarli pommels and grips are usually made of bone or ivory, two pieces sandwiching the tang and riveted in place. The khanjarli is thought to be Maratha in origin, and is usually associated with Vizianagaram in Orissa, a region famous for its elephants and ivory work. This has led to the suggestion that the distinctive ivory-handled khanjarlis come mainly from this part of India. The Marathas conquered Orissa in the 18th century, and undoubtedly the khanjarli design spread outside of its area of origin in subsequent campaigns.

BELOW Both the chilanum and its cousin the khanjarli were sometimes fitted with recurved blades like this fine example forged in wootz.

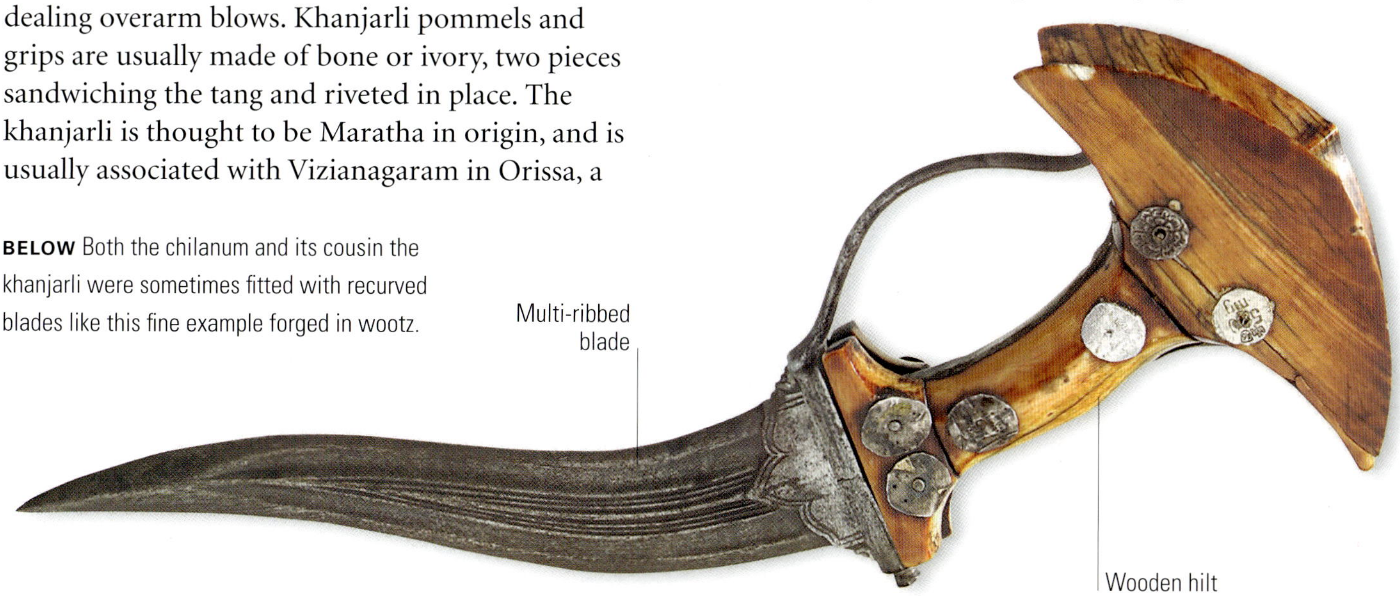

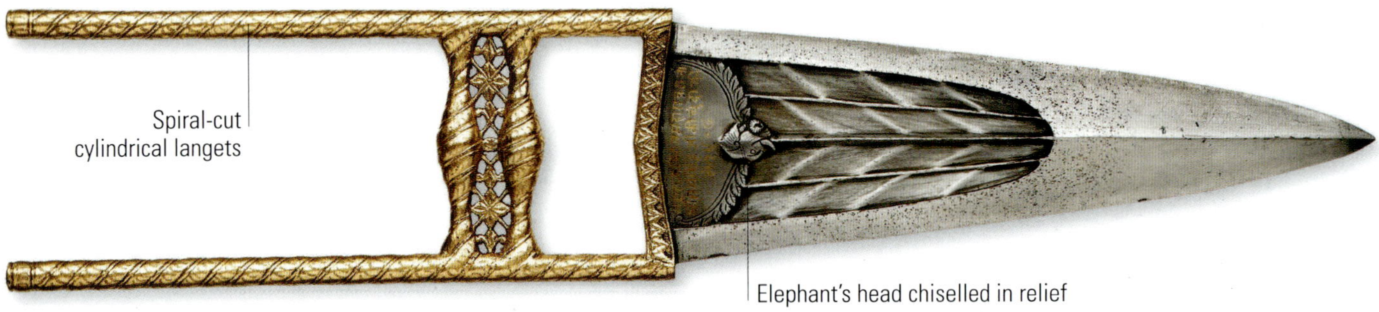

ABOVE This Rajasthani katar of about 1850 carries a typically heavy blade, thickened at the point and ideally suited to stabbing through the light armour typically worn in northwestern India.

The katar

The most famous Indian dagger is without doubt the katar, or jamdhar. The basic katar is composed of a short, wide blade from the base of which emanate two long, metal langets spaced apart from each other by the width of the user's hand. Between the langets is placed a pair of bars that form the grip of the weapon. So unlike most conventional daggers, which when held project their blades along a line approximately 90 degrees to that of the user's forearm, the katar places the blade in line with the arm, so that the striking action is essentially the same as a punch. Therefore, when striking correctly the user is able to put the whole weight of his body behind his dagger blows. Because the force of katar strikes could be so great, many examples have specially thickened points, to help prevent them bending or breaking. These points may also have improved the katar as an armour-piercing weapon, with which the user could literally punch through the textile, mail and perhaps even plate armour of his opponents on the battlefield.

One Indian fighting style, in evidence from the 16th century onwards, involved two katars, one held in each hand. With each fist armed with a lethal 1ft (30cm) or more of razor-sharp steel, the Indian warrior must have adopted a technique not unlike that of the pugilist, punching at the head and body of his opponent with sudden, lightning-fast attacks.

The katar seems to be of south Indian origin, earliest forms being closely associated with the Vijayanagara Kingdom, a south Indian empire in the Deccan founded in the 14th century. One of the most famous groups of these daggers came from the armoury at Thanjavur, which, with the armoury's dissipation in the late 19th century, has today come to be spread throughout many different museum collections. These early katars generally include a leaf or shell-like plate that protects the back of the hand, usually elaborately decorated with piercing and file-work.

Towards the end of the 16th and into the 17th century, European blades began to be imported into India in very large numbers and many katars dating from the late 1500s and early 1600s are fitted with such blades, which are often broken sword blades. By the second half of the 17th century the more enveloping hand guard was beginning to be discarded in favour of the simpler hilt that is now familiar as the classic katar form.

Stout, straight katar blades are common, but they are by no means the only type. Regional tastes led to a profusion of flamboyant katar designs. While the straight-bladed versions tended to be fashionable in the north of India, wavy or curved blades seemed more popular in the south. Multi-bladed weapons with two or even three blades were not uncommon. Other katars, sometimes referred to as "scissors" katars, were cleverly constructed so that when the grips were squeezed together, the blade split into three, rather like the European sword-catching parrying daggers of the late 16th and 17th centuries. Perhaps the most novel variation

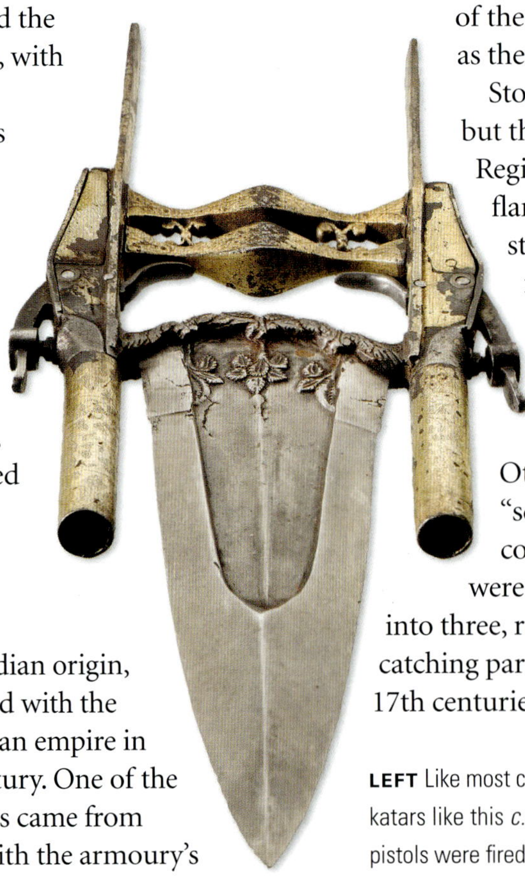

LEFT Like most combination weapons, the effectiveness of pistol katars like this *c.*1850 weapon is uncertain. The 9.5mm calibre pistols were fired by triggers pulled by the index and little fingers.

RIGHT Mughal miniatures provide vital evidence for the way weapons were worn by noblemen in India. Here a high-ranking boy wears a *katar* in his sash, prominently displayed and close to hand if needed.

on the katar theme was a Rajasthani type that was fitted with two very small flintlock or percussion pistols, one flanking each edge of the blade. The triggers were fitted inwards over the grip, which meant that they could be pulled by the index and little fingers, one at a time or simultaneously. Multiple katars are also known in which one or two smaller katars fit inside a larger one constructed as a sort of sleeve.

Katars were also important status symbols and many survive with extraordinarily varied forms of decoration. Hilts covered in enamel, gems and gold koftgari, blades chiselled with complex figures, scenes and abstract ornament, and sheaths covered in rich silk or velvet were the prize possessions of, for example, the famous Rajput warriors of northwest India. Many Rajput and Mughal princes and noblemen were portrayed with their katars tucked away safely at their waists, ready at all times if needed for self-defence but also an obvious sign of wealth and position. Katars were even used by the Mughal nobility to hunt tigers. Employed in pairs, one katar in each hand, this was without doubt the most impressive but also most hazardous of hunting practices.

ABOVE Early forms of katar like this Deccan piece, possibly made in the 17th century, often include a graceful knuckle-guard that sits over the back of the hand.

ABOVE Katar design varies greatly. Here the arms of the hilt are extended, and the blade has a gentle curve.

RIGHT When the forward grip-bar of the "scissors" katar is squeezed, the blade spreads apart into three.

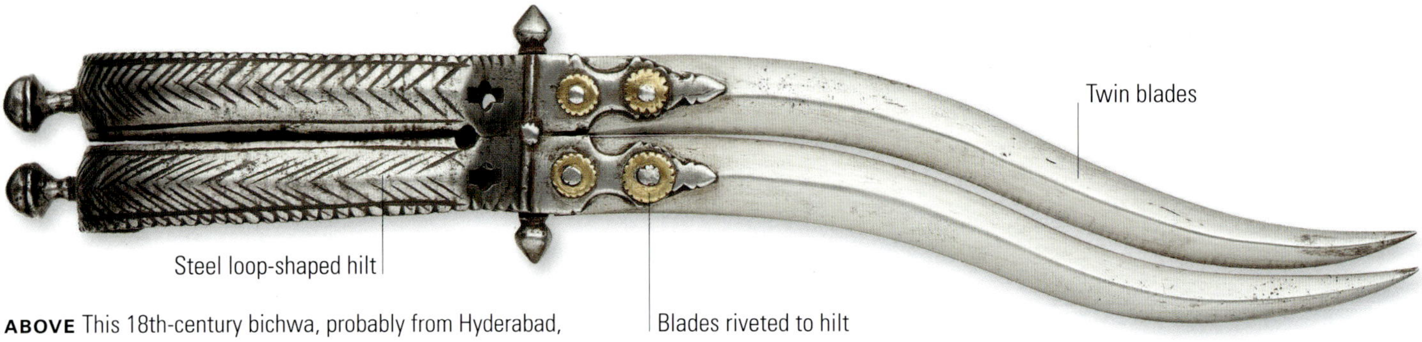

ABOVE This 18th-century bichwa, probably from Hyderabad, displays the typical flowing blade form and loop grip. The double-bladed configuration is less common.

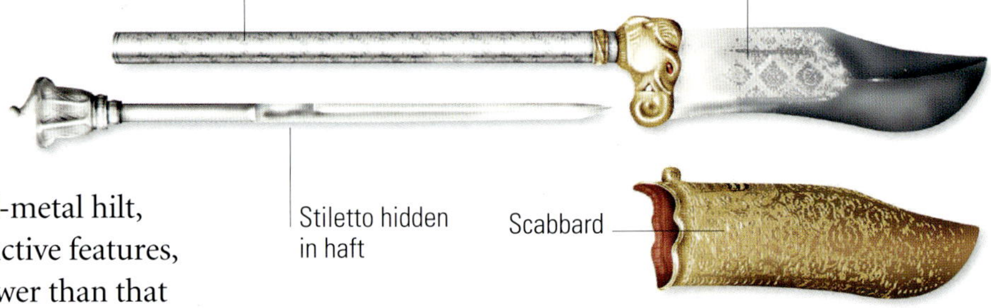

ABOVE The bhuj represents one of the most unorthodox dagger designs. The elegant dagger blade is mounted at a right angle to a short metal haft. The haft is usually hollow, inside which is often hidden another dagger of more conventional form, a short spike mounted onto the underside of the screw-threaded pommel.

The bichwa and bhuj

Two other distinctively Indian dagger types are the *bichwa*, or "scorpion" dagger, and the *bhuj*, or "elephant" dagger. The bichwa usually has a simple all-metal hilt, having a knuckle guard but no other distinctive features, and a recurved blade, but one much narrower than that found on most chilanums and khanjarlis. Like the latter, the bichwa is probably a Maratha design. This small dagger was easily hidden up a sleeve or in the qamarband, and was especially useful as a weapon for clandestine attack. It is perhaps most famous as the concealed weapon of the famous Maratha war-leader Shivaji (1630–1680), whose Robin Hood-like adventures are still told in the form of stories, poems and films. Shivaji is said to have had a bichwa named *Bhavani* ("giver of life"), which he used (although some accounts insist he used a *bagh-nakh*, or "tiger-claw") to disembowel Afzal Khan, a general in the service of the Mughal Emperor Aurangzeb (1618–1707), who tried to assassinate him during a supposedly friendly meeting.

The bhuj takes its name from the city in the Kachchh district of Gujarat (in the extreme west of India) where it was supposedly invented. It is sometimes also referred to as a *gandasa*, or "axe-knife", and is made up of a short, very heavy dagger blade that surmounts a short, axe-like haft (handle). The head of an elephant in profile is very often worked into the metal forming the base of the blade, hence the further nickname "elephant" dagger. Sometimes a small stiletto-like dagger is hidden in the haft of the bhuj, the butt cap of which unscrews to release it.

BELOW This Mughal khanjar is mounted with a classic horsehead grip of jade inlaid with gold. The blade is probably Persian, indicated by the palmette ornament at the ricasso and the recessed panels of the blade.

Koftgari decoration

One of the most popular techniques used for the decoration of fine daggers in India was koftgari, a particular type of gold inlay. The origin of the term is a brilliant evocation of the process; the Persian word *koft* means "interwoven", while a *gar* was a goldsmith or gold-beater.

The koftgari process starts with a piece of steel being cross-hatched with hundreds of tiny scratches, made with a special stout knife. Minute strands of gold wire are then worked into the surface, and are held there because the soft gold is pushed down into the scratches, becoming in a way interwoven with the steel.

This process was used to create all sorts of intricate designs, from simple plant forms and geometric patterns to complex scenes including gardens, buildings, trees and animals.

ABOVE The very elegant koftgari work on this Indian katar, which dates from the early 19th century, includes representations of cheetahs, water buffalo and lions.

LEFT Fine weapons made in Lucknow in northern India, such as this 19th-century peshkabz, usually include silver hilts embellished with brightly coloured enamelling.

The Persian influence

While the katar and chilanum originated in the south, the bhuj from the far west, and the khanjarli from the east, other dagger types were introduced from the north. The khanjar was perhaps one of the commonest forms throughout Indo-Persia, popular in Mughal India and Afghanistan but also within the rest of the Islamic world. It is probably of Persian origin, brought to India in the 15th century with the conquest of the first Mughal Emperor. The khanjar's most recognizable attribute is its supremely graceful recurved blade, often with a thickened reinforced stabbing point. Indian khanjar hilts, like those of the Middle East, lack a guard and are usually carved from a single piece of ivory, jade, agate or similar hard stone. Some especially fine examples are made of clear rock-crystal. The handles are often inlaid with precious and semi-precious stones and gold, and commonly carved into horses', rams' and tigers' heads. In depictions of Mughal noblemen these distinctive handles are often seen protruding from their sashes.

Some dagger forms were popular throughout India, but others were only found close to their areas of introduction. The peshkabz and the kard were Persian in origin, introduced by the Mughals. The peshkabz was never adopted with any regularity beyond the north. The kard caught on to some extent in central India, but remained perhaps less common as a fighting weapon. It was common throughout Rajasthan and down into central India, carried along, undoubtedly, by the progress of the Mughal Empire's incursions from the north.

The kris of South-east Asia

Most weapons are something more than a killing tool. They are symbols of status, signifiers of wealth and prestige, or badges of allegiance. But rarely are they believed to possess genuine supernatural powers and seldom is their physical appearance so conducive to such beliefs. The other-worldly appearance of the kris, and the mystical belief system that surrounds it, has promoted a unique relationship between the weapon and its world.

From the 1st century AD onwards, trade routes expanded east from India into Assam, Burma, Indonesia and Malaysia. With the accompanying migrations came also cultural and religious transmission. Hinduism became the dominant faith in some areas of the Malay Peninsula and Archipelago, while Islam and Buddhism prevailed in others. The major faiths intermingled with a bewildering variety of indigenous belief systems practised by many diverse ethnic groups, and so it is not surprising that the weapons found in this vast area are equally multifarious. Indian, Chinese and European influences combined with unique local styles and designs, creating a vast range of edged weapons.

ABOVE The belief in the magical power of the kris is not difficult to understand when one sees a kris blade of exceptional quality, such as these Javanese examples, rippling with swirling colour.

ABOVE A fine kris blade must be mounted with a hilt of equal quality. This example has been intricately carved in a highly individual and complex manner using very diverse materials.

The origins of the kris

This vibrant set of ethnic communities – where many belief systems existed side by side – might not seem like the most obvious environment for a single iconic weapon to evolve. After all, as we have seen, cultural diversity in India generated a great variety of weapons forms and designs. Yet one form of dagger did indeed rise above the many other types of knife and sword in use throughout the Malay Archipelago. The kris, or keris, achieved a cultural status unique in the world history of daggers. It was this weapon, thought to have originated in Java, that later spread throughout southeast Asia – perhaps the only weapon whose use was shared by the many peoples of that region.

RIGHT Gods and demons are frequent subjects for the carving of the kris handle, or *hulu*; this Sumatran weapon also features a graceful *wrangka* (scabbard throat) of highly-polished ebony.

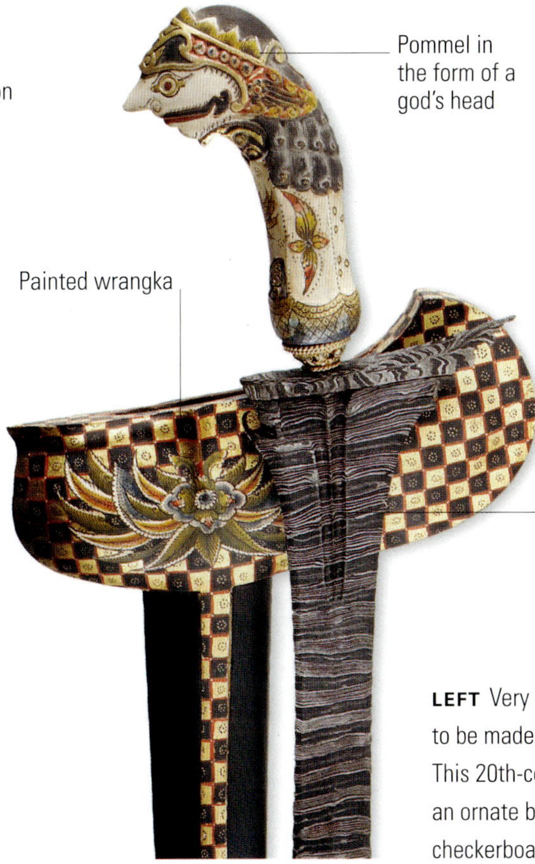

LEFT Very fine krises continue to be made in modern times. This 20th-century piece includes an ornate banded blade and checkerboard-pattern wrangka.

It has been suggested that the kris was inspired by the stingray's stinger, while other theories relate it to the ancient Chinese ko, or dagger-axe, which, like the kris, projects its blade at a right angle to the user's grip. Whatever the origin, it seems clear that the kris had defined itself as a distinctive Malay weapon by the 14th century. A carving at the mid-14th-century Hindu temple of Candi Sukuh in Java depicts a god forging a kris, while one of the earliest known examples bears a date corresponding to AD1342.

The kris blade

This knife is characterized by its long, narrow blade, which can be either straight or, more famously, wavy. Kris blades are pattern-welded works of art, made of up to seven types of iron (meteoric iron being highly prized) and steel braided and forged together. After being formed, the kris blade was carefully ground, polished, boiled in a potion of water, sulphur and salt, and rubbed with lime juice. These processes brought out the blade's welded pattern; not only did the different metals darken and discolour to different degrees, the citric acid also ate into them in varying amounts. Thus the pattern, or *pamor*, of the blade took on a striking, three-dimensional quality, like tiny meandering canyons and rivers. Malay smiths created around 150 different pamors, each being given a poetically evocative name, such as "tender coconut leaf", "spray of jasmine", "venerable serpent", "flowering of nutmeg", "snakeskin" and "rind of the watermelon".

Although kris forms vary enormously, most blades flare out at the base to form a pointed projection sometimes called the "elephant's trunk". They are fitted with a narrow metal band forming the *ganja*, or guard. A thin tang is forged out of the ganja and inserted into the *ukiran*, or handle, and secured with a gummy paste. The ukiran of the kris is usually a work of art in itself. Beautifully sculpted in ivory (elephant, walrus or even mammoth), horn, wood, bone, brass, silver or gold, kris handles take many forms. Hindu gods and demons, animals, scrollwork, phallic symbols and a number of basic ergonomic forms are all common.

In combat the kris was predominantly a thrusting weapon. The position and shape of the grip, not unlike that of a pistol, allowed the blade to project along the same line as the forearm. Like the Indian katar, it was not uncommon for two krises to be used in combat, one in each hand. The distinctive sheath could also be used to block an opponent's blows.

LEFT Two men in ceremonial dress unsheathe the long serpentine blade of a kris. This example from Java plays a symbolic part in traditional *wajang*, or shadow plays.

A magical relationship

A kris was, for its owner, an intensely personal object. It was washed and anointed during annual rituals, during which offerings were also made to it, in similar fashion to the sword worship practised by some Indian Hindus. A kris was considered one of a man's basic possessions, along with a house, a wife and a horse. It asserted a man's identity and associations, both within his family and in society in general. A kris passed down through a family was a tangible bond between a man and his ancestors, a link between the living and the dead. In Java the relationship between a kris and its owner was so strong that the weapon could actually stand in for a bridegroom at his wedding if for some reason he was unable to be present himself.

The kris was also believed to possess many mystical properties. Some have been said to fly out of their sheaths at night to kill unsuspecting victims. Others were thought to have healing powers. One of the most widely held ideas was that a kris could kill someone just by being pointed at them; great care was therefore taken in the handling of a kris to prevent accidental harm caused by someone inadvertently coming in line with the point. In Bali, specially designed kris stands in the form of animals or demons held the weapon vertically to minimize the danger from its projected magical energy. It is also said that the very best krises can kill simply by being driven into the footprint, shadow or a photo of the intended victim.

Foreign interest

Since westerners first became aware of the kris, it has been a source of fascination and curiosity. Sir Francis Drake (*c.*1540–1596) brought krises back to England from Java in 1580, while another was sent to King James I (1566–1625) as a gift in 1612. They also became popular with European artists in the 16th and 17th centuries. Rembrandt (1606–1669), for example, included krises in several of his works. He grasps one in an engraved and etched self-portrait (mistakenly titled *Self-Portrait with Raised Sabre*), while a soldier plunges another into Samson's eye in *The Blinding of Samson*.

An ancient weapon in a modern world

Krises featured in Indonesian warfare into the 20th century. During the Philippines Campaign (1899–1905), local kris-wielding warriors mounted many ambushes and nocturnal attacks against the American military. In 1903, the US Army fought a group of Moros near Jolo that included 4000 men armed with krises.

RIGHT Kris stands take an endless variety of forms. This particular stand has been carved and painted into an image of the Hindu elephant-headed god Ganesh.

Their leader was later captured, but the American force guarding him was in turn ambushed by men with krises; he was rescued and a number of the Americans killed or injured, including the commander, whose hand was so badly slashed that several of his fingers had to be amputated.

Since the 1960s, the kris has begun to lose much of its cultural and religious influence in Indonesian society. Although a small number of master smiths practising the traditional art form can still be found, they are now very few. Transmission of the skill of kris making has also been made difficult as the younger generation becomes increasingly westernized.

Efforts from the 1990s onwards have, however, revived the craft of kris making to some extent, and in 2005 UNESCO heralded the kris a Masterpiece of the Oral and Intangible Heritage of Humanity (Third Proclamation).

ABOVE Another kris appears in Rembrandt's *The Blinding of Samson* (1636); here a soldier plunges one into Samson's eye. It was undoubtedly thought to be suitably exotic and thus appropriate to the Biblical theme.

RIGHT This drawing made in 1864 gives some idea of what an Indonesian (Javanese) warband might have looked like. The leading warrior holds his kris, signifying his elite status, high in the air.

The Japanese tanto

Unlike the many different dagger forms that evolved elsewhere in Asia, those of Japan remained remarkably consistent in design throughout their long history. A short, single-edged, thick-backed blade, ground to a steep wedge shape in cross-section, remained the sidearm of samurai warriors for several hundred years. In that time the design changed very little, remaining essentially a miniature version of the swords with which it was partnered.

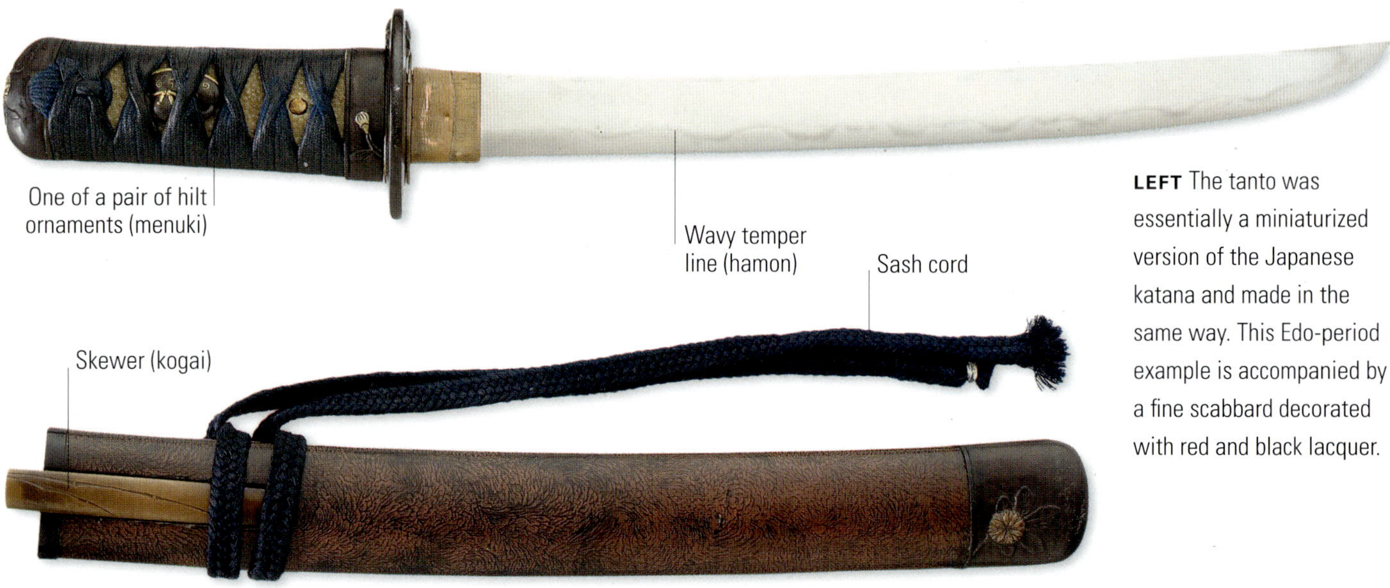

LEFT The tanto was essentially a miniaturized version of the Japanese katana and made in the same way. This Edo-period example is accompanied by a fine scabbard decorated with red and black lacquer.

The distinctive Japanese dagger, the tanto, is thought to have first appeared in the pre-medieval Heian Period (AD794–1185). Early tantos seem to have been very basic utilitarian implements, unworthy of note. It was not until the very end of that era that the tanto distinguished itself, as a work of art as well as a weapon, during the bloody Gempei War (1180–85) fought between the rival Minamoto and Taira clans.

By this time the warrior culture of the samurai had fully developed, and along with it, codified systems of combat. Warriors of the late Heian Period carried the bow, a long-bladed staff weapon called a naginata and the long sword, or tachi, as their primary weapons, along with the tanto as a weapon of last resort. These weapons, and the sequence of their use, are vividly described in an account of the first Battle of Uji (1180), the opening battle of the Gempei War. One passage from the epic *Tale of the Heike* (1371), as follows, relates how the warrior Tsutsui Jomyo Meishu fought the Taira samurai on the Uji bridge itself, in an attempt to prevent them crossing and destroying the fleeing Minamoto forces:

And loosing off twenty arrows like lightning flashes he slew twelve of the Taira samurai and wounded eleven more … throwing away his bow … With his naginata he cut down five of the enemy but with the sixth the blade snapped ... he drew his tachi … and cut down eight men. But as he brought down the ninth with an exceedingly mighty blow on the helmet, the blade broke at the hilt .... Then seizing his dagger, which was the only weapon he had left, he plied it as one in a death fury.

The tanto and ritual suicide

This dagger was not only the samurai's final option in hand-to-hand combat. It was also the weapon with which he killed himself when defeated in battle or dishonoured. After the destruction of his forces by the Taira at Uji, the Minamoto commander Yorimasa quickly wrote a death poem on the back of his war fan before using his tanto to cut two long slashes into his abdomen. This is the earliest known instance of a samurai committing *seppuku*, or ritual suicide after a battlefield defeat.

ABOVE This dramatic detail from an early 17th-century version of the Kamakura/Muromachi *gunki-mono* ("war-tales") shows the monk Mongaku attacking a samurai with a *tanto*.

A lethal work of art

Following the Gempei War and throughout the subsequent Kamakura Period (1186–1333), which marks the beginning of the Middle Ages in Japan, the tanto developed into a weapon pleasing to the eye and worthy of respect, as skilfully made and as beautifully decorated as any sword. The blade was constructed in the same way as that of the sword; it was single-edged and strong-backed, 15–30cm (6–12in) long, with an asymmetric point tapering diagonally to the back.

Early forms of the dagger were also termed *koshi-gatana*, or "loin-sword" and were worn tucked into the armoured samurai's sash, or *uwa-obi*. While the earliest forms had curved blades, by the Muromachi Period (1334–1572) nearly straight blades became more common. The dagger's companion, the sword, was also changing; the long tachi was increasingly being replaced by the shorter, handier katana. The katana was not slung like the tachi but thrust through the girdle along with the dagger. The mounts of these early sword and dagger sets often did not match, although later they would be decorated as a pair.

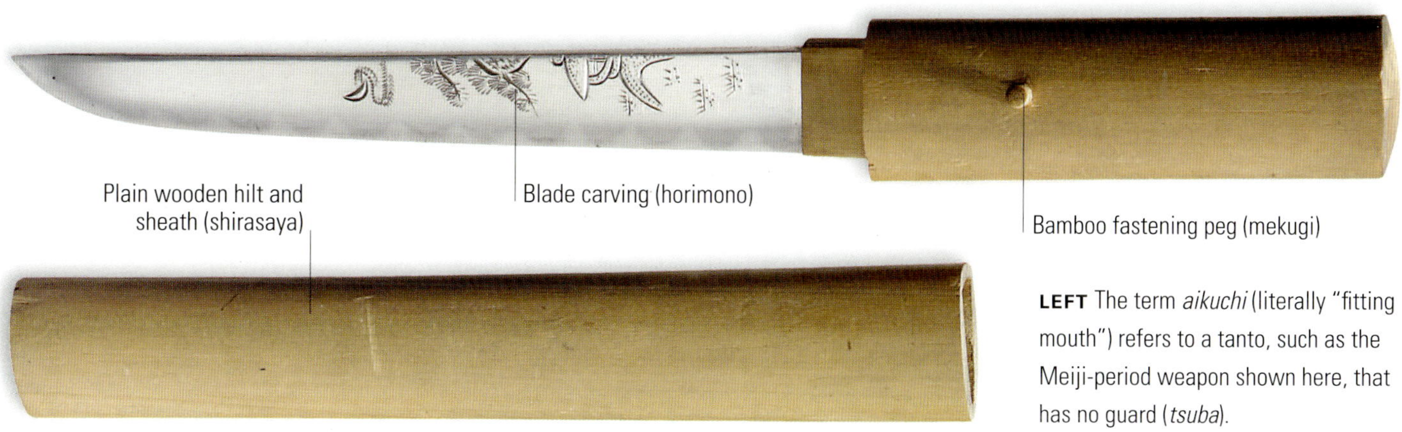

LEFT The term *aikuchi* (literally "fitting mouth") refers to a tanto, such as the Meiji-period weapon shown here, that has no guard (*tsuba*).

LEFT The Japanese samurai, like the western knight, was armed with a number of different weapons. In addition to a powerful bow and sharp arrows, he also carried a long sword (tachi) and short sword (tanto).

The kaiken

Noblewomen used a smaller version of the tanto called a kaiken to commit suicide with a swift thrust to the throat, especially in cases where the castle of their lord was taken by storm. In the Siege of Fushimi in 1596, the entire family of the castle's lord, Torii Mototada, killed themselves to avoid capture when this great fortress – near Kyoto – fell after a great battle. This desperate sacrifice was later held up as a powerful example of samurai honour and loyalty; the bloodstained floorboards from the room where the women and children died were later built into the ceiling of a nearby temple.

The decline of the tanto

The tanto was gradually being replaced as the companion weapon of the sword during the violent Momayama Period (1573–1603). The Edo (or Tokugawa) Period (1603–1867) that followed began with the unification of Japan under Tokugawa Ieyasu (1543–1616) and ushered in over 250 years of cultural development and relative peace. The tanto fell quickly out of use as the symbolism of weapons became as important as their application. Although the production of the more symbolic elements of the samurai's dress, namely his armour and sword, continued, the making of the tanto fell dramatically, and most of those made were imitations of the daggers of previous eras.

In 1868 the Medieval Period in Japan officially came to an end with the Meiji Restoration, which ended the rule of the Tokugawa shoguns and established a new line of imperial rulers. Members of the Imperial Court adopted ancient, pre-shogunate fashions, including the wearing of the tachi and tanto. Many daggers were produced before World War II, but Japan's defeat in 1945 and subsequent weapons ban meant that they ceased being made once again.

BELOW A yoroi doshi was a tanto fitted with a special type of narrower, armour-piercing blade. The scabbard is fitted with additional sleeves for a hair-pick (*kogai*) and byknife (*shirimono kodzuka*).

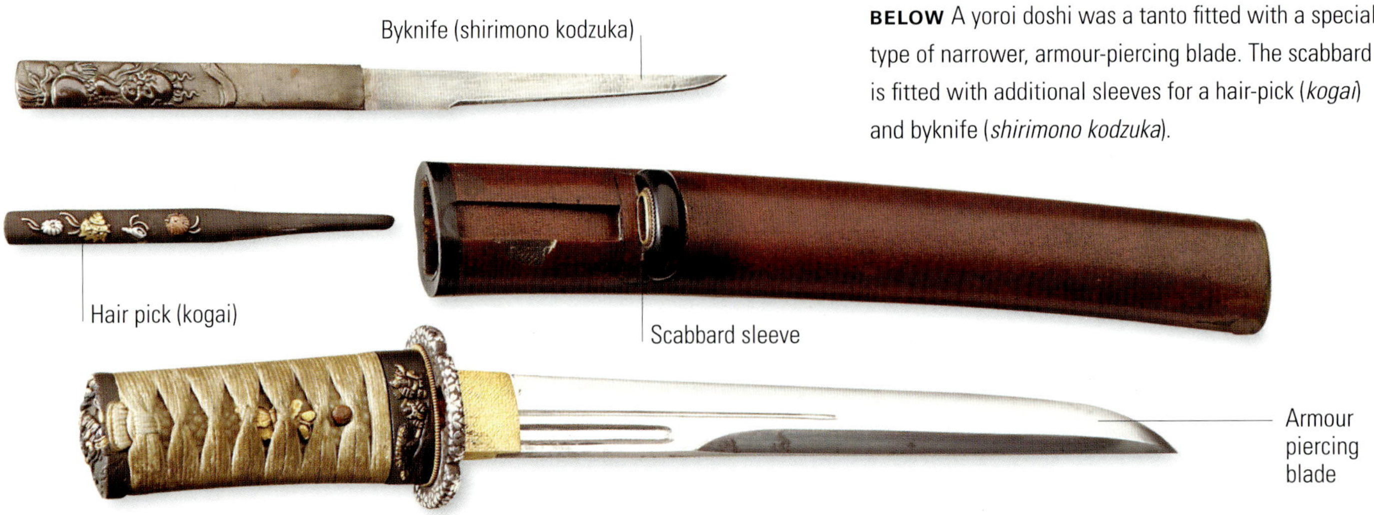

Seppuku

As *bushido* – the Japanese warrior code – developed in the 12th and 13th centuries, seppuku quickly became one of its central elements. Unlike the European code of chivalry, which required defeated and captured knights to be compassionately treated, bushido advocated contempt for one's defeated enemies; if taken prisoner, a samurai was tortured and killed. Seppuku initially evolved as an honourable way for warriors to avoid capture after defeat in battle, but later became a way to salvage and even increase one's honour in recompense for some disreputable or disgraceful act. It was also adopted as a more respectable alternative to execution granted to condemned samurai.

Seppuku provided perhaps the most iconic role for the dagger in Japan. It involved the seated samurai taking up his tanto and plunging it into the left side of his own abdomen. He then calmly cut a long slash across his stomach. The bravest samurai would sometimes attempt a second cut, either another horizontal slash or an even more excruciating vertical cut, before expiring in agony.

As late as the 1860s, Algernon Bertram Freeman-Mitford, the British ambassador to Japan, described in his book *Tales of Old Japan* a seppuku ritual witnessed by a colleague:

The case of a young fellow, only twenty years old, of the Choshiu clan, which was told me the other day by an eye-witness, deserves mention as a marvellous instance of determination. Not content with giving himself the one necessary cut, he slashed himself thrice horizontally and twice vertically. Then he stabbed himself in the throat until the dirk protruded on the other side, with its sharp edge to the front; setting his teeth in one supreme effort, he drove the knife forward with both hands through his throat, and fell dead.

BELOW This fabricated seppuku ritual was staged in about 1875. Two samurai act as witnesses while another acts as headsman.

The modern era

Today, knives, daggers and bayonets are found all over the world. Although the role of a separate fighting knife has diminished, the bayonet remains standard issue to every infantryman serving in a professional army. At the same time, fine-quality edged weapons have gained respect as an art form. Created by modern smiths drawing on 6000 years of experience, these art-object weapons are at once traditional and highly contemporary.

Outside the military world, specialist fighting knives are still produced for the purposes of self-defence, and the demand for survival knives and multi-use "sportsmen's" knives is as strong as ever. Additionally, many people around the world collect historic edged weapons, as much for their craftsmanship as their history. This concept of knives as objects of creative design as well as utility is a growing trend among many modern bladesmiths, especially in the United States.

The art of the knife

Craftsmen today have the huge advantage in their work not only of exact temperature and time control but also the knowledge of precisely why different metals behave the way they do, and exactly how their properties may be manipulated to produce a very wide range of forms and varying effects. Heat and chemical processes, for example, can now be used to create an extraordinary range of colours in steel, giving visual qualities to modern knives that were never possible before. A seemingly endless array of materials are at the disposal of the modern craftsman,

ABOVE Dated 2005, the etched, heat-tinted blade, crucible steel bolsters and handle made of blackwood burl and fossilized mammoth tooth of this fine specimen demonstrate the creativity of modern smiths, such as P.J. Ernest.

BELOW Richard Furrer's "Palm-leaf Bowie" combines a Javanese *Blarka Ngirdi* ("Palm-Leaf") pamor, typical Bowie "Spanish notch" and a Japanese-style *mokume-gane* wood-grain metal guard. The handle is a 30,000-year-old Walrus tusk.

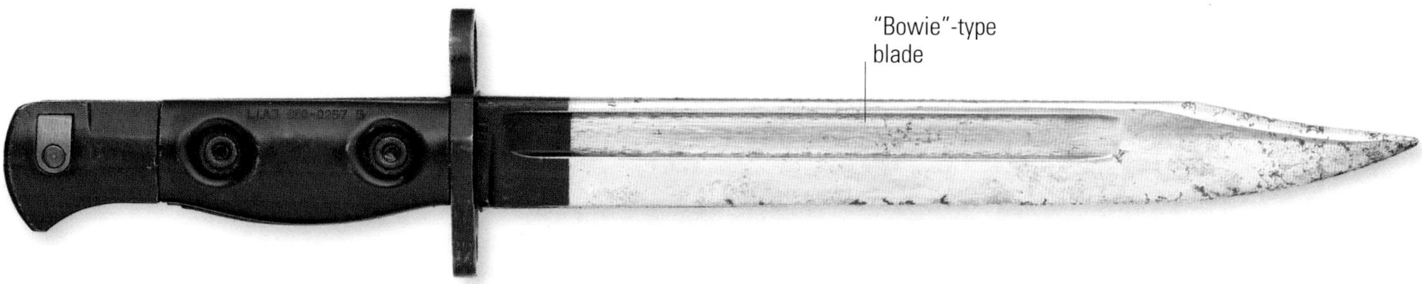

ABOVE The L1A3 knife bayonet for the British 7.62mm SLR was introduced in 1959 and remained in use for nearly 30 years. It was used with legendary effectiveness in the Falklands War.

ABOVE The old desire to design a bayonet that serves more than one function continues today; this knife bayonet for the British SA-80 assault rifle is also intended to convert for use as a wire-cutter.

not only modern or rare metals such as titanium, meteoric iron, and many forms of exotic watered steels, but also more unusual organic materials and minerals such as fossilized mammoth and mastodon ivory, hematite and tanzanite.

The modern bayonet

With advances in automatic weapons, one could easily assume that the bayonet would quickly become obsolete. However, bayonets are still issued to infantrymen in most modern armies. How could such an apparently outdated weapon as the bayonet, devised more than 400 years ago, continue to demand a special place in the soldier's arsenal?

The bayonet's functions in present-day war zones are diverse. Despite the increasing effectiveness of firearms in close combat, the bayonet remains an important alternative. In the Vietnam War, US Marines and the North Vietnamese Army fought each other with fixed bayonets at the Siege of Khe Sanh (30 March 1968). At the Battle of Mount Tumbledown (13–14 June 1982) during the Falklands War, British troops stormed Argentinean positions with fixed bayonets in a famous night attack. More recently, in the Second Gulf (Iraq) War (2003–11), soldiers from the Argyll and Sutherland Highlanders regiment of the British Army executed a bayonet charge against members of a Shi'ite militia who had ambushed them near the city of Amara (reported 15 May 2004).

The bayonet was not an uncommon sight during both Iraq wars. In the unpredictable environment of urban warfare, especially when clearing buildings or bunkers, an attack at close quarters is always a danger and a fixed bayonet a sensible precaution. The bayonet obviously becomes more important to a soldier who runs out of ammunition, but it can also prove a decisive weapon in the face of a surprise attack during reloading, or similar circumstances. Yet perhaps just as important as its practical fighting applications are the psychological advantages: the inexperienced soldier may feel more confident entering battle at close quarters with his bayonet in place; the fierce aspect of the edged weapon is just as strong today as it ever was. It serves to embolden the wielder and often terrifies the enemy. It also gives the modern soldier the sense that he is a part of a martial tradition and in possession of an ancient warrior skill that makes him better than his ill-disciplined opponent. These are advantages that cannot be overcome by technological change. At least, not yet.

Knives, daggers and bayonets come in an incredible variety of forms, depending on their historical period and origin.

A directory of knives, daggers and bayonets

In this informative catalogue, you will find details of some of the most important weapons from around the world and throughout history, along with information about their manufacture and use. Arranged chronologically as well as by geographical area, each of the weapons has a description and a specification that lists its country of origin, date and length.

TOP A Japanese Arisaka bayonet, 1939, with a heavily blued hilt.

MIDDLE TOP German Luftwafte Flying Officer's dagger, 1934.

MIDDLE BOTTOM Indian Coorg Tamil knife, mid-19th century.

BOTTOM A British bayonet for sappers and miners, 1st Pattern 1842, with sword-type guard.

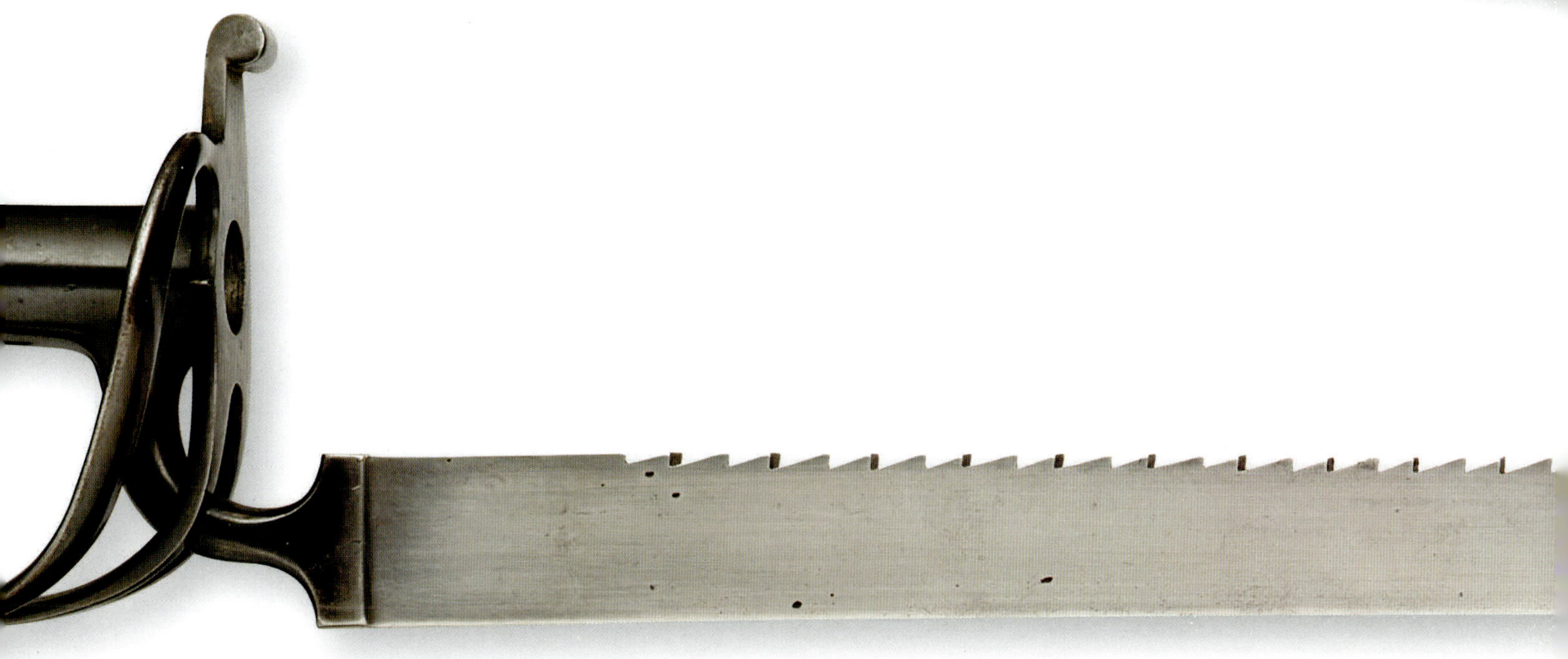

Design of knives, daggers and bayonets

The creation of an aesthetically pleasing and successful fighting knife, dagger or bayonet involves a number of considerations. Foremost of these is the intended method of use of the weapon. The size and shape of the blade are of primary importance here – for example, stabbing daggers require a slender blade, while daggers intended to be used in rapier combat need to be strong – although the balance and proportions of the weapon also contribute to its effectiveness for a particular use.

Types of knives and daggers

Stabbing

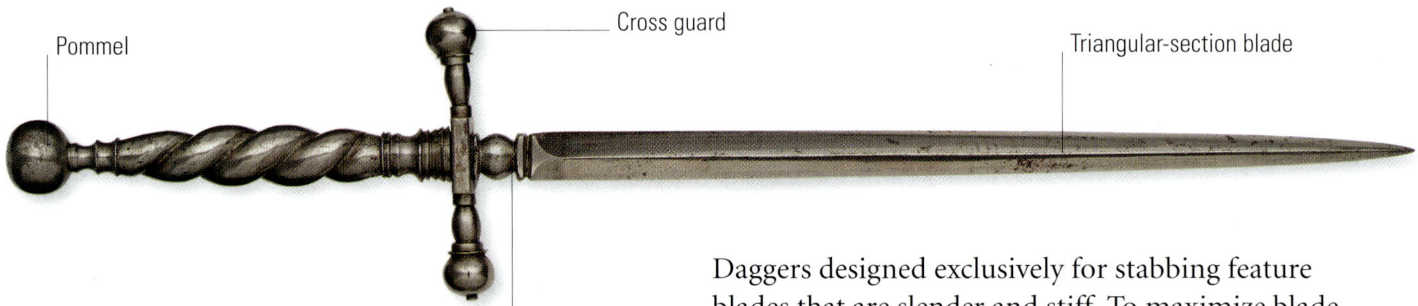

Daggers designed exclusively for stabbing feature blades that are slender and stiff. To maximize blade rigidity, cutting edges are sometimes sacrificed in favour of thickness and narrowness.

Cut and thrust

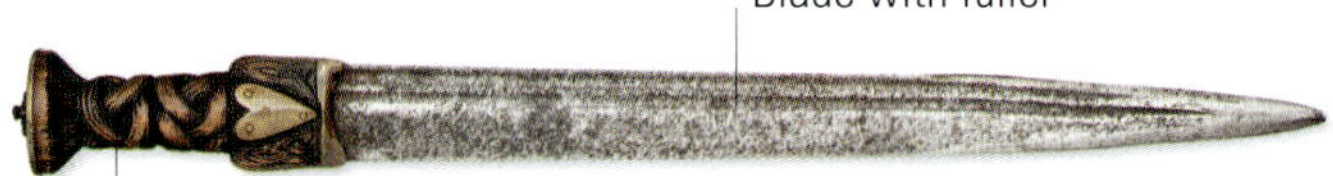

Most fighting knives and daggers are designed for both stabbing and slashing. These functions must be carefully balanced – a knife cannot do both perfectly.

Parrying

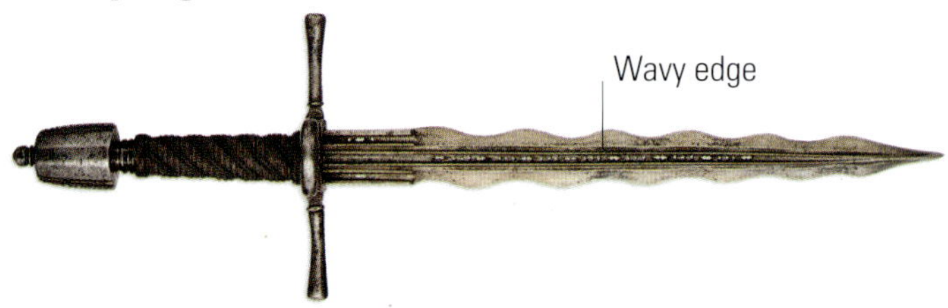

Daggers designed to be used in rapier combat have to be large and strongly built, so that they can stand up to blows from opposing sword blades.

Folding

Fighting knives which have blades folding down into the handle are easy to carry about one's person. They usually have single-edged blades.

Push

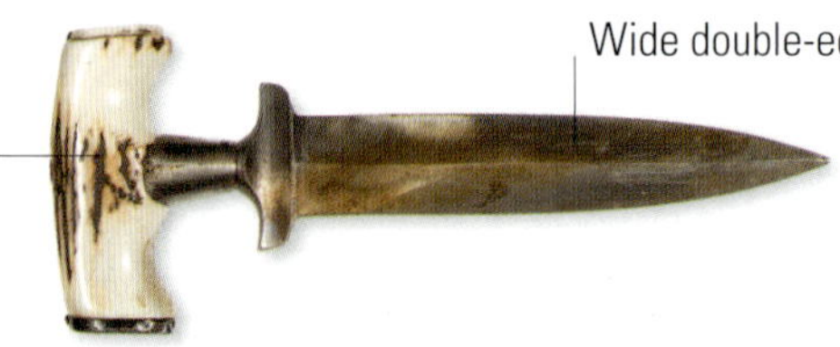

Push daggers are more unusual, perhaps because their method of use – a punching action with the blade projecting in front of the fist – is so specific.

African sickle blade

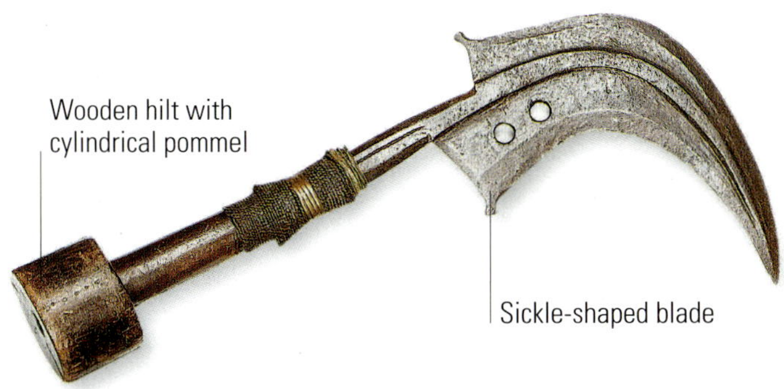

Large fighting knives with C-shaped blades are rare but not unknown; the cutting edge is on the concave side. These knives are often used to strike hammer-like blows with the point.

African throwing knife

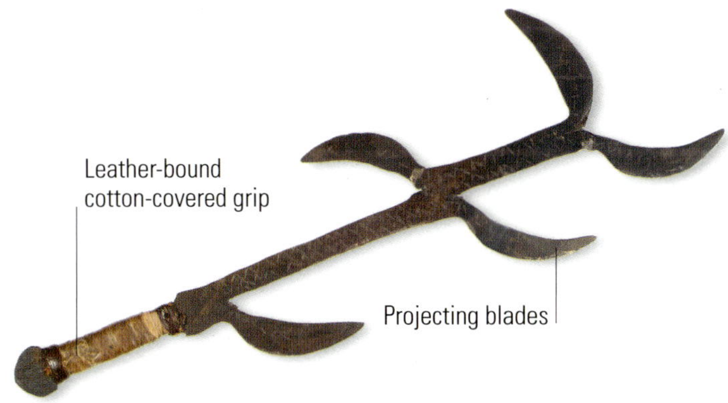

Single-blade throwing knives rely on the thrower accurately judging distance and rotation in the throw. Multi-bladed versions are designed to produce a blade-strike, whatever the point of impact.

Parts of a dagger and scabbard

The precise ways in which edged weapons are constructed varies tremendously. Likewise, the exact parts that make up a knife or dagger, and the names of those parts, depends on how and where the weapon has been built. Shown below are some of the basic elements that make up most forms of dagger and fighting knife.

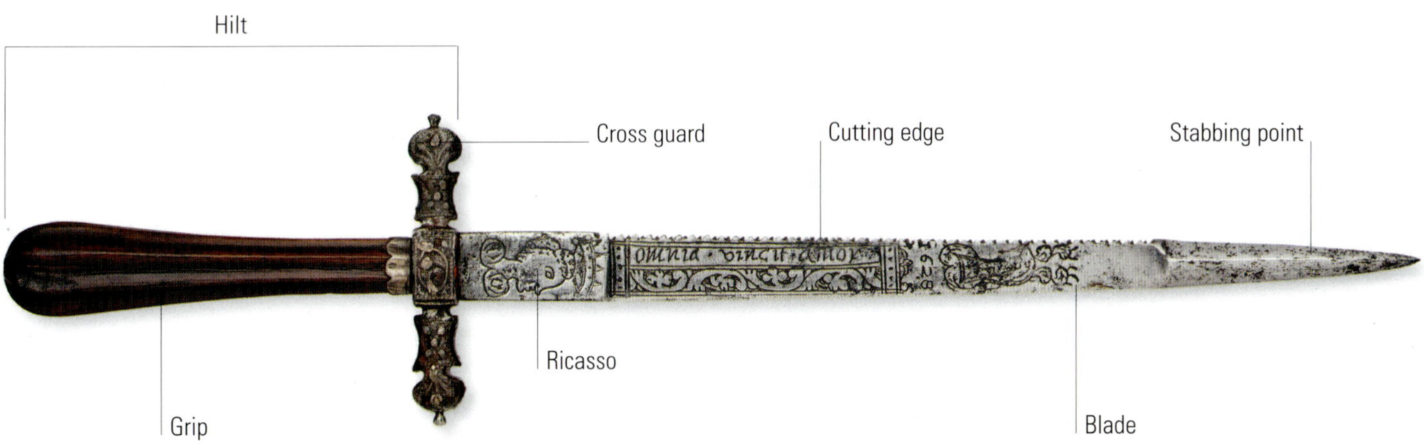

Types of bayonets

Plug

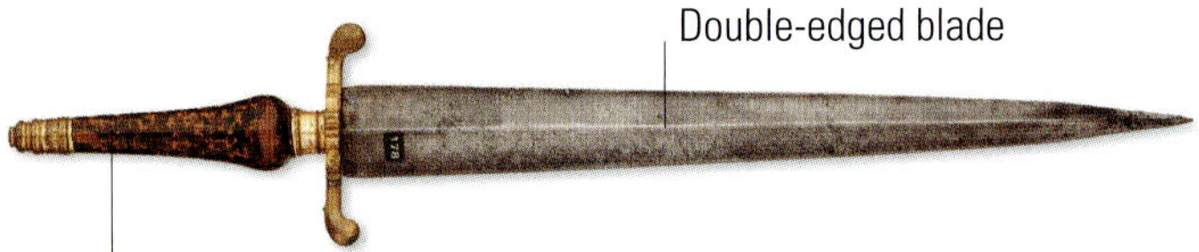

The earliest bayonet was simply a cross-hilt dagger with the handle tapered down so that it could be jammed into the end of the musket.

Socket

The socket bayonet fitted around the muzzle, with the blade slung underneath to the side, allowing the musket to be fired with the bayonet fixed.

Sword

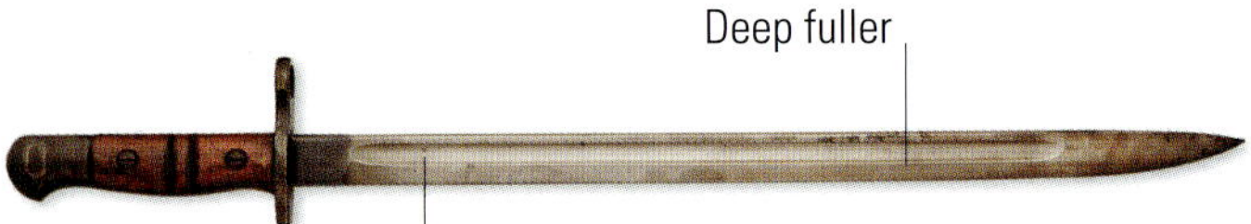

Sword bayonets were the result of an effort to combine the reach of a long blade with a hilt, allowing use as an independent weapon.

Knife

The knife bayonet was introduced in the late 19th century. Here the bayonet returned to its origins, coming to resemble a small all-purpose dagger again.

Parts of a bayonet

Bayonet terminology varies depending on the type of bayonet as, unlike most other small-edged weapons, different types of bayonet feature specific mechanical components – for example the devices for attachment to the firearm. Some of the most essential 19th- and 20th-century terms are given below.

Knife bayonet

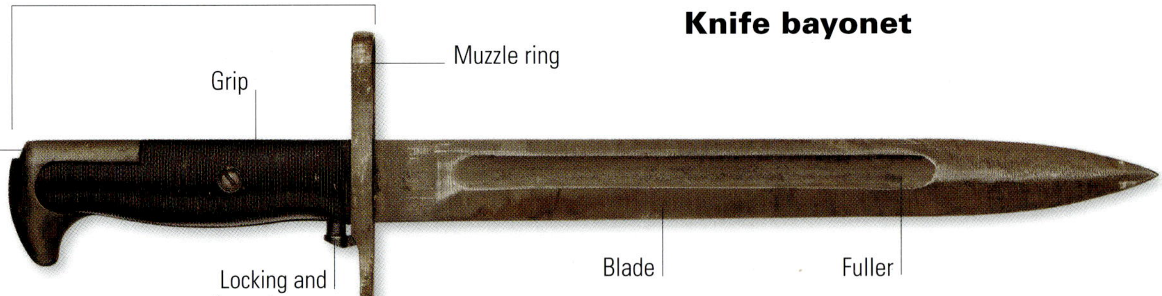

Socket bayonet

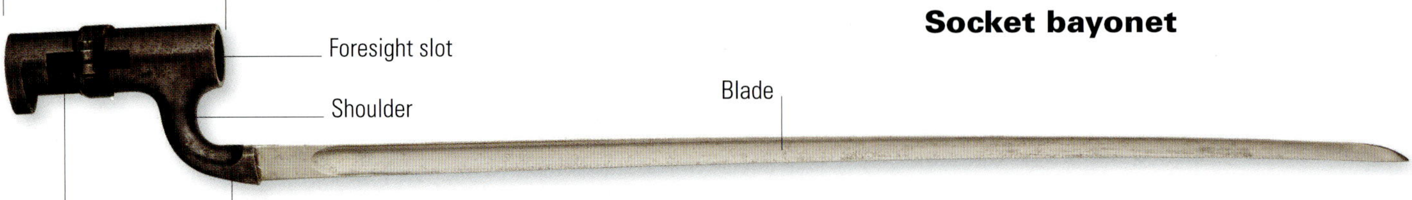

Types of blades

The form of the blade of an edged weapon determines everything about it – its method of use as well as the effects it can produce. The blade shape also gives the weapon its particular identity or "personality", bringing aesthetic attractiveness as well as deadly functionality.

Leaf

Mechanical blade

Triangular

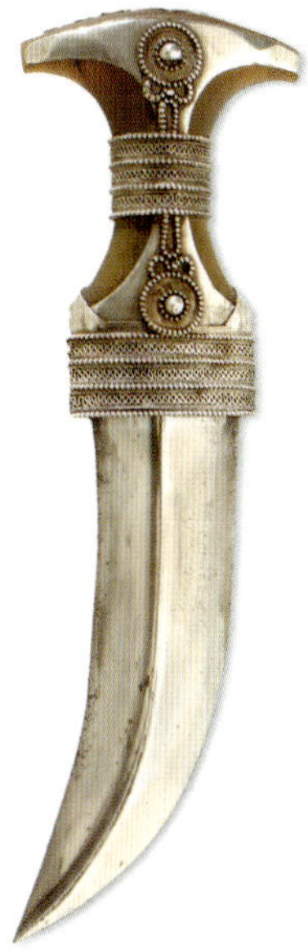
Double-edged curved

Double-edged straight

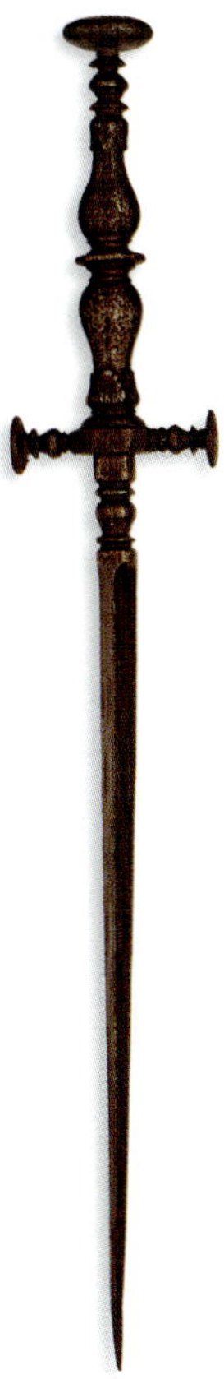
Thrusting

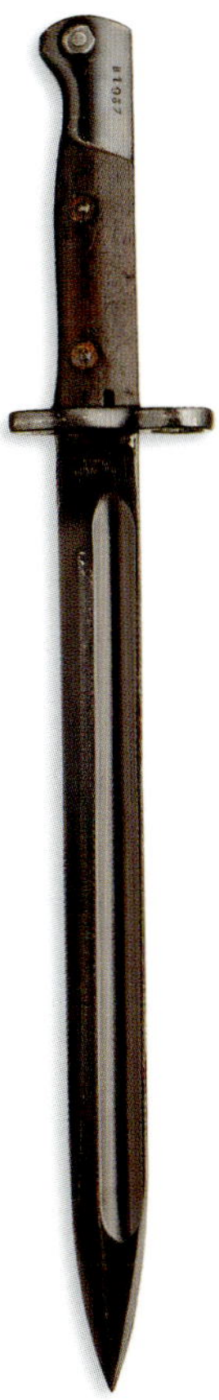
Single-edged straight

Single-edged with false edge

Single-edged curved

Variable section blade

Blade cross-sections

The cross-section shape of the blade of any edged weapon plays an essential role in determining the way in which that weapon performs. It determines whether the weapon is dedicated to one use, being better suited either to cutting or thrusting, or conversely, whether it is intended to provide a decent level of general effectiveness in both forms of attack. Cross-section shapes vary enormously; there are a small set of basic shapes, each of which has formed the basis for the development of more complex designs.

Basic blade sections

Flattened oval or lenticuler

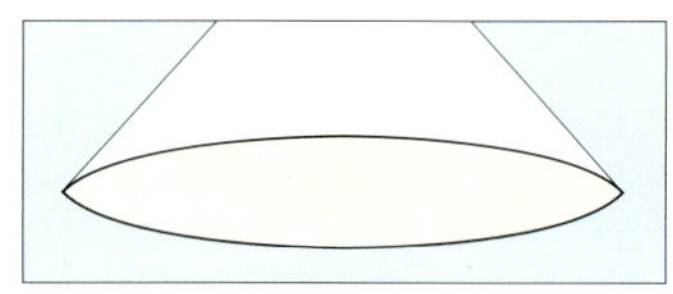

This is one of the most ancient blade sections, found on flint knives of *c.*2000BC and earlier. The middle of the blade is kept thick to retain strength, while each side is smoothly tapered down to the two cutting edges.

Spined flat section

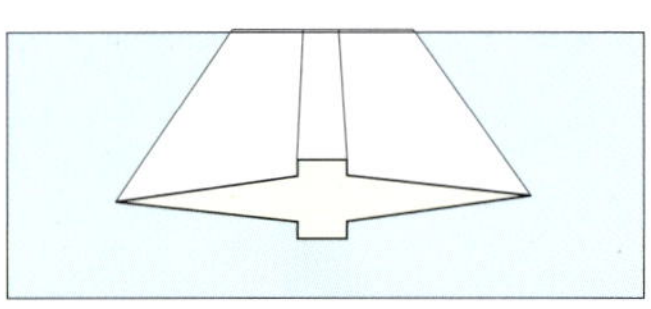

Blades with a simple flat section, though straightforward in design and easy to make, are very weak and therefore very rare. Most flat-sectioned blades of the Bronze Age, for example, have a specially thickened, straight-sided medial spine, to prevent the blade from simply collapsing on impact.

Wedge section

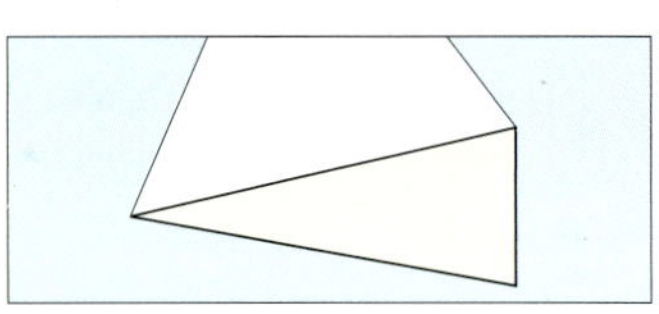

All single-edged or "backed" blades are of wedge section, with the thick unsharpened back providing the blade's strength and rigidity. The design is typically found on the early medieval scramasax, as well as on many medieval "cutting" daggers.

Diamond section

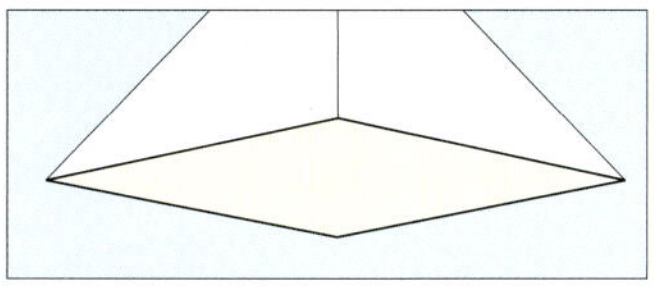

This is an excellent shape for daggers and knives intended primarily for stabbing because it provides very high rigidity at the cost of the cutting edges. Cutting edges can be retained with the flattened diamond section, but the decreased taper sacrifices some of the spine thickness.

Square section

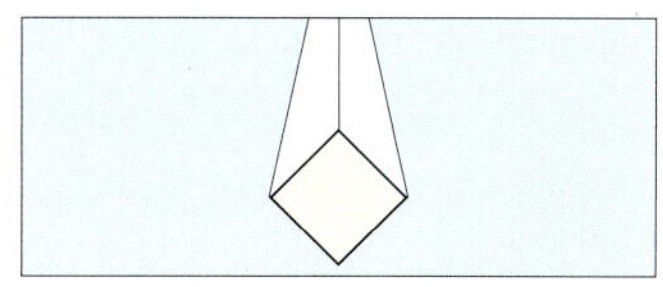

A more extreme move towards an exclusively thrusting capability, with no edges of any sort. It's ideal for stabbing but the lack of a cutting edge is somewhat limiting.

Triangular section

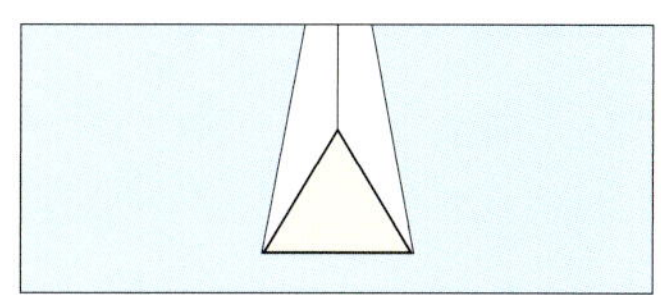

Another dedicated thrusting design, the triangular section is conceived to perform like the square section blade but with a reduced overall weight. For this reason it is commonly found on socket bayonets of the 18th and 19th centuries.

T-section

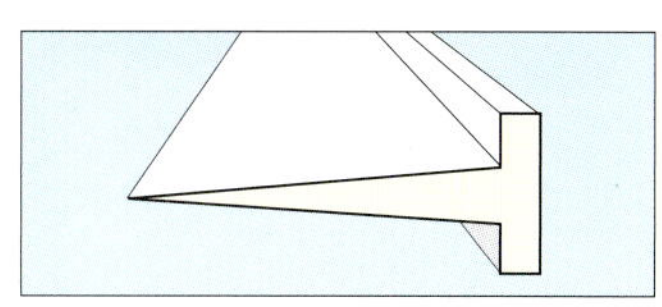

The T-section is an unusual variation of the wedge-section concept. The thickness of the back has been ground almost entirely away, leaving only a narrow shelf. This is a design unique to certain types of Indo-Persian peshkabz.

More complex sections

By the Medieval Period, blades started to develop with more than one cross-section. For example, the base of the blade might be made in a rectangular section to provide maximum strength at the guard; the middle of the blade could be shaped into a wedge section to give a long cutting edge; while the forward part might use a flattened diamond section to create a sharper point and better thrusting capability. These blades made up of more than one cross-section also reflect light in an interesting way.

BELOW Early 17th-century English daggers like this one usually include very fine etched blades, having three distinct cross-section areas.

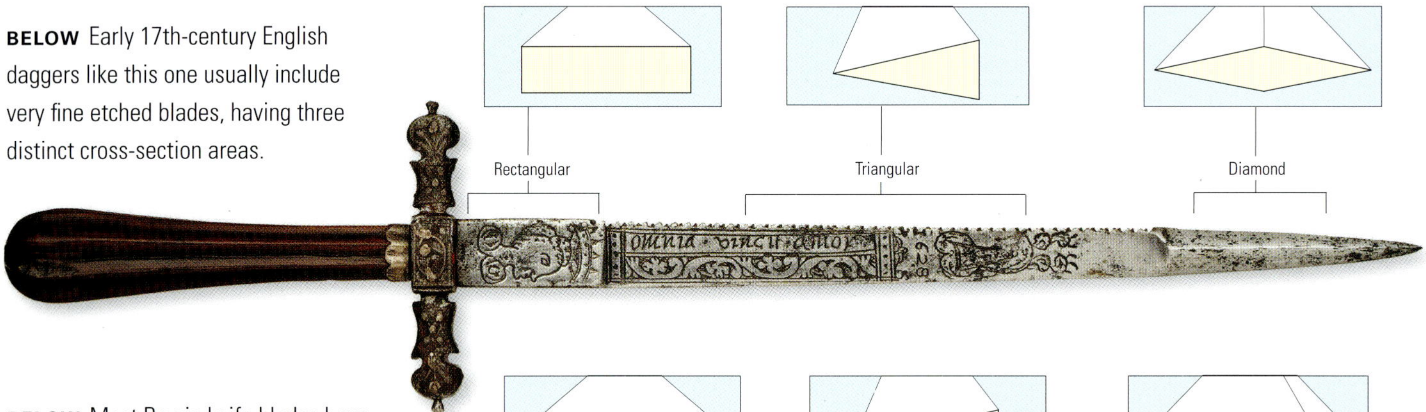

BELOW Most Bowie knife blades have a very thick and strong lower half of triangular section, while the upper section is sharpened on both edges.

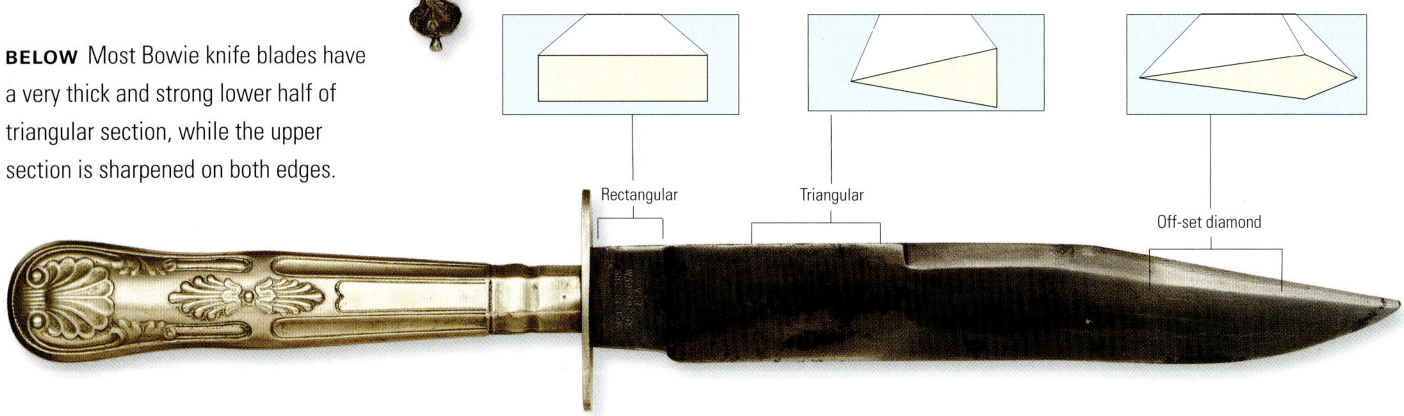

The fuller

Maintaining strength while reducing weight is important in blade design. The fuller is key to this. A shallow groove down a blade's length reduces its weight but does not weaken it. By the Medieval Period most blades had fullers, either down the middle or offset. The fuller was never a "blood-groove", nor did it make the weapon easier to pull out of an enemy's body. It was simply a way of optimizing weight. Some blades have multiple fullers – some very shallow and wide, others very narrow and quite deep.

Single-fullered flattened diamond section

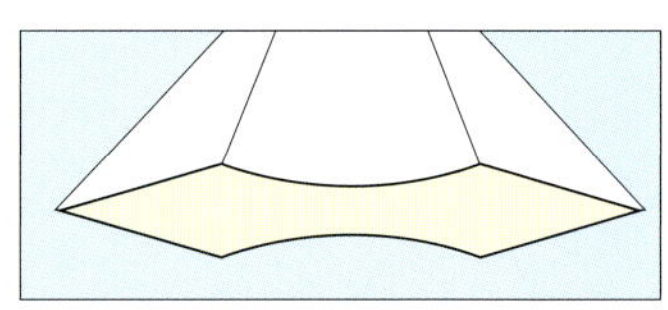

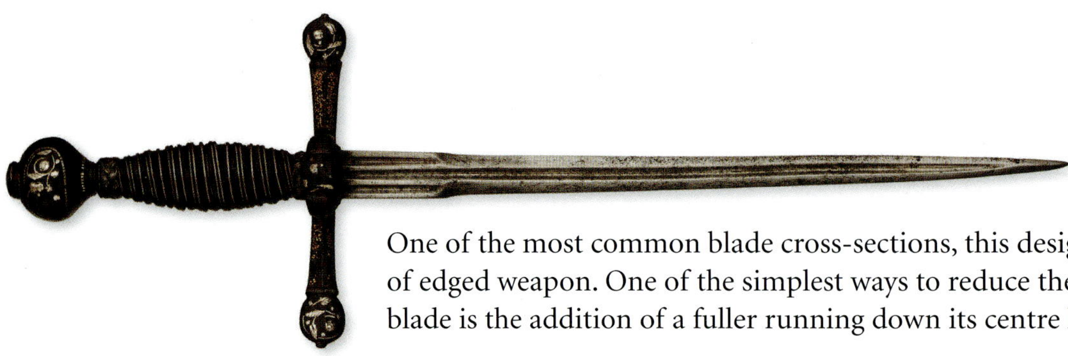

One of the most common blade cross-sections, this design is found on many types of edged weapon. One of the simplest ways to reduce the weight of a double-edged blade is the addition of a fuller running down its centre line on both sides.

Offset fullered wedge section

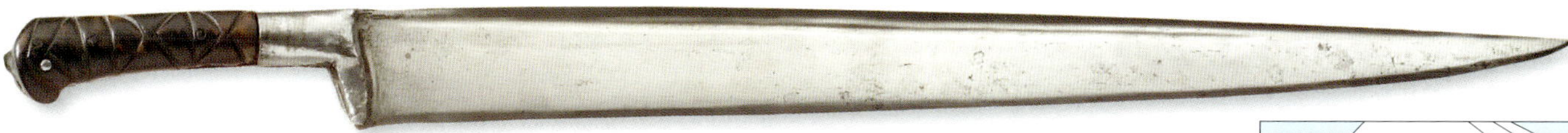

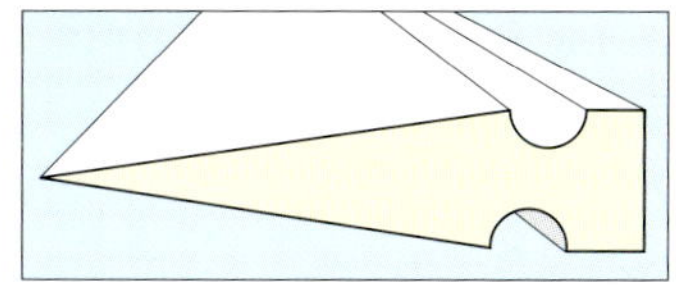

This is another very common design, one that takes some of the weight out of the thick back of the blade while retaining overall strength.

Multi-fullered wedge section

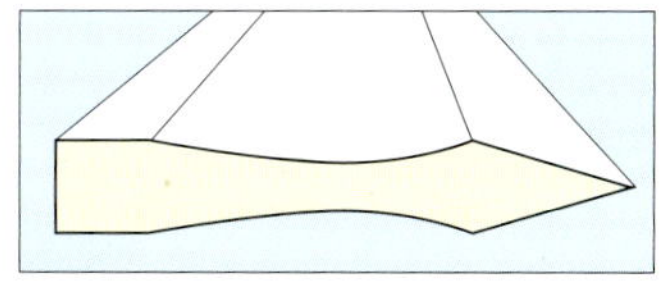

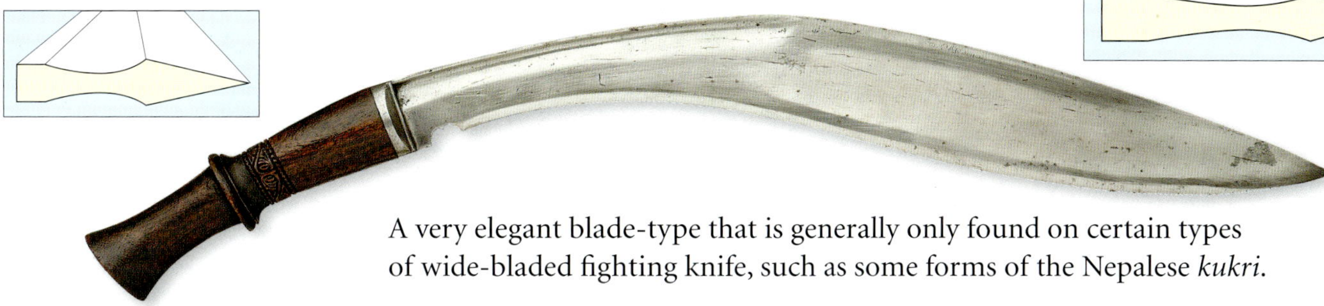

A very elegant blade-type that is generally only found on certain types of wide-bladed fighting knife, such as some forms of the Nepalese *kukri*.

Multi-fullered flattened diamond section

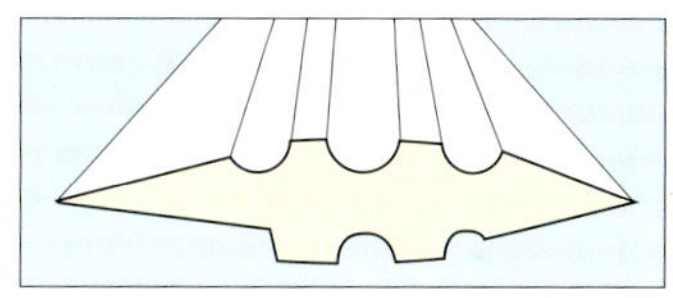

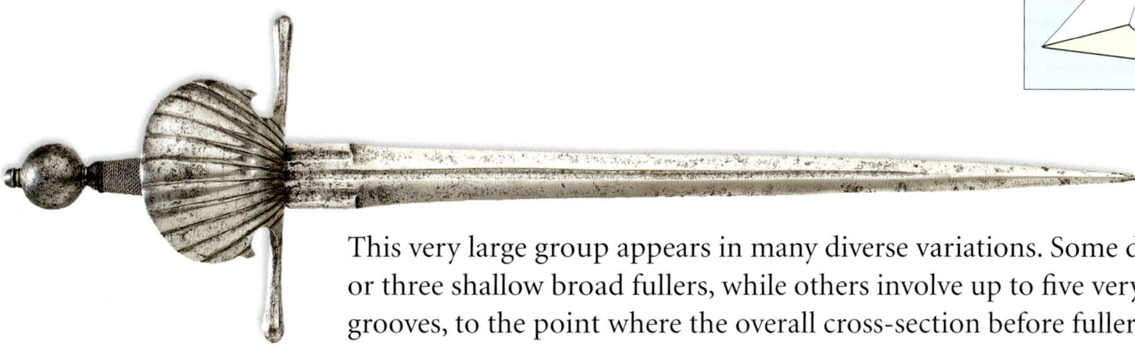

This very large group appears in many diverse variations. Some display only two or three shallow broad fullers, while others involve up to five very narrow and deep grooves, to the point where the overall cross-section before fullering is lost.

Hollow-ground triangular section

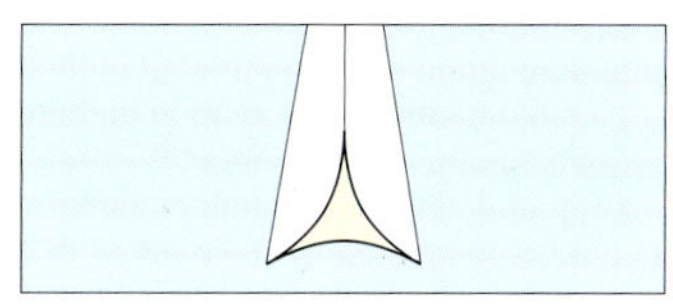

A hollow-ground blade involves one or more fullers that have been widened to take up the whole width of the blades' surface. Hollow-ground triangular sections are found on many socket bayonet patterns.

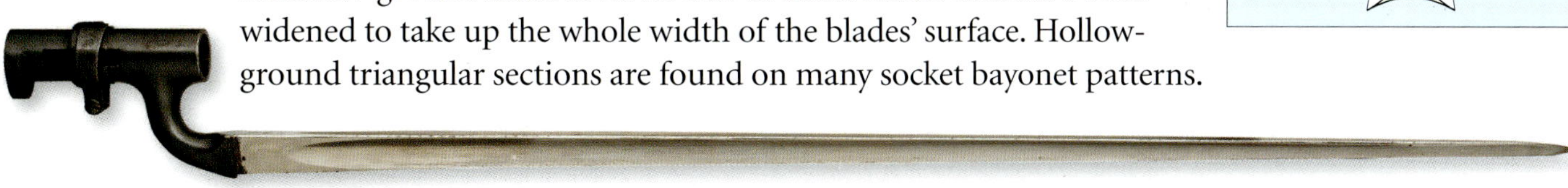

Cruciform section

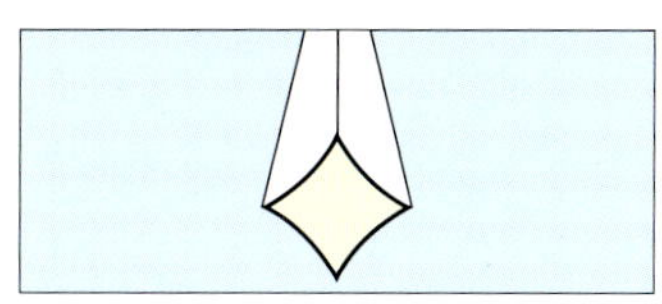

Found on several 19th-century bayonet types, this design is almost never used on any other sort of edged weapon; blades of this type are comparatively difficult to make and the benefits are minimal.

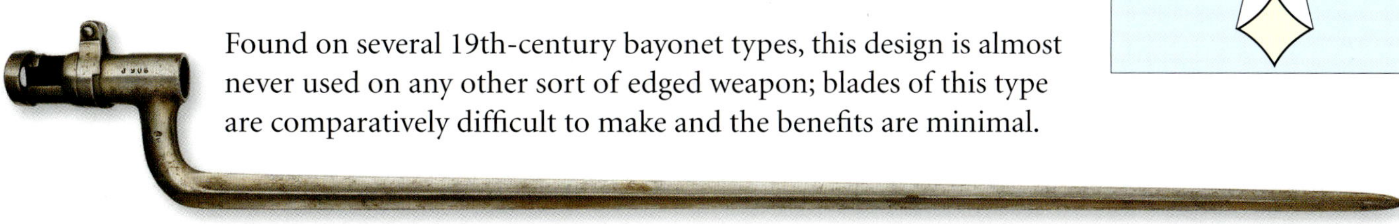

Decorations

Many decorative techniques were available to the makers of edged weapons, some spread by the export of the weapons themselves, others by the migration of their creators. The type and extent of the decoration was determined by the financial means of the person commissioning it, meaning that weapons were generally viewed as important indicators of social status. Most decorative processes were practised by specialists; decoration was almost never carried out by the weaponsmith himself. The finest and most beautiful weapons are often those that have been decorated by means of more than one process.

Engraving

A sharp graving tool is used to trace a design by cutting channels or furrows directly into a metal surface. In Europe this process was used throughout the Medieval and Renaissance Periods, although by the 15th century it had been largely superseded by etching, which was less difficult and time-consuming.

Etching

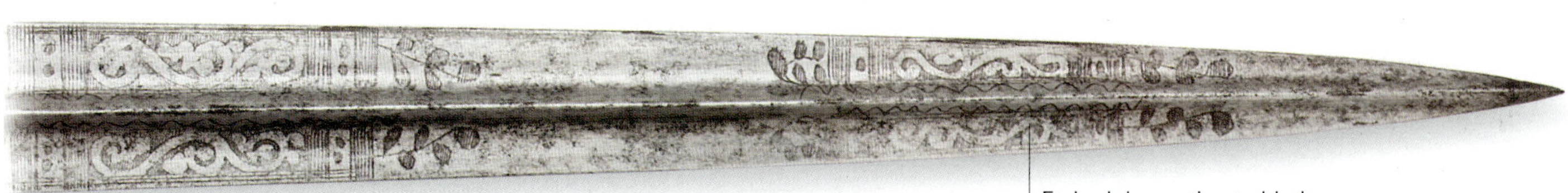

This is a process of producing a design on metal by "biting" it away with acid. The surface to be etched is covered with an acid-resistant coating (the "resist"), usually a wax or varnish. The design is then scraped out in the resist with a graving tool. When the object is washed in acid, the exposed design becomes permanently etched into the metal. In "raised" etching the design is painted on to the metal surface in the resist substance, leaving the background exposed. This produces a very bold three-dimensional effect.

Steel-chiselling

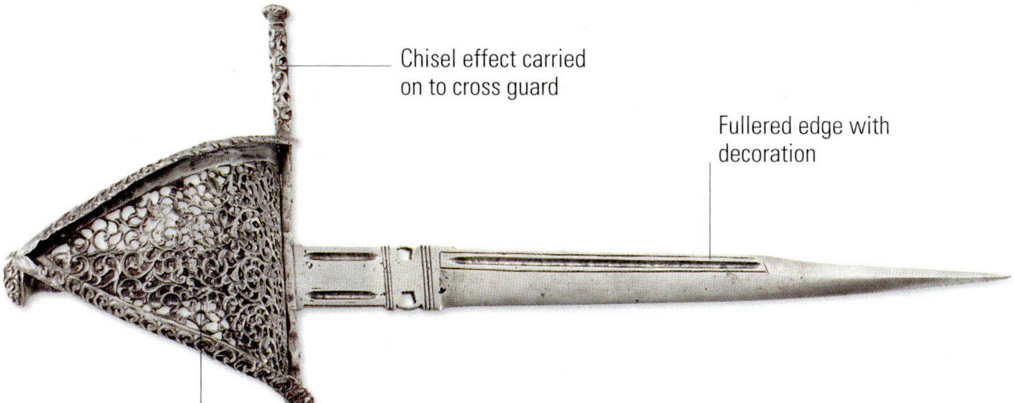

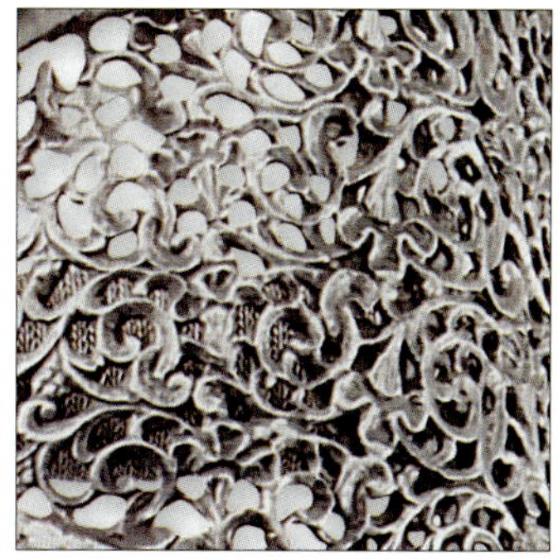
Intricate steel-chiselling

Steel-chiselling is the highly skilled art of carving steel into intricate ornamental forms. The process was mastered in Renaissance Europe, where it was used to decorate the hilts of fine swords and daggers, as well as the locks of firearms.

Punchwork

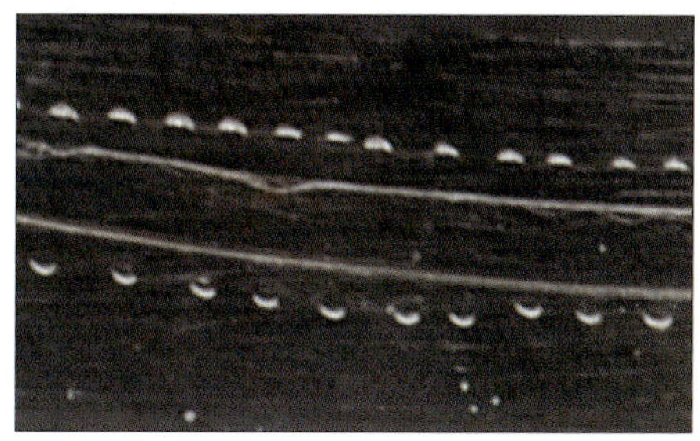
Punched decoration along the blade

A technique usually called *pointillé* is perhaps the simplest form of punchwork. This involves the formation of patterns on a surface by means of lightly punched dots, sometimes of varying sizes and depths. More complex effects were produced through the use of shaped punches.

Enamelling

Not to be confused with paint that is sometimes called enamel, true enamel is a brilliantly coloured vitreous substance applied in the form of a powder and heated until it begins to melt, coalescing into a smooth, glassy surface. Enamel is obviously very delicate and easily broken and is therefore usually found only on weapons intended purely for decorative or ceremonial use.

Blueing

When highly polished steel is heated, it changes colour, passing through darkening shades of blue, until it reaches purple and black. If a particular temperature can be maintained for a certain period of time, the colour produced will remain after the steel cools. The rich tints produced with heat processes – "blueing" – were often used to decorate the hilts of edged weapons.

Fire- or mercury-gilding

This is perhaps the most common traditional way of applying gold to steel. An amount of gold dust was first mixed with mercury. The gold dissolved in the mercury forming an amalgam or paste-like mixture. This substance was then applied to the steel surface. The piece was then heated to boil or "fume" off the mercury, leaving the gold permanently bonded to the steel. The same technique could also be used to apply silver to steel.

Encrustation

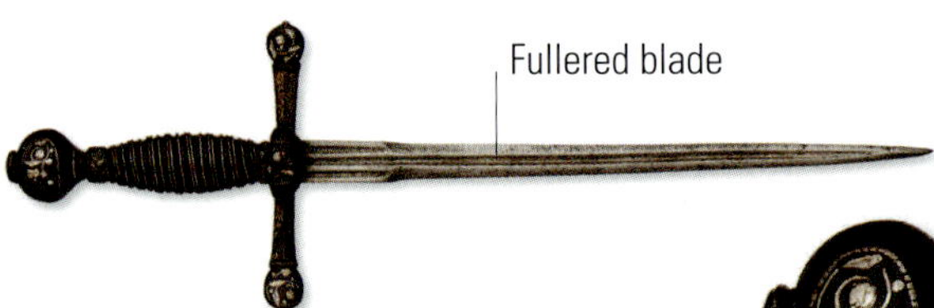

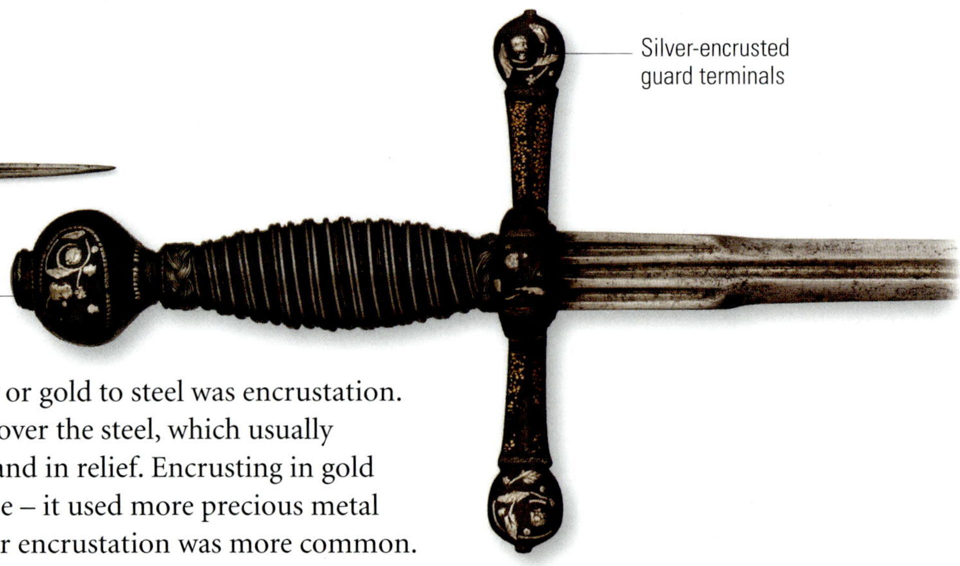

Another process used to apply silver or gold to steel was encrustation. Gold or silver foil was carefully laid over the steel, which usually featured designs "chiselled" beforehand in relief. Encrusting in gold was quite rare because of the expense – it used more precious metal than the mercury process – but silver encrustation was more common.

Inlay

Most true inlay is a development of the basic process of engraving. A channel was cut into the metal surface, after which small pieces of soft metal, usually copper alloy, gold or silver, were tapped into it. The inlaid metal was then burnished so that it sat flush with the steel around it.

Damascening

The use of the term "damascening" in English dates to at least the 16th century. True damascening is a form of inlay, wherein the precious metal, usually gold, is laid into a channel having a cross-section shaped like an upside down "Y". This technique was much rarer than "false" damascening with which it is often confused.

False or Counterfeit Damascening

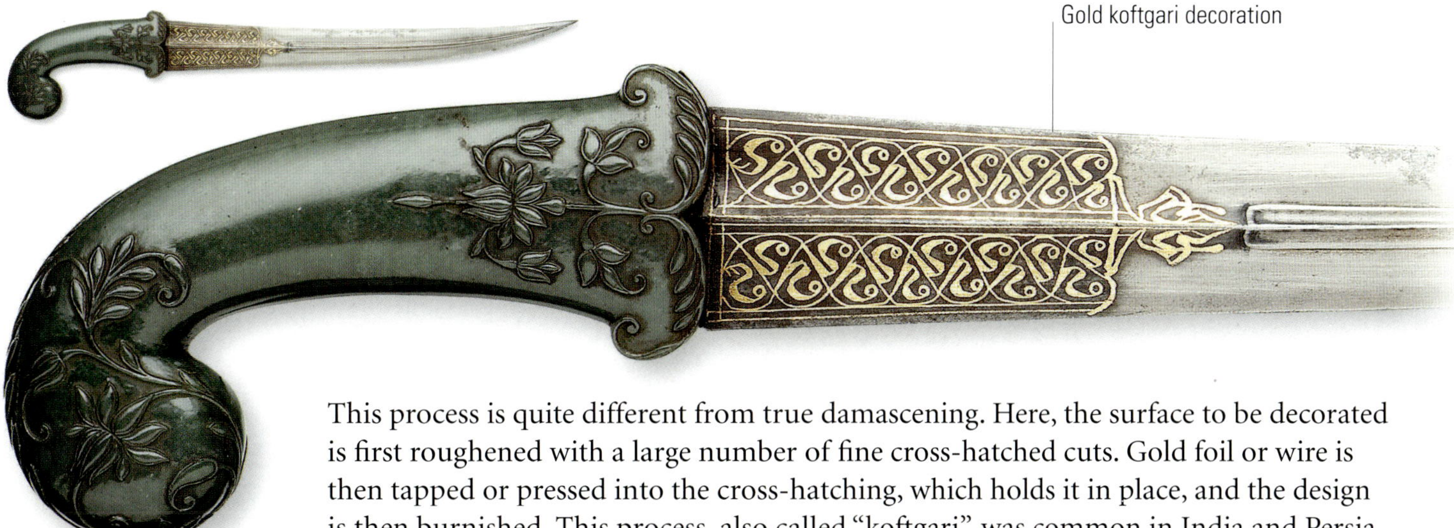

This process is quite different from true damascening. Here, the surface to be decorated is first roughened with a large number of fine cross-hatched cuts. Gold foil or wire is then tapped or pressed into the cross-hatching, which holds it in place, and the design is then burnished. This process, also called "koftgari", was common in India and Persia.

Stone Age blades

For thousands of years the only edged weapons available to prehistoric peoples were simple stone hand axes. These were grasped in the palm and used to strike overarm cutting blows. Over 2000 centuries, these tools slowly began to take on a more recognizable blade shape. Some of the finest flint knives were made as recently as 1500BC, after which point they were rendered obsolete by bronze weapons.

Palaeolithic hand axe, 300,000BC

This quartzite hand axe is a rare example of the precision knapping skills of Palaeolithic humans. The cutting edge is placed at a right angle to the line of direct force, and the butt has been shaped with a few perfect knap-strikes to sit comfortably in the palm.

DATE	300,000BC
ORIGIN	PALAEOLITHIC
LENGTH	17.8cm (7in)

Palaeolithic hand axe, 100,000–60,000BC

This flint core axe shows a very important development, for the maker's intention seems to have been to create a weapon or tool with a more prominent point. It is not in any sense a true stabbing blade, but the fact that a point will more effectively focus the force of a blow into a small area seems here to be well understood. The point and cutting edge have been skillfully pressure-flaked. Their patterns combined with the smooth white cortex produce a very beautiful sculptural effect.

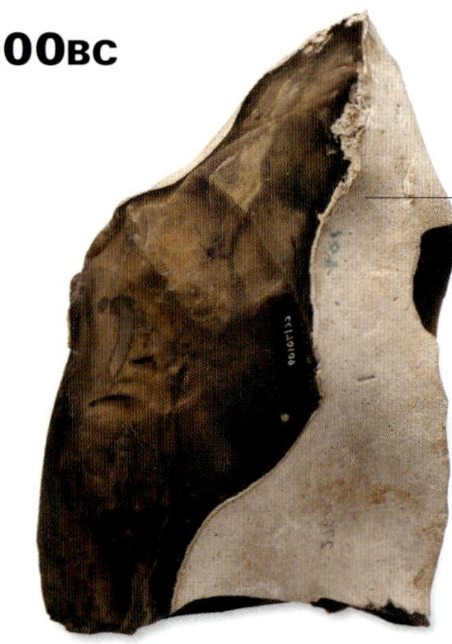

DATE	100,000–60,000BC
ORIGIN	PALAEOLITHIC
LENGTH	15.2cm (6in)

Neolithic chisel, 6000–3000BC

As the skills of the flint-knapper became more advanced, tools could be shaped into more specialized forms. This Neolithic mottled flint chisel has taken on a form that is much more blade-like, being much longer and narrower in comparison to earlier tools.

DATE	6000–3000BC
ORIGIN	NEOLITHIC
LENGTH	17cm (6.75in)

Dagger of the Iceman

This small dagger was among a number of perfectly preserved objects found with "Ötzi the Iceman", an extraordinarily well-preserved natural mummy of a Chalcolithic (Copper Age) man who died *c.*3300BC in the Ötztal Alps on the Italo-Austrian border. When he died, possibly of an arrow wound in his shoulder or a blow to his skull, the Iceman's body froze in glacial ice and was there preserved until its discovery in 1991.

The dagger is made of a short flint blade and a handle of ash wood. The scabbard is woven from fibrous plant bark. This is the fighting weapon of a man whose death was a direct result of violence; the blade still bears traces of the blood of one of the Iceman's enemies.

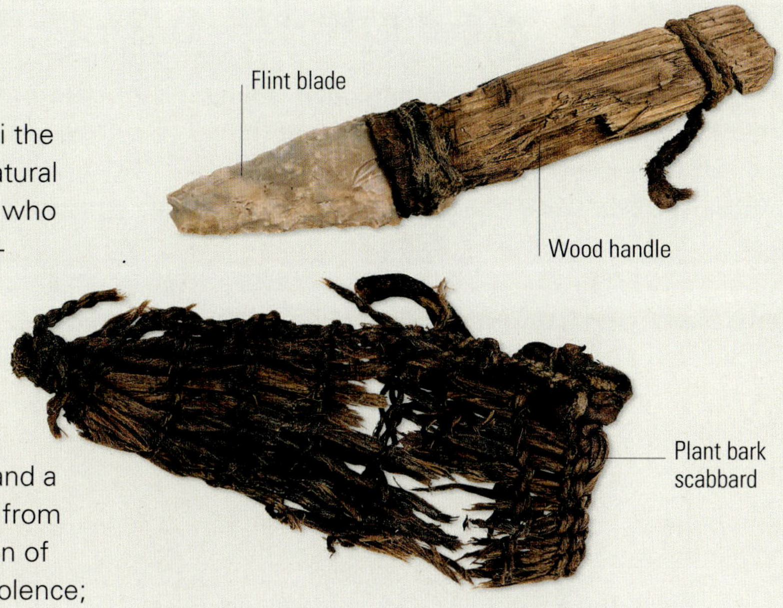

ABOVE Perhaps the most extraordinary aspect of this weapon is the fact that it survives with all of its organic material elements intact.

Bronze Age dagger, *c.*1800–1500BC

DATE	c.1800–1500BC
ORIGIN	BRONZE AGE
LENGTH	11.4cm (4.5in)

This late flint dagger, made as the use of metal was becoming more widespread, is a good example of a fully-fledged bladed weapon. Two pressure-flaking techniques have been used; larger flakes have been removed to form the grip, while much finer, tiny pieces have been taken away to create the edges of the razor-sharp blade.

Bronze Age dagger, 1600BC

DATE	1600BC
ORIGIN	BRONZE AGE
LENGTH	18cm (7.1in)

This beautiful weapon, typical of the best "Dagger Age" pieces, is a direct copy of a bronze knife. An impressive detail is the zigzag ridge that runs down the grip – an imitation of the stitching on the leather grip of this weapon's bronze counterpart.

Ancient Egyptian knives and daggers

The dagger had become a common weapon among ancient Egyptians long before the Early Dynastic Period (*c.*3150–2686BC). Fine flint daggers were produced, the best-known being cleaver-like ceremonial knives. Few Old Kingdom (2686–2134BC) daggers are known. More survive from the Middle (2040–1640BC) and New (1570–1070BC) Kingdoms, usually fitted with copper, bronze, or in a few cases, gold blades.

Egyptian ceremonial knife blade, *c.*3000BC

This object is one of several ceremonial knife blades dating from the Predynastic Period in Egypt (*c.*5000–*c.*3100BC). It is now less recognizable as a knife because of the loss of its handle. Weapons of this type are in fact very beautiful works of art, the wavy patterns on the blade created with great skill by a master flint-knapper.

DATE	*c.*3000BC
ORIGIN	EGYPTIAN
LENGTH	18cm (7.1in)

Egyptian dagger, New Kingdom, *c.*1570–1085BC

This bronze dagger from the 18th, 19th or 20th Dynasty is comparable to weapons from Bronze Age Europe and Asia. The blade is quite wide for its length, the hilt ergonomically shaped and stepped on its outer edge to hold the missing grip scales. In these ways it is similar to bronze daggers from ancient Persia.

DATE	*c.*1570–1085BC
ORIGIN	EGYPTIAN
LENGTH	unknown

Egyptian knife, New Kingdom, *c.*1570–1085BC

The wooden grip of this New Kingdom dagger may be original. It is fitted to a short blade of bronze, the profile of which shows it to be a serviceable cut-and-thrust weapon. The point may have become rounded due to wear, although it could have been made so. A rounded but razor-sharp tip would still slash flesh and split bone.

DATE	*c.*1570–1085BC
ORIGIN	EGYPTIAN
LENGTH	unknown

Egyptian thrusting dagger, New Kingdom, *c.*1570–1085BC

DATE	*c.*1570–1085BC
ORIGIN	EGYPTIAN
LENGTH	unknown

This spike-like weapon was designed for stabbing. But unlike later stabbing knives and stilettos of the Early Modern Era in Europe (*c.*1500–1800), to which it is not dissimilar, this dagger is made not of hardened steel but of softer bronze. To strengthen it, the smith has gracefully flared the blade just above the grip.

Egyptian funerary dagger, New Kingdom, *c.*1370–1352BC

DATE	*c.*1370–1352BC
ORIGIN	EGYPTIAN
LENGTH	31.8cm (12.5in)

Only Egyptian royalty could afford daggers with blades of pure gold. This ornately decorated solid gold weapon armed the boy-king, Tutankhamun, for the afterlife. A dagger and sheath of solid gold were also found among the tomb effects of Queen Ahhotpe, mother of Ahmosis I, founder of the 18th Dynasty of the New Kingdom during which Tutankhamun reigned.

Egyptian funerary dagger, New Kingdom, *c.*1370–1352BC

DATE	*c.*1370–1352BC
ORIGIN	EGYPTIAN
LENGTH	34.3cm (13.5in)

The iron blade of Tutankhamun's second dagger may seem plain compared to the gold of its companion, but it is even more precious. Its composition is 97 per cent iron and three per cent nickel. This means it is meteoric iron, very rare and more valuable than gold. The pommel is rock-crystal and the hilt is decorated with enamel.

Bronze Age edged weapons

For 2,000 years bronze was the most advanced metal available. Despite the fact that bronze work hardens, weapons made out of this alloy still had to be designed to take account of its softness and propensity to deform during use. Most bronze daggers are relatively short with a sharp taper to help maintain rigidity, a requirement often enhanced by a strong medial ridge running down the blade.

French Bronze Age dagger, 1800–1500BC

This fine bronze dagger was found at Mirabel in France, and dates from the French Early Bronze Age, 1800–1500BC. The triangular blade, the edges of which are decorated with a number of ridges and grooves, is riveted to a separate hilt. Daggers of this type may have inspired the cinquedea of Renaissance Italy.

DATE	1800–1500BC
ORIGIN	FRENCH BRONZE AGE
LENGTH	27cm (11in)

Luristan dagger, 1200BC

This beautiful dagger is one of many found at Luristan. It is elegantly designed to make the best use of the material while minimizing the effects of its limitations. The sharply tapered blade is strengthened with quite a wide medial ridge, whilst the thick, crescent-shaped hilt block strengthens the top of the grip against breakage.

DATE	1200BC
ORIGIN	LURISTAN (IRANIAN)
LENGTH	41.5cm (16.3in)

European knife blade, 1200–1000BC

This long blade demonstrates a different approach to the problem of how to build a sound edged weapon out of bronze. The strength and rigidity derive not from a steep taper and thick medial ridge, but from the overall thickness of much of the blade and its wedge-shaped section, with a thick back and single cutting edge.

DATE	1200–1000BC
ORIGIN	EUROPEAN
LENGTH	30cm (11.8in)

Luristan dagger, 1200–800BC

DATE	1200–800BC
ORIGIN	LURISTAN (IRANIAN)
LENGTH	27cm (11in)

This fine bronze dagger is another Luristan find. Dating from 1200–800BC, it falls within the Ancient Persian Iron Age. The finely shaped handle is designed to fit perfectly into the hand, with finger grooves for a comfortable grip. It was also originally fitted with grip scales of wood or some other organic material.

Weapons from Luristan

Some of the largest groups of Bronze Age objects ever found come from sites in Luristan (also Lorestan), in what is now northwestern Iran. Excavations in the 20th century uncovered tools, ornamental objects and very large numbers of weapons made by the ancient semi-nomadic people who lived in this mountainous part of the Middle East. Along with many swords, axes and spearheads, the weapons included a great many daggers, cast in bronze and usually fitted with grip scales of wood, horn or bone. Some of the best bronze daggers from Luristan in fact probably date from the Iranian Iron Age, *c.*1200–650BC, although many others have been found that belong to the Iranian Bronze Age, *c.*3500–1250BC.

BELOW Many ruined settlements like this one are preserved all over northwestern Iran, and have been extensively excavated yielding a large number of weapons, tools and other objects.

Daggers of the Classical World

We often imagine Greek and Roman warriors armed with shining bronze arms and armour. It is, however, important to remember that iron was well known by this time. Bronze and iron coexisted as weapons materials for centuries. Bronze was harder than early iron, but iron was cheaper. Almost all Roman weapons had iron blades. Roman smiths also made use of a new alloy of iron and carbon: steel.

Hallstatt "antennae" dagger, *c.*750–450BC

DATE	*c.*750–450BC
ORIGIN	HALLSTATT CULTURE
LENGTH	unknown

This classic Hallstatt "antennae" dagger is an excellent example of its type, not only because of the distinctive form of the hilt but also because it is made of iron. The Hallstatt were the first Bronze Age Europeans to master this metal.

Villanovan dagger and scabbard, 600–300BC

This exquisite Villanovan dagger, from tomb 11 at the Necropolis at Villanueva de Teba, is a beautiful example of the best ornamented bronze-work. The aesthetic influence on later Roman pugios is also apparent in the banded construction of the scabbard and in the overall proportions of the weapon.

DATE	600–300BC
ORIGIN	VILLANOVAN
LENGTH	unknown

English or German dagger and scabbard, 600–300BC

The design of this iron-bladed dagger is associated with southern Germany. It closely resembles the Roman pugio and may be one of its precursors. It was found in the River Thames, but was most likely imported into Britain rather than made there. The bronze-banded scabbard is probably the work of a local metalworker.

DATE	600–300BC
ORIGIN	ENGLISH/GERMAN
LENGTH	35.6cm (14in)

Roman pugio and scabbard, AD100

DATE	AD100
ORIGIN	ROMAN
LENGTH	unknown

By the 1st century AD the Roman pugio had assumed a very consistent form and construction. Both hilt and blade were usually made of iron, the hilt being decorated according to the particular owner's status and either left plain or tinned, silvered or gilded.

Roman pugio, AD100

DATE	AD100
ORIGIN	ROMAN
LENGTH	26.5cm (10.4in)

This worn, bent example has a less pronounced point than many other examples, but otherwise it is fairly typical, having a narrow medial ridge running down the whole length of the blade. The grip displays the usual central swelling and wheel pommel, while the guard is decorated with incised lines and beading.

Roman officer's pugio, *c.*AD100–300

DATE	C.AD100–300
ORIGIN	ROMAN
LENGTH	unknown

Pugios of this type remained in use until the middle of the 2nd century AD. With its silvered and finely worked hilt, it is clear this weapon belonged to a Roman officer, a centurion or perhaps a navarch. The decorative rope motif on the grip may indicate an association with a commander in the Roman Navy. This dagger survives in exceptional condition, one of the finest remaining Roman examples.

Daggers of the Medieval Period

The dating of the Medieval Period is very difficult. Working exclusively in the context of weapons history, it is possible to consider the Medieval Period, or "Middle Ages", as beginning with the collapse of the western Roman Empire in the 5th century (the Early Medieval Period, often wrongly called the "Dark Ages"), continuing through the early 14th century (the "High" Middle Ages), and ending sometime in the 15th century (the "Late" Middle Ages). Daggers developed a great deal during these ten centuries.

Central European scramasax blades, 500–600

Although they are now in a heavily corroded "excavated" condition, these two Early Medieval sax blades still give a very good impression of their original shape. The wide, thick-backed form, ideal for cutting and slashing, angles sharply down in the upper third to form a very long stabbing point. It is not surprising that this impressive, multifunctional design remained popular throughout central, northern and western Europe for nearly 1,000 years.

DATE	500–600
ORIGIN	CENTRAL EUROPEAN
LENGTH	26cm (10.2in)

English cross-hilt dagger, *c.*1200–1300

This classic High Medieval dagger carries a distinctive type of pommel, made essentially as a mirror of the cross guard. Medieval daggers of this type recall the "anthropomorphic" designs of the Hallstatt and La Tène Celts. A number of these daggers survive, many of which have been found in London. The type is probably not exclusively English and was undoubtedly also popular on the Continent.

DATE	*c.*1200–1300
ORIGIN	ENGLISH
LENGTH	30.5cm (12in)

English cross-hilt dagger, 1400

DATE	1400
ORIGIN	ENGLISH
LENGTH	29cm (11.4in)

The guard and pommel of this fine dagger are made of a copper alloy instead of iron or steel. The missing grip may have been covered with a colourful textile. The blade is purely for stabbing, although the bladesmith has gone to some trouble to shape it into a more elegant form than a simple square-section spike. The blade's deeply fullered lower half transitions gracefully into the square-section upper half.

English or Scottish cross-hilt dagger, *c.*1300–1400

DATE	c.1300–1400
ORIGIN	ENGLISH/SCOTTISH
LENGTH	33.8cm (13.3in)

Although its blade is relatively short, its narrowness and very sharp taper indicate that this dagger is undoubtedly what medieval people would recognize as a *couteau à pointe*, or "stabbing knife". The guard is of an interesting type, the arms drooping diagonally down towards the blade and swelling towards the ends. The guard block also extends down to sit flush with the wooden grip, which like those of most other surviving medieval daggers is not lost. Guards very similar to this are one of the characteristic features of Scottish medieval swords, of which this may be a diminutive.

German cross-hilt dagger, late 15th century

DATE	late 15th century
ORIGIN	GERMAN
LENGTH	44cm (17.3in)

This very ornate dagger probably dates from the very end of the Medieval Period and may be of German origin. The pommel and guard are of copper alloy. The blade is especially interesting in that along its length the cross-section changes four times, beginning with a double-edged section at the guard to single-edged a few centimetres above the guard, and alternating back and forth to the point.

Rondel daggers

By the middle of the 14th century the rondel dagger was becoming the most fashionable type worn by all classes, both in war and for self-defence in daily life. Some have single-edged blades, while others are stabbing tools, the blades being merely long steel spikes. The disks or rondels were constructed of diverse materials – wood, horn, copper alloy, iron or steel – and can vary greatly in diameter. Nevertheless, they always grip the user's hand tightly, giving a solid seat for a powerful downward thrust.

English rondel dagger, *c.*14th century

This weapon was found in the River Thames in London. It shows one of the characteristic features of the earliest forms of rondel dagger: while the guard is composed of a metal disk, the pommel is not, but is instead a heavy half-round "tea cosy" form found on many 12th- and 13th-century swords.

DATE	*c.*14th century
ORIGIN	ENGLISH
LENGTH	unknown

The suicide of Lucretia

Since weapons rarely survive in pristine, undamaged condition, it is vital to look at depictions of weapons in art. Most artists attempted to represent weapons as faithfully as possible. They can be seen as the artist himself saw them – bright, polished, with all decoration intact. Some artistic themes are very useful to weapons researchers. In the study of daggers, the tragic subject of Lucretia, a semi-mythical Roman noblewoman, is especially relevant. Her rape and subsequent suicide by stabbing was thought to have led to the foundation of the Roman Republic. Botticelli, Raphael and many other artists painted pictures of her, and these works usually include excellent renderings of daggers from the artist's time, usually of a very high quality to emphasize Lucretia's noble status.

RIGHT Lucretia supposedly stabbed herself to death after being dishonoured by the son of the last king of Rome. The popular outrage that followed brought the overthrow of the ancient Roman monarchy.

English (?) rondel dagger fragment, *c.*1400

DATE	*c.*1400
ORIGIN	POSSIBLY ENGLISH
LENGTH	9.6cm (3.8in)

This broken piece of gilt metal is the grip and pommel of a once extremely fine rondel dagger, undoubtedly the weapon of a knight. The ornate geometric decoration is typical of knights' daggers as depicted on English funerary effigies of the late 14th and early 15th centuries. The squared, four-petal flower motif on the pommel is especially common in late medieval English metalwork; the same pattern was used to decorate copper-alloy boxes, candlesticks and armour.

English or Scottish rondel dagger, 15th century

DATE	15th century
ORIGIN	ENGLISH/SCOTTISH
LENGTH	35.4cm (13.9in)

This is a well-preserved example of a rondel dagger with a hilt made largely of wood, the only metal element being the slightly domed cap-plate on the bottom rondel. The stout, lozenge-section blade has no cutting edges; attacks were delivered with the point exclusively. The good quality of the blade is indicated by its mark – a letter "I" standing on a letter "O", inlaid in copper alloy.

English (?) rondel dagger, 15th century

DATE	15th century
ORIGIN	POSSIBLY ENGLISH
LENGTH	51.6cm (20.3in)

Its considerable length indicates that this dagger is undoubtedly a weapon of war, made long to pierce with lethal effect the multilayered armour of plate, mail and textile worn at the time. The metal rondels are quite thick and of a comparatively small diameter. Also unusual is the original wooden grip – the grips of most medieval daggers have long since rotted away, leaving only the exposed tang.

English rondel dagger, 15th century

This small dagger is interesting because the original wooden grip survives, as do the wooden rondels which are capped with metal washers. Also, the single-edged wedge-section blade is unusual in that the back curves gently forward towards the cutting edge as it tapers to the point. This specimen was found in the River Thames in London under Southwark Bridge.

DATE	15th century
ORIGIN	ENGLISH
LENGTH	unknown

German rondel dagger, *c.*1500

The copper-alloy hilt of this weapon is unusual in that the guard, rather than being a simple disk – like that fitted to the end of the tang – is formed into three knobs, or lobes. This form is very similar to certain types of German, so-called "landsknecht" daggers fashionable in the early to mid-16th century. The thick, heavy blade is triangular in section and entirely suited to such common medieval fighting techniques as stabbing blows to the opponent's skull.

DATE	*c.*1500
ORIGIN	GERMAN
LENGTH	34cm (13.4in)

English rondel dagger, *c.*1510

This late rondel dagger was found in the River Thames near Southwark in London. The heavy iron pommel is unusual and recalls the earliest forms of rondel dagger which had similar rounded pommels instead of the wide disk. The dagger was discovered along with the remains of its leather scabbard, and two small byknives for eating and other utilitarian purposes.

DATE	*c.*1510
ORIGIN	ENGLISH
LENGTH	unknown

Baselards

There was considerable variation in the size of baselards, some being small daggers, others short swords. The hilt always displays the distinctive I-shape, being two plates of wood sandwiching the tang, which is forged to the same shape. The small dagger baselards were most common in Italy during the late 14th and early 15th centuries. The longer sword baselards were closely associated with Germany and Switzerland.

European baselard dagger, *c.*1400

DATE	*c.*1400
ORIGIN	EUROPEAN
LENGTH	33.3cm (13.1in)

The smaller dagger version of the baselard seems to have appeared first, the longer versions appearing later. This example is for the most part representative of late 14th- and early 15th-century baselards, apart from the ergonomic finger grooves carved into the guard and pommel cross pieces, which are perhaps more atypical.

English long baselard, *c.*1490–1520

DATE	*c.*1490–1520
ORIGIN	ENGLISH
LENGTH	68.2cm (26.9in)

This rare English baselard indicates that the long type was popular outside Switzerland and Germany. It is an excellent cut-and-thrust blade. The hilt includes an asymmetrical pommel with an extended forward section; this allowed the user to make deadly whipping cuts, using his little finger as a fulcrum.

Swiss or German long baselard, 1520

This standard early 16th-century baselard features the more usual symmetrical hilt, the cross guard being slightly wider than the pommel, which in this case has been widened into a roughly lenticular form. Unlike the English example above, this weapon is fitted with a plain, double-edged blade of flattened diamond section.

DATE	1520
ORIGIN	SWISS/GERMAN
LENGTH	unknown

Ballock daggers

Often referred to as "kidney" daggers even today, the form of these uniquely recognizable knives makes their true inspiration fairly obvious. While ballock knives shocked Victorian scholars of weapons into renaming them, to the medieval mind the open and public display of a phallic icon was not necessarily erotic at all. Rather it may have been an apotropaic defence intended to ward off evil.

English or Scottish ballock dagger, 14th century

This ballock dagger clearly foreshadows the dudgeon daggers of the 17th century. It is a very early example of the placement of a metal spacer between the top of the lobes and the base of the blade. The spacer is secured by means of two rivets, one passing through each lobe, a method found on most surviving dudgeon daggers.

DATE	14th century
ORIGIN	ENGLISH/SCOTTISH
LENGTH	25.1cm (9.9in)

English ballock dagger, 15th century

This very long 15th-century example already looks something like its late 17th-century descendant, the Scottish Highland dirk. The hilt appears to be carved out of some very hard root or bogwood, while the thickly backed, single-edged blade is similar to the later Highland dirk blades in terms of its size and proportions.

DATE	15th century
ORIGIN	ENGLISH
LENGTH	29.2cm (11.5in)

English or Scottish ballock dagger, 15th century

Like many examples of its type, this flared-base ballock dagger is fitted with a copper-alloy base plate. This plate is not only a convenient opportunity for incised decoration; it also provides a secure seat for the end of the tang, which passes down the centre of the wooden grip and out through a hole in the base plate, to be peened over, thus holding hilt and blade together.

DATE	15th century
ORIGIN	ENGLISH/SCOTTISH
LENGTH	39cm (15.4in)

English or Scottish ballock dagger, 15th century

DATE	15th century
ORIGIN	ENGLISH/SCOTTISH
LENGTH	36.5cm (14.4in)

The lobes of ballock daggers with flared, trumpet-like grips are generally smaller in proportion to the blade than those of daggers with bulbous ends, the lobes of which are usually significantly wider than the base of the blade. This example also has a metal spacer between lobes and blade, with teeth above and below the blade to ensure a snug fit in the scabbard. The flared trumpet hilt appeared in the 15th century and remained popular into the 16th century. It may have been intended to provide a platform similar to that of the rondel dagger, allowing a firmer grip.

English or Scottish ballock dagger, 15th century

DATE	15th century
ORIGIN	ENGLISH/SCOTTISH
LENGTH	unknown

This fairly standard ballock hilt, carved in the usual way from a single piece of wood, is fitted to a noteworthy single-edged blade. In its form and especially its point, the blade closely resembles the earlier medieval dagger of the type called in textual sources *couteau à tailler*, or "cutting knife", the single sharpened edge of which curves gently upward towards the straight, unsharpened back to form an asymmetric point, not unlike that of a typical kitchen knife.

English (?) ballock dagger, 15th century

DATE	15th century
ORIGIN	POSSIBLY ENGLISH
LENGTH	34.7cm (13.7in)

This purposefully lifelike ballock hilt, the grip slightly curved, is fitted to a remarkable blade. The lower third of the blade is of a standard triangular construction, but it changes quite suddenly, and the upper two-thirds of the blade consists of a skilfully hollow-ground diamond section. This produces a blade that is extremely strong at the base but still narrow enough at the point to slide with ease between the ribs of an enemy. Elaborate blades like this are rare on ballock daggers, being perhaps more commonly found with rondel hilts.

Daggers of the Renaissance

The 16th century was an important turning point in the history of weapons. While traditional fighting methods, with swords, daggers and staff weapons, were still essential, new gunpowder-weapon technology was evolving rapidly. As the 1500s progressed, edged weapons started to become less important on the battlefield. But in civilian life they became much more significant. Duelling became common, and the dagger formed an integral part of most self-defence, or "fencing", systems of the time.

Italian ear dagger, *c.*1500

The ear dagger is closely associated with Spain and Italy. It is a strongly built design, the thick-spined blade continuing into a strong tang with increased thickness towards the pommel. This shape makes it nearly impossible to break the blade and also perfectly balances it, making it seem feather-light in the hand.

RIGHT The ear plates are a perfect opportunity for ornamentation, as they are the most visible part of the dagger.

DATE	*c.*1500
ORIGIN	ITALIAN
LENGTH	unknown

German rondel dagger, early 16th century

This weapon is a good example of a late rondel dagger, the final form that this type assumed before falling out of use around the middle of the 16th century. It displays two key improvements that were made to the rondel dagger design around 1500: the rondel guard has been folded down at a 90-degree angle on the side, allowing it to rest against the body during routine wear. In addition, the blade is not located centrally in the guard but is offset towards its folded section; this also helps the weapon to rest flat against the hip.

DATE	early 16th century
ORIGIN	GERMAN
LENGTH	36cm (14.2in)

German "Landsknecht" dagger, 16th century

DATE	16th century
ORIGIN	GERMAN
LENGTH	unknown

This exquisite and typologically important dagger is a very rare example of one made in the same style as the legendary *katzbalger* ("cat-fighter") short swords of the feared German and Swiss mercenaries known as Landsknechts. Hilts of this type were made not only for Landsknecht daggers and short swords, but also for their famous giant two-handed swords. The key features are the circular guard composed of a single bar forged into a tight S-shape, the slightly tapered grip flaring towards the pommel area and the small beaks on either side of the pommel.

Saxon side-ring dagger, *c.*1570

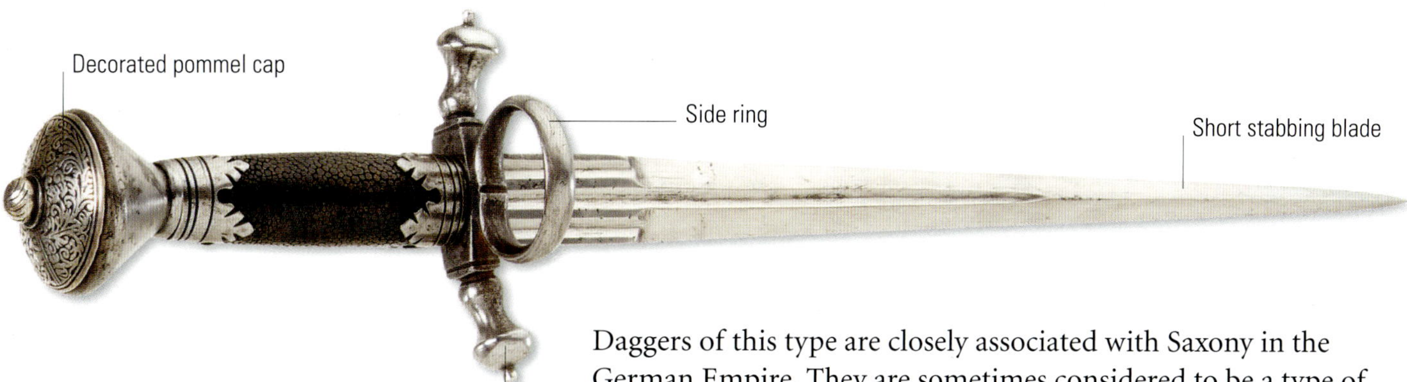

DATE	*c.*1570
ORIGIN	GERMAN (SAXON)
LENGTH	38cm (15in)

Daggers of this type are closely associated with Saxony in the German Empire. They are sometimes considered to be a type of Landsknecht dagger, although they were undoubtedly employed on a much more general level, both by soldiers and civilians. This specimen, from the Royal Armoury in Dresden, may date from about 1570, although the type first appeared in the early 16th century and remained largely unchanged for most of the century.

Italian cross-hilt dagger, late 16th century

DATE	late 16th century
ORIGIN	ITALIAN
LENGTH	37.2cm (14.6in)

This is a very curious form of cross-hilt dagger, quite unlike most other Renaissance designs. The very fine inlaid handle includes an integral pommel. The guard is very narrow in proportion to the length of the blade, which is quite extreme. The profile of the blade seems to be a forerunner to later types of Mediterranean fighting knife, especially the navaja.

Cinquedeas

Because their blades tend to be short and narrow, almost all forms of dagger are stabbing and slashing weapons. They cannot be used to deliver cutting blows, as their smallness rules out any sort of concussive potential. A unique exception to this rule, the cinquedea, appeared in the mid-15th century in Italy. Many cinquedeas could be described either as a dagger or short sword. They were designed primarily for dealing blows with their sharp edges rather than the point. Therefore the blade was usually very wide.

Italian short cinquedea, *c.*1500

The range of sizes in which cinquedeas were made was very wide. Although many are quite long and very effective as short cut-and-thrust swords, others, like this one, are quite small. The broad, sharply tapered blade, with its thick central spine, is ideally suited to thrusting. Here an ancient Bronze Age idea has been improved upon through its rendering in hardened steel.

DATE	*c.*1500
ORIGIN	ITALIAN
LENGTH	42cm (16.5in)

Italian short cinquedea, *c.*1500

Although it is in an excavated condition, this elegant little weapon is an excellent example of the smaller form of cinquedea. The hilt is designed in the usual way for this style, being the same size as most of the larger forms, and has a copper-alloy pommel cap. The small but fearsome blade displays a needlelike reinforced point. This weapon was once in the collection of the British arms and armour scholar Charles Alexander, Baron de Cosson (1843–1929).

DATE	*c.*1500
ORIGIN	ITALY
LENGTH	37cm (14.5in)

Italian cinquedea, early 16th century

DATE	early 16th century
ORIGIN	ITALIAN
LENGTH	unknown

This typical cinquedea exhibits a grip of ivory with circular inserts, swelling in the middle with an integrated pommel area capped with gilt copper alloy. The boomerang-shaped guard projects beyond the blade on both sides. The plain blade does not have the staggered numbers of fullers as do the finest examples, but displays two deep fullers travelling the whole length of the blade.

North Italian cinquedea, early 16th century

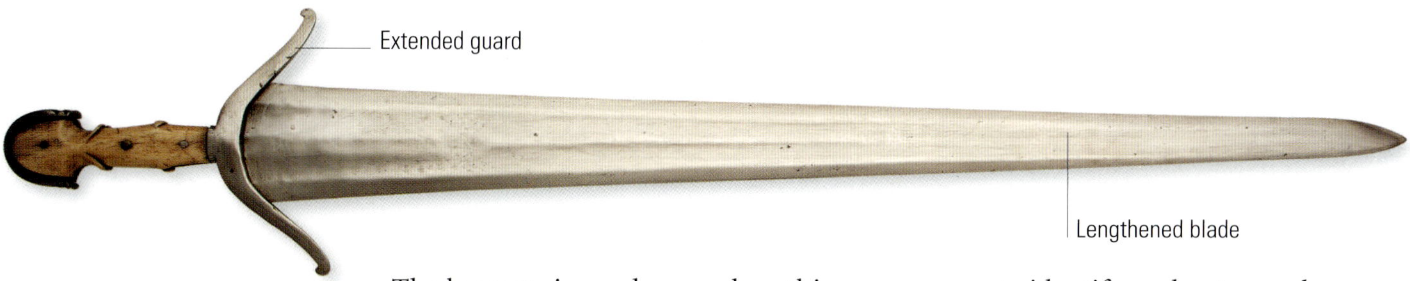

DATE	early 16th century
ORIGIN	NORTH ITALIAN
LENGTH	unknown

The longest cinquedeas, such as this one, are easy to identify as short-swords. In this example, the cinquedea design has been modified so that the weapon will function better as a sword. The guard has been lengthened to protect the hand better, while the blade has been significantly extended to the point where it has nearly lost the characteristic triangular form.

Replica cinquedea, 19th century

DATE	19th century
ORIGIN	UNKNOWN
LENGTH	unknown

Cinquedeas were very popular with 19th-century collectors. Their desirability led to a flood of fakes. Some were complete fabrications, others made up of original parts. This one has been constructed using a 16th-century rapier pommel, a 19th-century grip and guard, and the blade of a 16th- or 17th-century staff weapon.

"Side ring" parrying daggers

By the second half of the 16th century, rapier fencing almost always required a parrying dagger held in the left hand. Until the mid-17th century, parrying daggers were almost always of the "side ring" type, having a simple cross guard onto which was attached a metal ring that protected the outside of the hand. Parrying daggers were often decorated to match their rapiers, although very few matching sets survive.

German parrying dagger, late 16th century

The most noticeable aspect of this dagger is its wavy blade. The waves look intimidating, but they may also have had a practical function. With a firm grip it is possible to grab a straight blade and take the weapon away from its user. A wavy blade makes a firm grip impossible.

DATE	late 16th century
ORIGIN	GERMAN
LENGTH	unknown

English parrying dagger, late 16th century

This rare English parrying dagger was found in the River Thames in London. After several hundred years underwater, the surface is now heavily pitted, but the fluted pommel and guard are still recognizable. This was a weapon of quality, although unusually it lacks a side ring.

DATE	late 16th century
ORIGIN	ENGLISH
LENGTH	unknown

German parrying dagger, *c.*1600

This dagger exhibits two design traits that started to appear after 1600. To counter lighter and faster rapiers better, parrying dagger blades became longer and narrower. The guards became more protective against thrusts, with solid plates in place of the side ring.

DATE	*c.*1600
ORIGIN	GERMAN
LENGTH	64.5cm (25.3in)

German parrying dagger, *c.*1600

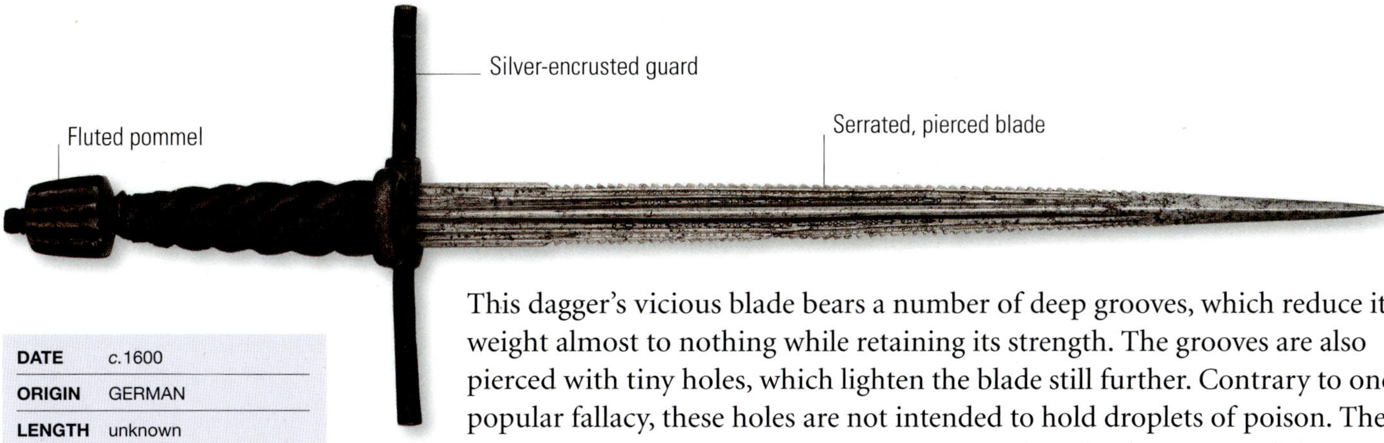

DATE	*c.*1600
ORIGIN	GERMAN
LENGTH	unknown

This dagger's vicious blade bears a number of deep grooves, which reduce its weight almost to nothing while retaining its strength. The grooves are also pierced with tiny holes, which lighten the blade still further. Contrary to one popular fallacy, these holes are not intended to hold droplets of poison. The edges are also serrated, the saw-teeth biting when the dagger is withdrawn.

German parrying dagger, *c.*1600

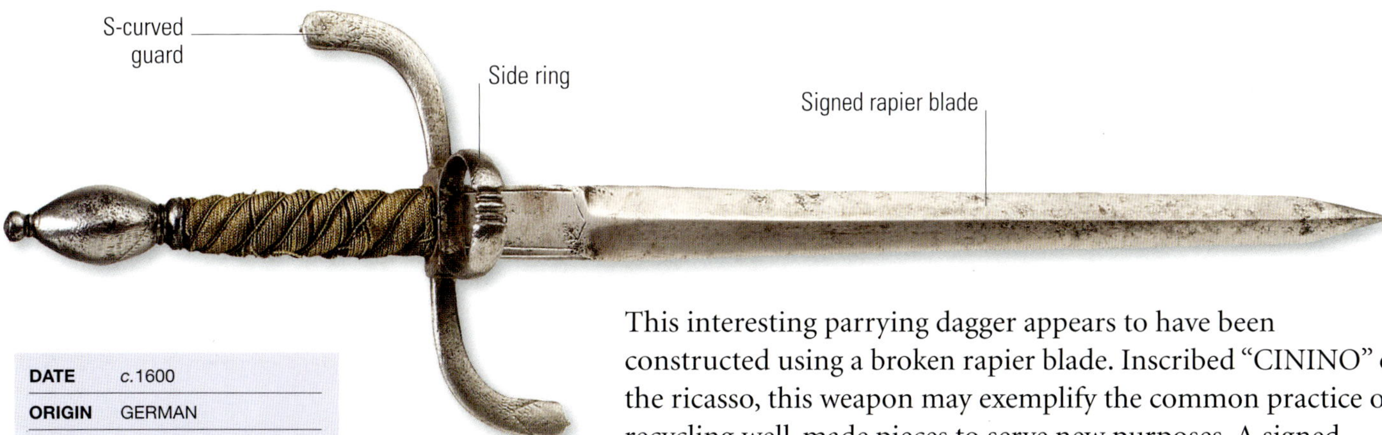

DATE	*c.*1600
ORIGIN	GERMAN
LENGTH	46cm (18.1in)

This interesting parrying dagger appears to have been constructed using a broken rapier blade. Inscribed "CININO" on the ricasso, this weapon may exemplify the common practice of recycling well-made pieces to serve new purposes. A signed rapier blade was too valuable to throw away, even if broken.

Italian left-handed dagger, *c.*1600

DATE	*c.*1600
ORIGIN	ITALIAN
LENGTH	44cm (17.3in)

By the end of the 16th century, parrying daggers were being built with an increasing variety of customized features to make them more effective in civilian combat. This blade has been pinched into a puncturing point like a sharp nail, and it may have been designed to pierce more easily the leather and textile doublets worn at the time.

Spanish sword-catcher, *c.*1600

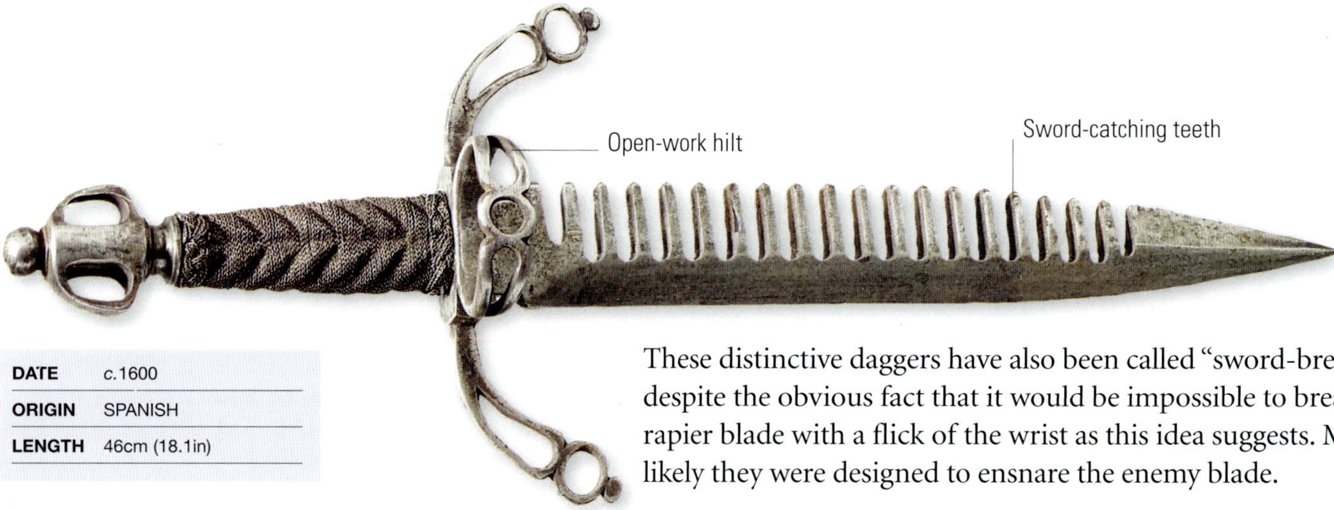

DATE	*c.*1600
ORIGIN	SPANISH
LENGTH	46cm (18.1in)

These distinctive daggers have also been called "sword-breakers", despite the obvious fact that it would be impossible to break a rapier blade with a flick of the wrist as this idea suggests. More likely they were designed to ensnare the enemy blade.

English parrying dagger, blade dated 1608

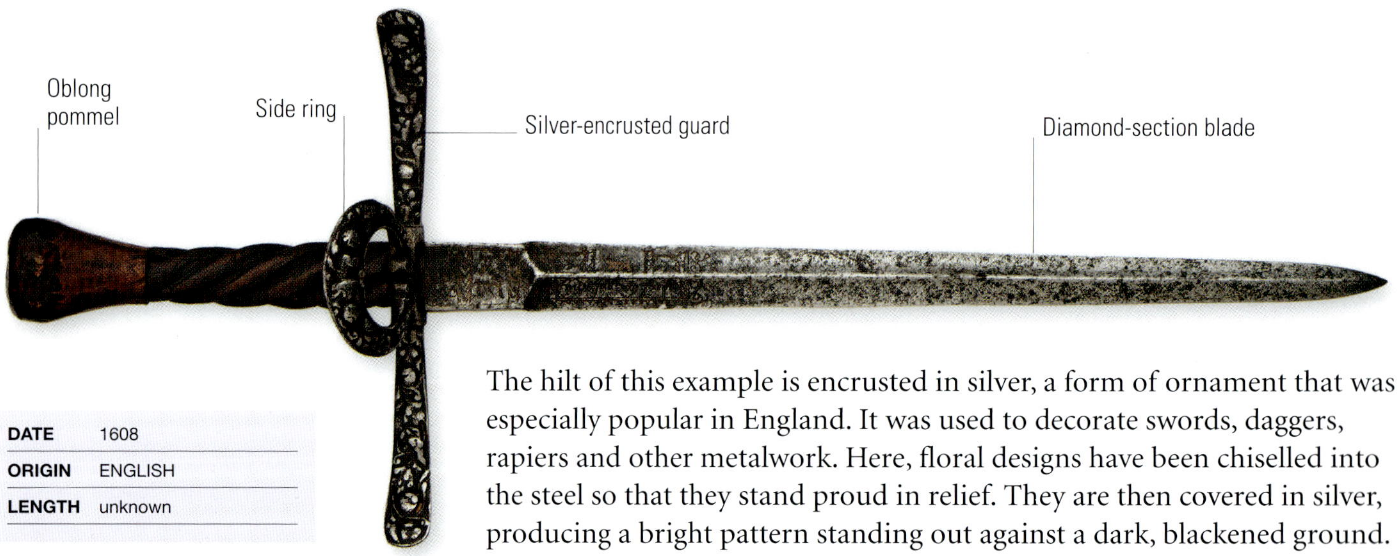

DATE	1608
ORIGIN	ENGLISH
LENGTH	unknown

The hilt of this example is encrusted in silver, a form of ornament that was especially popular in England. It was used to decorate swords, daggers, rapiers and other metalwork. Here, floral designs have been chiselled into the steel so that they stand proud in relief. They are then covered in silver, producing a bright pattern standing out against a dark, blackened ground.

German parrying dagger, *c.*1610

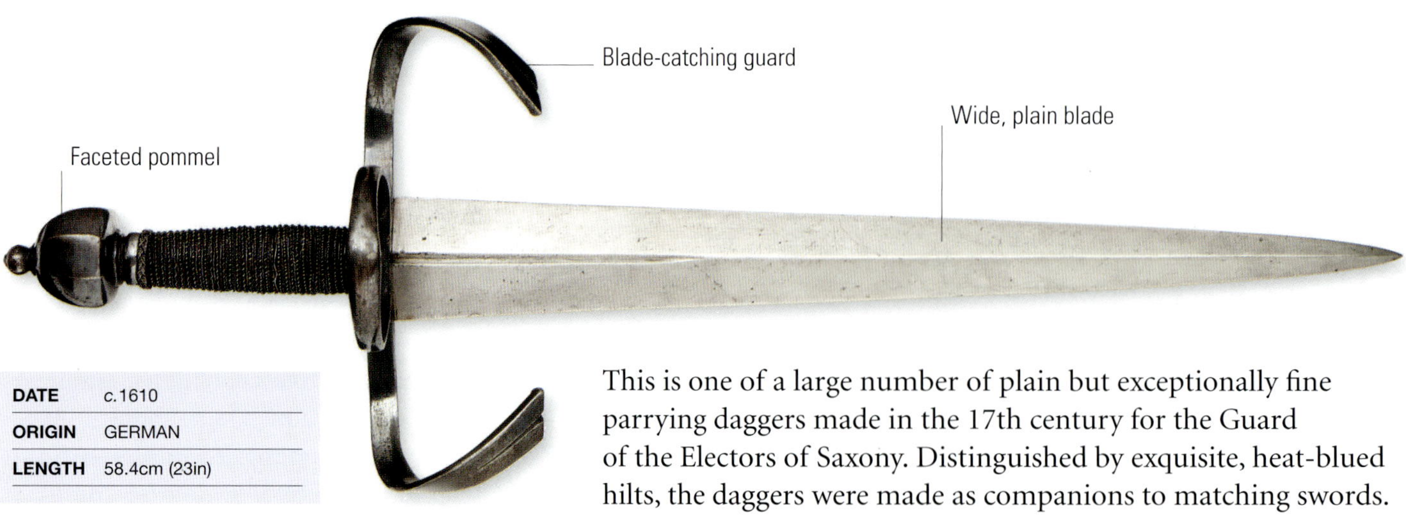

DATE	*c.*1610
ORIGIN	GERMAN
LENGTH	58.4cm (23in)

This is one of a large number of plain but exceptionally fine parrying daggers made in the 17th century for the Guard of the Electors of Saxony. Distinguished by exquisite, heat-blued hilts, the daggers were made as companions to matching swords.

English parrying dagger, early 17th century

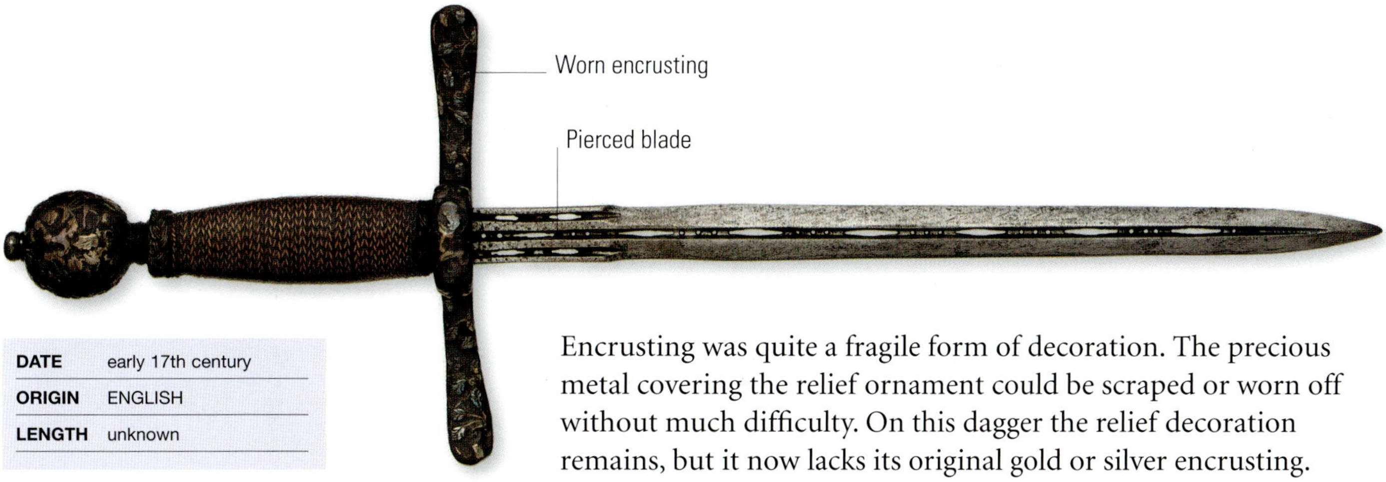

DATE	early 17th century
ORIGIN	ENGLISH
LENGTH	unknown

Encrusting was quite a fragile form of decoration. The precious metal covering the relief ornament could be scraped or worn off without much difficulty. On this dagger the relief decoration remains, but it now lacks its original gold or silver encrusting.

German (?) parrying dagger, *c.*1600–20

DATE	*c.*1600–20
ORIGIN	POSSIBLY GERMAN
LENGTH	unknown

This parrying dagger has the straight guard and side ring typical of earlier 16th-century examples. But the blade exhibits the 17th-century trend towards a longer, narrower profile, built with a very thick spine. The weight is reduced through the use of several deep grooves and piercings.

English dagger, *c.*1610–25

DATE	*c.*1610–25
ORIGIN	ENGLISH
LENGTH	unknown

The style of the English hilt of this dagger is typical of the Jacobean period (1603–1625). The large, rounded pommel and straight cross guard with large, knob-like terminals, as well as the encrusting in silver, is typical of English taste of the early 17th century. The same design features are also found on contemporary dress swords.

17th-century main-gauche daggers

Main gauche simply means "left hand", and is therefore no more specific a term than "parrying dagger". It originally denoted a dagger that was meant for rapier and dagger fencing, as opposed to more general uses, as well as self-defence. However, over time it has come to be applied more specifically in English. Today it is used, rightly or wrongly, to refer to this quite late class of Italo-Spanish fencing dagger.

Spanish main-gauche dagger, *c.*1640

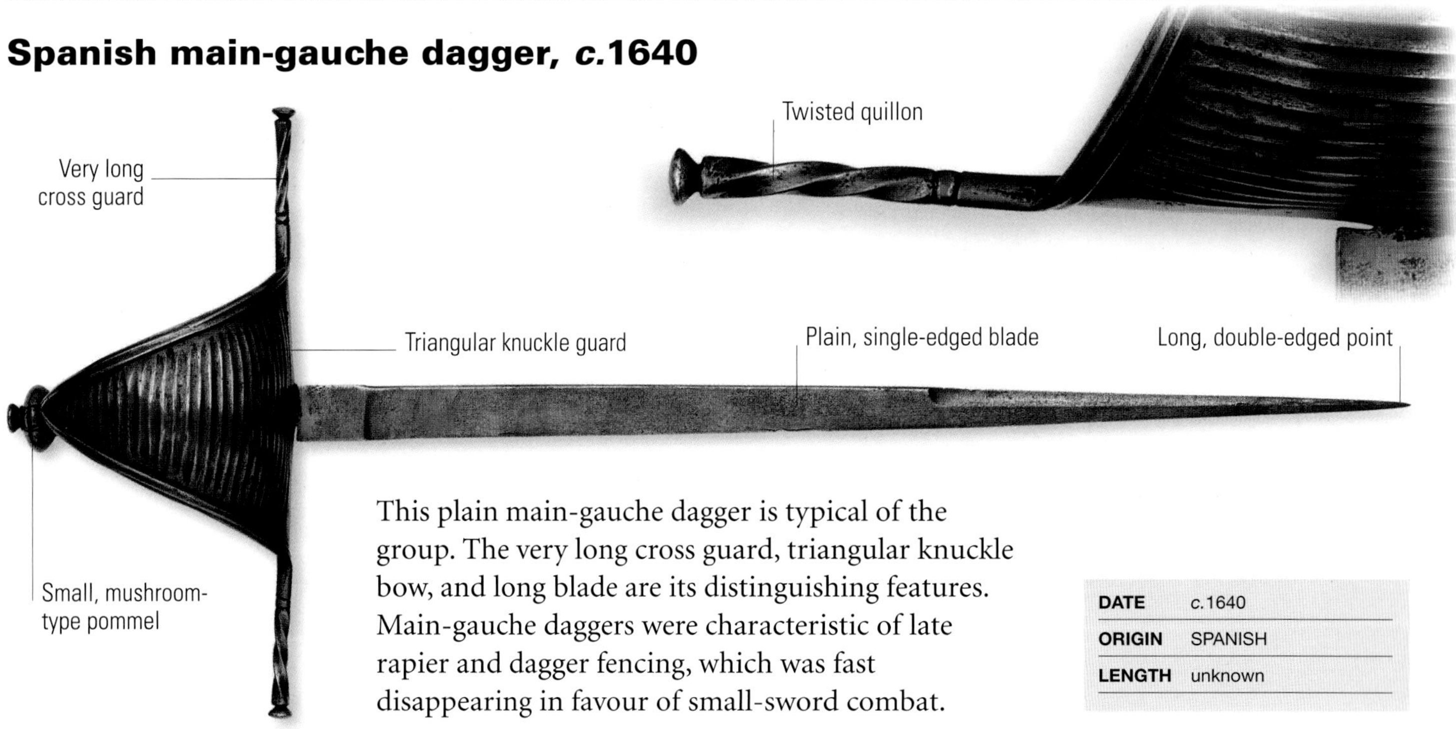

This plain main-gauche dagger is typical of the group. The very long cross guard, triangular knuckle bow, and long blade are its distinguishing features. Main-gauche daggers were characteristic of late rapier and dagger fencing, which was fast disappearing in favour of small-sword combat.

DATE	*c.*1640
ORIGIN	SPANISH
LENGTH	unknown

Southern Italian main-gauche dagger, *c.*1650

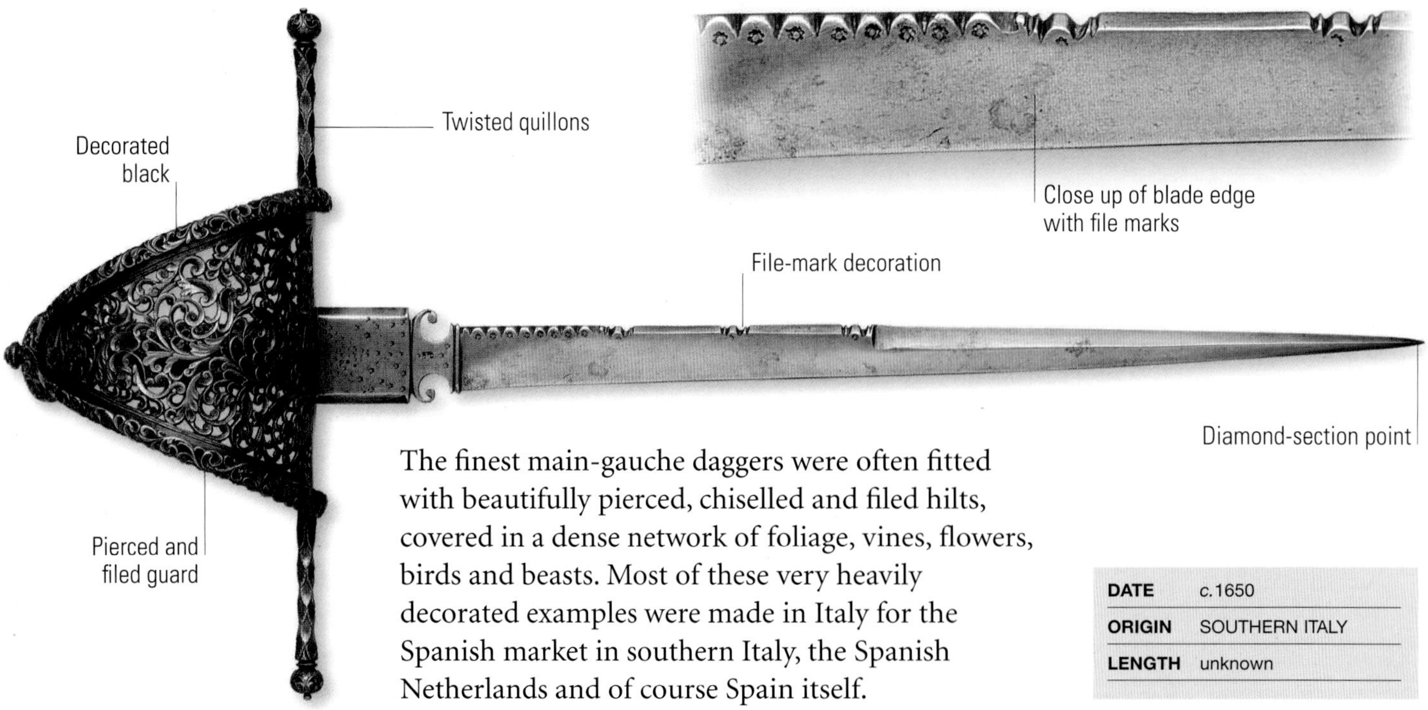

The finest main-gauche daggers were often fitted with beautifully pierced, chiselled and filed hilts, covered in a dense network of foliage, vines, flowers, birds and beasts. Most of these very heavily decorated examples were made in Italy for the Spanish market in southern Italy, the Spanish Netherlands and of course Spain itself.

DATE	*c.*1650
ORIGIN	SOUTHERN ITALY
LENGTH	unknown

Italian main-gauche dagger, *c.*1650

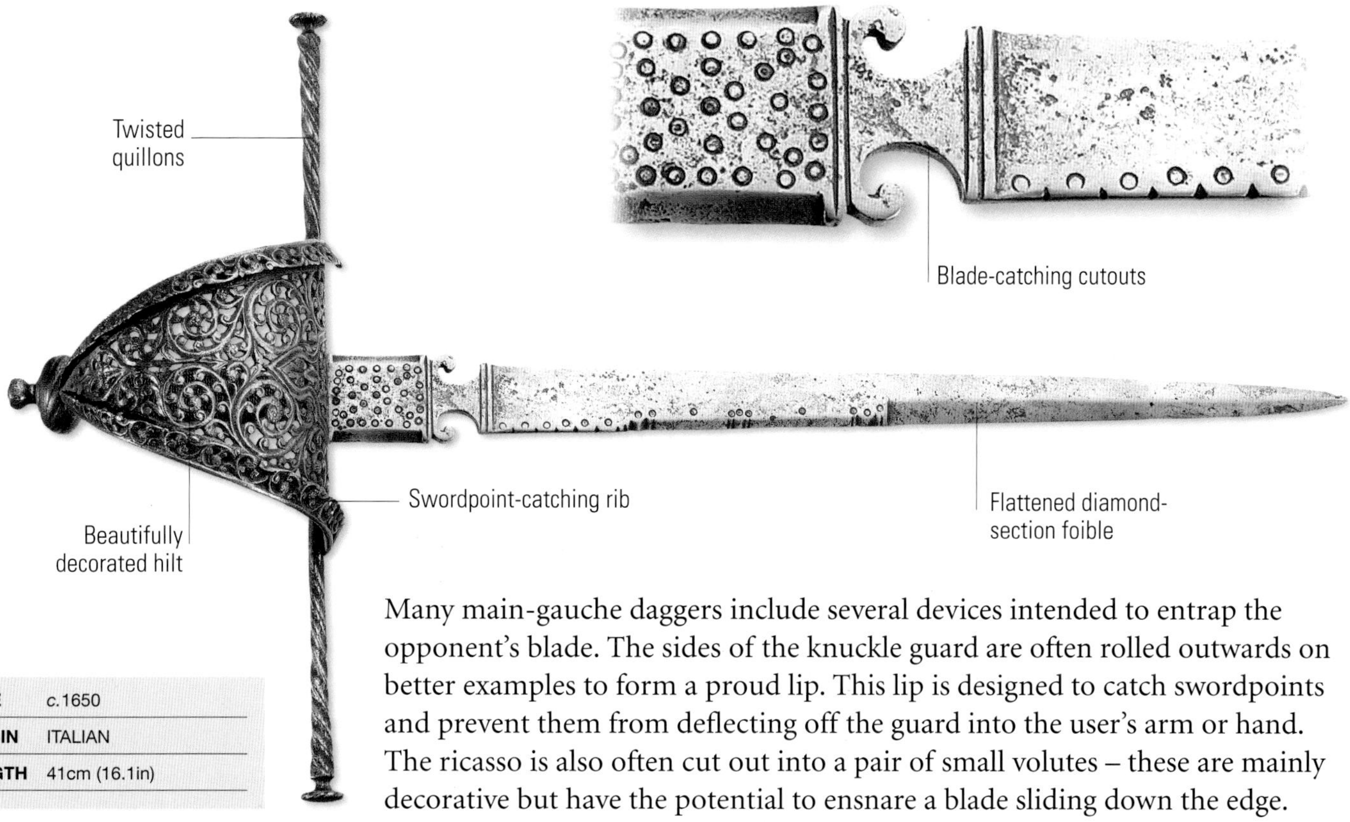

Many main-gauche daggers include several devices intended to entrap the opponent's blade. The sides of the knuckle guard are often rolled outwards on better examples to form a proud lip. This lip is designed to catch swordpoints and prevent them from deflecting off the guard into the user's arm or hand. The ricasso is also often cut out into a pair of small volutes – these are mainly decorative but have the potential to ensnare a blade sliding down the edge.

DATE	*c.*1650
ORIGIN	ITALIAN
LENGTH	41cm (16.1in)

German main-gauche dagger, *c.*1660

This is an interesting German variation on the main-gauche theme. Rather than the usual triangular knuckle guard, this weapon is fitted with a rounded dish guard, acid-etched in the typical German manner, with additional bars at the edges. This piece was undoubtedly made as an en suite mate to a cup-hilt rapier with a guard having similar specific features, now lost. The blade is also typically German: very narrow with a deep central fuller along the lower half, in the trough of which is the maker's signature.

DATE	*c.*1660
ORIGIN	GERMAN
LENGTH	unknown

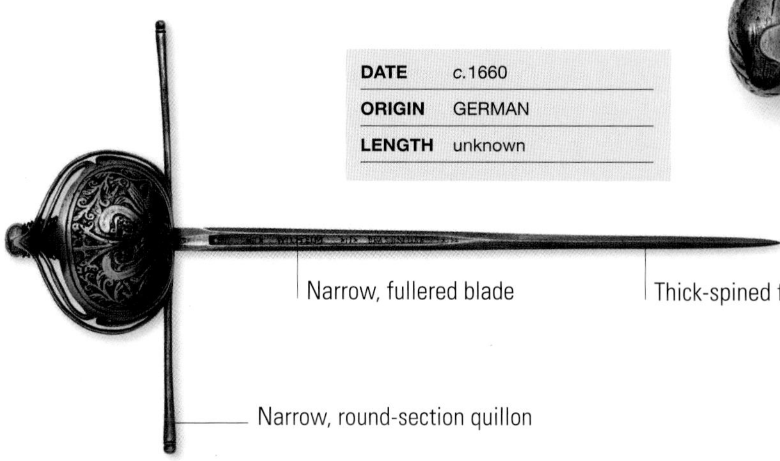

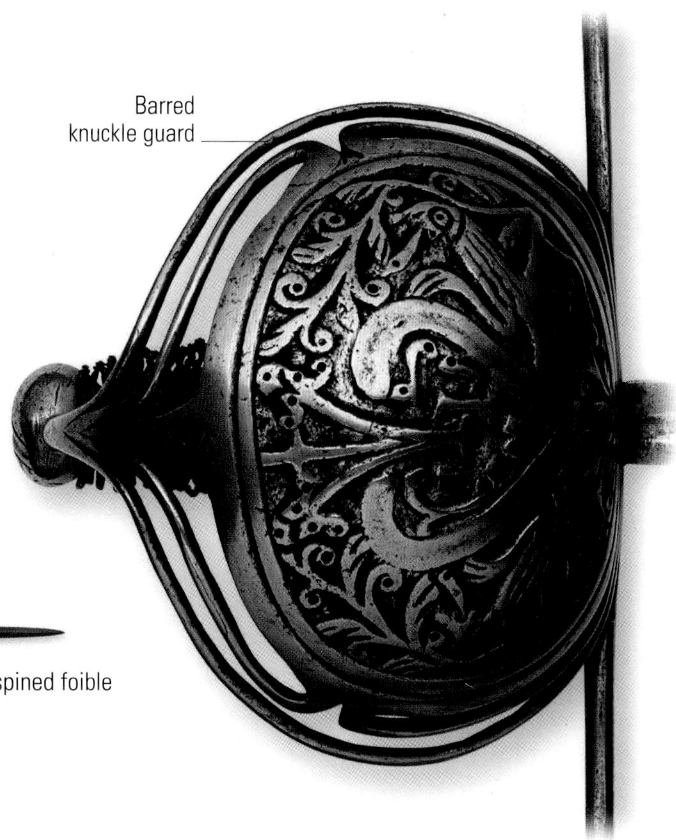

17th-century stilettos

The stiletto or stylet appeared late in the 16th century. Its development probably began with the production of miniature side-ring daggers. One of these little daggers would have been too small for fencing, but it nevertheless adhered to the fashion of the time. Since it was useless as a fencing implement, this new form of dagger quickly lost its resemblance to the larger parrying dagger. At the height of its popularity in the mid-17th century, the all-metal stiletto was a weapon purely of last resort and of assassination.

Spanish stiletto, late 16th century

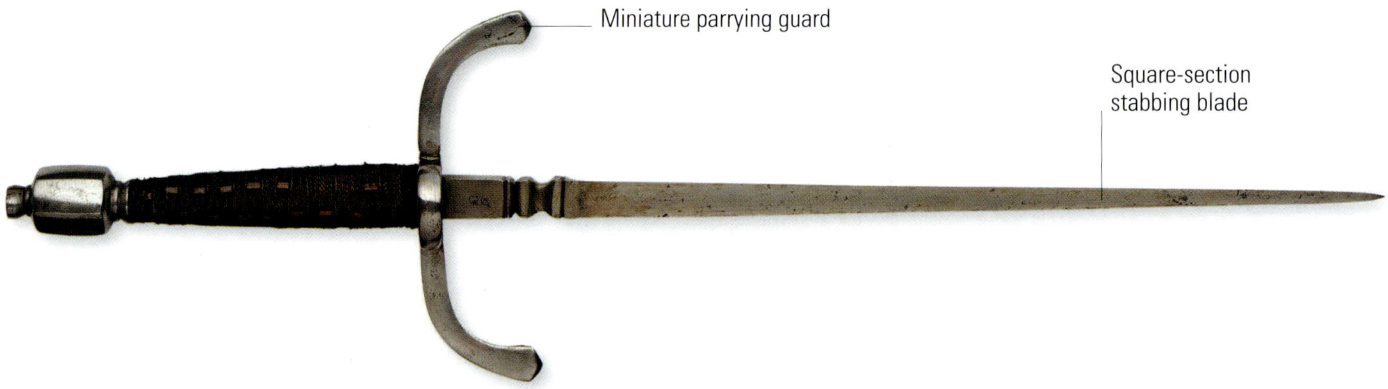

This weapon could easily be mistaken for a typical late 16th-century parrying dagger, if not for its size and blade-type. It is perhaps three-quarters the size of a full-size parrying dagger, and thus is too small and delicate for sword-fighting. Its blade also has no sharp edges, being square in cross-section. The base or ricasso of the blade also exhibits a new decorative feature, a turned area just forward of the guard that emphasizes the delicate refinement of the weapon's lines. This "baluster-turning" quickly became a standard feature of 17th-century stilettos.

DATE	late 16th century
ORIGIN	SPANISH
LENGTH	unknown

Italian stiletto, late 16th century

This weapon is a superb demonstration of steel cutting, the hilt turned into a beautifully proportioned piece of architecture in miniature. The grip mutates skillfully from discoidal knobs into flowing tulip-like forms and continues seamlessly on to the strong needle-like blade. These all-metal weapons were accompanied by equally elegant scabbards, made entirely of steel or wood; three or four narrow lengths glued together to house the either triangular- or square-section blade and covered in paper-thin leather.

DATE	late 16th century
ORIGIN	ITALIAN
LENGTH	unknown

Italian stiletto, early 17th century

DATE	early 17th century
ORIGIN	ITALIAN
LENGTH	20cm (7.9in)

The hilt of this stiletto is quite different from the baluster-turned types. Instead of being cut out of a single piece of steel, the hilt of this weapon has been modelled in wax and then cast in copper alloy. The grip takes the form of an ape standing on its hind legs, and on its head stands a small animal, probably a dog.

Italian stiletto, *c.*1600

DATE	*c.*1600
ORIGIN	ITALIAN
LENGTH	unknown

Despite their overall smallness, most stilettos have a blade that makes up around three-quarters of their total length. This example is somewhat unusual in that its total length is divided nearly equally between blade and hilt. Such a small weapon would be especially easy to hide about one's person.

Italian stiletto, *c.*1600

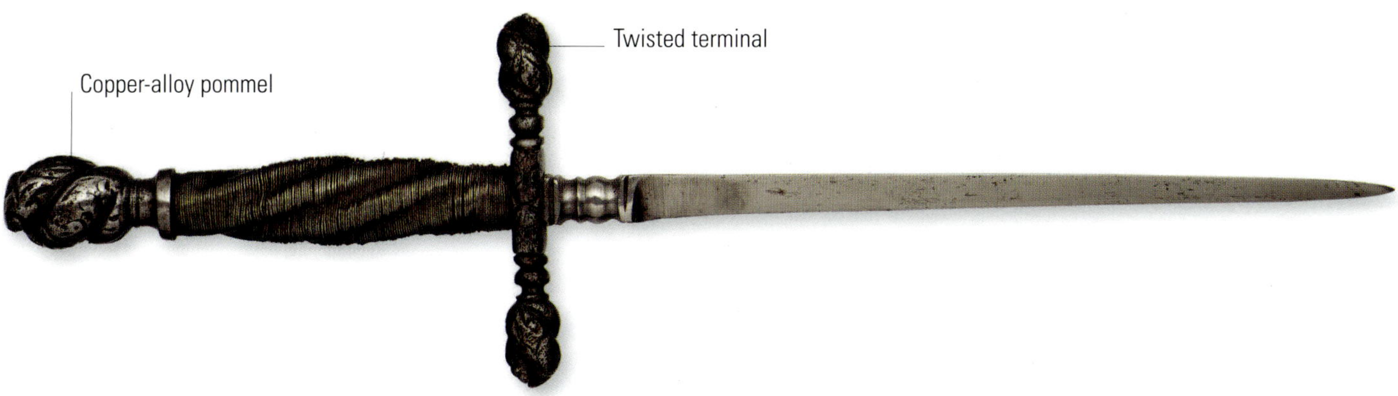

DATE	*c.*1600
ORIGIN	POSSIBLY ITALIAN
LENGTH	unknown

This weapon shows a different construction to many other stilettos of the time. Here the pommel and guard are made in copper alloy, while the grip is wrapped in fine wire. The hilt seems out of proportion to the blade; it may be that the blade and hilt did not originally belong together.

Italian stiletto, *c.*1600

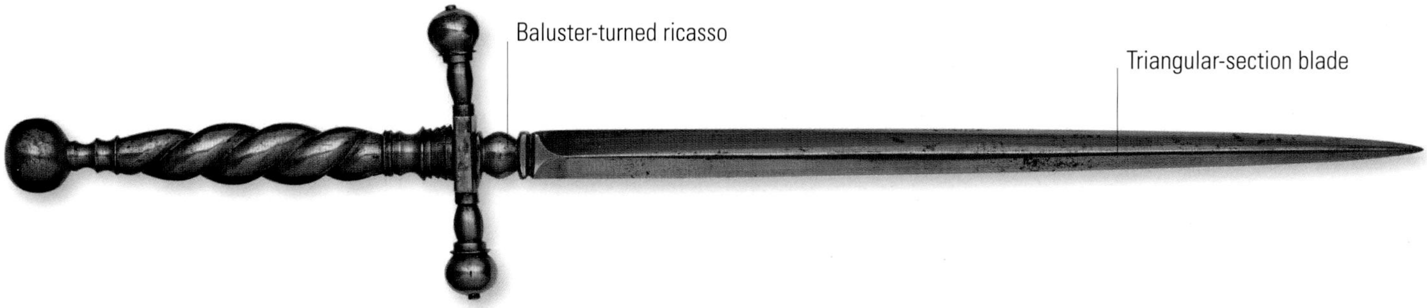

While the blades of some stilettos are entirely plain, many of the finer examples display baluster-turnings on the base of the blade as well as the hilt. This produces an attractive unity between hilt and blade, a detail seen on very few forms of edged weapon. The grip of this example has been cut into a fluid, twisting form.

DATE	*c.*1600
ORIGIN	ITALIAN
LENGTH	unknown

Italian stiletto, *c.*1600

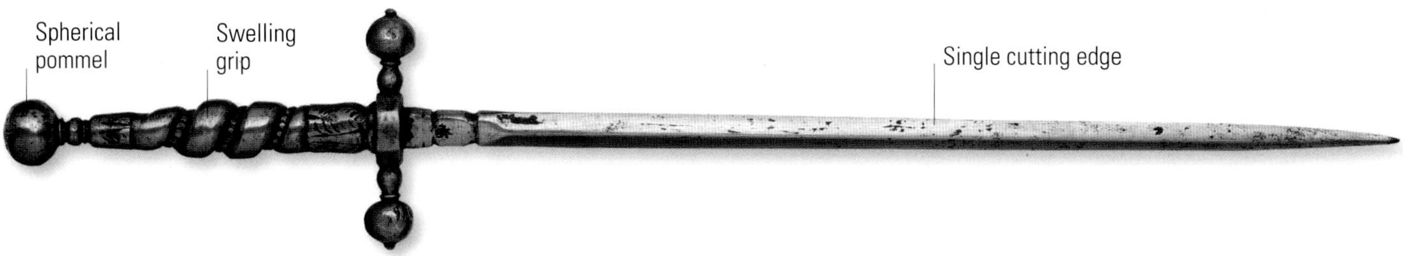

Most all-metal stilettos with baluster-turned hilts have a spherical, discoidal or ovoid pommel, the size of which is carefully designed to balance the blade in the hand. When the perfect balance is achieved, the weapon seems almost weightless in the hand. The shape of the guard terminals usually matches that of the pommel, while the grip is usually twisted into graceful architectural forms.

DATE	*c.*1600
ORIGIN	ITALIAN
LENGTH	unknown

Italian gunner's stiletto, 1600

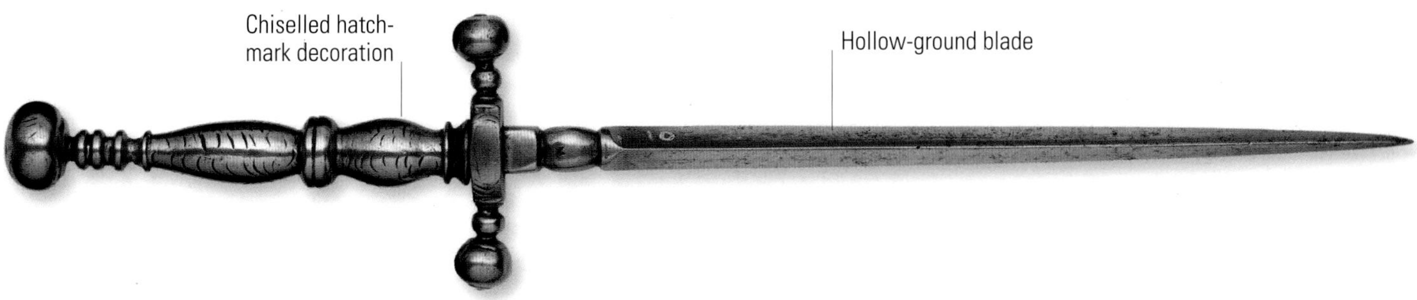

Although the plainly smooth-surfaced stilettos are the most common, a number of examples show chiselled or punched decoration as well, such as the hatch-marks on the grip of this piece. The back of this blade is numbered, supposedly to enable the owner to determine the weight of a cannon ball so that he could range a shot effectively. However, the numbering is non-functional, and the blade is too short to be used as a measuring device.

DATE	1600
ORIGIN	ITALIAN
LENGTH	unknown

Italian stiletto, early to mid-17th century

DATE	early to mid-17th century
ORIGIN	ITALIAN
LENGTH	unknown

Here we find yet another variation on the stiletto theme, the guard terminals and pommel taking on a faceted conical form, with delicately undercut bases. The ricasso is cut with a similar knob. The handle, swelling in the middle, is of wood strengthened with narrow metal straps.

Spanish stiletto, late 17th century

DATE	late 17th century
ORIGIN	SPANISH
LENGTH	45.2cm (17.8in)

This later stiletto takes a very unusual form. While the grip flares towards the pommel, in a manner not unlike some earlier 16th-century daggers, the guard is really that of a small-sword in miniature; it is, however, too small to be an actual sword that has been broken and cut down.

Spanish stiletto dividers, *c.*1700–50

DATE	*c.*1700–50
ORIGIN	SPANISH
LENGTH	unknown

It was very popular in the Renaissance to draw parallels between the fighting arts and the sciences. Fight masters often saw themselves as scientists as well as martial artists, and they strove to communicate their skills in a learned, scientific way. This led to a fashionable association between weapons and scientific instruments, and thus noblemen often liked to collect both. The idea of combining the two into a single object, the stiletto that split apart to form a pair of architect's dividers, first occurred in the 16th century and was repeated many times.

17th-century plug bayonets

At some early date someone had the idea of whittling down the wooden haft of a knife and plugging it into the muzzle of a gun, turning it into a thrusting spear. This probably happened in Europe, and some believe the term "bayonet" is derived from the name of the French cutlery town, Bayonne. The gun was of course disabled, but if a spear was needed then the enemy were too close for the lack of a gun to be a problem.

British officer's or sporting bayonet, *c.*1660

The elaborate and decorated bone or ivory hilt suggests this bayonet was for an officer or for sporting use. With such hard material, it is doubtful whether the hilt could have been secured in the muzzle and there are no marks to indicate its use in this way. The weapon was probably used merely as a knife.

DATE	*c.*1660
ORIGIN	BRITISH
LENGTH	41cm (16.1in)

British officer's or sporting bayonet, *c.*1660

This is another example of a decorated bone or ivory hilt but slightly less elaborate than the one above. While this weapon has a more conventional blade, both have a number of features that are almost identical, such as the tang buttons on the pommels and the cross guards, suggesting that they may be by the same maker.

DATE	*c.*1660
ORIGIN	BRITISH
LENGTH	45.1cm (17.8in)

British military bayonet, *c.*1680

Common to all plug bayonets is a slender, round, tapering handle with a bulbous swelling near where it joins the blade. The handle has to be resilient enough to allow it to be pushed into the muzzle and stay there, but not so tightly that it can't be removed. Most handles are therefore wooden as this material is slightly elastic.

DATE	*c.*1680
ORIGIN	BRITISH
LENGTH	45.8cm (18in)

British officer's bayonet, 1686

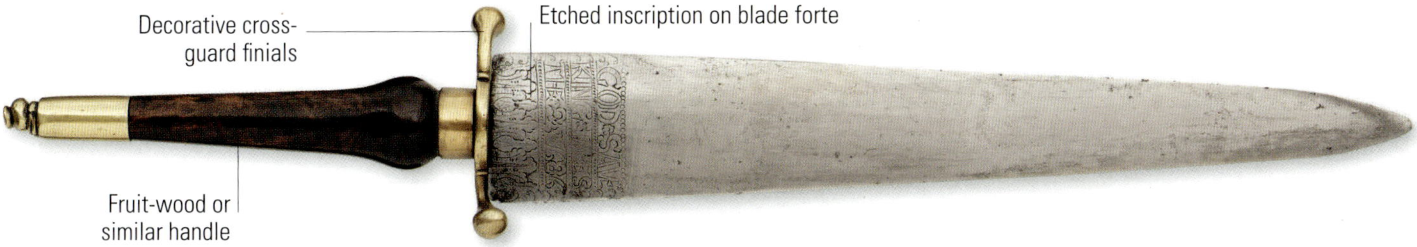

DATE	1686
ORIGIN	BRITISH
LENGTH	46cm (18.1in)

This plug bayonet conforms more to the general type of serviceable military bayonet with its wooden handle, but it is of better quality than usual, suggesting that the weapon may have belonged to an officer. This is supported by the fact that the blade is inscribed "GOD SAVE KING JAMES THE 2 1686", which is an unusual feature on any type of bayonet and is useful for dating this general style.

British officer's bayonet, 1686

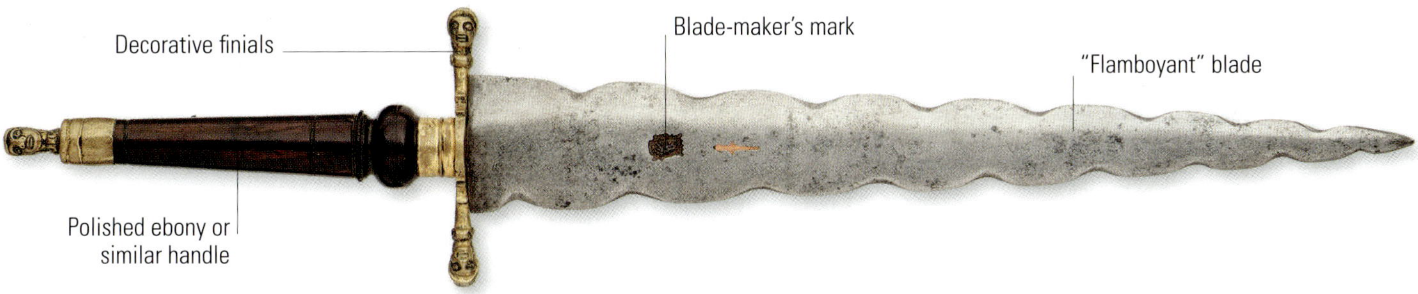

DATE	1686
ORIGIN	BRITISH
LENGTH	45.4cm (17.9in)

A bayonet as distinctive and of such quality as this one, with its highly polished grip of either ebony or other exotic wood and its gilded brass fittings, was undoubtedly used by an officer. The pommel, tang button and cross guard show close similarity to those of the two officer's bayonets on the previous page. The most distinctive feature is obviously the blade with its sinuous wavy edges, often referred to as "flamboyant" because of its likeness to a flickering flame.

Scandinavian officer's bayonet, 1700

DATE	1700
ORIGIN	POSS. SCANDINAVIAN
LENGTH	48.7cm (19.1in)

A good-quality, possibly Scandinavian, bayonet. It has a wooden grip, painted possibly in imitation of tortoiseshell or an exotic wood, and gilded decorated brass hilt fittings. The cross guard with its downturned finials is more reminiscent of many 19th-century sword bayonets than of the typical English plug bayonet. Like others of this class, it shows few if any signs of having been thrust into a muzzle.

17th- and 18th-century civilian daggers

Walking-out and dress-type swords and daggers became a prominent feature among the rising classes in the period following the Reformation. Although such weapons were still very expensive, there was a larger class of people who could now afford them.

Daggers and knives that were primarily intended for functional use were often completed to a level of decoration that suggested the object might also be worn as an item of jewellery or statement of rank, as well as having a more practical day-to-day use.

English dagger, 1628

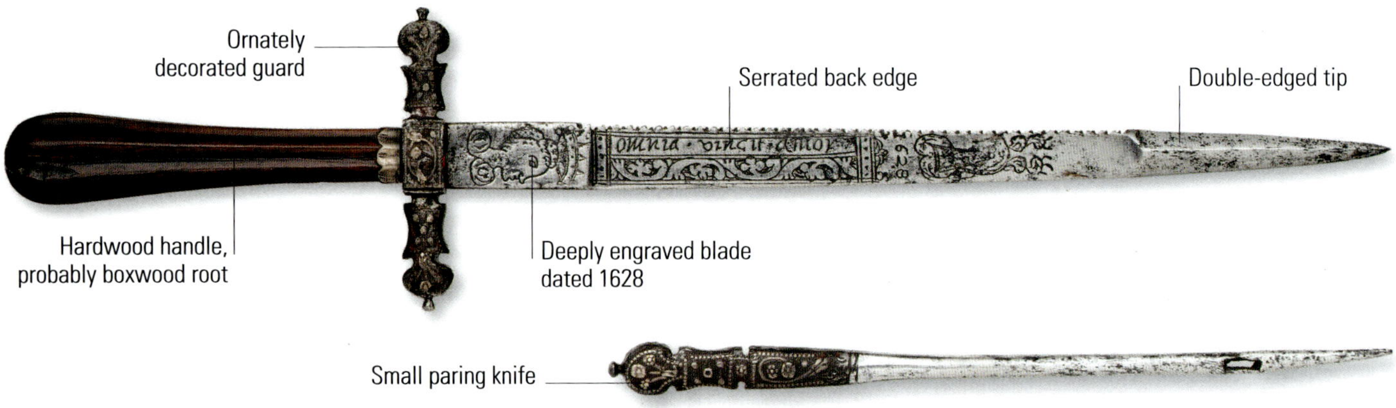

This very fine, high-quality combination set comprises a main dagger and matching paring knife, both of which fit together in the same scabbard. The blade of the main knife is beautifully decorated with deep engraving. The serrated edge had a practical application in that when cutting a joint of meat it could sever through the toughest parts; the paring knife was used to secure the treated item in position.

DATE	1628
ORIGIN	ENGLISH
LENGTH	32.7cm (12.9in)

The cutler's trade

In 17th- and 18th-century Europe, improved trade routes meant that raw materials such as iron were transported more easily to the main commercial towns and cities. Aided too by advances in industrial power, Solingen in Germany and Sheffield in England became important centres of blade production.

It took many craftsmen to produce a good-quality edged weapon. The manufacture of the blade was a highly skilled art and there were also specialist cross-guard and pommel makers, scalers (grip makers) and scabbard and sheath makers.

RIGHT A German bladesmith in his workshop. Many of Europe's best cutlers worked in Solingen, Germany and Sheffield, England.

English dagger, 1631

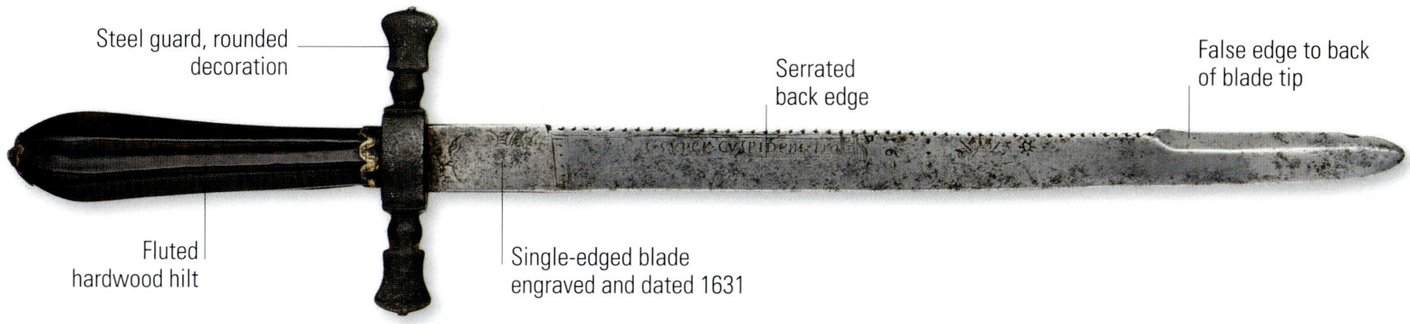

DATE	1631
ORIGIN	ENGLISH
LENGTH	26.3cm (10.4in)

This is a fine example of a gentleman's utility knife, having a fluted wooden grip, and a steel ferrule and cross guard. The latter is simplistically decorated with rounded finials. The blade is flat and single-edged, yet has a sharpened false edge at the tip. The back edge of the blade is serrated. Engraved decoration on the blade indicates that it dates from 1631.

English dagger, mid-17th century

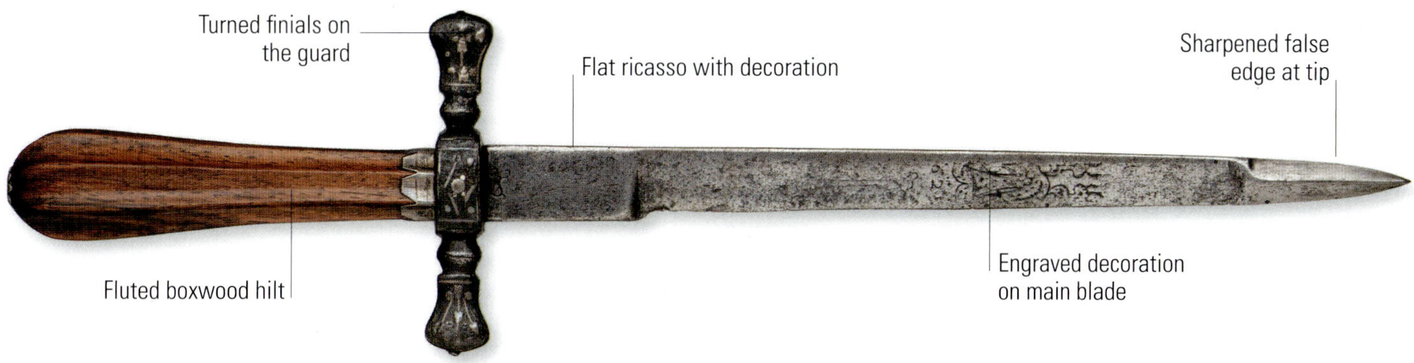

DATE	mid-17th century
ORIGIN	ENGLISH
LENGTH	31.4cm (12.4in)

This dagger has an interesting blade construction. The flat ricasso extends the back flat of the blade along almost the full length, effectively making this a single-edged knife with a double-edged tip. The steel guard is nicely formed with domed terminals and decoration on the quillon block. The fluted boxwood hilt is typical.

English quillon dagger, 1678

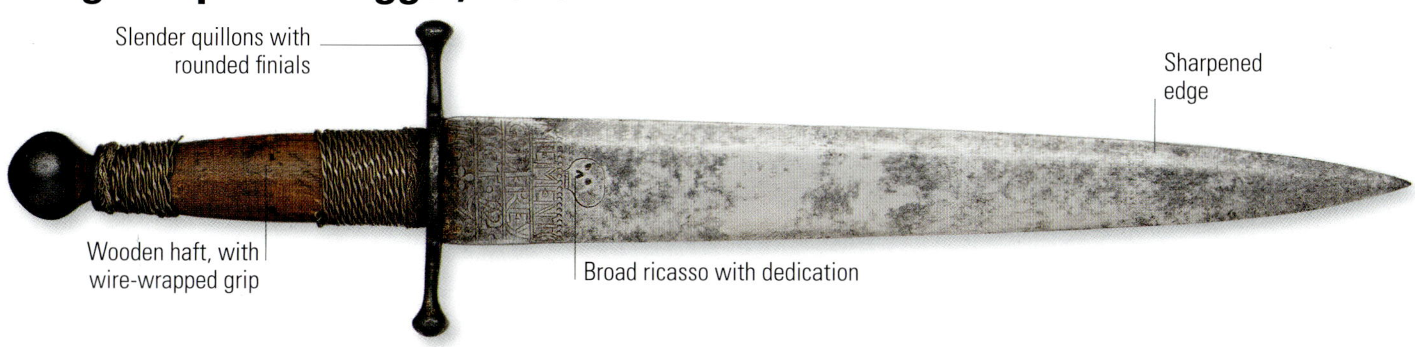

DATE	1678
ORIGIN	ENGLISH
LENGTH	31.4cm (12.4in)

This English quillon dagger is inscribed on the blade "Memento Godfrey...1678". The long blade is single-edged for most of the length, and the ricasso area is broad and flat with the inscribed decoration. The tang of the blade is concealed by an ovoid-section wooden grip, which is covered with a twisted-wire wrapping.

Dutch or German quillon-form hunting dagger, *c.*1700

The structure and style of the grip on this weapon suggests that it is a hunting knife, and most probably Dutch or perhaps German in origin. It dates from the latter part of the 1600s or possibly the early 1700s. The ornate cross guard is brass, S-shaped and decorated with miniature lion's-head finials. The long, narrow, tapered blade has an inscribed decoration and is single-edged along most of its length, narrowing to a double-edged tip.

DATE	*c.*1700
ORIGIN	DUTCH/GERMAN
LENGTH	40.8cm (16.1in)

French or German stiletto, early to mid-18th century

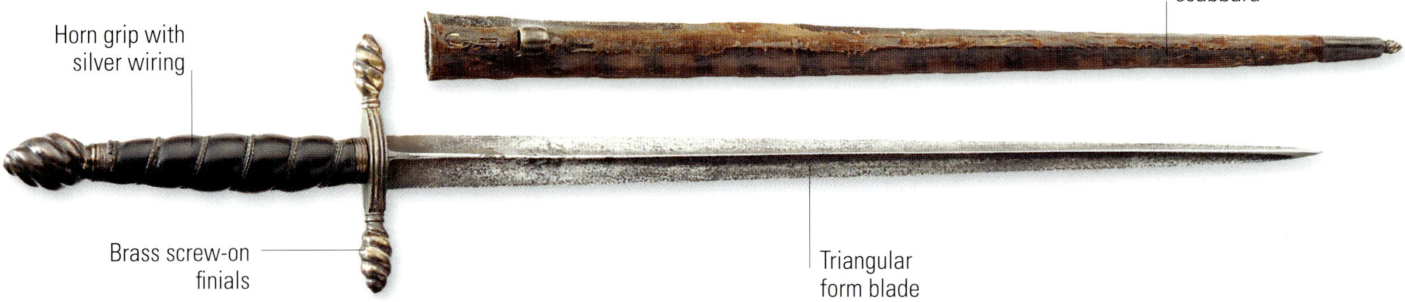

This stiletto is French or possibly German. The triangular-section blade has a forte with remnants of decorative etching and gilding and the point has been lightly resharpened. Grooved finials are screwed onto quillons, the grip covered with silver-wire winding. The front of the brass scabbard has a leather cover; the rear is engraved with scrolling vine patterns.

DATE	early to mid-18th century
ORIGIN	FRENCH/GERMAN
LENGTH	48cm (18.9in)

Spanish or Italian short stiletto, mid-18th century

This short thrusting stiletto is possibly the accompanying knife to a larger hunting weapon. It has an interesting horn, or narwhal, grip with decoration and wiring. The steel pommel cap has engraved decoration, and the steel ricasso of the blade a chiselled decoration. The blade has a long fore edge and a short false edge.

DATE	mid-18th century
ORIGIN	SPANISH/ITALIAN
LENGTH	24.9cm (9.8in)

Italian or Dalmatian Schiovona dagger, 1790

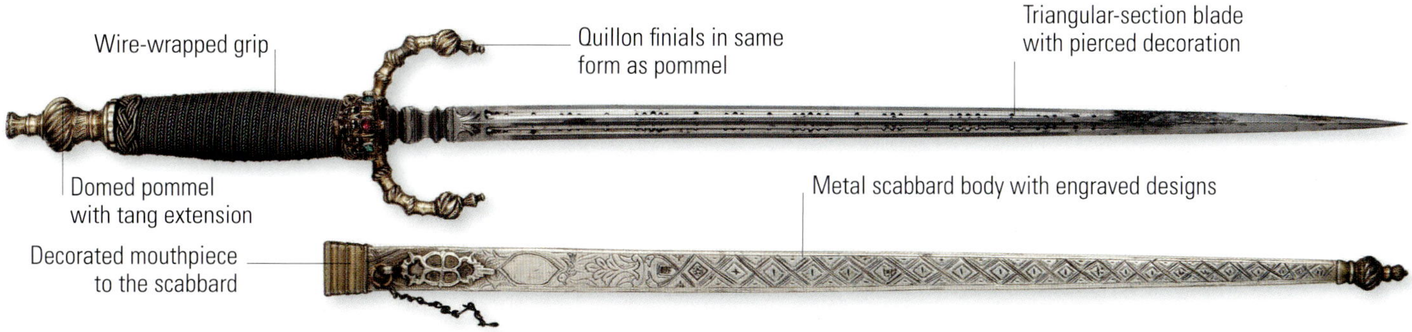

The slender blade of this dagger is triangular in section with pierced decoration on the facings. The ricasso of the blade is decoratively segmented and may disguise a join where a new tang has been added. The pommel and cross-guard terminals are of matching design and the centre section of the guard is decorated with coloured, semi-precious stones. The grip is of wood with wire wrapping.

DATE	1790
ORIGIN	ITALIAN/DALMATIAN
LENGTH	45cm (17.8in)

Italian dagger, late 18th century

DATE	late 18th century
ORIGIN	ITALIAN
LENGTH	35cm (13.8in)

This late 18th-century knife is of a pattern popular around the Mediterranean. It has a distinctive blade with a double fuller, which converges towards the blade tip, and the ricasso features a relief-engraved emblem of a cockerel. The fluted wood grip has polished steel mounts, and the leather scabbard has steel mounts.

Italian utility knife, late 18th century

DATE	late 18th century
ORIGIN	ITALIAN
LENGTH	24.5cm (9.6in)

This utility knife has the very distinctive feature of an open-frame ricasso, used to receive the forefinger and ease movement of the blade when cutting fresh meat on the bone. The blade shape is designed for both cutting and filleting. It is possibly the accompanying knife to a larger hunting knife set and probably Italian in origin.

18th- and 19th-century naval dirks

It was in the latter half of the 18th century that some short swords and dirks started to be carried by midshipmen and officers of the English Navy, and often these were conversions from other, broken weapons. Such damaged weapons were far too valuable to be discarded, but instead could be resurrected as short swords, and the evolution into short dirks appears to have been influenced by this trend.

French long-bladed dirk (conversion), late 18th century

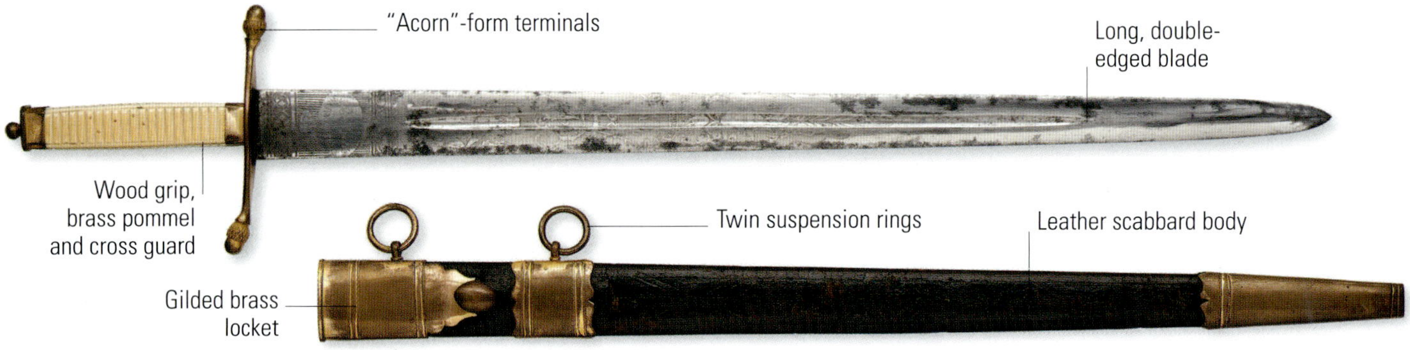

The blade of this conversion dirk appears to be from a hunting sword and it is engraved with scrolling designs. The grip's square form could be French and the leather scabbard appears to have gilded brass fittings. The "acorn" decoration on the cross guard doesn't seem to fit "naval traditions".

DATE	late 18th century
ORIGIN	FRENCH
LENGTH	58cm (23in)

British (?) long-bladed naval dirk (conversion), late 18th century

This interesting dirk is composed partially from a short sword, possibly a spadroon. The assembly of the blade, cross guard, grip and pommel is secured by drawing the tang of the blade through the pommel cap and peening (hammering) it into place.

DATE	late 18th century
ORIGIN	POSSIBLY BRITISH
LENGTH	61cm (24in)

British naval dirk (conversion), early 19th century

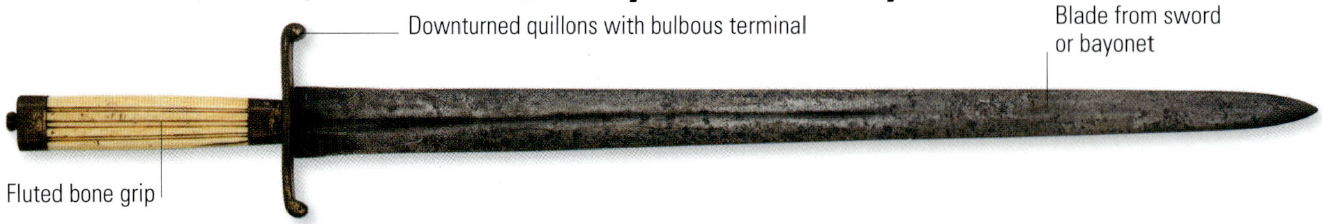

This is quite a substantial item, and appears to be more similar to a short sword than a dirk. The blade is not dissimilar to some of the variations found on the bayonet for the English Baker rifle, although it is by no means certain that this is what this weapon has been converted from.

DATE	early 19th century
ORIGIN	BRITISH
LENGTH	58cm (23in)

American naval dirk, early 19th century

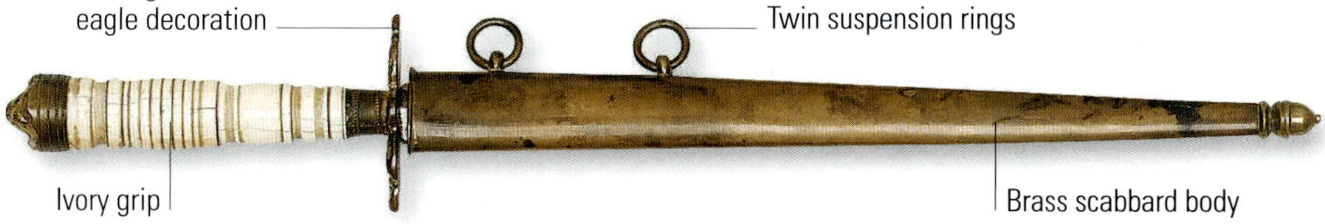

DATE	early 19th century
ORIGIN	AMERICAN
LENGTH	19cm (7.5in)

This American Naval dirk has a brightly polished, slender, double-edged blade with a flattened diamond section. There are gilt-copper hilt fittings and a lion's-mask pommel, and an embossed cross guard with an eagle head holding a ball in its beak. The grip is turned ivory. The gilded brass scabbard has twin suspension rings.

Spanish naval officer's hanger sword, early 19th century

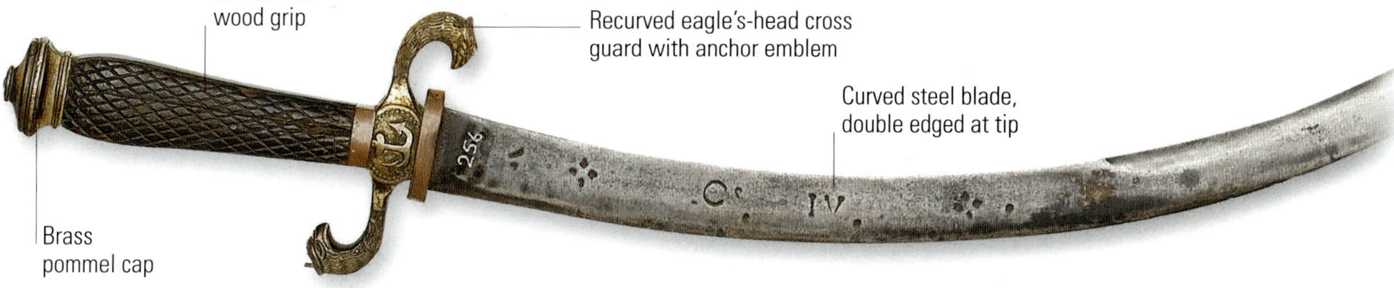

DATE	early 19th century
ORIGIN	SPANISH
LENGTH	44.5cm (17.5in)

The curved blade of this Spanish naval officer's hanger sword from the early 1800s is single-edged with a double-edged tip. Stampings on the blade indicate "Cs IV" (Carlos IV, who died in 1819). The hilt fittings are brass, the pommel is in the form of a flattened urn, and the cross guard is decorated with eagle's-head terminals and an anchor emblem on the quillon block.

British long-bladed naval dirk, early 19th century

DATE	early 19th century
ORIGIN	BRITISH
LENGTH	60.7cm (24in)

This unusual form of dirk has an exceptionally long blade and is probably a conversion that has used the blade from some other weapon. The wood grip is square in cross-section, with grooved fluting on all sides. There is a copper or brass square-form pommel cap on the hilt, with the blade tang drawn through and peened. There is a metal ferrule at the base of the grip, and a cross guard with upturned and downturned quillons.

French boarding dagger, mid-19th century

Although commonly called a "boarding dagger", this is actually an "on-board" utility knife. Whereas knives were not normally carried on deck (for safety reasons), they were often required for work on the rigging. The lanyard ring was secured to a cord tied to the belt, as a prevention against loss if dropped.

DATE	mid-19th century
ORIGIN	FRENCH
LENGTH	35.6cm (14in)

British naval hanger, *c.*1850

This naval hanger has a long, curved blade of the "cut-and-thrust" form, being mostly single-edged with a flat back and long fuller. The last third of the blade is double-edged. The pommel, backstrap, ferrule and cross guard are made of brass, the pommel decoration being that of a lion's head. There is no record of this pattern of hanger being issued to the English Navy; it is probable that they were sold to privateers, or even as export items to foreign naval powers.

DATE	*c.*1850
ORIGIN	BRITISH
LENGTH	45.7cm (18in)

Spanish naval dirk, 19th century

This is not strictly a naval dirk but more of a maritime knife used by sailors. The blade has a long, flat ricasso which tapers to a point to form the central spine of the blade. The cross guard is plain, flat and tapered, and the hilt is composed of an elongated ferrule and pommel cap connected by the central grip made of bone. The fluted grooves are not simply decoration but intended to improve the grip.

DATE	19th century
ORIGIN	SPANISH
LENGTH	32cm (12.6in)

Georgian dirks

The term "Georgian dirk" really embraces weapons from the mid-1700s to the start of Queen Victoria's reign. The Industrial Revolution had evolved, and more efficient means for the production of metal wares had come into being, as well as a growing middle class of people who could afford expensive items. The Georgian dirk offered a form of weapon that was also ornate enough to be considered a form of male jewellery.

British Georgian naval dirk, early 19th century

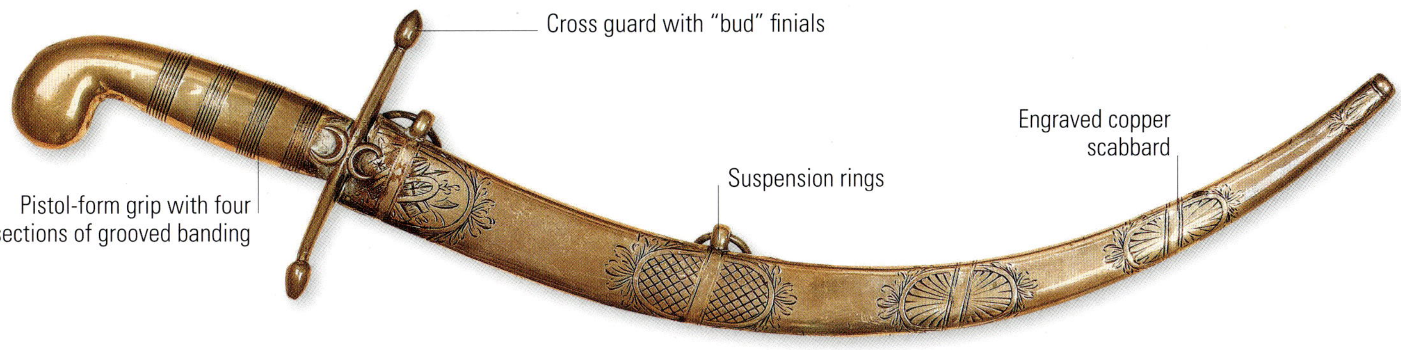

DATE	early 19th century
ORIGIN	BRITISH
LENGTH	22.8cm (9in)

The scabbard carrying the slender, curved, single-edged blade is engraved copper, with gilding featuring scrolling and checkering designs. Metal portions of the hilt are made of copper with gilding. The cross guard features "bud"-type finials and a double-crescent langet at the centre of the guard.

British Georgian dirk, early 19th century

This broad, single-edged blade has etched, blued and gilt decoration. The blade has a flat back, with a single fuller running along most of the back edge. Metal portions of the hilt are gilded copper, comprising a pommel with lion's-mask motif, ferrule and a cross guard with shell emblem finials.

DATE	early 19th century
ORIGIN	BRITISH
LENGTH	27.4cm (10.8in)

British Georgian naval dirk, early 19th century

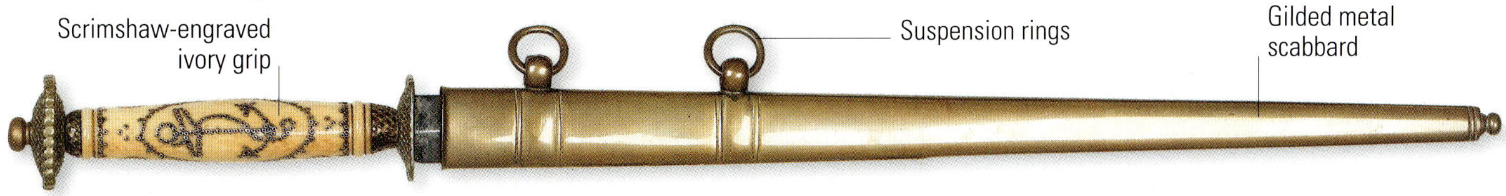

DATE	early 19th century
ORIGIN	BRITISH
LENGTH	18.4cm (7.25in)

This unusual Georgian naval dirk has a scrimshaw-decorated ivory grip depicting a rope and anchor. The blade is of shallow diamond section, etched with trophies, wreaths and flourishes. There are gilded copper fittings with a screw-on pommel and an unusual cross guard in the form of an elongated eight-pointed star.

British Georgian naval dirk, *c.*1820

The blade of this unusual Georgian naval dirk has a plain, flattened diamond section. The turned ivory grip has a silver pique-work design of a fouled anchor in an oval, and the initials "RC" in scrolls. The small, rounded rectangular brass guard has a matching pommel embossed with tiny scales within a studded border. The brass scabbard is ornately engraved with a button chape and two suspension rings.

DATE	*c.*1820
ORIGIN	BRITISH
LENGTH	21.6cm (8.5in)

British Georgian naval dirk, *c.*1820

This Georgian naval dirk has a blade of shallow diamond section. The blade is etched with a crown, anchor and foliage designs. The grip is turned ivory, topped with a metal pommel bearing the unusual design of a coiled snake. The cross guard is formed as a small oval disc, engraved with the legend *Palmam Qui Meruit Feriat* ("Let him who merits bear the palm").

DATE	*c.*1820
ORIGIN	BRITISH
LENGTH	17.8cm (7in)

British Georgian dirk hanger, *c.*1820

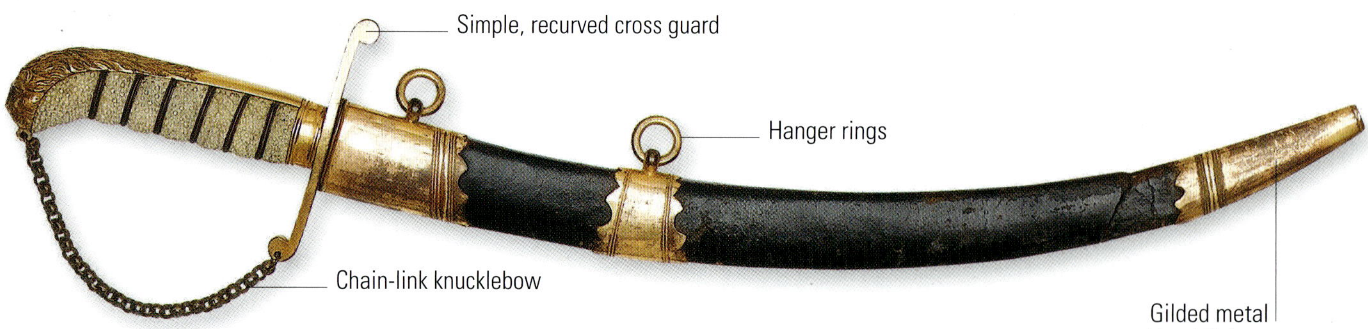

This dirk is like a small-sized hanger featuring a curved, single-edged blade etched with a decoration consisting of scrolled foliage, and a panel with the engraved initials "CLP" – presumably those of the former owner. The hilt comprises a brass backstrap in the form of a lion's head, with a segmented bone grip and gold wiring. The chain-link knucklebow appears to be a contemporary addition. The scabbard is made of black leather, with gilded metal fittings.

DATE	*c.*1820
ORIGIN	BRITISH
LENGTH	30.5cm (12in)

British Georgian naval officer's dirk, *c.*1820

DATE	*c.*1820
ORIGIN	BRITISH
LENGTH	27.4cm (10.8in)

This extremely handsome naval dirk is reputed to have belonged to a member of the Suckling family. The blade is etched with the manufacturer's details: "Drury, sword cutler, 32 Strand, London". The blade is also etched with designs of a rope and fouled anchor, military trophies and scrolling foliage. There are gilded metal fittings to the hilt and to the black leather scabbard.

The Georgian Era

The period of British history known as the Georgian era spanned 1714–1830 and is named after its four monarchs, George I, George II, George III and George IV. It also included the nine-year Regency period presided over by the Prince Regent (later George IV). A time of huge social, political and economic change in Britain, it was an era that saw the agricultural revolution and the birth of the industrial age. Overseas, the battle for the American colonies was lost but the acquisition of foreign lands heralded an expanding empire.

The British throne had passed to the Hanoverian George I (1714–27) on the death of Queen Anne. His disinterest in ruling led to the appointment of the first Prime Minister. George II's reign (1727–60) saw territorial gains in America and Africa during the Seven Years War with France. Bouts of insanity rendered George III (1760–1820) unstable and in 1810 his son George became Prince Regent. A flamboyant figure famous for his extravagant lifestyle, his reign marked the start of social, legal and electoral reforms. His brother William IV succeeded him to the throne in 1830.

RIGHT A portrait of King George I painted by Sir Godfrey Kneller (1646–1723). The German-speaking king never learned English and preferred ministers to rule on his behalf.

Highland daggers and dirks

The distinctive Scottish dirk evolved from the early style "kidney dagger", which in turn had been developed from the "ballock knife". Two bulbous kidney-shaped lobes in the place where the quillons of the guard might exist were a characteristic feature. The knife was originally intended as an all-round survival and utility item, and some early examples had a serrated back edge. In later years, this feature became a symbolic series of indentations on the back of the blade, rather than being a serviceable sawtooth.

English or Scottish dudgeon-hilted dirk, 1603

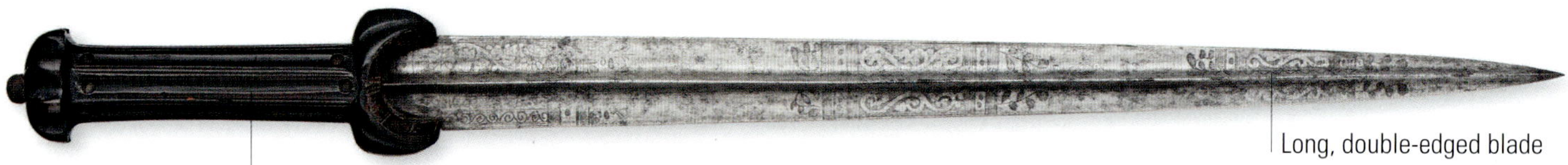

This is a fine example of an early English, or probably Scottish, dirk having the characteristic "kidney-shaped" lobes covering the shoulders of the blade. The hilt is made of dudgeon, or boxwood root, with the tang of the blade drawn through and peened over. The blade is long, with a strong central spine running the entire length.

DATE	1603
ORIGIN	ENGLISH/SCOTTISH
LENGTH	46cm (18.1in)

Scottish dirk, *c.*1740

This dirk, from the time of the Scottish Uprisings, has a long, single-edged blade, double-edged at the tip, and with a flat back and long fuller. The tang of the blade is drawn through the hilt and secured through a metal disc that protects the top of the wood grip. The grip itself is carved in a Celtic form of entwined design. The guard of the hilt forms an elliptical sleeve covering the shoulders of the blade.

DATE	*c.*1740
ORIGIN	SCOTTISH
LENGTH	41.5cm (16.3in)

Scottish dirk with ivory grip, mid-18th century

This fine dirk has an ivory, or walrus tusk, hilt comprised of three sections. The pommel portion features a protective metal plate on the top, through which the tang of the blade has been drawn and secured. The grip is carved with a curved fluting, and the guard comprises an oval sleeve fitting over the shoulders of the blade.

DATE	mid-18th century
ORIGIN	SCOTTISH
LENGTH	50.3cm (19.8in)

Scottish military dress dirk, 1879

DATE	1879
ORIGIN	SCOTTISH
LENGTH	37cm (14.6in)

This dirk is the military form as adopted by the Highland regiments from the mid-1800s and is intended for parade and dress wear. The carved wood grip mimics the design of woven straps secured in place with steel pins. The base of the grip features a metal ferrule with the words “GORDON HIGHLANDERS”.

Scottish full dress Highlander dirk, *c.*1900

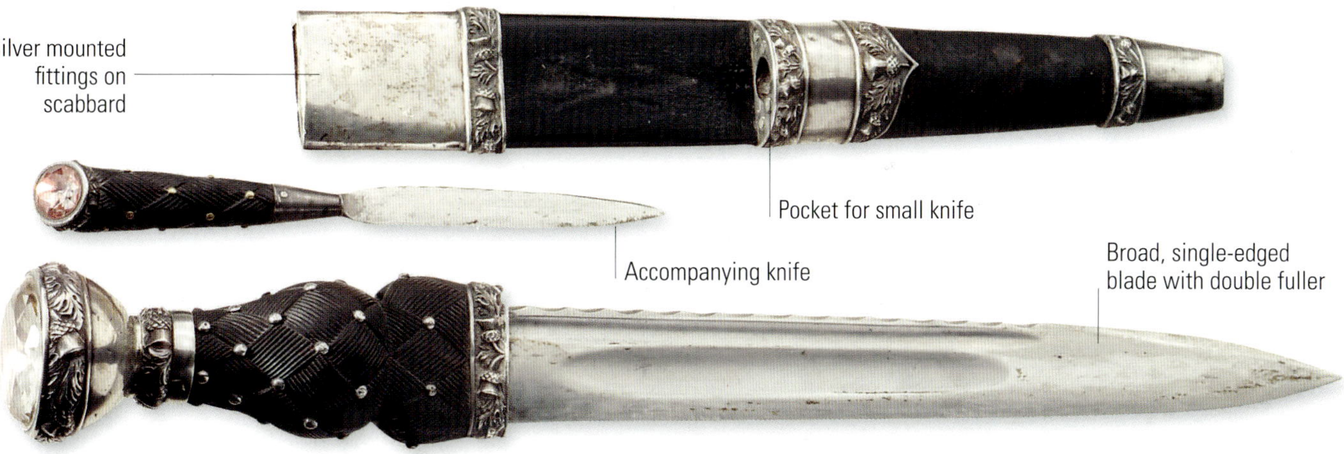

DATE	*c.*1900
ORIGIN	SCOTTISH
LENGTH	40cm (15.7in)

A full dress dirk with Cairngorm stones set in the pommel of both the dirk and the small knife. An interesting feature of the blade is the flat back with implied serration, and the two fullers – one thin and long close to the back, the other broader and shorter on the main body. Metal fittings are of finely chiselled silver.

Scottish Highland dirk with Cairngorm, *c.*1900

DATE	*c.*1900
ORIGIN	SCOTTISH
LENGTH	47cm (18.5in)

This is a full dress Highland dirk. The carved wood grip has silver mounts, the pommel mount featuring a faceted quartz stone (Cairngorm), and a basket-weave design to the grip with silver pins. The single-edged blade bears a scalloped design on the back (symbolic of a serrated edge). The scabbard pockets are for a knife and fork.

19th-century hunting and Bowie knives

The period from the end of the Napoleonic Wars in 1815 until the early 20th century heralded a boom period for European knife-makers. New markets were being established, primarily in the newly formed United States of America. In the aftermath of the American Civil War, economic development was fast expanding and the demand for commercial products was higher than could be supplied by the domestic economy. Europe took advantage of the new American market and exports of cutlery soared.

British knife by Wostenholm, Sheffield, mid-19th century

A deluxe-quality British knife, manufactured by the firm of George Wostenholm – at one time the second-largest knife manufacturer in Sheffield. The blade and tang are constructed of a single piece of steel, the tang area (hilt) being faced with stag-horn scales secured by three rivets. The middle rivet is covered by a metal escutcheon (which could be engraved with an owner's name or initials). The steel guard is decorated with a scalloped design and is polished and nickel-plated. The straight, double-edged blade features an elongated ricasso which tapers into a central spine.

DATE	mid-19th century
ORIGIN	BRITISH
LENGTH	34cm (13.4in)

American CSA fighting knife, 19th century

This roughly formed knife, emulating the famous "Bowie blade", is typical of the type of weapon produced by working smiths, particularly when utilizing broken implements. The heavy, broad flat blade would serve well as a type of machete and the improvised guard appears to be made of sheet metal. The grip scales are roughly made but functional, and this example is marked "CSA" (Confederate States of America).

DATE	19th century
ORIGIN	AMERICAN
LENGTH	32cm (12.6in)

British coffin-handled hunting knife, mid-19th century

DATE	mid-19th century
ORIGIN	BRITISH
LENGTH	unknown

The "coffin-handle" knife was so named because of its superficial resemblance in shape to wooden coffins of the time. The design of this knife was particularly popular in the mid-19th century, and the British concern of George Nixon, etched on the blade, was an established knife-maker in this style. The Nixon name later changed to Nixon & Winterbottom.

British Bowie knife by Rodgers, mid- to late 19th century

DATE	mid- to late 19th century
ORIGIN	BRITISH
LENGTH	31.1cm (12.2in)

A fine example of a Bowie knife by Joseph Rodgers of Sheffield. The typical blade broadens slightly towards the tip, where the flattened back edge forms a sharpened false edge. The body of the blade is sharpened for the entire length, except at the ricasso where it narrows and thickens. The simple straight hilt has stag-horn grip scales. The cross guard is steel and nickel-plated with ball-end finials. The leather scabbard has a belt loop, and nickel-plated fittings to the locket and the chape.

British Sheffield-made Bowie knife, mid-19th century

This knife pattern, made famous by the legend of James Bowie and the Alamo, is typical of the many pieces produced in Sheffield in the mid-19th century, and mainly intended for the American market. This specimen, manufactured by Edward Pierce and Co., is etched with the somewhat pious legend: "Never draw me without reason nor sheath me without honour".

DATE	mid-19th century
ORIGIN	BRITISH
LENGTH	32cm (12.6in)

British Raj personalized hunting knife, late 19th century

This is a well-made hunting knife, but seemingly of a type produced in British India during the days of the Raj. The tang of the blade has been curved to fit the stag-horn grip, and secured firmly with a large metal cap at the pommel. The blade bears the stamped legend "Bodrau Aurungabad", presumably the arsenal in India where it was manufactured. The side face of the grip has been smoothed, and then engraved with the name: "The Honble [Honourable] Cecil Cadogan".

DATE	late 19th century
ORIGIN	BRITISH RAJ
LENGTH	30cm (11.8in)

British Raj double-edged hunting knife, late 19th century

DATE	late 19th century
ORIGIN	BRITISH RAJ
LENGTH	32cm (12.6in)

A stylishly manufactured hunting knife, apparently made under British rule in India. A wide fuller runs for most of the length of the substantial double-edged blade. The grip is made of horn and has a sturdy steel cross guard. The steel cap forming the pommel has the tang drawn through and peened over.

German single-edged hunting knife, late 19th century

DATE	late 19th century
ORIGIN	GERMAN
LENGTH	31cm (12.2in)

A typically styled hunting knife by Friedrich Neeff and Son, Solingen. The underside of the grip is contoured for the fingers, the steel cross guard is nickel-plated and the single-edged blade is double-edged at the tip. It was a form made in similar style by many of the German arms companies in the Ruhr Valley.

British Bowie-bladed knife, late 19th century

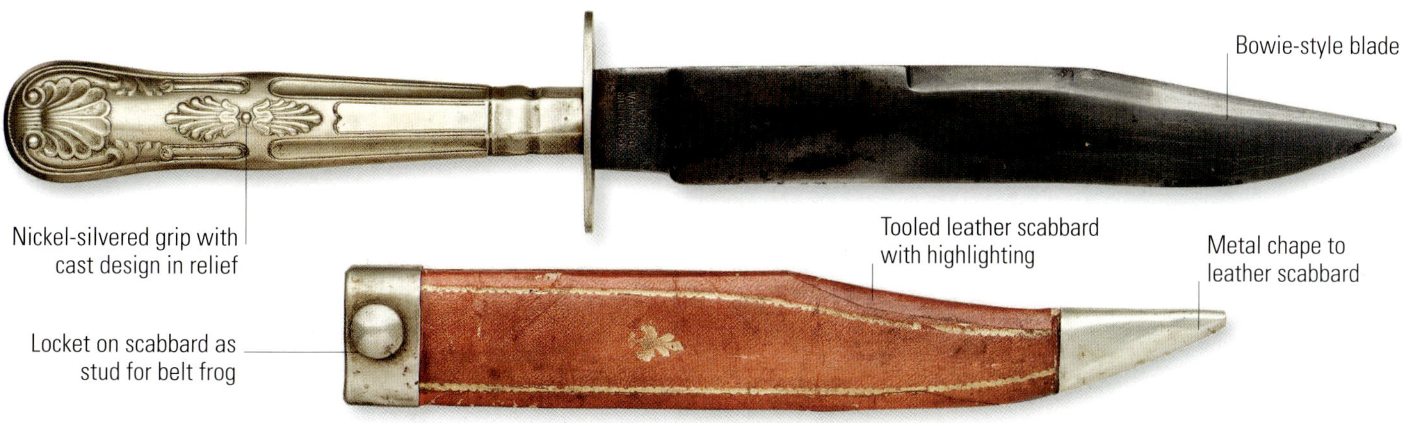

DATE	late 19th century
ORIGIN	BRITISH
LENGTH	32cm (12.6in)

This is an unnamed example of a Bowie-bladed knife – not a true Bowie in the sense of being a workable hunting knife, but an example of a weapon designed as an ornament. The hilt style, with the classical decoration in relief, is reminiscent of the cutlery styles popular during the closing years of the 19th century.

19th-century folding knives

Folding knives, or clasp-knives, were one of the great innovations of the 19th century, for now it was possible to carry a knife where the blade was safely contained out of harm's way when not in use. Folding knives were very popular among the northern Mediterranean countries where they were known as navaja knives, the word *navaja* being Spanish for "clasp-knife". The usefulness of this design ultimately manifested itself in its most prolific form – the "pocket knife" or "penknife" as we know it today.

Italian or Corsican navaja knife, 19th century

When opened, the blade of this 19th-century navaja knife is locked into position via a long spring on the back edge of the hilt. The clip of the spring can be released by pulling on a ring, which frees the blade for folding into the hilt. The above example has a metal hilt inset with silver inlay that features engraved decoration.

DATE	19th century
ORIGIN	ITALIAN/CORSICAN
LENGTH	35cm (13.8in)

Spanish (?) navaja folding knife, 19th century

This navaja, possibly of Spanish origin, is shown with the blade both open and closed, and demonstrates that even a folding knife can have a blade as long as the hilt. Some examples of this knife pattern had a sliding tube at the top end of the hilt, which could be passed over the tip of the blade to firmly lock it in the closed position.

DATE	19th century
ORIGIN	POSSIBLY SPANISH
LENGTH	35cm (13.8in)

Spanish navaja knife, late 19th century

This mass-produced navaja knife bears the stamped marking "Navajas de Toledo", the city of Toledo being the main producer (and exporter) for the Spanish cutlery industry. The hilt portions are made of steel with horn scales pinned into recesses. The exposed blade, when opened, is just under 25.4cm (10in) in length.

DATE	late 19th century
ORIGIN	SPANISH
LENGTH	54.5cm (21.5in)

German large folding knife, late 19th century

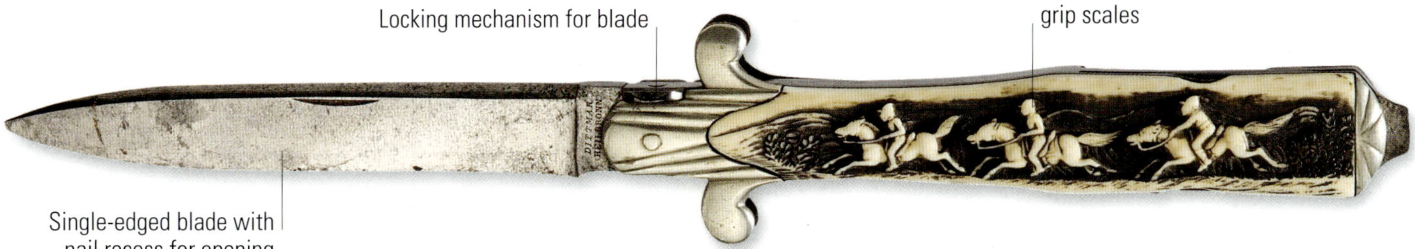

DATE	late 19th century
ORIGIN	GERMAN
LENGTH	25cm (9.8in)

Metal portions of the hilt on this folding knife are silver-coloured white metal, and the blade is marked "Dittmar, Heilbronn", a knife manufacturer founded in 1789. The grip scales are made of antler and inset with three figures of mounted horsemen in the chase. When opened, the blade is locked into position with a spring clip. When closed, the same spring tension keeps the blade folded into the hilt.

Corsican navajas, late 19th century

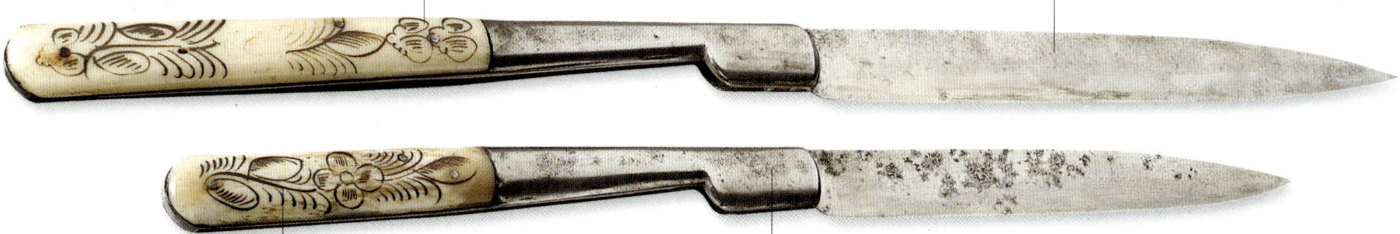

DATE	late 19th century
ORIGIN	CORSICAN
LENGTH	37.5cm (14.8in)

These Corsican folding knives from the latter half of the 19th century were intended to serve as practical cutlery knives that could be folded for transporting. Marketed under the trade name of "76 Veritable Bernard", the steel hilts were designed so that when the blade was opened the fingers were protected from the sharp edge by the bolster shape. The grip scales are made of polished horn.

Indian folding clasp-knife, 1875–1930

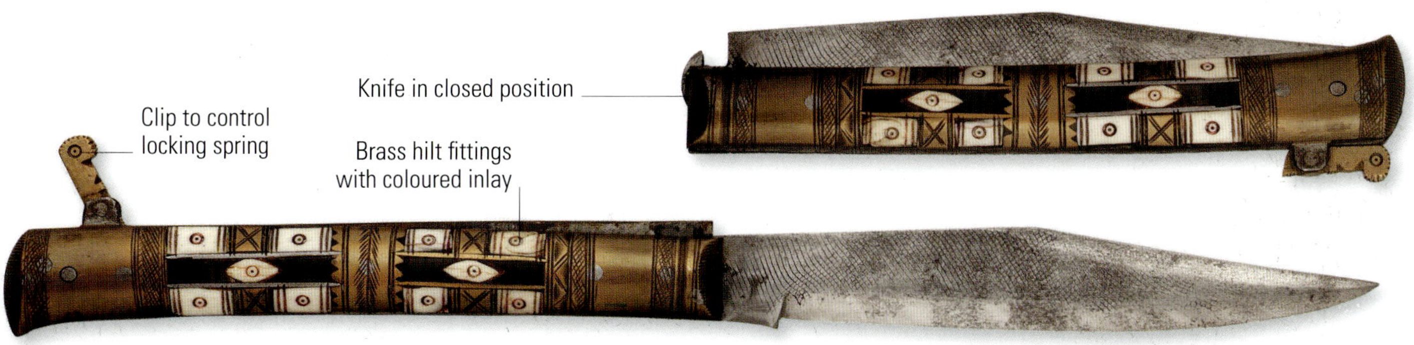

This clasp-knife was one of many patterns mass-produced for the export markets of the British Raj during the late 19th and early 20th centuries. The short steel blade, with clipped point, folds out and is locked into position by a spring and clip that form the back section of the hilt. At the top end of the hilt is a hinged lever, which when raised depresses the spring and unlocks the blade, in readiness for closing.

DATE	1875–1930
ORIGIN	INDIAN
LENGTH	25cm (9.8in)

19th-century civilian fighting knives

The knife in its various forms has always found favour as a weapon of offence by the criminal and been used for self-defence by the citizen. Unlike a firearm, especially in the era of muzzle loading, a knife did not require special skills for loading, cleaning and maintenance. A knife was cheaper than a firearm. There was no ammunition supply to worry about. Except in the case of the switchblade, there was no risk of mechanical malfunction at a crucial moment. And, for those who might benefit, it was silent in use.

British daggerstick, *c.*1800

Disguising a weapon always gave its user an advantage and the practice was not confined to the underworld. Most gentlemen in Georgian and Victorian England carried walking canes and were always at risk from attack on the badly lit streets. When not wearing a weapon, it made sense to carry one in the shaft of a cane.

DATE	*c.*1800
ORIGIN	BRITISH
LENGTH	25cm (9.8in)

African flywhisk dagger, 1870

The nature of this dagger suggests that it could have been used by a plantation owner, government official or military officer somewhere in the African colonies. Alternatively, it could have been used by a tribal chieftain, both to keep away flies and as a symbol of rank. In either case, one can imagine the need to have a weapon to hand.

DATE	1870
ORIGIN	AFRICAN
LENGTH	22cm (8.7in)

Spanish fighting knives, 19th century

DATE	19th century
ORIGIN	SPANISH
LENGTH	unknown

A pair of knives such as these wielded by someone practised in their use make him an opponent to be feared. The naturally ridged hilts give a very firm grip and their pointed tips, along with the very sharp blades with a second cutting edge towards the tip, enable them to inflict serious injury in a variety of ways.

Italian knife with ivory grip, 19th century

DATE	19th century
ORIGIN	ITALIAN
LENGTH	28cm (11in)

The broad pointed blade of this dagger is similar to many kitchen knives of today but it leaves little doubt as to what its real purpose was. The plain functionality of the blade is made up for by a silver inlaid ivory hilt elaborately carved to represent acanthus leaves and with a pommel in the form of a Turk's head.

American push dagger, *c.*1870

DATE	*c.*1870
ORIGIN	AMERICAN
LENGTH	12.7cm (5in)

Daggers such as this are usually associated with dishonest gamblers of the American West. It was easily concealed and could be produced surreptitiously. The handle was held in the fist, and the blade between the fingers, allowing a fatal punch to be delivered.

19th-century combination knives

The combination of a gun with a knife was not a new concept. Military guns with bayonets, or civilian pocket pistols with folding bayonets, were commonplace to give an added degree of protection. With the advances in gun technology during the 19th century, and the development of the self-contained cartridge, a new type of weapon with multi-shot capability evolved alongside traditional knife pistols.

French knife pistol, 19th century

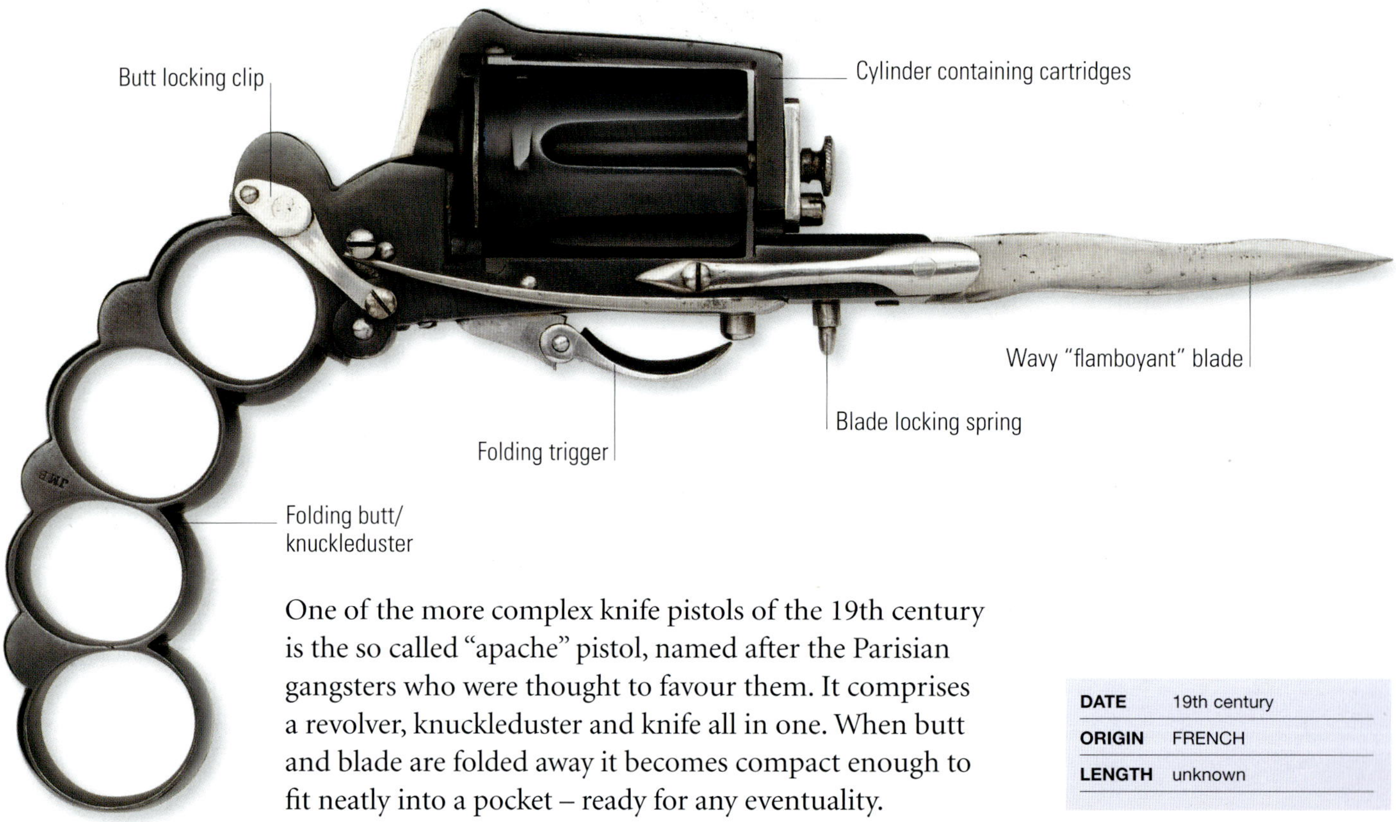

One of the more complex knife pistols of the 19th century is the so called "apache" pistol, named after the Parisian gangsters who were thought to favour them. It comprises a revolver, knuckleduster and knife all in one. When butt and blade are folded away it becomes compact enough to fit neatly into a pocket – ready for any eventuality.

DATE	19th century
ORIGIN	FRENCH
LENGTH	unknown

Belgian pin-fire dirk pistol, *c.*1870

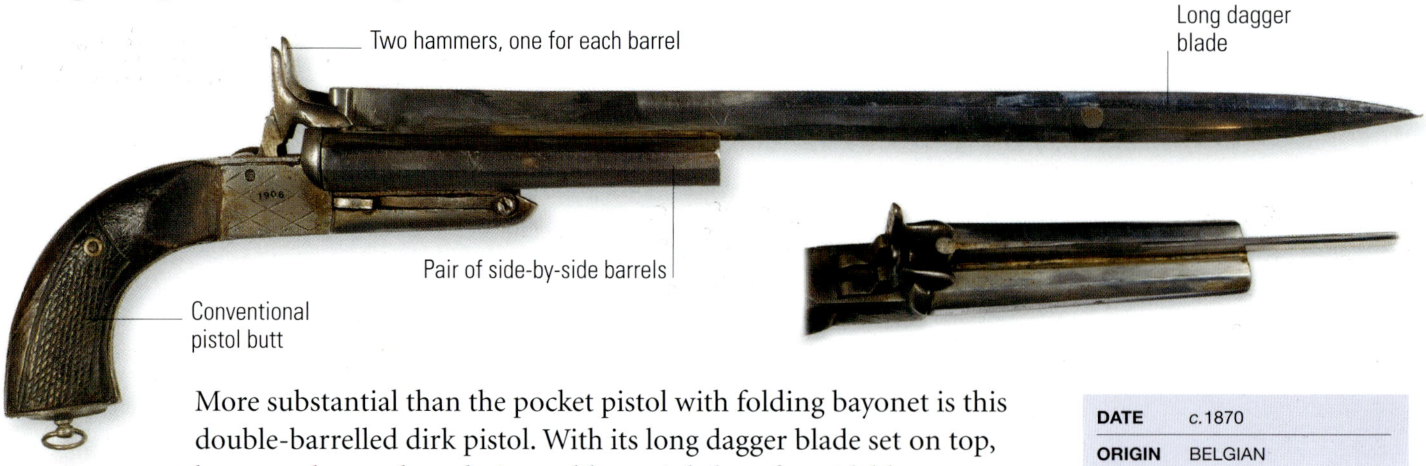

More substantial than the pocket pistol with folding bayonet is this double-barrelled dirk pistol. With its long dagger blade set on top, between the two barrels, it would certainly be a formidable weapon but, for a civilian, difficult to conceal and carry safely.

DATE	*c.*1870
ORIGIN	BELGIAN
LENGTH	34cm (13.4in)

Belgian knife pistol, *c.*1870

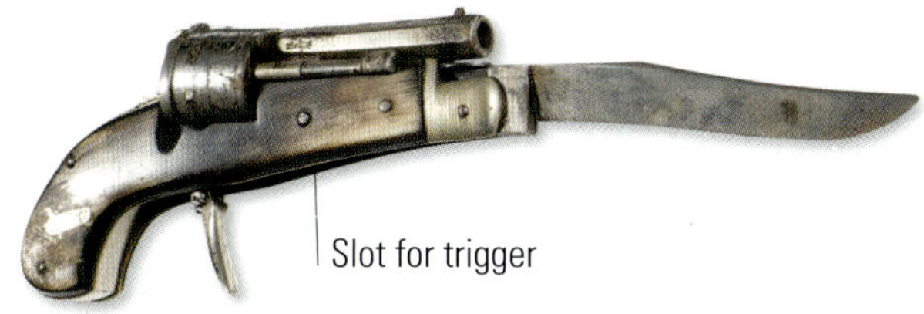

DATE	*c.*1870
ORIGIN	BELGIAN
LENGTH	unknown

This combination weapon features a six-shot double-action cartridge revolver built in the form of a large pocket knife. Weapons like this do not offer a comfortable or secure grip for use as a revolver and are much less common than their single-shot counterparts. But perhaps it was sufficient to scare a victim or would-be attacker.

European knife-pistol-club, late 19th century

DATE	late 19th century
ORIGIN	EUROPEAN
LENGTH	unknown

This multipurpose European weapon is almost medieval in concept. As a club, with spiked steel studs, it would be lethal in itself, but add a stiletto-like blade and a single-shot pistol and it becomes a formidable close-quarter weapon for either offence or defence. Similar devices without the pistol component were resurrected in the trenches of World War I.

The "apaches" of Paris

Every major city had its underworld members, whether engaged in petty theft or major crime. Victorian London had its "Bill Sykes" characters as portrayed by Dickens, the early 1900s United States had its immigrant Mafia and Paris was terrorised by gangs of "apaches", many wielding their unique revolver-knuckleduster-knives. Often lampooned for what is perceived as their characteristic dress of hooped shirt and black beret, these gangsters were notorious for their ruthlessness.

RIGHT The "apaches" were famous for their disregard of law and order as this illustration from a 1907 edition of *Le Petit Journal* clearly shows.

18th- and 19th-century socket bayonets

The problem with plug bayonets was that they literally plugged the muzzle, rendering the gun incapable of being fired. Nor were they really secure; a good wrench could pull them out of the muzzle, leaving the soldier at a disadvantage. The breakthrough was the socket bayonet – a blade fitted to a tube that slid over the muzzle and could be secured in place, allowing the gun to be fired.

British socket bayonet, *c.*1690

DATE	*c.*1690
ORIGIN	BRITISH
LENGTH	unknown

This unusual bayonet is an early example of a socket bayonet. With its elaborate design and decoration, however, it was more likely a sporting accessory than a battlefield weapon. A spring catch allows the pommel cap to be removed, opening up the tubular hilt and enabling it to fit on the muzzle of a gun.

British socket bayonet, *c.*1700

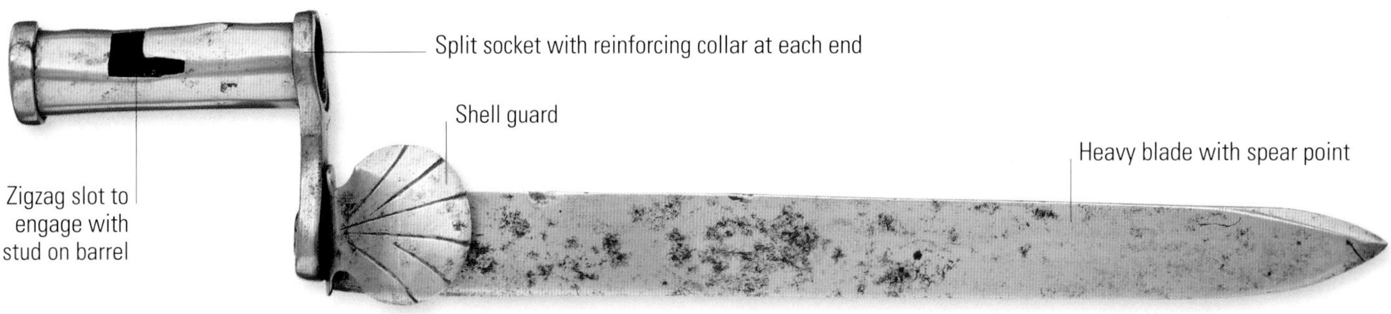

At the time the socket bayonet was introduced, manufacture of gun barrels was not a precise art. To overcome this, sockets had reinforcing collars at each end and were split along their length so their diameters could be adjusted to fit the musket. This socket bayonet with its dagger-like shell guard is typical of its period.

DATE	*c.*1700
ORIGIN	BRITISH
LENGTH	44.3cm (17.4in)

British socket bayonet, East India Company, 1797

With a plain zigzag slot, the bayonet was not locked in place, and could easily be removed accidentally during use by pulling and twisting. The East India Company introduced this simple spring, possibly the design of Ezekiel Baker, which latches against the fixing stud once the bayonet is in place.

DATE	1797
ORIGIN	BRITISH
LENGTH	51.5cm (20.3in)

British bayonet for India Pattern musket, 1800

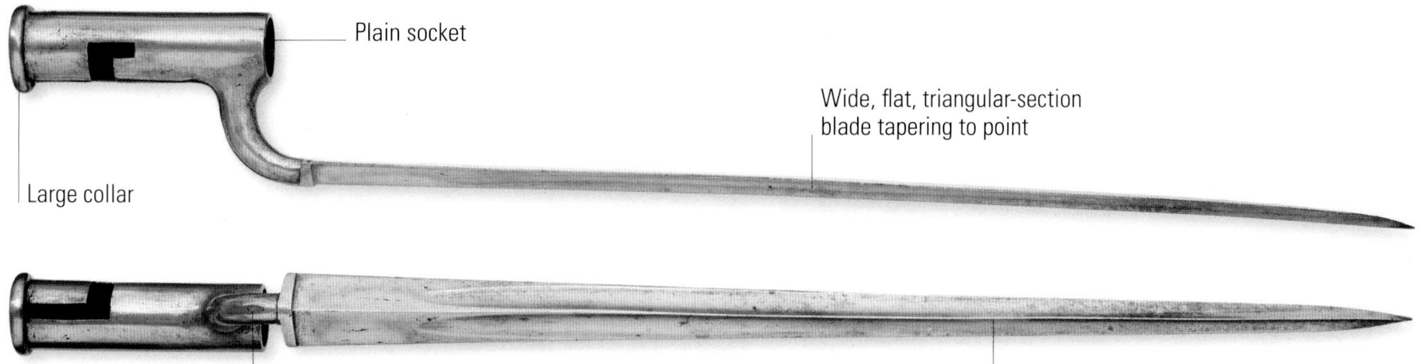

DATE	1800
ORIGIN	BRITISH
LENGTH	53.3cm (21in)

The introduction of a new musket in the late 18th century, based on those used by the army in India, brought with it a new bayonet. The bayonet differed little from its predecessors except in having a thicker collar on the socket. This bayonet and musket were widely used throughout the Napoleonic Period.

British bayonet with Gill's experimental locking system, *c.*1800

DATE	*c.*1800
ORIGIN	BRITISH
LENGTH	50.5cm (19.9in)

This standard service bayonet was modified by having a spring-loaded lever fitted to the socket collar. The nose of the lever is held in place behind the front sight when the bayonet is fitted, preventing its accidental removal. The old zigzag slot has been filled and a new one cut, bringing the bayonet below the barrel.

British bayonet for sea service musket, *c.*1805

This bayonet is unusual in having a flat blade as opposed to the more usual flattened, triangular section. Although dated to the Napoleonic Period, the weapon may derive from the 18th century. Surviving records show that at that time the only bayonets that could fit this description were a number commissioned for naval use.

DATE	*c.*1805
ORIGIN	BRITISH
LENGTH	54cm (21.2in)

German or Swedish (?) bayonet, Model 1811, *c.*1811

This bayonet is of unusual proportions and uncertain origin, though it closely resembles the Model 1811 for the Swedish infantry musket. The long, slender neck connects to an unusually long blade, offset much further from the socket than most other bayonets of this type. Its most interesting feature is the beautifully made locking ring, hinged at the bottom to facilitate assembly and replacement, and which is guided in its movement by a pin riding in a slot.

DATE	*c.*1811
ORIGIN	GERMAN/SWEDISH (?)
LENGTH	70cm (27.6in)

French bayonet, Model 1822, 1822

This bayonet is based on the model of 1777, introduced under General Gribeuval (1715–1789) as part of his programme to standardize French military equipment. It was the first to employ a locking ring placed in the centre of the socket to secure the bayonet. The Model 1822 bayonet differs only in being slightly longer and by having a slightly different pattern of locking ring which provides a more secure attachment.

DATE	1822
ORIGIN	FRENCH
LENGTH	53.1cm (21in)

Austrian bayonet, System Augustin rifle, Model 1842, 1842

DATE	1842
ORIGIN	AUSTRIAN
LENGTH	56.5cm (22.2in)

This is a most unusual bayonet. The socket looks unfinished, having no slot, since the bayonet does not have to engage with the foresight of the musket or a stud beneath the muzzle. Instead, it has a collar thickened at one point in which a notch is cut. When the bayonet is fitted, it is slid over the muzzle to the forend, from which a spring clip projects, and then it is rotated. The thickened collar acts as a cam, lifting the spring catch which falls into the notch and secures the bayonet.

British bayonet for sappers and miners, 1st Pattern 1842, 1842

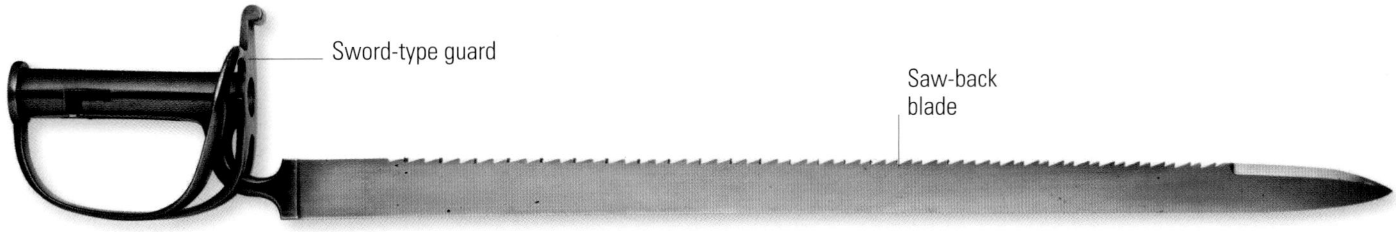

DATE	1842
ORIGIN	BRITISH
LENGTH	77.9cm (30.7in)

As can be seen, this bayonet has a very elaborate hilt, similar in style to many swords of the period, and a tubular socket which acted as the grip. It is equipped with a heavy blade, having a double row of saw-teeth along its wide back edge. This feature was intended to be used for cutting wood, though if used on anything other than shrubbery it must have been hard and exhausting work. These weapons never actually went into production and this one, probably the sample pattern, is thought to be the only one ever made.

British bayonet for sappers and miners carbine, 2nd Pattern 1842, 1842

DATE	1842
ORIGIN	BRITISH
LENGTH	71.7cm (28.2in)

This is a much simpler affair than its predecessor but still possesses a long, heavy blade. The idea of having it serve also as a saw had been abandoned due, no doubt, to complaints from those who were expected to use it. It has a projecting step on the collar to allow it to be secured by a spring beneath the barrel known as the Lovell's Spring Catch. The small notch that can be seen on the collar was to give a clear view of the front sight.

British bayonet for Enfield rifle, Pattern 1853, 1853

A good wrought-iron socket fitted with a locking ring and a narrow, sharply pointed, triangular-section blade of the best Sheffield steel gave the Pattern 1853 bayonet a superb quality and singularity of purpose. It was by far the finest bayonet ever to enter British military service up to that time.

DATE	1853
ORIGIN	BRITISH
LENGTH	51.5cm (20.3in)

American bayonet, Winchester Model 1873 musket, 1873

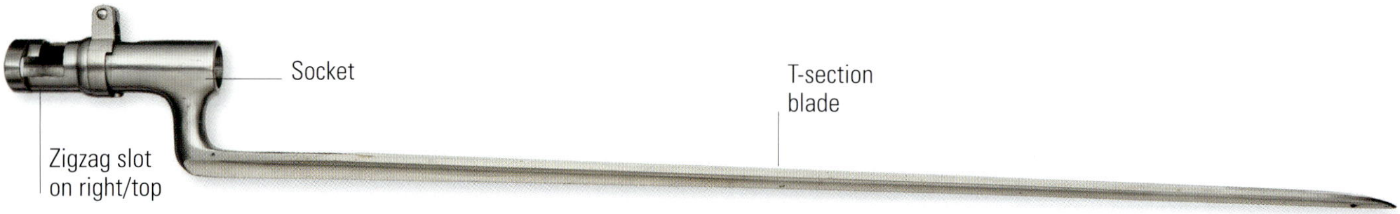

Unusually, these bayonets lack any markings. However, they are distinguished by being arranged to sit beneath the barrel when fitted, are finished bright all over, and have a long taper between the blade and the neck. They were not used in the US armed forces but were supplied with muskets to many South American countries.

DATE	1873
ORIGIN	AMERICAN
LENGTH	54.5cm (21.5in)

American bayonet, Springfield Model 1873 rifle, 1873

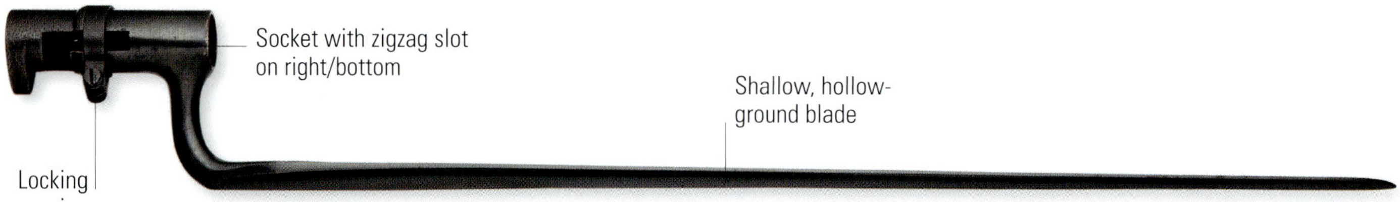

The bayonet for the new Model 1873 Springfield "trapdoor" rifle so closely resembled the models of 1855 and 1870 that these were often converted by having the sockets resized to fit the smaller-diameter barrel of the 1873 rifle. It was the first American bayonet to be blued all over.

DATE	1873
ORIGIN	AMERICAN
LENGTH	54.1cm (21.3in)

British bayonet for Martini-Henry, Pattern 1876, 1876

The new Pattern 1876 bayonet was modelled on the Pattern 1853 but with some adjustments. The smaller-diameter barrel of the Martini-Henry rifle required a smaller diameter socket and, to compensate for it being a shorter rifle, the blade was made longer to maintain the "reach".

DATE	1876
ORIGIN	BRITISH
LENGTH	65.8cm (25.9in)

Dutch bayonet, Beaumont-Vitali rifle, Model 1871/88, 1888

DATE	1888
ORIGIN	DUTCH
LENGTH	57.1cm (22.5in)

When the 1871 Beaumont rifle first entered into military service, the bayonet designed for it included a complex locking ring attachment with two adjusting screws. With the transition in 1888 from the single-shot rifle to magazine loading on the Vitali principle, the locking ring design was amended to a more conventional form with a single adjusting screw.

The 54th Massachusetts Volunteer Infantry

The Pattern 1853 Enfield rifle and bayonet was created for the British soldier using technology largely developed and perfected in the United States. Ironically, it played a significant role in the bloodiest war of the mid-19th century, the American Civil War. This was perhaps the first and last conflict in which this fine weapon was used in such large numbers – over 1 million were supplied in roughly equal numbers to both sides by British arms manufacturers. The 54th Massachusetts Volunteer Infantry was one of the more famous regiments to carry the rifles. It was the first military unit composed of African-American soldiers and it led one of the most legendary exploits of the Civil War, the assault on Fort Wagner. The heroism of one soldier, Sergeant William Carney, led to his becoming the first African-American to be awarded the Congressional Medal of Honor.

BELOW This lithograph by Currier & Ives, *The Gallant Charge of the 54th Regiment from Massachusetts*, depicts the assault by Union African-American troops on the Confederate-held Fort Wagner.

19th-century sword bayonets

The 19th century was a time of great innovation. It witnessed a complete transformation of the firearm, from the single-shot, muzzle-loading flintlock at its outset to the self-contained metallic cartridge and magazine-loading multi-shot rifles at its end. This innovation and diversity was not limited to the firearm itself but also found expression in a great diversity of bayonet designs.

British volunteer sword bayonet, *c.*1810

The style of hilt on this bayonet is similar to the 1796 Pattern light cavalry sword, and was perhaps modelled on that since these bayonets were for use by mounted volunteers. They were not official issue and several varieties exist, some having brass hilts. They were generally used with rifles similar to the Baker rifle.

DATE	*c.*1810
ORIGIN	BRITISH
LENGTH	77.7cm (30.6in)

British Baker rifle sword bayonet, *c.*1815

The S-shaped cross guard differs from any of the official military-issue varieties and suggests this might be a prototype or experimental bayonet, or even one for volunteers. Its blade with a fuller that runs to the tip is also an unusual feature since most Baker sword bayonets had plain blades.

DATE	*c.*1815
ORIGIN	BRITISH
LENGTH	75.2cm (29.6in)

British Baker rifle "hand" bayonet, *c.*1825

In 1825 the Rifle Brigade complained their "hand" or knife bayonets were too heavy. Their colonel submitted an alternative with a buckhorn handle which was much lighter. It was rejected by the Ordnance Board as being too fragile, and this one, with a smaller brass hilt, may have been created in its place for trial.

DATE	*c.*1825
ORIGIN	BRITISH
LENGTH	54.4cm (21.4in)

British Baker rifle sword bayonet with saw-back, *c.*1850

In 1815 a sawback bayonet for the Baker rifle was suggested but seems not to have been developed. The one illustrated is probably a Second Pattern sword bayonet from around 1805 modified at a much later date, since it carries the royal monogram of Queen Victoria stamped on the pommel.

DATE	*c.*1850
ORIGIN	BRITISH
LENGTH	75.2cm (29.6in)

French Sabre-lance du Mosqueton des Cent Gardes, 1854

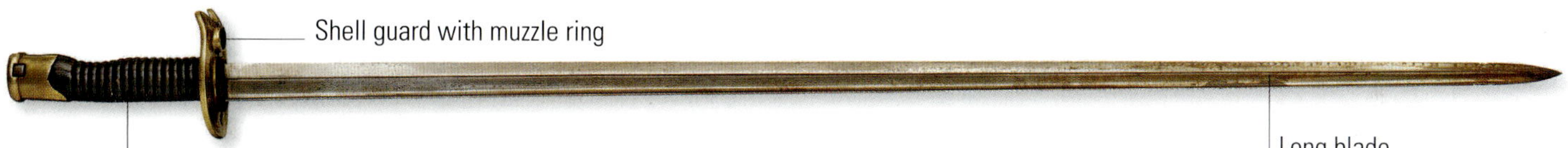

DATE	1854
ORIGIN	FRENCH
LENGTH	115.5cm (45.5in)

With a blade length of more than a metre, this Model 1854 bayonet is one of the longest ever produced. It is also one of the rarest of French bayonets. Only a few hundred were made for the emperor Napoleon III's personal guard, and most were shortened after the presenting of arms one evening at the imperial residence, the Château de Compiègne, when they pierced the ceiling!

British Lancaster bayonet, Pattern 1855, 1855

DATE	1855
ORIGIN	BRITISH
LENGTH	73.2cm (28.8in)

In 1855 the Corps of Sappers and Miners adopted Lancaster's oval-bored carbine and with it this very distinctive bayonet. Unlike most other British bayonets it has a brass pommel and cross guard, reminiscent of continental practice, and a so-called "pipe-back" blade. In this type of blade, the rounded back extends as a rib across the centre of the tip, creating a second or "false" edge. The bayonet was later adopted by the Royal Army Medical Corps as a sidearm.

American bayonet for Harper's Ferry rifle, 1855

This new service rifle with a calibre of .58 inches closely followed the British .577 inch Enfield Pattern 1853 rifle. The bayonet, representative of the early stages in the adoption of sword bayonets by the US military, also exhibits European influence with a brass hilt. It has a curious upturn at the point of the blade, rarely seen on bayonets of any nationality.

DATE	1855
ORIGIN	AMERICAN
LENGTH	67.3cm (26.5in)

British bayonet for Jacob's double-barrelled rifle, *c.*1859

These bayonets were not official British military issue. They were designed by John Jacob for use with his double-barrelled rifle by the Indian Scinde Irregular Horse, which he commanded. Both rifle and bayonet were made by Swinburn and Son of Birmingham. With twin fullers and spear point, the blade resembles Scottish broadswords, and it has a heavy-gauge "half-basket" type of guard, making it weigh more. It would have made an ungainly weapon when fitted to the heavy rifle.

DATE	*c.*1859
ORIGIN	BRITISH
LENGTH	90.7cm (35.7in)

British naval cutlass bayonet, 1859

This is the second type of cutlass bayonet designed for use with the Pattern 1858 Naval Rifle. The first bayonet had ribbed wooden grips whereas this model has the more conventional checkered or "knurled" leather variety. It may have been successful as a cutlass but, as with the Jacob bayonet, when fitted to a rifle it must also have created a very unwieldy combination.

DATE	1859
ORIGIN	BRITISH
LENGTH	81.9cm (32.3in)

American sword bayonet for Navy rifle, Model 1861, 1861

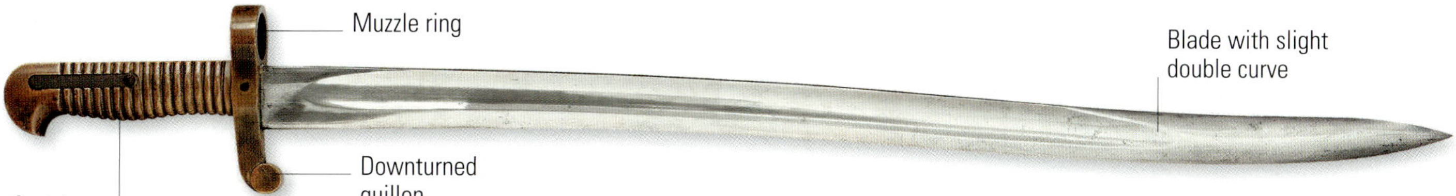

DATE	1861
ORIGIN	AMERICAN
LENGTH	71cm (28in)

This bayonet was designed by Admiral John A. Dahlgren for use with the Plymouth/Whitneyville naval rifle. It was manufactured by the Collins Company of Hartford, Connecticut, who had a reputation for the great variety and high quality of axes they produced. With its heavy muzzle ring and cross guard with a slightly downturned quillon, it closely resembles the bayonets for the Spencer, Merrill and Zouave rifles. With their ribbed cast-brass grips and varying degrees of double curvature in their blades, these all reflect the trend in Europe, especially France, for "yataghan"-bladed sword bayonets. This bayonet was equipped with a heavy black leather scabbard fitted with a brass "top locket", or mouthpiece, a stud for securing it in a carrying "frog" and a brass tip or "chape".

French sword bayonet for Chassepot rifle, 1866

DATE	1866
ORIGIN	FRENCH
LENGTH	70cm (27.6in)

Following the example set by Prussia in adopting Nicholas von Dreyse's new breech-loading needle-fire rifle with self-contained cartridge, the French responded by developing what was to become known as the Chassepot rifle. This rifle brought with it one of the world's most familiar bayonets. Their decorative hilts with cast-brass grips and polished-steel cross guard with a large hook quillon, combined with a stylish "yataghan" blade, heralded a new fashion in bayonet design which was copied almost worldwide. Add to that the allure of the name of the maker and date of manufacture engraved in script on the wide back edge of the blade, and it is easy to understand why they have adorned innumerable walls. But their true value lies in their representing the beginnings of a new era in firearms evolution.

British naval cutlass bayonet, 1872

The Pattern 1872 was the third and final cutlass bayonet to be put into service, differing from its predecessors with its narrower, straight blade. This certainly made it lighter but still created an unwieldy combination when fitted to a rifle. Few were newly manufactured, most being converted from the Pattern 1859 cutlass bayonet.

DATE	1872
ORIGIN	BRITISH
LENGTH	79.5cm (31.3in)

British Elcho bayonet for Martini-Henry, *c.*1872

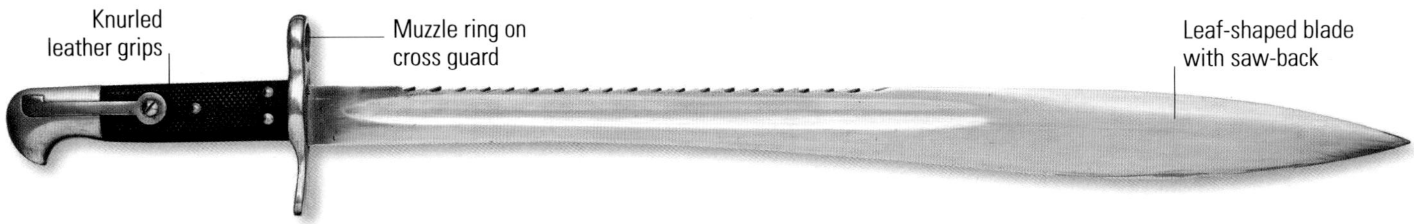

One of the most distinctive and unusual of British bayonets, designed by Lord Elcho, this seems to place greater emphasis on its effectiveness as a tool for sawing wood or hacking shrubbery than as a weapon. The leaf or spear shape of the blade perhaps inspired the German bayonet at the end of the century. This weapon was only partially successful as a tool and its function as a bayonet was questionable. Few were made and issued, and more conventional bayonets were used instead.

DATE	*c.*1872
ORIGIN	BRITISH
LENGTH	64.1cm (25.2in)

Austrian sword bayonet, Werndl rifle, 1873

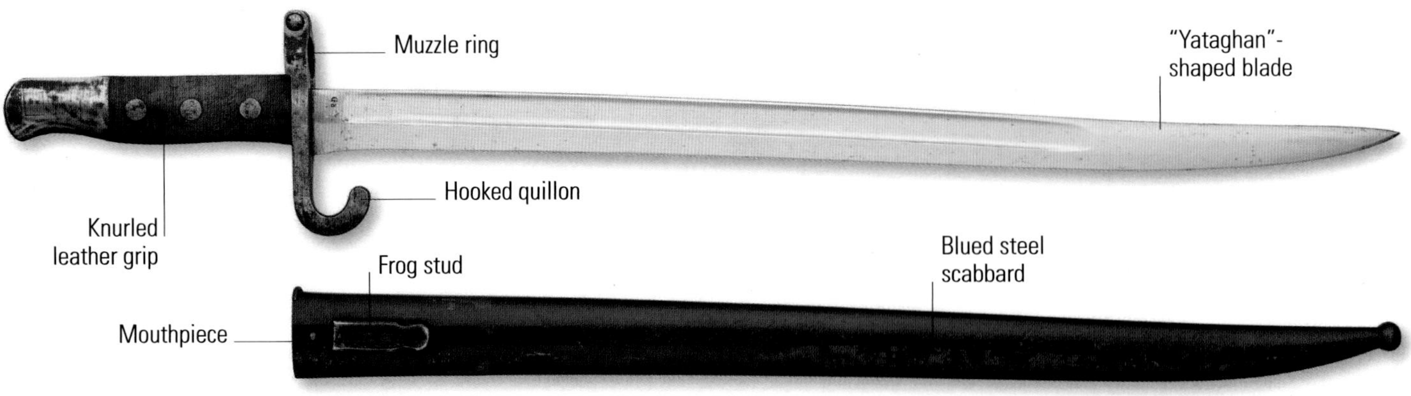

This bayonet was used with various models of the Austrian Werndl military rifle and was basically a modification of its forerunner, the model of 1867. It used a coil spring in place of the leaf spring to operate the locking catch. Like the Chassepot of 1866, it has a distinctive "yataghan"-shaped blade.

DATE	1873
ORIGIN	AUSTRIAN
LENGTH	60.6cm (23.9in)

French bayonet, Gras rifle, Model 1874, 1874

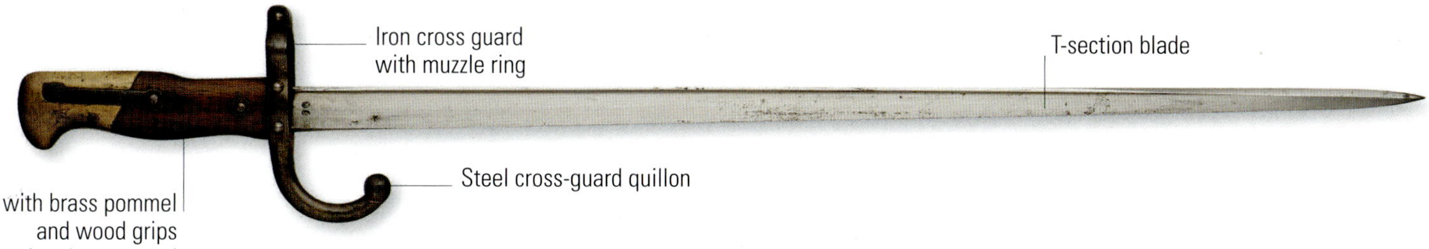

DATE	1874
ORIGIN	FRENCH
LENGTH	64.3cm (25.3in)

This bayonet marks the French departure from sword bayonets and the creation of the "epee" bayonet. Its most important feature is the T-section blade with its needle-like point, similar to the fencing epee. Its design makes it strong and light, an ideal combination for a bayonet. It was copied in the last of the British cavalry swords, the 1908 Pattern, and was the forerunner of the later Lebel bayonet.

British artillery sword bayonet, 1879 Pattern, 1879

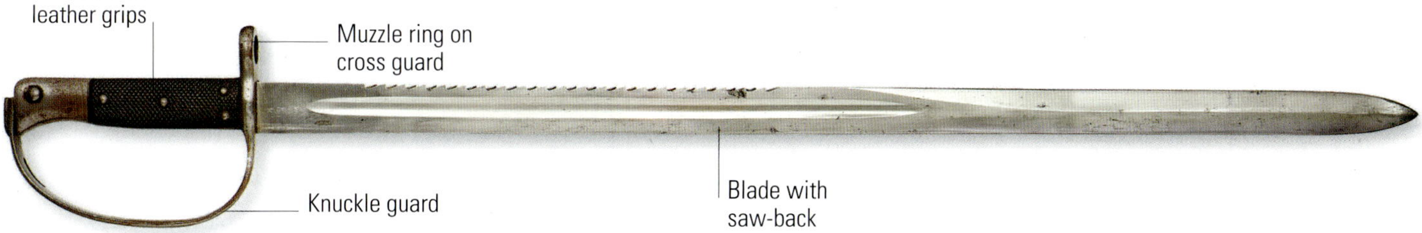

DATE	1879
ORIGIN	BRITISH
LENGTH	75.6cm (29.8in)

This was produced as one alternative to the Elcho bayonet. In view of its length and the nature of its hilt, the term "sword bayonet" is very apt. The knuckle guard made it easier to grip for use as a saw, and its longer blade made it more effective as a sword or as a bayonet when fitted to the short artillery carbine. However, its double row of teeth made its use as a saw very hard work, and like many dual-purpose bayonets it was never completely successful in either role.

Portuguese sword bayonet, Guedes rifle, Model 1885, 1885

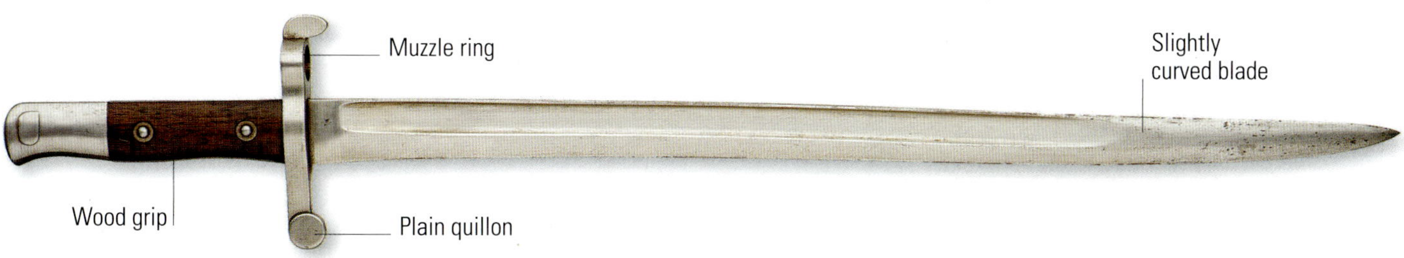

DATE	1885
ORIGIN	PORTUGUESE
LENGTH	60.8cm (23.9in)

The "yataghan" shape of this bayonet is less pronounced, as the trend was now towards straight blades. Although for Portuguese use, these bayonets and their rifles were manufactured at the Steyr factory in Austria. The bayonets are usually marked with the place and date of manufacture on the back edge. The decorative hilt of an earlier era has been replaced with a more functional but finely engineered hilt.

British Lee-Metford bayonet Mk I, 1888

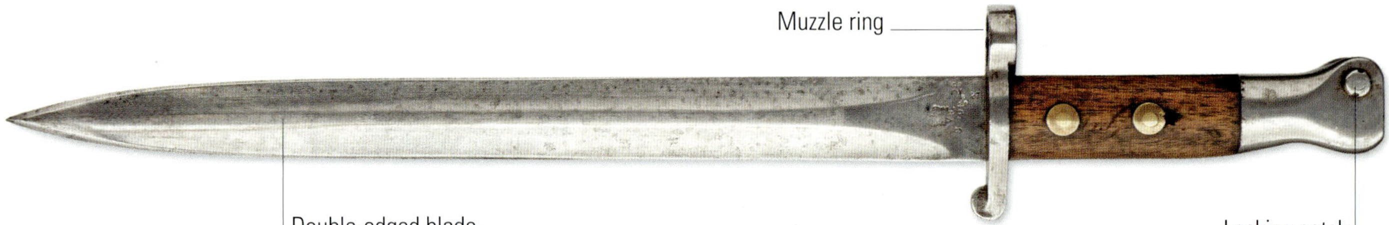

This Model 1888 was the second pattern bayonet adopted for the Lee-Metford rifle, the first having the grips secured by three rivets. This rifle was fitted with a cleaning rod which projected from the bayonet mounting stud beneath the barrel. As a consequence, the hilt had a cavity within it to accommodate the end of the rod, and a drain hole at the bottom of this cavity was provided, adjacent to the upper grip rivet.

DATE	1888
ORIGIN	BRITISH
LENGTH	42.2cm (16.6in)

British sword bayonet Mk IV, 1887 Pattern, 1891

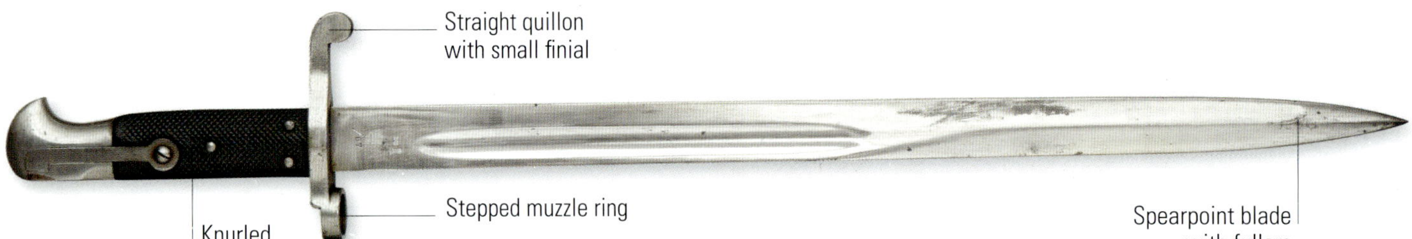

The last of a series of bayonets developed for the Martini-Henry rifle, it evolved from experimental bayonets developed in 1886 for a proposed smaller-bore Martini-Henry rifle. This rifle was abandoned following the adoption of the Lee series of small-bore, bolt-action, magazine-loading rifles in 1888. The days of the Martini as a mainline weapon were numbered, but the experimental rifles were modified to standard Martini calibre, these 1887 Pattern bayonets being adapted to fit. As secondary arms, many of these rifles and bayonets were issued to the Navy.

DATE	1891
ORIGIN	BRITISH
LENGTH	60.3cm (23.7in)

German Mauser bayonet, 1884–1945

This bayonet, the third model, became the prototype for most bayonets used on Gewehr 98 and Kar 98 rifles until 1945. While following the same basic design, numerous variations occur. This example has plain wood grips secured by screw bolts, and on the back of the hilt a flash guard to protect the wood grips.

DATE	1884–1945
ORIGIN	GERMAN
LENGTH	39cm (15.4in)

19th-century knife bayonets

Many soldiers throughout the 19th century carried their own personal knives for use in a difficult situation, since none were officially issued. But the idea of combining the function of a bayonet with that of a knife is always a compromise. To make it handy enough to be used as a knife means the weapon has to be short. By making it short enough, the important element of "reach" is lost, which puts a soldier at a disadvantage when confronted by an enemy with a long bayonet fixed to his rifle.

Japanese bayonet for Murata rifle, Type 20, 1887

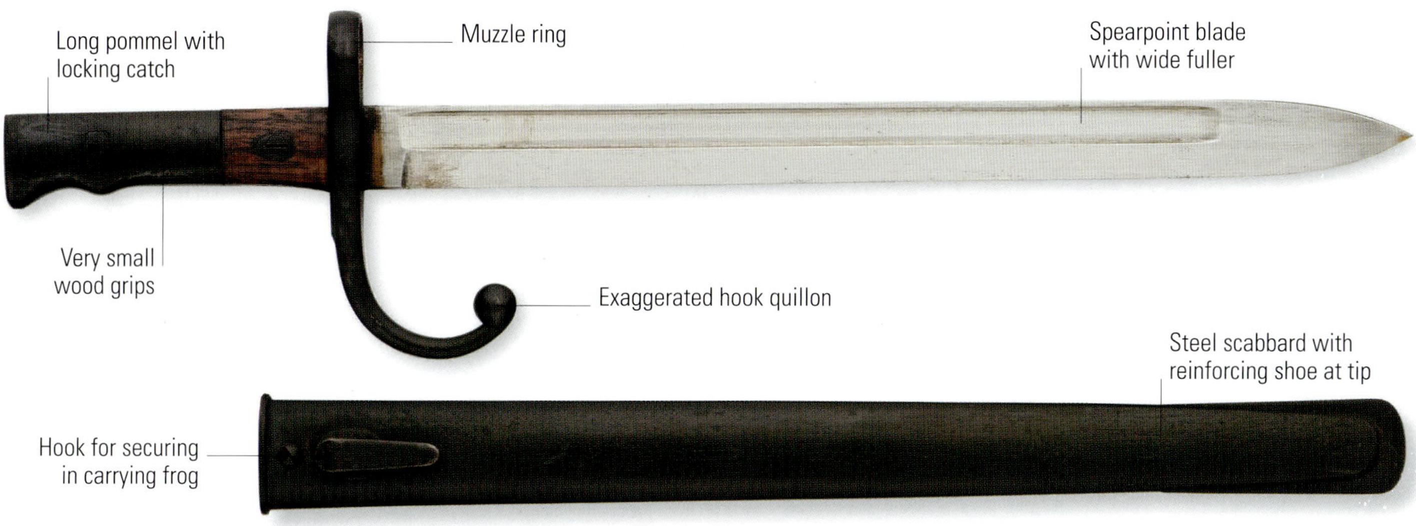

DATE	1887
ORIGIN	JAPANESE
LENGTH	37cm (14.6in)

This bayonet was developed for the Murata Type 20 rifle and carbine, although it could also fit the Type 22 rifle. The whole hilt is very short, barely 90mm (3.5in), making it difficult to grasp despite the supposed shaping to fit the fingers, and giving the impression of an overly large hooked quillon.

Dutch Mannlicher carbine bayonet, 2nd type, 1895

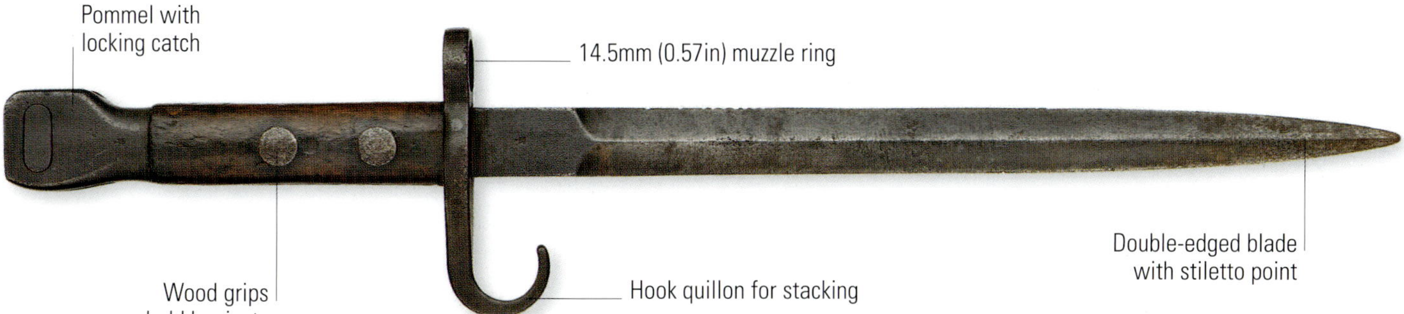

DATE	1895
ORIGIN	DUTCH
LENGTH	37.5cm (14.8in)

This bayonet was produced in two models for the Mannlicher cavalry carbine. The first had a short straight quillon, while this one, the Model 1895, has the stacking hook. Without the hook it is loosely reminiscent of the British 1888 Patterns. Its size and slender double-edged blade made it a useful fighting knife.

Presentation knives and daggers

Compared with the presentation of swords as marks of military achievement or personal respect, the presentation of knives of any form is a far more unusual occurrence. In the Third Reich in Germany, however, the reverse was true, and presentation of daggers based around the standard service patterns was widely practised. Even rarer are those knives presented to civilians to mark various occasions.

German presentation hunting hanger, mid-19th century

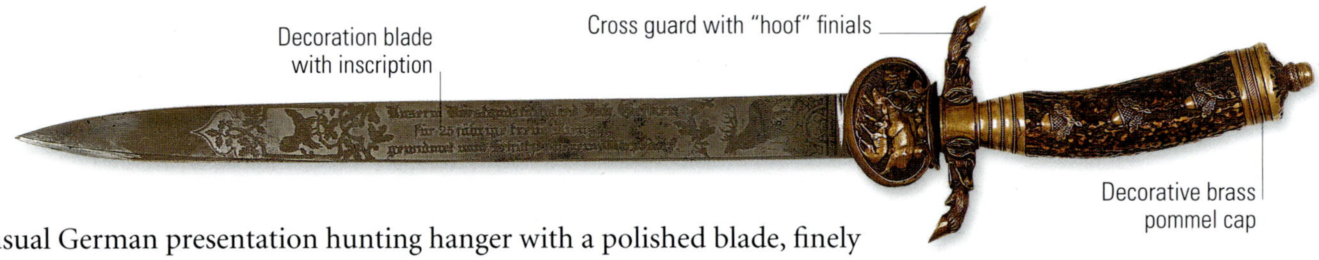

An unusual German presentation hunting hanger with a polished blade, finely frost-etched to depict huntsman, deer and game birds. It also carries the inscription: *Urerm Vorstandsmitglied Jon, Gefken fur 25 Jahrige treue Dienste gewidmetvon Schutzen-verein worpedorf*, which means it was presented to a founder or first director, Jon Gefken, of the Worpedorf Rifle Club, for 25 years' faithful service.

DATE	mid-19th century
ORIGIN	GERMAN
LENGTH	35.6cm (14in)

South African presentation Bowie knife, 1885

The blade of this knife by H. Herder, Solingen has the inscription: *N. J. Smit Vice President van de B.-A. Republiek*. Smit became Vice President of the Transvaal Republic in 1886, having led the Boer commandos to victory at Majuba Hill in the First Boer War (1880–81).

DATE	1885
ORIGIN	SOUTH AFRICAN
LENGTH	34cm (13.4in)

German Imperial dagger, 1900

DATE	1900
ORIGIN	GERMAN
LENGTH	47cm (18.5in)

This dagger is of standard form with its gilt brass scabbard and hilt with open crown pommel. What distinguishes it are the buttons of lapis lazuli set into the quillons and the richly decorated blade, with anchor and sailing ship, inscribed with the Frisian sailor's motto: *Rüm Hart – Klaar Kimming* or "Bold Heart – Clear Horizon".

British RN midshipman's presentation dirk, 1897 pattern, 1905

DATE	1905
ORIGIN	BRITISH
LENGTH	37cm (14.6in)

This Royal Navy midshipman's presentation dirk, with blued and gilt blade, carries the inscription: "Chief Captain's Prize Awarded to R. C. R. Peploe HMS Britannia, December 1905". Although of standard overall pattern, such presentation dirks, especially from such a notable ship, are very rare. Supplied by J. R. Gaunt and Sons.

Saudi Arabian presentation jambiya, 20th century

DATE	20th century
ORIGIN	SAUDI ARABIAN
LENGTH	25.4cm (10in)

In style, this is a typical jambiya of Saudi Arabia with its boot-shaped scabbard and wide, curved and sharply pointed blade. What makes it unusual are its hilt and scabbard, each elaborately decorated with gold wire filigree. A jambiya such as this would only be worn by the highest-ranking members of society.

German Third Reich naval officer's dirk, 1933–45

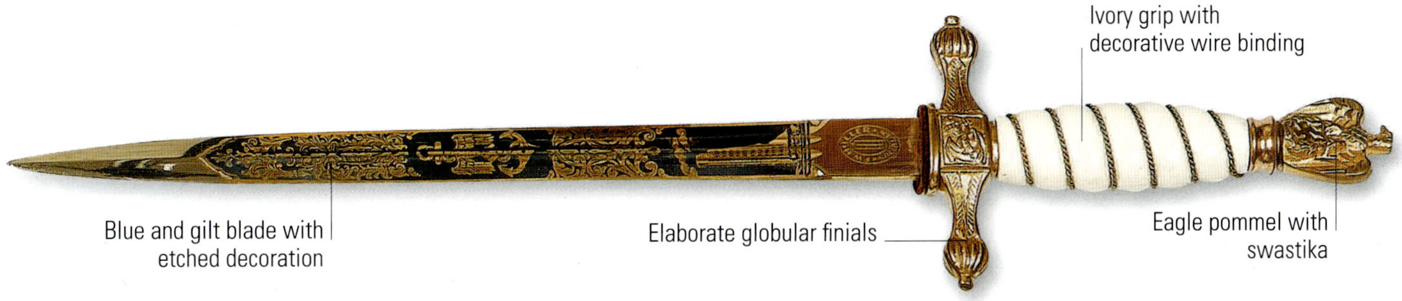

DATE	1933–45
ORIGIN	GERMAN
LENGTH	24.9cm (9.8in)

This is a rare presentation dagger to a Third Reich *Kriegsmarine* (Navy) officer. It differs from the standard-issue dagger in having blued and gilt panels of etched decoration on the blade depicting a warship and the eagle and swastika. Unfortunately, it has no presentation inscription so the recipient is unknown. Supplied by a well-known maker, E W Holler of Solingen.

Unusual bayonets

Most bayonets, though they may differ in details such as the shape and material of the hilt, the method of locking on to the gun, or the shape and length of the blade, still conform to a more or less conventional overall pattern. There are those, however, that differ widely from the conventions of their time. For example, some bayonets may have been developed for special purposes; some may be the first tentative steps into a new form ahead of their time; while others are just simply bizarre with no obvious explanation.

British socket bayonet, 1680

Plain split tube with zigzag slot to engage with stud on barrel

Semicircular hollow blade welded to socket

This is probably one of the simplest, though most likely experimental, bayonets developed at a time when the socket bayonet was first coming into existence. It consists of an iron-tube socket split along its full length, and locking slots that could fit over the muzzle and lock onto a rectangular stud. Attached to the socket is a tapered, hollow, pointed blade. The design was resurrected, again experimentally, by BSA in 1948 for use on submachine guns.

DATE	1680
ORIGIN	BRITISH
LENGTH	50.6cm (19.7in)

British plug bayonet, 1686

Flat blade thickened in the centre

Maker's mark

This is a most unusual plug bayonet by any standards and the reason behind its design can only be guessed at. With a blade 65mm (25.6in) wide, it could even function as a trowel, but entrenchment was not a feature of 17th-century warfare. The Rose and Crown mark suggests it was made by William Hoy about 1686.

DATE	1686
ORIGIN	BRITISH
LENGTH	29.4cm (11.6in)

British spear bayonet for Egg's carbine, 1784

Conventional socket with zigzag slot

Spear point

DATE	1784
ORIGIN	BRITISH
LENGTH	84.5cm (33.3in)

One of the most unusual bayonets produced for British military service was this spear bayonet. It was designed for use with a new breech-loading flintlock cavalry carbine produced in 1784 by Durs Egg at the request of the Duke of Richmond, Master General of Ordnance. The bayonet's length made it impossible to carry it in the normal way of a scabbard attached to the belt. So it was designed to be reversed on the muzzle when not in use and, as a further refinement, the trigger guard had a shaped pocket at its forward end into which the tip of the spearhead could be lodged. It was not widely issued and was more experimental in nature.

American trowel bayonet, 1873

Hollow socket handle with swivelling pommel to act as locking ring

Sharp-edged blade with central stiffening rib at rear

DATE	1873
ORIGIN	AMERICAN
LENGTH	35.7cm (14.1in)

Viewed as a weapon, this Model 1873 bayonet could be considered barbaric. However, it was not a weapon. It was designed as a spade, or for use in the hand as a trowel. It was the third of its type used in American service, and it has the elegance of simplicity and good design.

18th- to 20th-century integral bayonets

The idea of a bayonet permanently attached to a firearm has been explored with varying success over two centuries. It is only practical if the bayonet can be stowed away when not in use but easily deployed as needed. It was used in the 18th and 19th centuries on civilian weapons like blunderbusses and pistols, where the blade was folded away and held against a spring, and could be opened by a trigger. It was tried on some military firearms but never extensively. It has regained popularity in some military circles more recently.

British flintlock blunderbuss by Grice with spring bayonet, *c.*1780

The blunderbuss, a muzzle-loading firearm, was a popular means of self-defence in the homes of the gentry. Being a single-shot weapon, the fitting of a spring-loaded bayonet that could be brought into use simply by moving a catch gave the user a second line of defence if a shot failed to achieve its purpose.

DATE	*c.*1780
ORIGIN	BRITISH
LENGTH	24.9cm (9.8in)

British Elliott's carbine with folding bayonet, 1785

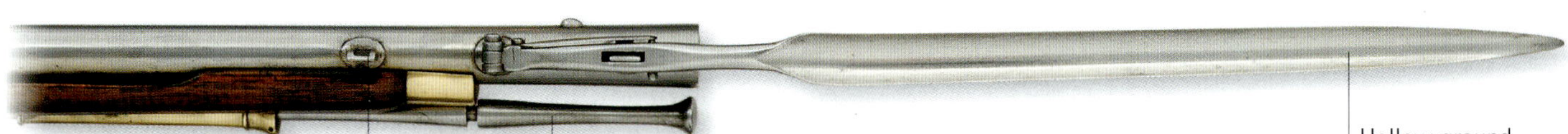

The folding bayonet was also experimented with by the military authorities in Britain for use by cavalry, but it was never adopted. In comparison with a socket bayonet mounted on the muzzle, the mountings of a folding bayonet were flimsy and would hardly stand up to the rigours of extended use in battle.

DATE	1785
ORIGIN	BRITISH
LENGTH	39.9cm (15.5in)

American ramrod bayonet, Springfield rifle, Model 1884, 1884

A clearing rod that could double as a bayonet had been used on the North-Hall musket in 1833 but was resurrected for use on this Springfield rifle. A notch cut in the sharpened rod, combined with a catch beneath the barrel of the gun, allowed the bayonet to be pulled forward and locked firmly in position.

DATE	1884
ORIGIN	AMERICAN
LENGTH	59.2cm (23.3in)

Japanese military carbine, Arisaka Type 44, 1911

DATE	1911
ORIGIN	JAPANESE
LENGTH	43.9cm (17.2in)

This Japanese bayonet was developed for the Arisaka Type 44 carbine used by mounted troops. It could be locked in the open or closed position by a simple catch, and when not in use was folded away beneath the barrel. Carbines with these bayonets saw service until the end of World War II.

Chinese AK47 assault rifle, Type 56, 1980

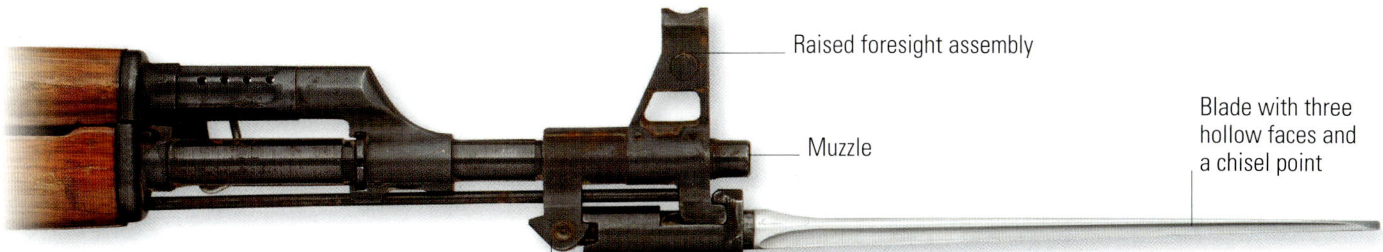

DATE	1980
ORIGIN	CHINESE
LENGTH	36.2cm (14.3in)

The simple, reliable and rugged AK47 has become ubiquitous, continuing to find many adherents more than 60 years after it was developed by Mikhail Kalashnikov in 1947. This one, made in China, was used by Iraqi forces during the Gulf War of 1990–91. It is fitted with a short folding bayonet.

Italian Fascist Youth (*Balilla*) Carbine with folding bayonet

The Italian Fascist Youth organization was created shortly after the rise to power of Benito Mussolini. It replaced the traditional boy scout movement for boys between the ages of 8 and 14 years. The age range was later extended up to 18 years. Like the later Hitler Youth movement, its main objective was to indoctrinate young Italians in the principles of fascism. But it was also intended to provide basic military training and to this end, the older boys were issued with rifles. Only 750mm (29.5in) long and complete with a 250mm (9.8in) folding bayonet, blunted at the tip to avoid accident, these rifles were fully functional miniature versions of the Mannlicher Carcano cavalry carbines.

ABOVE The Italian Fascist Youth organization shared many of the same ideals as the later Hitler Youth movement. During military exercises, older boys were armed with bayonet rifles.

Fighting knives of World War I

When Europe went to war in 1914, it was not foreseen that a new form of combat would emerge – trench warfare. The dilemma experienced by all sides when overrunning an enemy position was that the long length of a rifle with fixed bayonet quickly became a dangerous hindrance. To fight and survive in a narrow trench, a soldier needed a more compact fighting knife: the trench dagger was about to evolve.

German fighting knife, 1914

Known by the Germans as the *Nahkampfmesser* ("Close-combat knife"), a wide range of patterns was created for the German war effort. This example is a style that was widely reproduced by many companies, such as Gottlieb Hammesfahr and Erfurt Gewehrfabrik, although many examples are unmarked.

DATE	1914
ORIGIN	GERMAN
LENGTH	28cm (11in)

German fighting knife, 1914

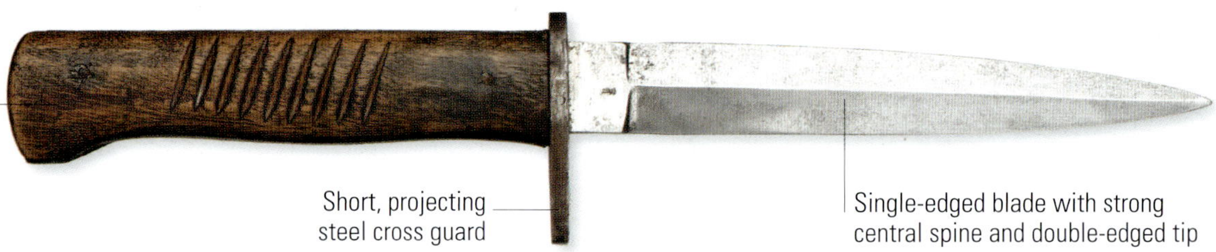

A variation pattern of the close-combat knife, with a wooden grip. This specimen was possibly made by the company of Ernst Busch, Solingen, which is known to have manufactured an identical specimen with a solid-steel hilt. Both patterns are considered to be quite uncommon variations.

DATE	1914
ORIGIN	GERMAN
LENGTH	28.6cm (11.3in)

British push dagger, by Robbins of Dudley, 1916

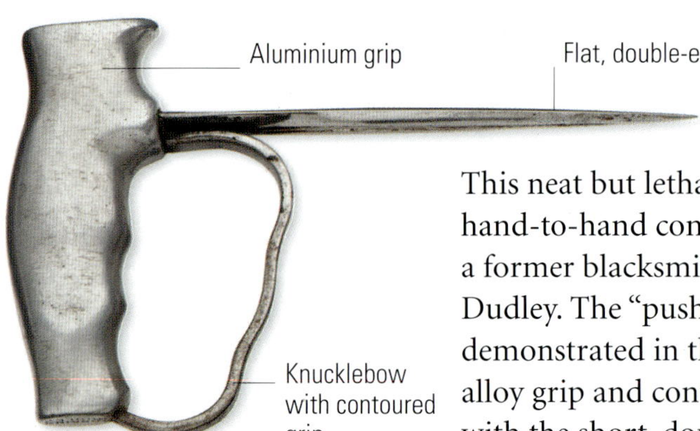

This neat but lethal British Army weapon for hand-to-hand combat was manufactured by a former blacksmithing company, Robbins of Dudley. The "push dagger" design is clearly demonstrated in the combination of the large alloy grip and contoured steel knucklebow with the short, double-edged blade.

DATE	1916
ORIGIN	BRITISH
LENGTH	17.5cm (6.8in)

French fighting knife, 1916

DATE	1916
ORIGIN	FRENCH
LENGTH	unknown

Early "trench daggers" utilized broken bayonets and spikes but it was soon recognized that robust, professionally made knives were to become essential weapons for Allied soldiers. This knife, by the French Au Lion company, features a wooden grip covering the tang of the double-edged blade and a steel cross guard with extended quillons.

American Model 1917 knucklebow knife, 1917

DATE	1917
ORIGIN	AMERICAN
LENGTH	37cm (14.6in)

This close-quarter fighting knife was issued to US troops when they joined the European campaign. It is distinguished by a bayonet-style blade and knucklebow guard.

American knuckle knife, Model 1918, 1918

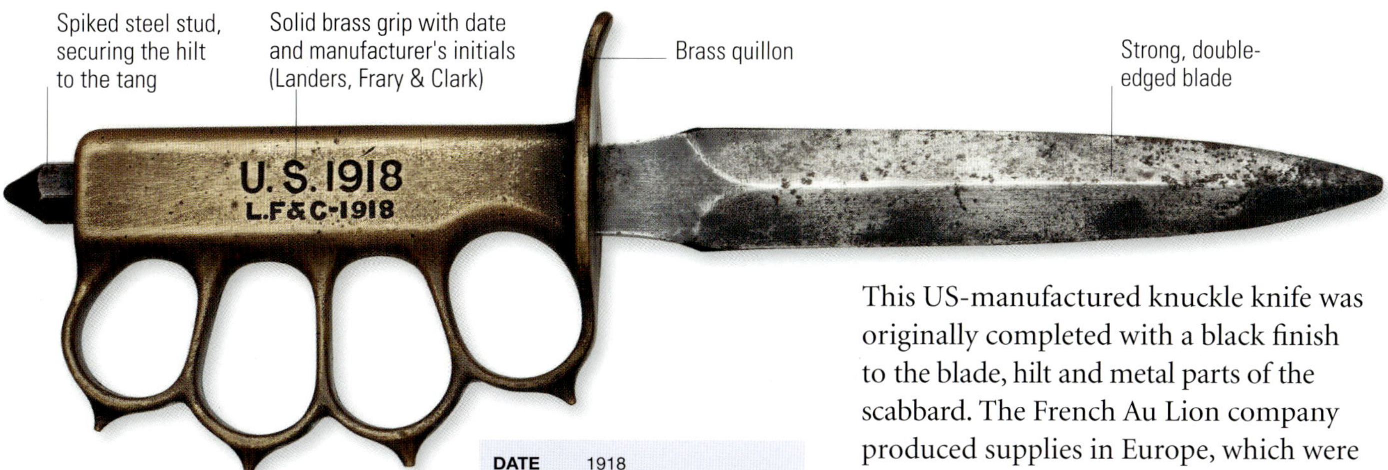

DATE	1918
ORIGIN	AMERICAN
LENGTH	29.6cm (11.6in)

This US-manufactured knuckle knife was originally completed with a black finish to the blade, hilt and metal parts of the scabbard. The French Au Lion company produced supplies in Europe, which were distinguished by their bright polish (with the Au Lion stamp on the ricasso). The hilts were marked only with the U.S. 1918 mark.

Bayonets of World War I

At the outbreak of World War I, military thinking had changed little since the mid-19th century, despite the advent of vastly improved firepower. It was still thought that troops could be deployed in massed ranks and engage in bayonet charges. But this was a war of entrenchment and little mobility, and the fields of Flanders showed the deadly futility of the fixed-bayonet charge across No Man's Land against a barely visible dug-in enemy defended by barbed wire, machine guns, mortars and artillery.

French Lebel epee bayonet, 1886

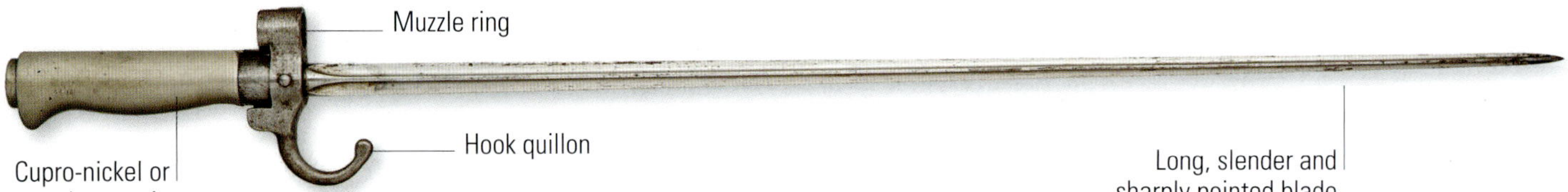

The Lebel bayonet with its long, slender, cruciform blade, resembling the fencing sword, or epee, is probably one of the most distinctive bayonets from its era. It was first introduced in 1886 for use with the new Lebel rifle, the world's first small-calibre, high-velocity rifle utilizing a smokeless propellant.

DATE	1886
ORIGIN	FRENCH
LENGTH	64cm (25.2in)

American Springfield bayonet, 1905

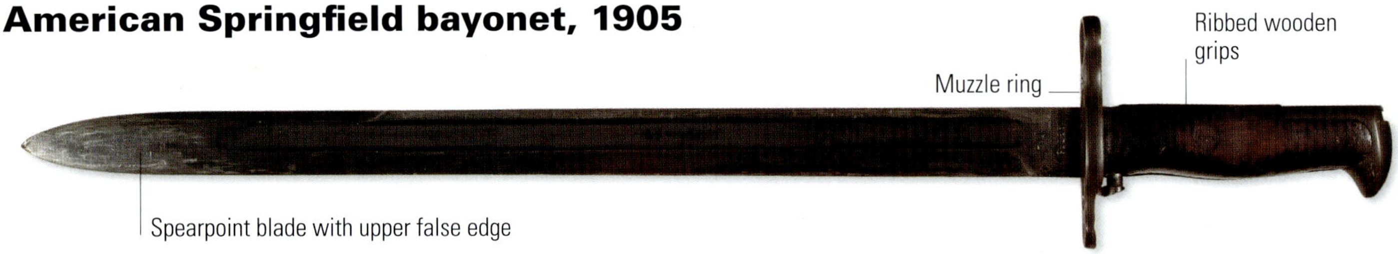

This was the second bayonet adopted for the newly introduced Springfield Model 1903 rifle, which initially used the bayonet of its predecessor, the Krag. However, President Theodore Roosevelt insisted a new bayonet with a longer blade be designed to compensate for the shorter length of the rifle.

DATE	1905
ORIGIN	AMERICAN
LENGTH	52.6cm (20.7in)

British SMLE bayonet, Pattern 1907, 1907

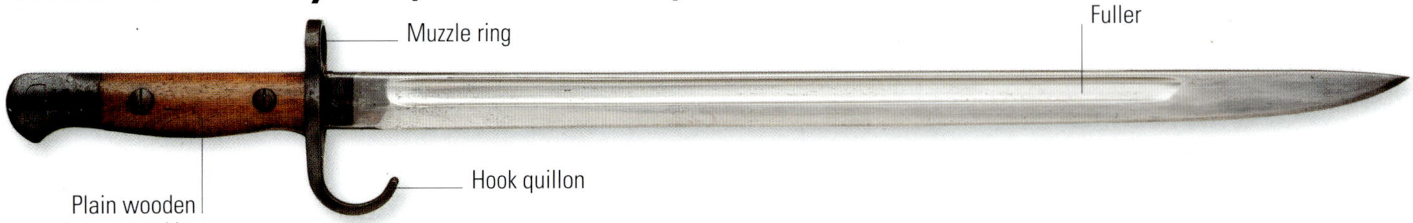

DATE	1907
ORIGIN	BRITISH
LENGTH	55.3cm (21.8in)

When introduced in 1903, this rifle had a short bayonet modelled on the 1888 pattern. However, this was felt to be too short for use with a shortened rifle so a longer pattern, inspired by the Arisaka Type 30, was introduced. The hooked quillon was eventually deemed to be too cumbersome and was abandoned in 1913, but many of this pattern saw service during World War I. Unusually, the muzzle ring does not actually fit on the muzzle but on a stud mounted beneath it.

British bayonet Pattern 1913, 1914

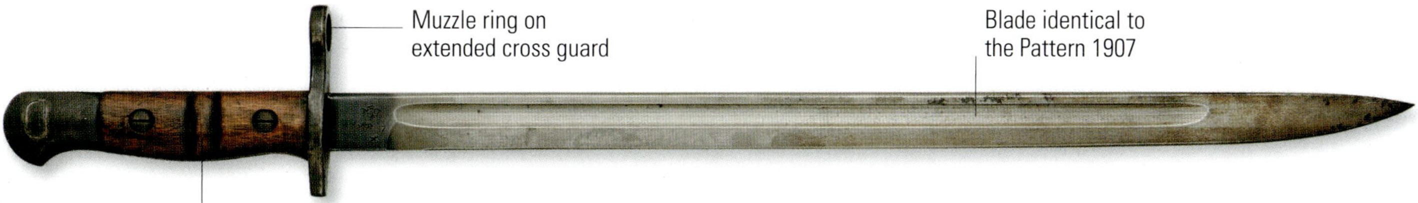

DATE	1914
ORIGIN	BRITISH
LENGTH	55.6cm (21.9in)

This Pattern 1913 bayonet, whilst very similar to the Pattern 1907, was designed to fit the Pattern 1914 rifle, a rapid adaptation of the Pattern 1913 experimental rifle discontinued at the outbreak of war and modified to .303in calibre. Unlike the SMLE, this rifle had a muzzle projecting beyond the end of the stock, and so this bayonet was designed so that the muzzle ring actually fits on the muzzle. It therefore has an extended cross guard to enable it to do that.

American bayonet for American Enfield rifle Model 1917, 1914

The British Pattern 1914 rifle and bayonet were already being manufactured under contract in America when it entered the war. Adapted to .30-06 calibre, the Pattern 1914 rifle became the Model 1917. Both rifle bayonets are identical, except for the US ownership marks and date on the American blade.

DATE	1914
ORIGIN	AMERICAN
LENGTH	54.4cm (21.4in)

German Mauser bayonet Model 98/05, 1915

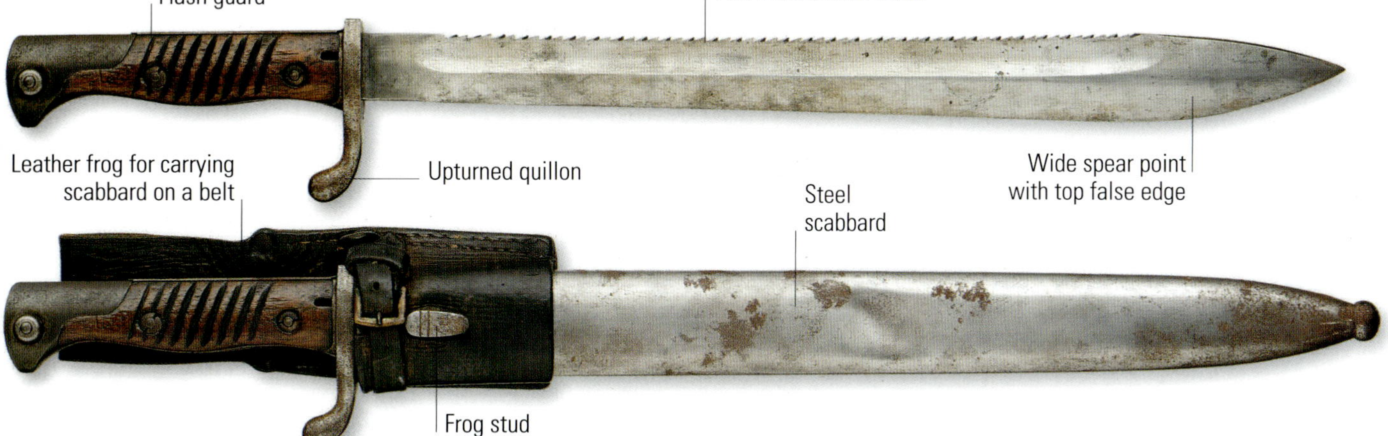

Numerous bayonets exist for the German Gewehr 98 rifle of 1898. This model with saw-teeth originated in 1905 for issue to infantry NCOs. The more durable scabbard dates from 1914. Saw-teeth were provided for cutting brushwood, not for inflicting more severe wounds, a popular misconception at the time.

DATE	1915
ORIGIN	GERMAN
LENGTH	50.8cm (20in)

American Model 1915 bayonet, 1915

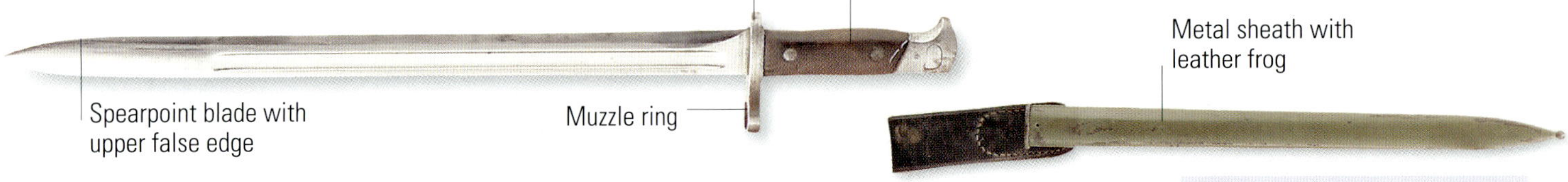

A Russian contract for 300,000 Model 1895 rifles and bayonets was placed with the Winchester company in 1915, and in Russia this bayonet is referred to as the Model 1915. The steel parts are polished bright and the Winchester name appears on the blade side of the cross guard.

DATE	1915
ORIGIN	AMERICAN
LENGTH	51.7cm (20.4in)

Canadian Ross rifle bayonet, 1915

DATE	1915
ORIGIN	CANADIAN
LENGTH	38.5cm (15.2in)

This bayonet was first introduced in 1912, but in the early stages of World War I the slightly hollow-ground blade was modified by having a portion of the tip ground away and the top edge reduced in thickness. These changes were undertaken to enable the blade to penetrate its target more easily. In addition, the once polished bright blades gave way to a dull matt finish. Whether this was done simply to ease manufacture or to reduce reflection is open to question.

German Mauser ersatz bayonet, 1916

The term "ersatz" means a substitute or makeshift, in this case indicating that it was constructed using metal grips riveted together, on the grounds of speed and convenience. The hilt was usually painted field grey and the blade polished bright. This bayonet also functioned as a convenient trench knife.

DATE	1916
ORIGIN	GERMAN
LENGTH	26.1cm (10.3in)

German Mauser ersatz bayonet, 1916

DATE	1916
ORIGIN	GERMAN
LENGTH	43cm (17in)

This is another example of the many ersatz bayonets produced, again for use with the Model 88 and 98 Gewehr rifles or captured French Lebel and Russian Mosin-Nagant rifles. The pressed-steel hilt is a little more elaborately formed, although on this example the quillon has been bent further backwards subsequent to manufacture. Like the other bayonets, this would have had a hilt and scabbard painted field grey, and a polished blade.

British mountable revolver bayonet for Webley Mk VI, 1916

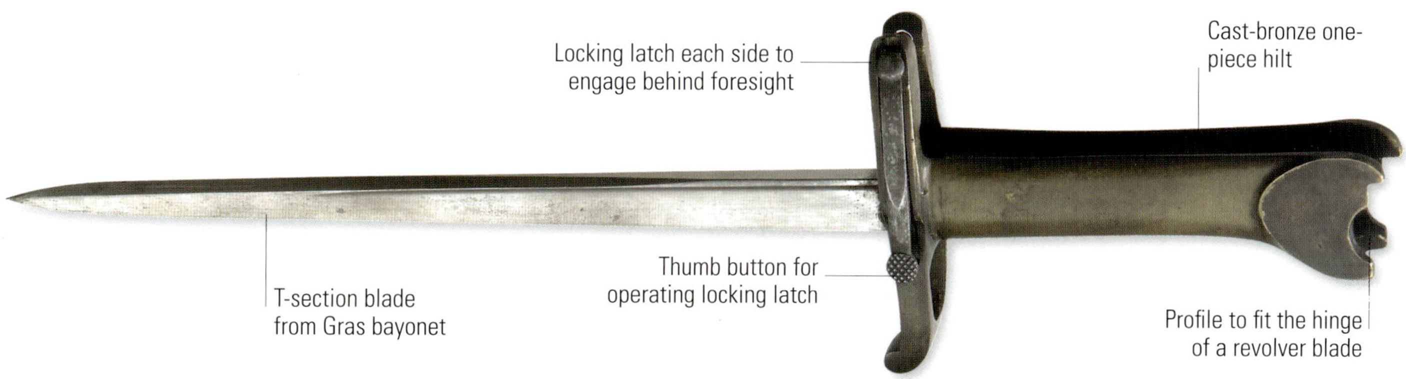

DATE	1916
ORIGIN	BRITISH
LENGTH	32.4cm (12.8in)

This bayonet was the brainchild of Lieutenant Arthur Pritchard. Made by Greener of Birmingham, it used a Gras bayonet blade and was only for private purchase. The pommel sits tightly up against the revolver frame. The muzzle ring slides over the foresight and is locked in place by two sprung levers on the cross guard.

German Mauser ersatz bayonet, 1917

DATE	1917
ORIGIN	GERMAN
LENGTH	43.9cm (17.3in)

These ersatz versions of the Model 88/98 bayonets were designed to fit the Model 88 and 98 rifles and, by using adapters, captured Russian Mosin-Nagant and French Lebel rifles too. The all-steel hilt reflects the grooved wooden grips of the standard bayonet and was originally painted field grey. It has the open muzzle "ring" common on many ersatz bayonets.

Survival weapons of World War II and after

As the world went to war in 1939, fighting knives and other survival weapons were redesigned to fill a variety of purposes, depending upon the conditions under which they would be used. Some pieces were designed solely as assassination items, while others were intended to double as working tools for building shelter or finding food. Part of the early training for British Commandos was for each man to take his turn locating food – namely, to find an animal or bird, kill it, butcher it, cook it and supply it to his colleagues.

American Carlson's Raiders machete (Collins Pattern No 18), 1934 onward

Issued to the 2nd Marine Raider Battalion during the Guadalcanal Campaign in the Pacific, this knife's "machete-style" hilt is common to a number of Collins' weapons; its distinctive "beaked" pommel ensures a firm grip. The single-edged blade, with false edge tip, makes it an excellent all-round tool as well as a weapon.

DATE	1934 onward
ORIGIN	AMERICAN
LENGTH	36cm (14.2in)

German flight utility knife, 1936 onward

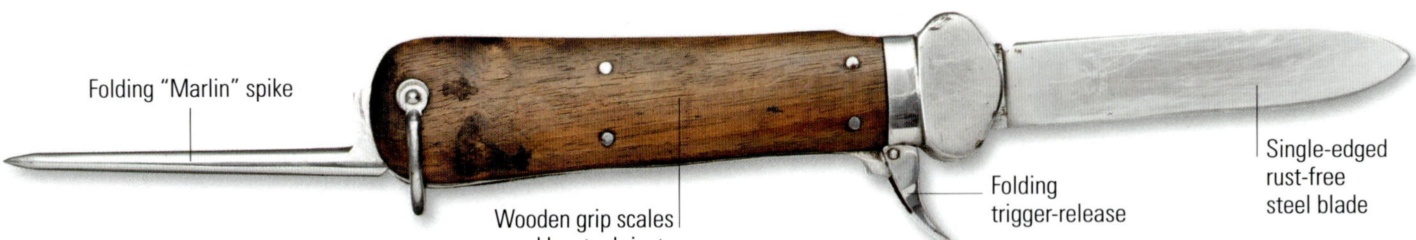

DATE	1936 onward
ORIGIN	GERMAN
LENGTH	35.2cm (13.9in)

Originally introduced for the army parachute units, the knife was subsequently adopted by all Luftwaffe parachute units. The knife blade was normally retracted, to keep it out of the way and prevent accidental injury to the wearer; it could be released by one hand. By holding the knife down and pushing the trigger, the blade drops into position, useful if a parachutist is trapped in a tree.

Soviet fighting knife, Armenian pattern, 1940 onward

DATE	1940 onward
ORIGIN	ARMENIAN
LENGTH	26cm (10.2in)

Manufactured in Armenia for the Soviet Armenian troops fighting alongside the Red Army, this weapon was intended as a general service knife, although its usefulness as a close-combat weapon was not overlooked. The blade is single-edged, with a double-edged tip and a fuller close to the back of the blade. This specimen has a ferrule between the main grip and the guard. In post-war years, the Armenian contingents continued to equip their troops with a similar dagger, although the main Russian troops preferred to have dual-purpose knife-bayonets.

English Fairbairn-Sykes commando knife, 2nd pattern, 1941 onward

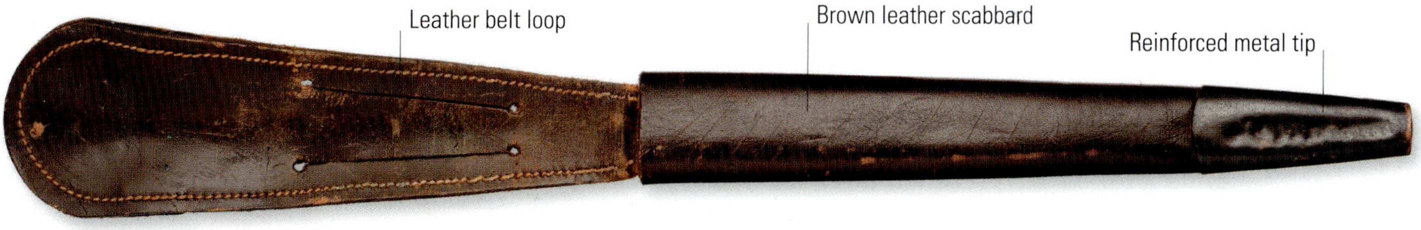

DATE	1941 onward
ORIGIN	ENGLISH
LENGTH	30cm (11.8in)

The classic fighting knife of the Commando, the Fairbairn-Sykes knife is perhaps the most identifiable commando knife in the world, and its design features were copied by many other nations for their own special troops. The blade is a straight stiletto form, double-edged with a central spine, and the tang of the blade projects through the hilt and is secured at the other end with a locking button. The finely checkered grip is made of turned brass, while the guard is made of steel and rounded at the end of the quillons. This specimen is an example of the Fairbairn-Sykes 2nd pattern (the 1st pattern had a recurved cross guard and a more acutely pointed blade with flat ricasso). It appears to be a private purchase example, as the scabbard is shown without the usual leather side tags.

American USMC KA-BAR (USN Mk 2) fighting-utility knife, 1941 onward

One of the most successful fighting-utility knives ever made, the KA-BAR was created by the Union Cutlery Company of Olean, New York State. Designed as an all-purpose survival tool, it is equally effective as a hammer, can opener or defensive weapon. Initial manufacture was exclusive to Government Order, and the knife was adopted by the US Marine Corps and the Navy.

DATE	1941 onward
ORIGIN	AMERICAN
LENGTH	32cm (12.6in)

British and American OSS/SOE dart and wrist dagger, 1942 onward

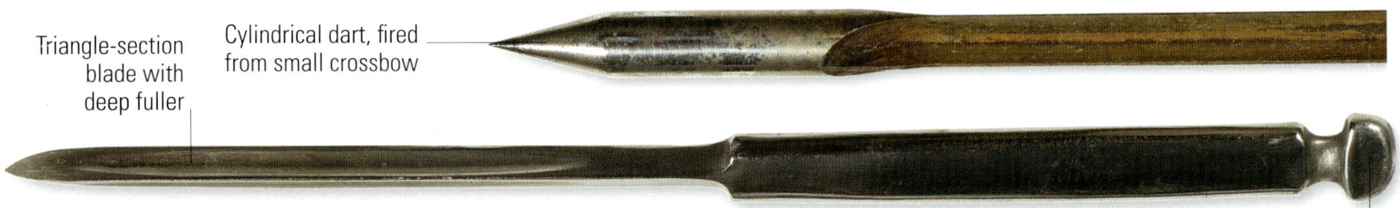

Specially manufactured out of surgical steel, these weapons were designed for dispatching an opponent quietly. The dart could be fired from a folding, pistol-sized crossbow, while the wrist dagger was carried in a leather sheath with arm or leg straps for concealment. The weapons were mainly deployed behind enemy lines.

DATE	1942 onward
ORIGIN	BRITISH & AMERICAN
LENGTH	17.5cm (6.8in)

English Fairbairn-Sykes commando knife, 3rd pattern, 1942 onward

The 3rd pattern Fairbairn-Sykes knife was the version that was most widely manufactured, both during World War II and well into the postwar years. Following the production of the original pattern by Wilkinson Sword, the design was modified and improved in the following models, and then contracted out to other manufacturers. The ringed grip is the distinguishing feature of the the 3rd pattern dagger, more than 1 million of which are thought to have been produced.

DATE	1942 onward
ORIGIN	ENGLISH
LENGTH	29.6cm (11.7in)

American Mk 3 trench knife with M8 scabbard, 1943 onward

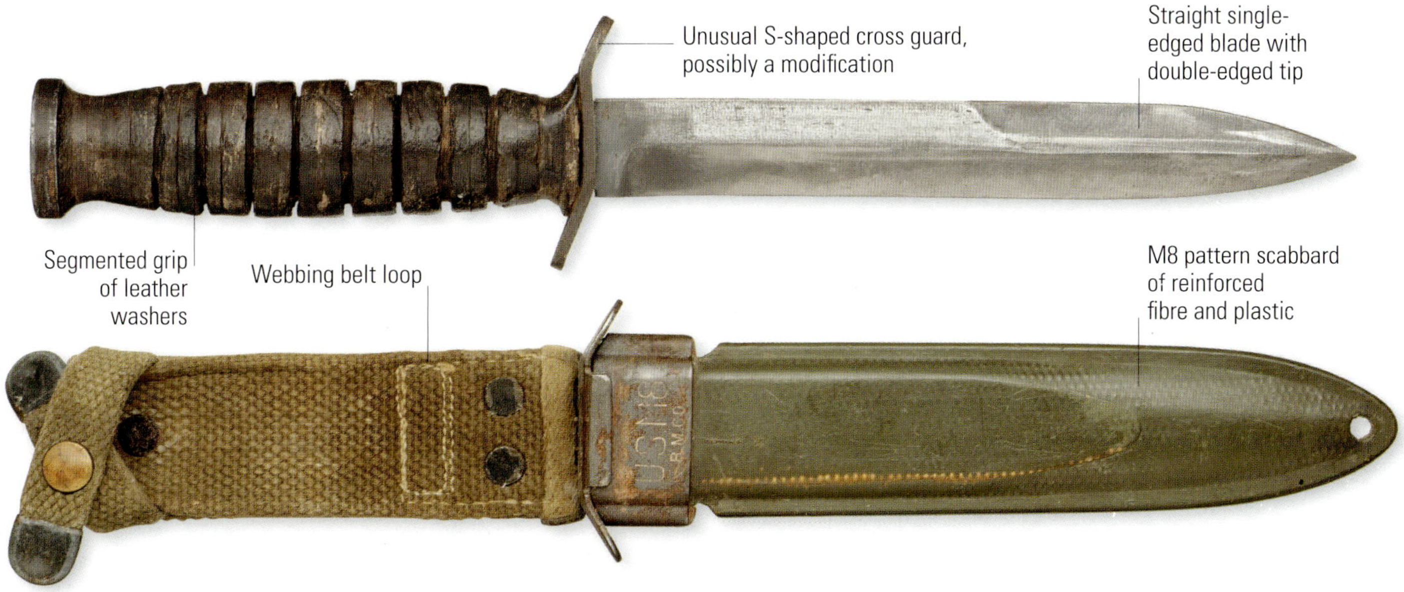

DATE	1943 onward
ORIGIN	AMERICAN
LENGTH	29cm (11.4in)

The Mk 3 trench knife was based on the knife bayonet for the 1936 M1 Garand rifle, the main difference being that the trench knife did not have the locking mechanism or the barrel ring. The blade and grip, however, were identical. The cross guard, which normally projects forward on this pattern, appears to have been modified with an upsweep on the underside.

German utility-fighting knife for the Bundeswehr, *c.*1970s

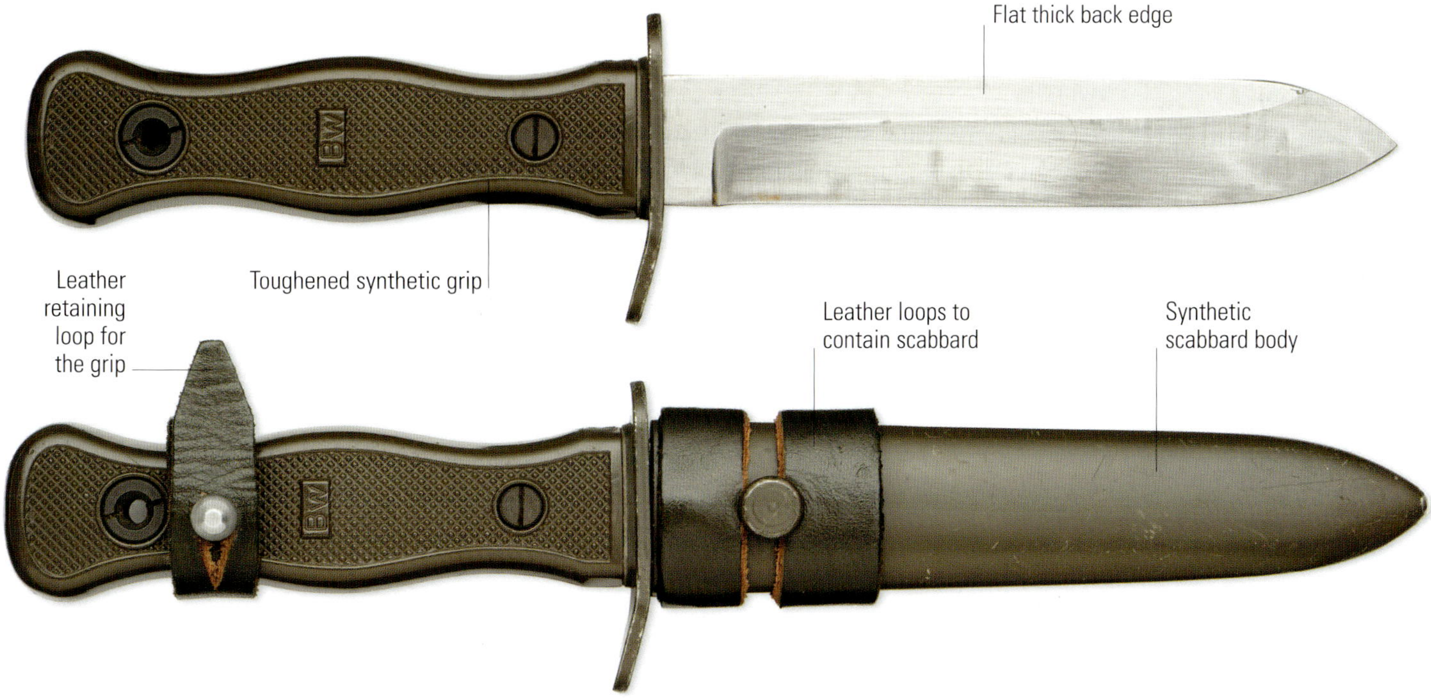

DATE	*c.*1970s
ORIGIN	GERMAN
LENGTH	26cm (10.2in)

Although the role of the fighting knife in modern armies has diminished, military thinking still holds that a neat general-purpose knife is a useful tool. Advances in materials now mean that non-rusting and non-degrading components can be used to assemble knives capable of lasting for years without any visible deterioration.

German Third Reich edged weapons

The city of Solingen, in the Ruhr Valley, has been recognized as a centre of excellence in the production of edged weapons for over 700 years. Following the German surrender and disarmament after World War I, its edged-weapons industry experienced a period of steep decline. Swords and daggers, which had been prevalent in the Imperial Period, had always been viewed as symbols of authority and officialdom, particularly in Prussian culture. The emergence of the National Socialist Government (NSDAP) in 1933 created an opportunity to develop weapons of a new design to reflect the culture of the Third Reich.

German Hitler Youth knife, *c.*1933

The Hitler Youth knife (HJ Fahrtenmesser, "Hiking Knife") was put into production in 1933. The blade is short and single-edged (examples made before 1938 featured the *Blut und Ehre!* motto) and the hilt is steel with a nickel plate finish. The knife would usually feature the Hitler Youth swastika emblem.

DATE	*c.*1933
ORIGIN	GERMAN
LENGTH	24.8cm (9.8in)

German SA service dagger, *c.*1933

The SA, or *Sturm Abteilung* ("Storm Detachment"), were the militia who kept order at Nazi Party meetings. This service dagger was introduced in 1933 and based on a south German medieval design. The wood-and-steel hilt is emblazoned with National Socialist and SA emblems. The accompanying brown metal scabbard would have been ornamented with nickel trimmings.

DATE	*c.*1933
ORIGIN	GERMAN
LENGTH	35.4cm (14in)

German SS officer's dagger, 1936

DATE	1936
ORIGIN	GERMAN
LENGTH	37cm (14.6in)

Introduced in December 1933, the SS dagger was based on the same design as the SA dagger, but with minor differences. The grip is made of hardwood which is stained black and has silver finish insignia, including the SS runic symbol at the top of the grip. The cross guards are finished in a nickel silver plating.

German RAD hewer, *c.*1934

DATE	*c.*1934
ORIGIN	GERMAN
LENGTH	37.7cm (14.8in)

The RAD (*Reichs Arbeit Dienst*, "Reich's Labour Service") aimed to give young people experience of manual labour in the community. The design of this heavy-duty hewer, which was carried by full-time personnel only, was based on a traditional German hatchet. A heavily ornamented black metal scabbard carried the broad steel blade, which was falchion shaped with a short fuller close to the back edge. The organizational motto, *Arbeit adelt*, is etched on the blade. The hilt is made of iron, with nickel plating and stag horn grip scales. The steel scabbard has decorated steel fittings: the upper one bears a scroll design, while the lower one features a version of the national emblem of the RAD service – a spade head with swastika and corn stalks.

German Luftwaffe Flying Officer's dagger, 1934

DATE	1934
ORIGIN	GERMAN
LENGTH	50.5cm (20in)

This dagger design was originally created for the *Deutsche Luftsportverband*, or "German Airsports Organization", which was a secret means of training air personnel while Germany was forbidden to operate a military air force under the terms of the Treaty of Versailles of 1919. In March 1935, the Luftwaffe came into existence and Germany declared its intention to begin rapid military expansion. This dagger would have been carried in a blue leather-wrapped scabbard with chain suspension.

The restoration of German pride

Uniforms and edged weapons had long been regarded as symbols of rank and status in Germany. The German love of order and discipline seemed to have come to the fore at around the time of Bismarck and the creation of the Second Reich (1871–1918). In this period of industrial growth and new prosperity, virtually every organization and service within Germany wore a uniform and carried a sword or dagger. This kind of adornment extended beyond the navy and army to hunters, postal workers, railway officials and so on.

In the years following World War I, most of this was swept away with the austerity of the new Weimar Republic and the heavy reparations imposed upon the defeated Germany. One of the key promises made by Hitler, sensing the people's resentment at the outcome of the war, was that he would restore German pride. The adoption of dress weapons for the Nazis' militarist formations was one aspect of this. New Nazi-inspired uniforms and daggers were created for other services, too, such as the German Red Cross and the Civil Service. The psychological effect was palpable. People started to feel important again; they were being given recognition and status.

ABOVE Adolf Hitler taking the salute at the 1938 Party Rally in Nuremberg. In the foreground is Reichs Labour Service leader Konstantin Hierl, wearing his own special RAD hewer. Another officer wears the 1937 Pattern RAD officers' hewer.

German army officer's dagger, 1935

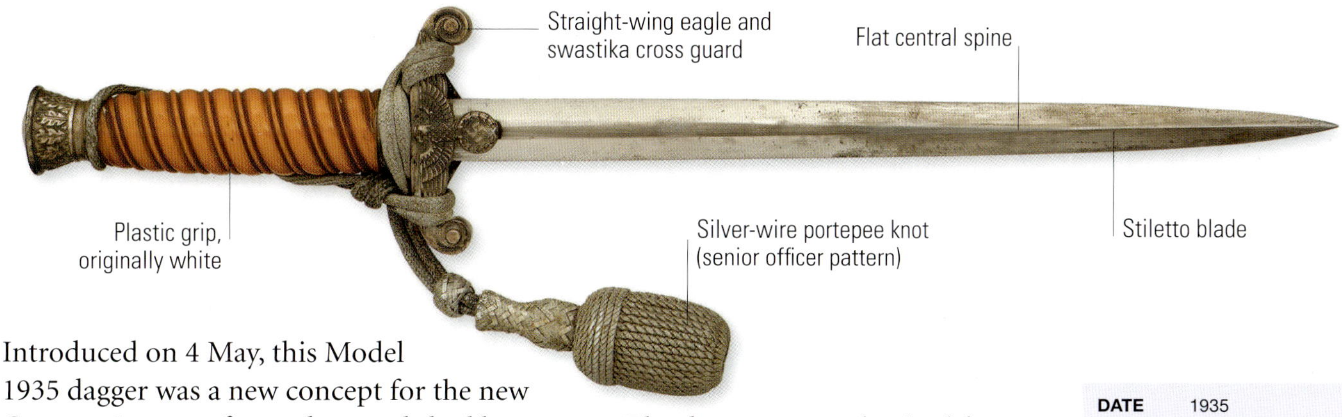

Introduced on 4 May, this Model 1935 dagger was a new concept for the new German Army, as formerly swords had been worn. The dagger was authorized for all officers, general staff officers, medical and veterinary officers, and musicians and officials with officer rank. It originally had a white ivory or plastic grip.

DATE	1935
ORIGIN	GERMAN
LENGTH	40cm (15.7in)

German Luftwaffe dagger, 1937

DATE	1937
ORIGIN	GERMAN
LENGTH	40cm (15.7in)

Introduced in 1937 for Luftwaffe officers, this stylish new dagger features a cross guard in the form of the Luftwaffe eagle. The thin stiletto blade is unsharpened and is secured to the hilt with the tang passing through the grip and screw-locked with a globe pommel. The pommel is decorated with oak leaf motifs and a swastika. Some deluxe examples of this dagger had an ivory grip with a Damascus steel blade.

German state official dagger, 1938

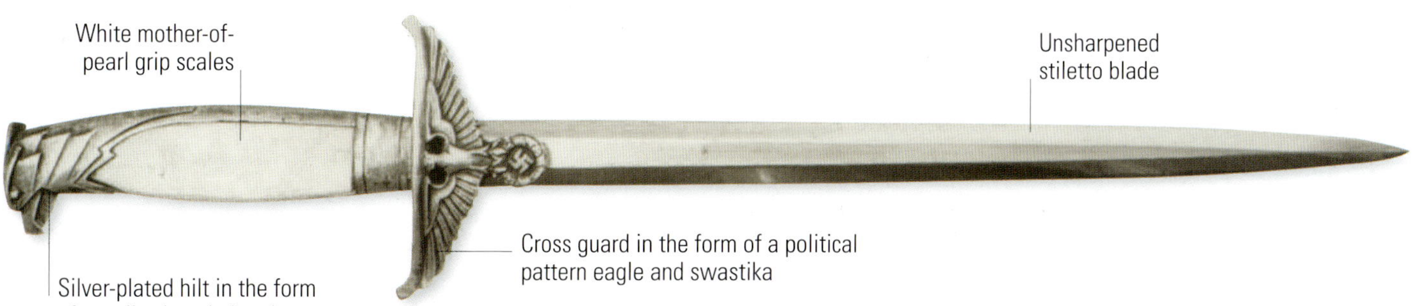

DATE	1938
ORIGIN	GERMAN
LENGTH	40cm (15.7in)

Introduced in March 1938 for all State and Civil Service Leaders, this dagger is very stylish, having an elegant hilt in the form of an eagle's head, with mother-of-pearl grip scales. All the hilt metal parts are made of brass, with a silver plate finish. The cross guard is very distinctive, featuring a political form spread-wing eagle, with upturned tips to the wings and a wreath with a swastika emblem clutched at the talons.

Bayonets of World War II

By the time World War II erupted, warfare had become much more mechanized. Soldiers were also more mobile and the widespread adoption of the submachine gun and automatic rifle meant that troops had greater individual firepower. But the need for close-quarter engagement still arose, in street fighting or commando operations, where the bayonet, especially the shorter versions, came into its own.

German or Belgian Mauser export bayonet, 1920s–30s

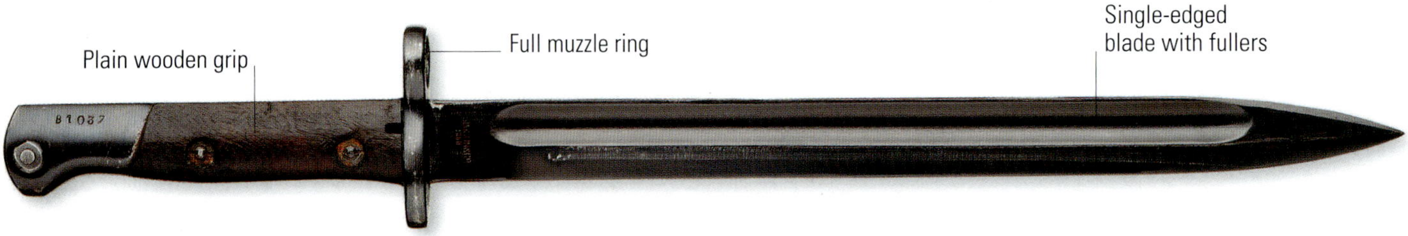

This is a typical Mauser "export" bayonet, manufactured in vast quantities in both Germany and Belgium and exported around the world during the interwar years. Unlike the majority of German service bayonets at this time, the export bayonets often had a complete muzzle ring and were either deeply blued or polished all over.

DATE	1920s–30s
ORIGIN	GERMAN/BELGIAN
LENGTH	38.5cm (15.2in)

Japanese Arisaka bayonet, 1939

This bayonet was created to fit the Type 99 Arisaka rifle introduced in 1939. It is almost identical to the original Arisaka bayonet, the Type 30 of 1897, and at the time of production had a heavily blued hilt and either a bright or blued blade.

DATE	1939
ORIGIN	JAPANESE
LENGTH	73.5cm (28.9in)

British entrenching tool/bayonet, 1939–45

This was not designed as a weapon. As a wartime expedient, the helve of the entrenching tool was adapted to accept the No. 4 bayonet so it could be used as a probe for detecting landmines. The spade portion could easily be removed for this type of work and to simplify carrying.

DATE	1939–45
ORIGIN	BRITISH
LENGTH	unknown

British bayonet for the No 4 rifle, No 4, Mk II, *c.*1940

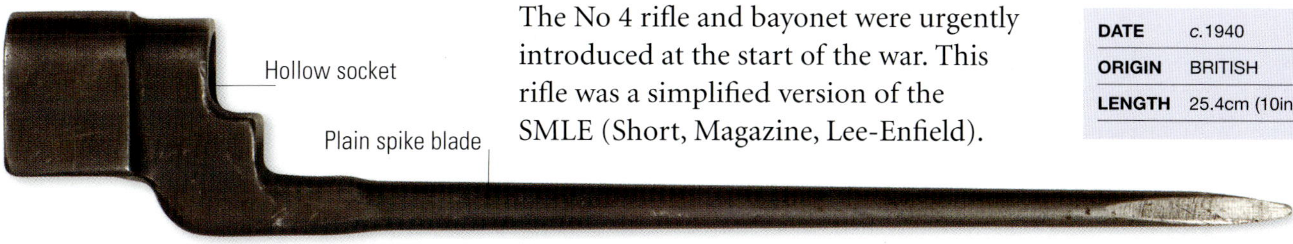

The No 4 rifle and bayonet were urgently introduced at the start of the war. This rifle was a simplified version of the SMLE (Short, Magazine, Lee-Enfield).

DATE	*c.*1940
ORIGIN	BRITISH
LENGTH	25.4cm (10in)

British Sten machine carbine bayonet, Mk I, 1942

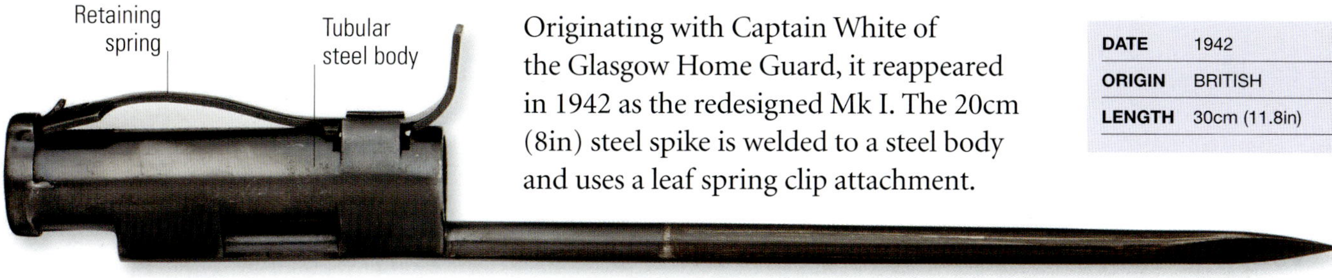

Originating with Captain White of the Glasgow Home Guard, it reappeared in 1942 as the redesigned Mk I. The 20cm (8in) steel spike is welded to a steel body and uses a leaf spring clip attachment.

DATE	1942
ORIGIN	BRITISH
LENGTH	30cm (11.8in)

American bayonet for Garand M1 rifle, Model M1, 1943

DATE	1943
ORIGIN	AMERICAN
LENGTH	36.7cm (14.5in)

New manufacture of this American bayonet model commenced in 1943. This is evidently not a conversion from previous models because the fullers which lighten the blade terminate properly before the tip. In converted examples, the fullers run to the very point, indicative of a blade that has been shortened.

American bayonet for M1 carbine, Model M4, 1944

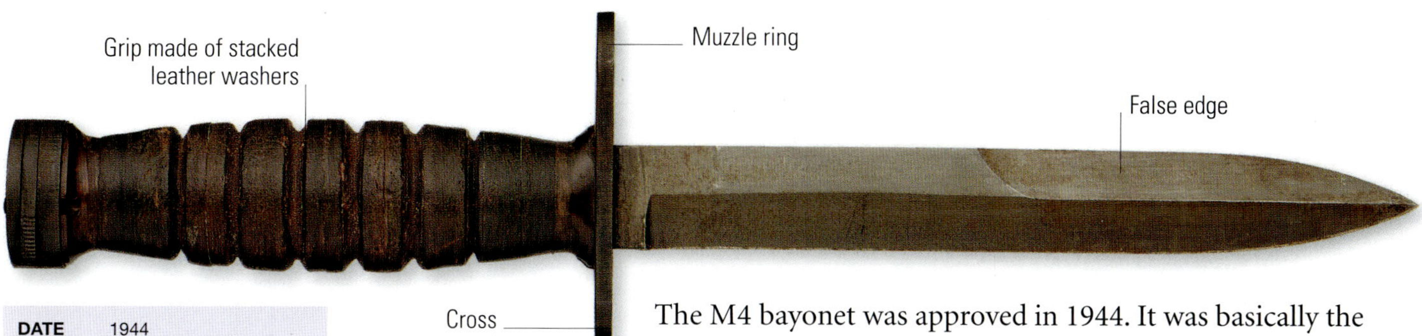

DATE	1944
ORIGIN	AMERICAN
LENGTH	30cm (11.8in)

The M4 bayonet was approved in 1944. It was basically the M3 fighting knife which was adapted to fit the M1 carbine by fitting a cross guard with a muzzle ring and a retaining catch in the pommel.

Bayonets up to the present day

Despite the increasingly hi-tech nature of warfare, reliance still has to be ultimately placed on the soldier at the battlefront. When all else fails, the bayonet, used in its traditional role on the rifle, or used with stealth as a fighting knife, or used as a combination tool, is probably more an essential piece of equipment than it was in the past. Even now, a soldier on parade would be incomplete without one.

Czech VZ/24 knife bayonet, *c.*1926

Introduced around 1926 for the VZ/24 rifle, this is a shortened version of the VZ/23, and several variants exist. Unusually, the cutting edge of the blade is on the upper side. It was widely exported to Europe, the Middle East and South America.

DATE	*c.*1926
ORIGIN	CZECH
LENGTH	43.3cm (17in)

British knife bayonet, No 7, Mk I, 1945

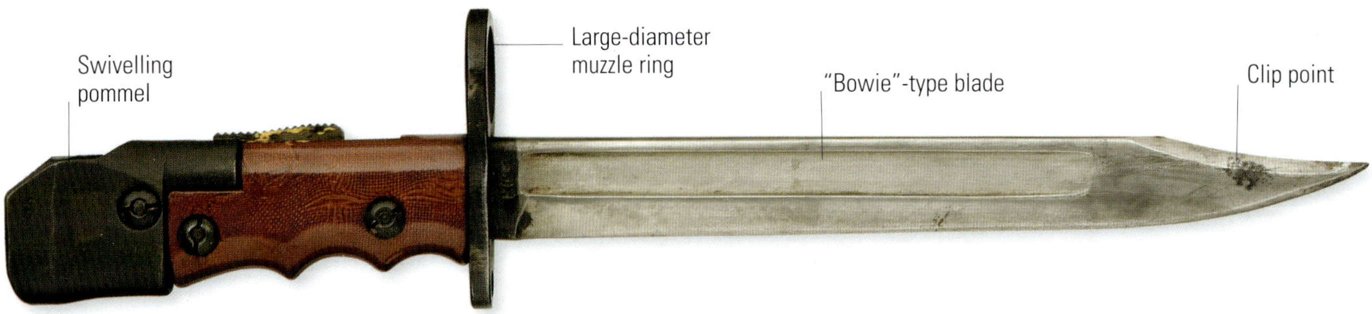

Designed for the No 4 rifle, this knife bayonet was first used on the Sten gun Mk V. After limited use, around 1947 the Guards began to use it for parade duty and this continued until the 1970s. The unusual swivelling pommel allowed the weapon to be used as a bayonet or, in the position shown, as a fighting knife.

DATE	1945
ORIGIN	BRITISH
LENGTH	32.3cm (12.7in)

Russian knife bayonet for AK47 assault rifle, 1947

DATE	1947
ORIGIN	RUSSIAN
LENGTH	32.6cm (12.8in)

This is a bayonet of very distinctive appearance. The pommel has two projections that partially wrap around the barrel, and slide along it when fitted, to give extra support. The cross guard has a traditional muzzle ring; immediately to the rear of this are the two locking catches that engage in recesses on the barrel.

British L1A3 bayonet for L1A1 SLR, 1957

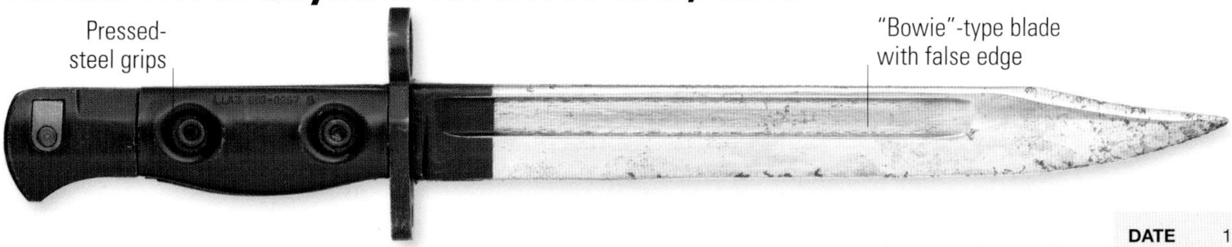

One of a series of bayonets for this rifle, all with minor differences and all evolving from the No 5 bayonet. This one has a recessed lock-release button on the other side of the pommel and a fuller which terminates close to the hilt. All have blackened hilts.

DATE	1957
ORIGIN	BRITISH
LENGTH	30.5cm (12in)

South African pattern No 9 socket bayonet, *c.*1960

This hybrid, consisting of the No 4 rifle type of socket and the blade of the S1 (Uzi) submachine gun bayonet, was issued to local defence groups.

DATE	*c.*1960
ORIGIN	SOUTH AFRICAN
LENGTH	17cm (6.7in)

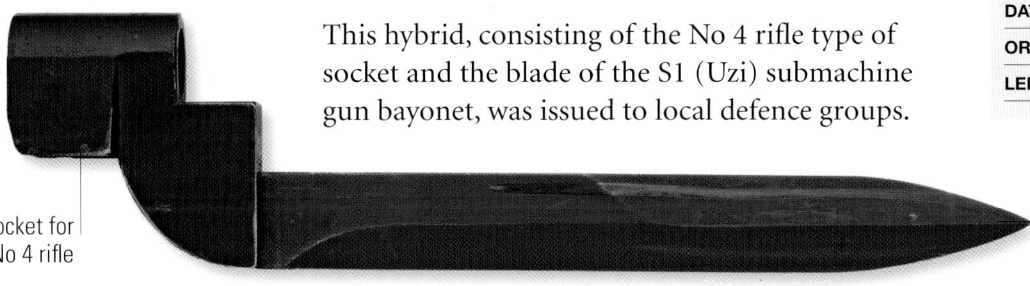

British knife bayonet L3A1 for SA80 (L85A1) rifle, 1985

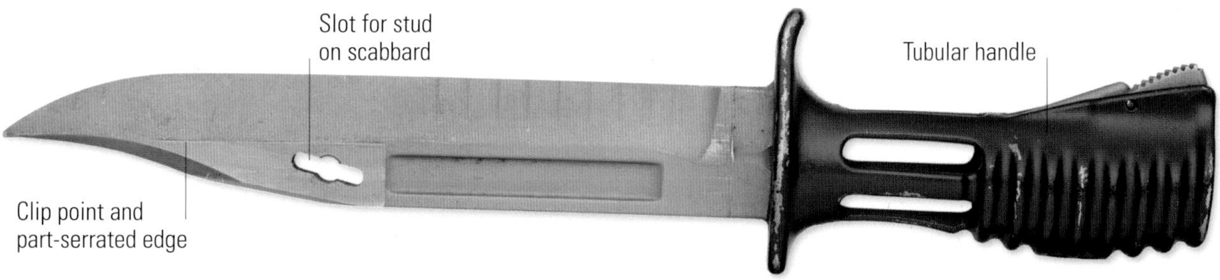

DATE	1985
ORIGIN	BRITISH
LENGTH	28.6cm (11.3in)

This bayonet, a stainless-steel investment casting with tubular hilt, departs widely from earlier concepts. The blade is serrated like a kitchen knife and has a hole to engage with a stud on the scabbard, for use as a wire-cutter. Later, a bottle-opener was built into the hilt.

French knife bayonet for SIG 540/542 rifle, 1985

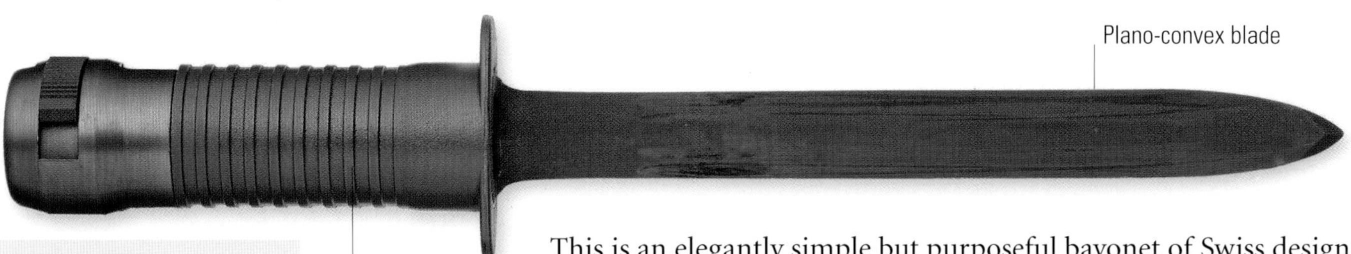

DATE	1985
ORIGIN	FRENCH
LENGTH	unknown

This is an elegantly simple but purposeful bayonet of Swiss design for the SIG rifle used by the Foreign Legion. It has a tubular steel hilt, partly encased in plastic with a catch built into the pommel, and a slender blade that is flat on one face and convex on the other.

Civilian knives to the present day

From the 19th century to the 21st century, the development of the modern knife has seen many novel interpretations. Revised and modified variations of some ancient knife styles came into being, together with "automatic" knives which flick open mechanically. Today, the classic Bowie knife endures in numerous updated forms alongside expressive, free-flowing styles that make the most of modern technology, such as the extravagant designs of Spanish knife-maker Martinez Albainox.

British bichwa double-bladed parrying knife, late 20th century

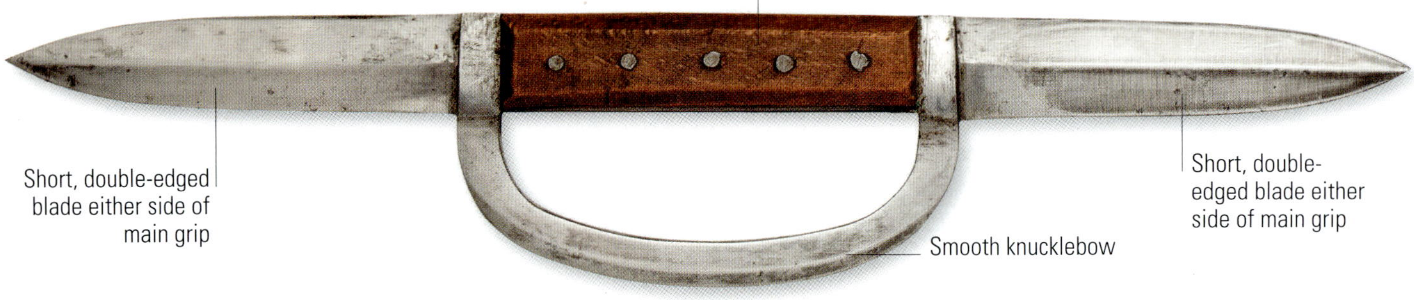

Wood grip scales mounted on central tang, secured by rivets

Short, double-edged blade either side of main grip

Smooth knucklebow

Short, double-edged blade either side of main grip

The bichwa (sometimes spelled bich'hwa) originated in India and usually had slightly curved, or wavy, blades. Some examples had two blades either side of the central grip. It was designed as a parrying knife, used in the left hand to thwart an opponent's blade, while the right hand retained a longer offensive weapon (sword or long dagger). This example appears to be a privately manufactured item, European and of modern construction.

DATE	late 20th century
ORIGIN	BRITISH
LENGTH	36.4cm (14.3in)

German flick knife, late 20th century

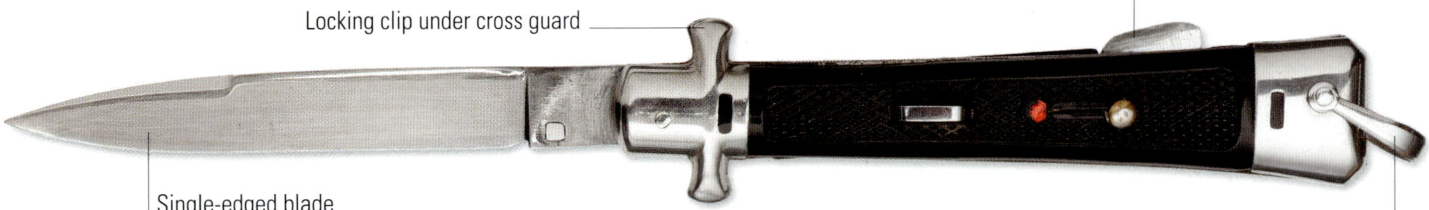

Release spring for locking clip

Locking clip under cross guard

Single-edged blade with double-edged tip

Lanyard ring

The flick-knife is, in reality, a spring-operated lock-back knife. The design has been known since the latter part of the 19th century, although its widespread popularity (and notoriety) seems to be encapsulated in the "Teddy boy" era of the early 1950s. The blade is folded into a hilt like a regular clasp-knife, and locked into position – under spring tension – with a clip. Depression of the button on the face of the grip releases the blade which swings out and into the open position, locked there by a spring clip inside the cross guard. Depressing a release spring on the side of the grip allows the blade to be folded back into a safe, closed position.

DATE	late 20th century
ORIGIN	GERMAN
LENGTH	24cm (9.4in)

West German Bundeswehr gravity knife, 1970s onward

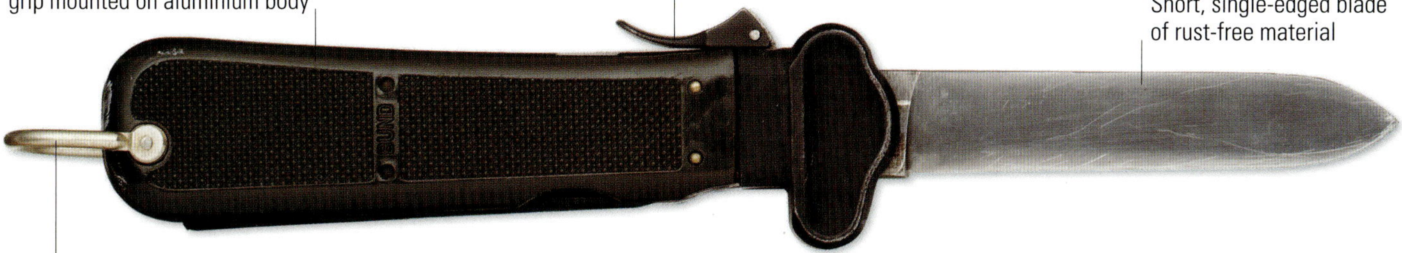

DATE	1970s onward
ORIGIN	WEST GERMAN
LENGTH	25.7cm (10.1in)

The design of this item has been clearly influenced by the World War II flight utility knife for the *Fallschirmjäger* (Paratroopers). Construction features have been improved, and the knife is lighter than the original wartime version. It is also designed to be stripped down for easy maintenance and repair work. The original examples were not designed to strip down, and were prone to fracturing on the spring.

West German spring-operated switchblade knife, 1970s onward

DATE	1970s onward
ORIGIN	WEST GERMAN
LENGTH	21.5cm (8.4in)

The "switchblade", so called because it is controlled by a switch on the outer grip, is wholly contained inside the hilt and held in place by a spring. The forward movement of the switch causes the blade to eject forward, then snap into position locked by a spring clip. Retraction of the switch causes the spring clip to release the blade, and the spring mechanism propels the blade back into the grip.

American Applegate-Fairbairn knife, 1980s

DATE	1980s
ORIGIN	AMERICAN
LENGTH	28cm (11in)

This knife was a joint venture by Rex Applegate, America's leading exponent of military close-combat knife-fighting, and W. Fairbairn, of the famous Fairbairn and Sykes design team. It appears that only commemorative copies were produced, for collectors interested in the historical association.

American keyring punch dagger and sheath, late 20th century

Intended as a personal self-defence item, this punch dagger is an evolutionary development of the punch daggers designed in the United States in the mid-1800s. Although not designed to create a knife-like slash wound, it is a formidable item when held in the clenched fist – capable of breaking a bone with a direct hit.

DATE	late 20th century
ORIGIN	AMERICAN
LENGTH	7.2cm (2.8in)

Taiwanese butterfly knife, late 20th century

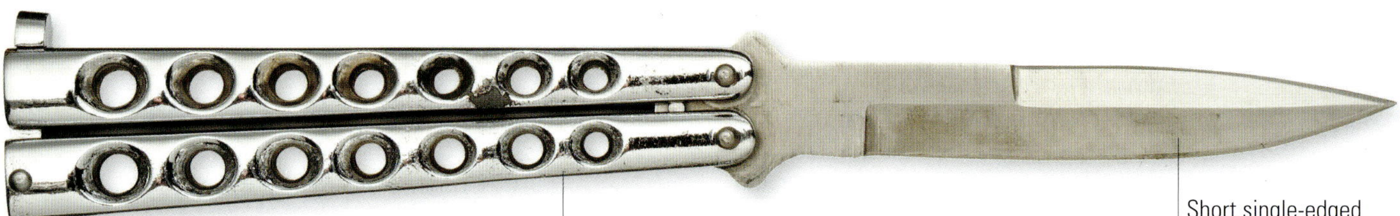

This folding knife does not have a tang. The blade is riveted to the two halves of the grip, each rivet acting as a hinge. Separating the halves of the grip at the base causes one half and the blade to swing around so that the blade faces down and insets into the grip. The second part of the grip follows round and covers the rest of the blade – now totally enclosed within the two halves of the grip.

DATE	late 20th century
ORIGIN	TAIWANESE
LENGTH	23.4cm (9.2in)

American Damascus steel knife, present day

This vibrantly coloured fixed-blade knife, by the California knife-maker P. J. Ernest, is made from Damascus steel in the ladder pattern. Both the knife and bolsters were heat-coloured to bring out the intricate pattern of the steel. The handle scales are made from Siberian mammoth tooth.

DATE	present day
ORIGIN	AMERICAN
LENGTH	17.5cm (6.8in)

American bodyguard knuckleduster knife, present day

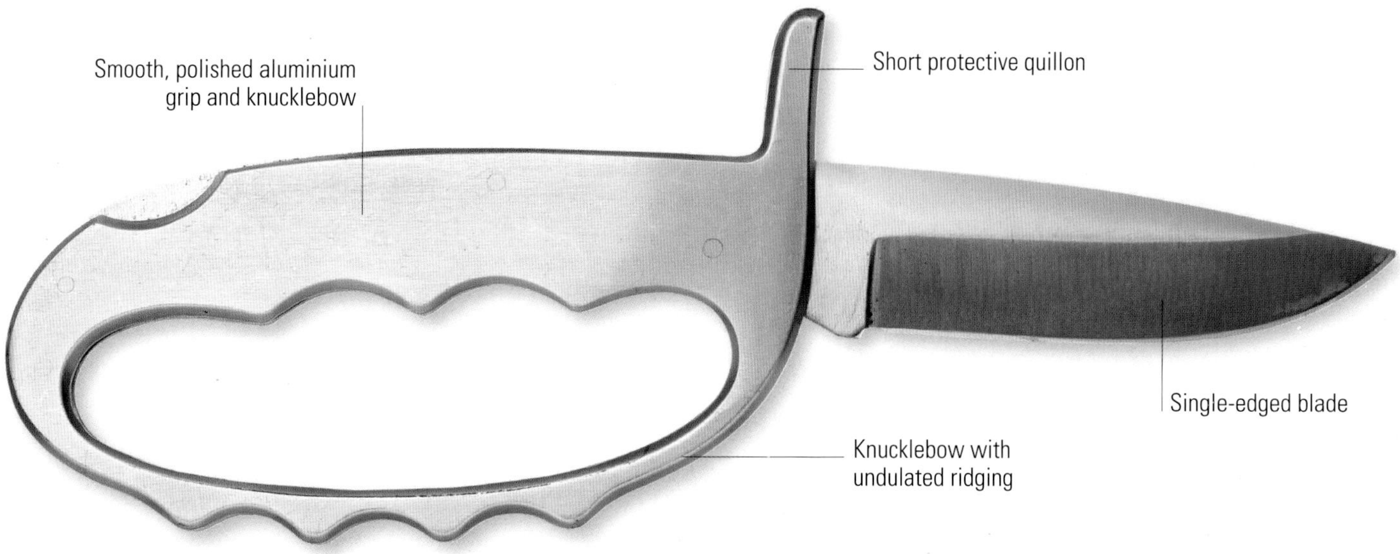

DATE	present day
ORIGIN	AMERICAN
LENGTH	23cm (9.1in)

The interpretation of what is permissible to carry as an item of self-defence is quite different in the United States compared to Europe. The above item is clearly of very modern manufacture, and is a very clean, 20th-century style. Designed as a "bodyguard" item, the intended market is unclear. Trained personnel, licensed as bodyguards, would be permitted to carry such a defensive weapon. If carried by an unlicensed person it carries the risk of being presumed to be a weapon of assault rather than defence.

Spanish Martinez Albainox knife, present day

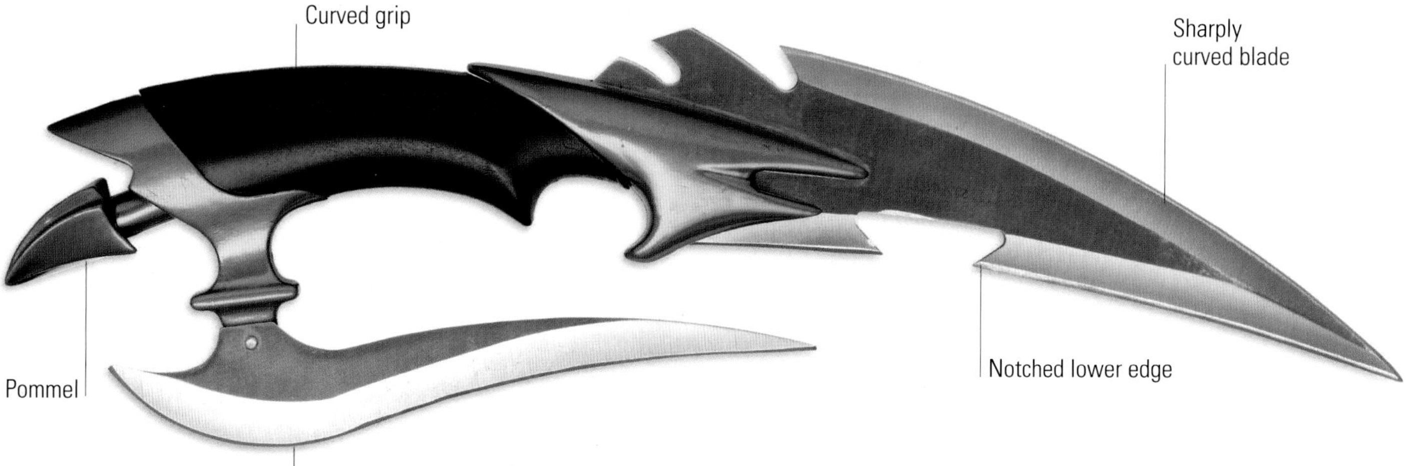

DATE	present day
ORIGIN	SPANISH
LENGTH	28.5cm (11.2in)

There is a school of modern knife-making that promotes the concept of knives of somewhat fantastical form – seemingly more rooted in the world of science-fiction than practical knife design. The above specimen by the Spanish company Martinez Albainox is clearly an impressive example. Intended purely as a collector's piece, the artistic sweep of the blade and the flow of the metal present a surreal appearance when compared to the utter simplicity of design of the Applegate-Fairbairn knife, for example. There are so many exposed points and edges on the item that any bearer might be advised to wear a suit of chain mail before unsheathing this weapon!

African knives and daggers

It is not surprising that the forms of knives and daggers found in Africa are almost infinitely diverse, given the size of the continent, the tribal nature of the people, and pervasive influences from the ancient Egyptians, Romans and other invader/trader nations. Although the workmanship cannot compare with that of other continents, the artistic style with which African smiths have designed their weapons is unsurpassed. The abstract nature of African art, its originality and vitality, attract worldwide admiration.

Yakoma or Ngbandi knife, mid-19th century

The tribal knives of the Yakoma and Ngbandi are similar and difficult to tell apart. In addition to their formal function, they were also used as currency, in particular to pay a "bride price". This blade has some nicely incised decoration; the hilt is bound with copper and it is made with a leather-covered pommel.

DATE	mid-19th century
ORIGIN	ZAIREAN
LENGTH	48.3cm (19in)

Mangbetu knife, mid-19th century

The Mangbetu of northeastern Zaire called this weapon a "trumbash", and its very particular shape is said to derive from ancient Egypt. In fact, a contemporary illustration of Rameses III (king of Egypt 1184–1156BC) shows him using a very similar "sickle-sword" when in the act of executing his enemies.

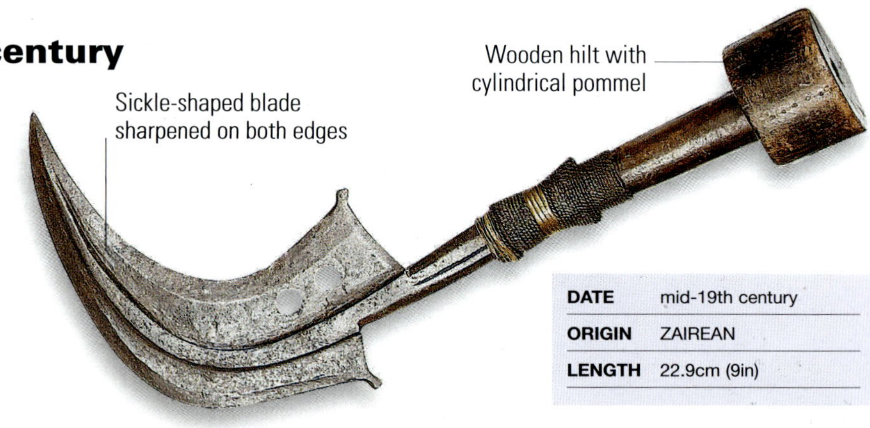

DATE	mid-19th century
ORIGIN	ZAIREAN
LENGTH	22.9cm (9in)

Konda shortsword, mid-19th century

This handsome knife was produced by the Konda of Haute-Zaire. Although its general shape commends it to close fighting, there is no doubt that in peaceful times it would have doubled as a particularly useful general-purpose knife. The wooden hilt and sheath are studded with brass nail heads forming a dense covering.

DATE	mid-19th century
ORIGIN	ZAIREAN
LENGTH	31.2cm (12.25in)

Ngala knife, late 19th century

DATE	late 19th century
ORIGIN	ZAIREAN
LENGTH	43.2cm (17in)

These Ngala swords from Zaire, with their unique form of sickle-shaped blade, were sometimes used for a particularly gruesome form of execution. The victim was secured to the ground with his head tied to a supple tree bent over for the purpose. At the moment of decapitation the head was catapulted into the distance.

Sudanese dagger, late 19th century

DATE	late 19th century
ORIGIN	SUDANESE
LENGTH	26.7cm (10.5in)

This dagger from Sudan is typical of those carried by followers of the Mahdi during the last quarter of the 19th century. It was intended primarily for stabbing, and the blade swells out towards the tip, which is slightly thickened in section. The blade is sharp on both edges and is contained in a leather sheath lined with cotton.

Sudanese double dagger, late 19th century

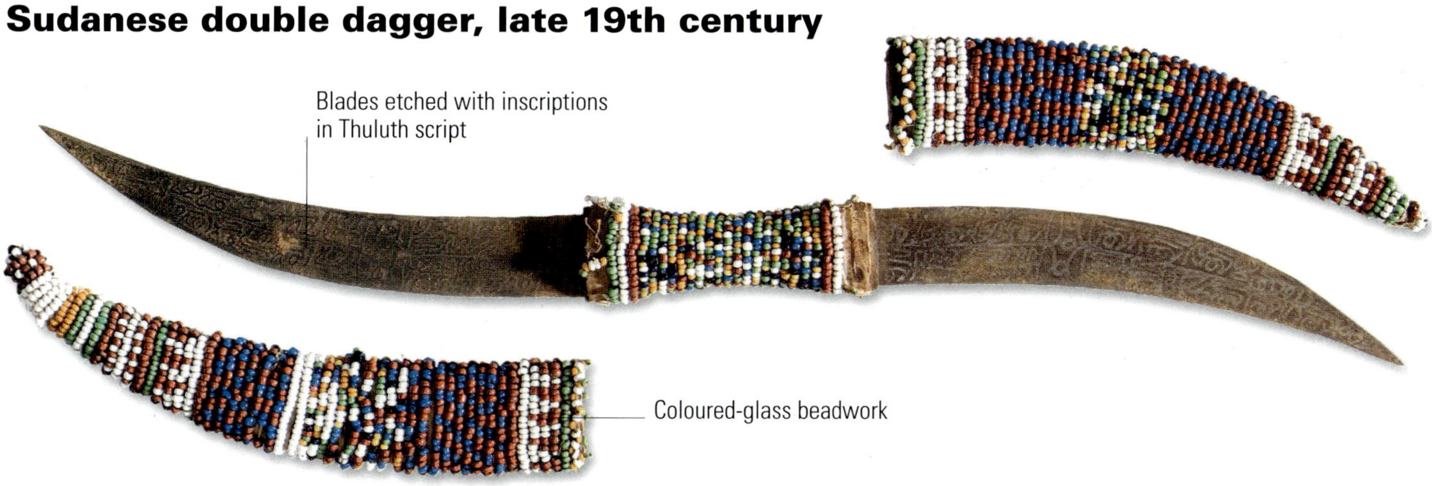

DATE	late 19th century
ORIGIN	SUDANESE
LENGTH	56cm (22in)

This double dagger comes from Sudan and is associated with followers of the Mahdi during the 1880s. The blades are etched with inscriptions in Thuluth script, which derives from that used by the Mamluks for monumental inscriptions. The wooden grip and sheaths are covered with multicoloured beadwork.

Hadendoa dagger, late 19th century

DATE	late 19th century
ORIGIN	NORTHEAST AFRICAN
LENGTH	19.5cm (7.7in)

The Hadendoa are a Nilotic people from Sudan, Egypt and Eritrea. Their unique style of dagger has an H-shaped ebony hilt, sometimes with silver-wire binding and fittings; it was carried in a leather sheath. It was extensively used when fighting against the British in support of the Mahdi in Sudan at the end of the 19th century, and was sometimes used to "hamstring" British horses.

Nubian arm dagger, *c.*1900

Nubia is a region of Sudan close to the River Nile. These daggers are found in leather sheaths which have woven leather straps to bind them to the wearer's arm. The circular pommel is lathe-turned and looks very similar to the counter used in the game of draughts. Often the dagger hilts have a pommel made of ivory.

DATE	*c.*1900
ORIGIN	NUBIAN
LENGTH	27.4cm (10.8in)

Somali "Billa" knife, *c.*1900

This Somali knife was produced by Arab cutlers who imported the skills of silversmithing from Oman. Arab interaction with Africa's east coast occurred through trade and traders; indeed, Zanzibar was ruled by Oman and Muscat during the 18th and 19th centuries. Only the finest of these knives have hilts of ivory and silver; others are made from horn or wood.

DATE	*c.*1900
ORIGIN	SOMALI
LENGTH	43.4cm (17.1in)

Sudanese throwing knife, *c.*1900

These multi-bladed throwing knives do not seem to have been produced for use, and may have had a ceremonial function or even have been made purely for the souvenir market. Sometimes stamped with geometric ornament, they have grips often bound with leather over cotton cloth.

DATE	*c.*1900
ORIGIN	SUDANESE
LENGTH	unknown

Moroccan jambya or koummya, early 20th century

These daggers are among the most numerous ever to have been produced in Africa, and their design conforms very closely. However, the grips can be made from wood, bone or ivory, while the mounts are of brass, silver and even gold. The blades are mostly plain or undecorated.

DATE	early 20th century
ORIGIN	MOROCCAN
LENGTH	31cm (12.2in)

Central African arm knife, 20th century

DATE	20th century
ORIGIN	CENTRAL AFRICAN
LENGTH	unknown

This type of arm dagger is commonly encountered all over Central and North Africa, from Nigeria to Sudan, and from the Sahara Desert to Cameroon. They are distinguished by the woven leather bindings to the hilt and by the protruding flattened iron pommel. They were and still are made by a large variety of tribes and craftsmen, perhaps the finest being Mandingo leatherworkers.

Persia, Middle East and Turkey

This geographic area has been home to a multitude of peoples and dynasties possessing fabulous wealth and artistry, and this is reflected in their weapons. The best knives and daggers came from the court workshops set up to reflect the majesty, wealth and reputation of their patrons. The quality of production would tend to diminish with distance from court, where function and cost were critical considerations.

Venetian or Turkish khanjar dagger, *c.*1520

This most unusual dagger was made in Venice for the Turkish market. The blade shape is found on daggers from the Mediterranean to Scotland. Venetian craftsmen specialized in the manufacture of weapons and armour for export to Turkey, and they were very accomplished at interpreting Turkish ornament.

DATE	*c.*1520
ORIGIN	VENETIAN/TURKISH
LENGTH	38.6cm (15.2in)

Ottoman Turkish knife, 17th century

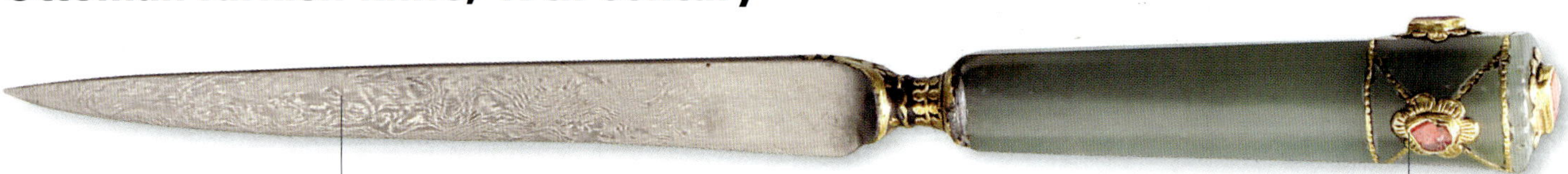

The blade of this dagger comes from Persia or India, and is made from watered steel. The jade hilt is only inlaid with gold at the top and the rest of the hilt is plain to enable the dagger to slide down deep into its sheath, with only the decorated pommel showing. The hilt is Turkish and dates from the 17th century.

DATE	17th century
ORIGIN	OTTOMAN TURKISH
LENGTH	19cm (7.5in)

Persian khanjar, *c.*1800

This fine Persian khanjar has a walrus-ivory hilt of the best quality. It is beautifully carved with a naked couple standing between two trees; at their feet are three naked children. It was made during the Qajar Dynasty, *c.*1800. The depiction of naked human figures is unusual in Persian art, but other daggers with similar subjects are known. It is possible they were made for the prurient, or for non-Muslims. The blade is made from finely watered steel.

DATE	*c.*1800
ORIGIN	PERSIAN
LENGTH	39cm (15.4in)

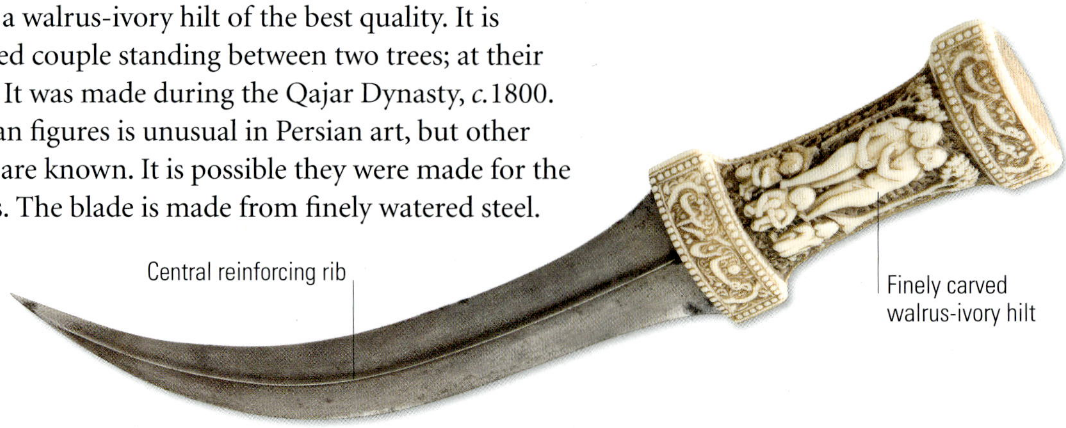

Ottoman Turkish khanjar with nephrite grips, early 18th century

DATE	early 18th century
ORIGIN	OTTOMAN TURKISH
LENGTH	34cm (13.4in)

The two-piece grips are made of jade. There are two different types of jade called nephrite and jadeite respectively; the former is slightly harder than the latter. This classic Ottoman dagger dates from the early 18th century, although the shape of the hilt is more commonly found on daggers of the 17th century.

Ottoman Turkish silver-mounted khanjar dagger, *c.*1740

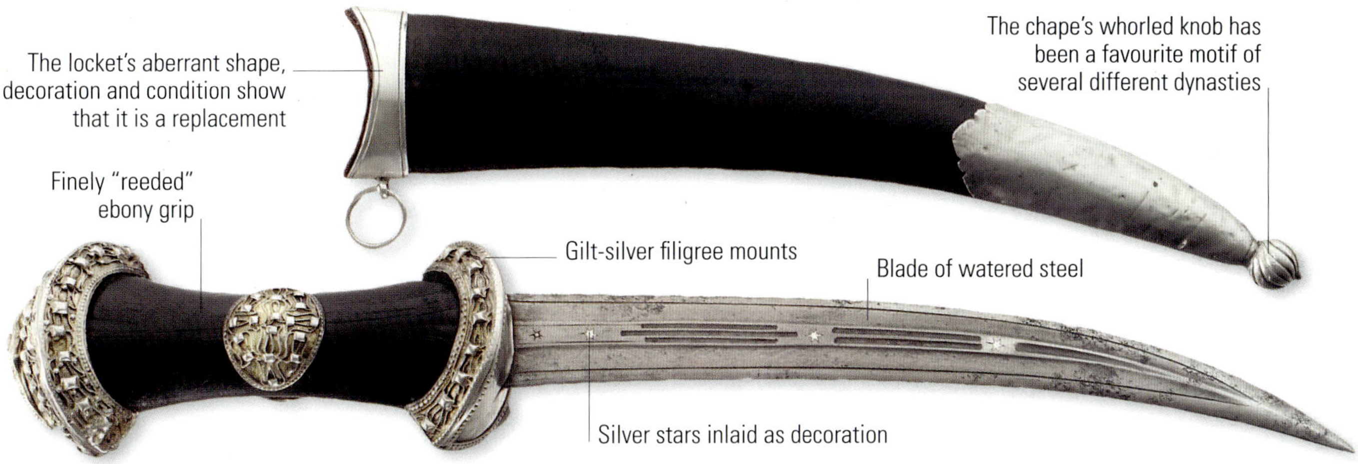

DATE	c.1740
ORIGIN	OTTOMAN TURKISH
LENGTH	42cm (16.5in)

Silver stars are found inlaid into Turkish blades from the 17th to the 19th centuries. This dagger, dating from *c.*1740, has a "reeded" ebony grip and is fitted with fine-quality filigree mounts made from gilt silver. This is a large dagger, and the original owner would have worn it in a prominent position.

Ottoman Turkish bichaq knife with agate grip, early 19th century

DATE	early 19th century
ORIGIN	OTTOMAN TURKISH
LENGTH	33cm (13in)

The bichaq serves principally as a knife, although it could be called into service as a dagger. This Ottoman example has an agate hilt with a gold-set jewel inlaid into the pommel. The blade has a false-damascened inscription, and it retains its original silver-mounted sheath. It dates from the early 19th century.

Ottoman Turkish khanjar, early 19th century

The shape of this dagger was found across Ottoman Turkey during the 18th and 19th centuries, but it is particularly associated with the Kurds. The grip is made from brass, and the double-edged blade is carved with a central rib and forms two shallow "fullers" between it and the slightly raised edges.

DATE	early 19th century
ORIGIN	OTTOMAN TURKISH
LENGTH	40.5cm (15.9in)

Uzbek kard, early 19th century

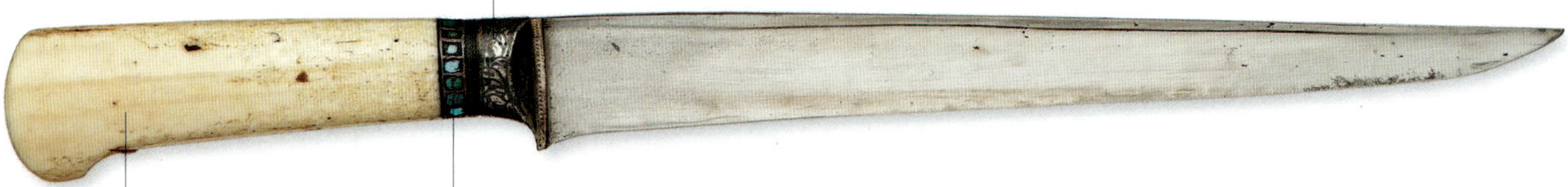

This dagger comes from Bukhara in Uzbekistan (formerly Turkestan), which was an important city on the Silk Road. Their weapons production famously employed the use of turquoise, either cut or polished, or as polished chips. The silver ferrule is decorated with niello (a shiny black alloy) and the grip is made from walrus tusk.

DATE	early 19th century
ORIGIN	UZBEK
LENGTH	unknown

Ottoman Turkish stiletto, early to mid-19th century

This unusual dagger dates from the period during the 19th century when Turkey was intensely influenced by Western Europe (especially France). It is Turkish-made, but this particular type of dagger is known as a stiletto in Europe. The hilt and sheath mounts are made from gilt brass, whilst the blade is a simple, slender but strong spike designed for maximum penetration.

DATE	early to mid-19th century
ORIGIN	OTTOMAN TURKISH
LENGTH	33.5cm (13.1in)

Persian khanjar, early to mid-19th-century

An attractive Qajar khanjar built to create an impression, this dagger is fitted with a dark-coloured watered blade that has been chiselled and false damascened with an allegorical scene of a lion attacking an antelope. The hilt features two cabochon turquoises in gold mounts; the use of gold on the black blade combines with the light-coloured walrus-ivory hilt to produce a rich effect.

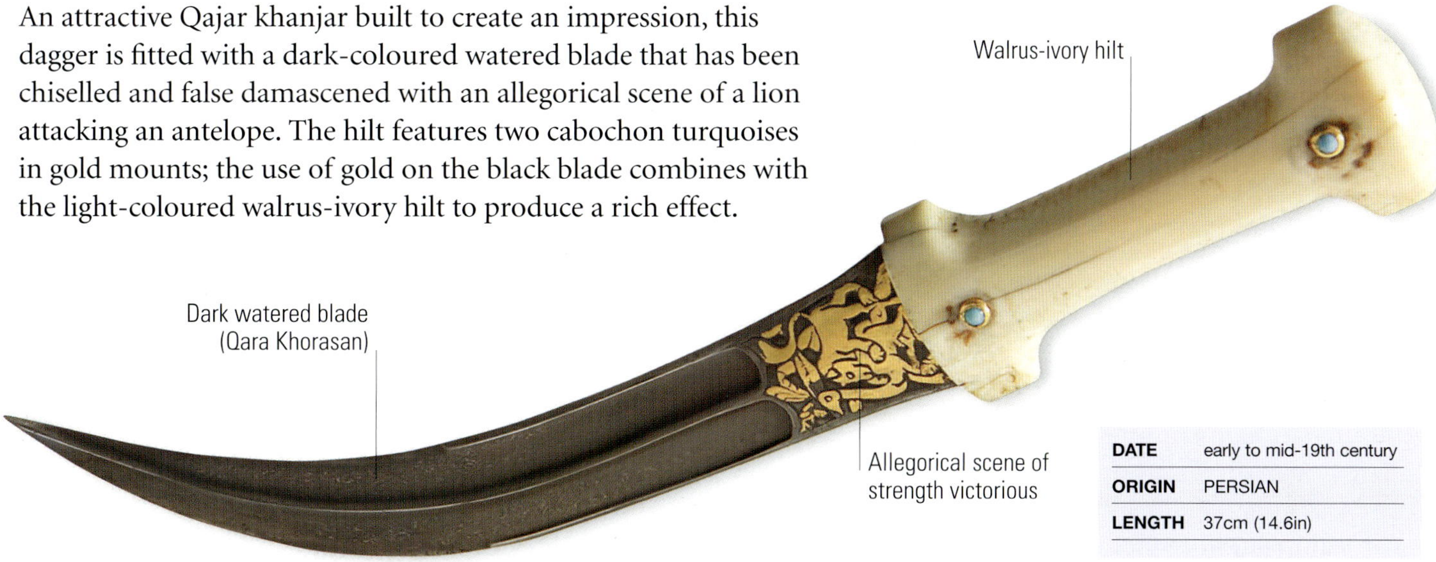

DATE	early to mid-19th century
ORIGIN	PERSIAN
LENGTH	37cm (14.6in)

Lawrence of Arabia

T.E. Lawrence ("Lawrence of Arabia") famously led an army of Arab tribes to victory against the Turks during World War I. Many depictions of Lawrence, such as this portrait, show him wearing Arab dress and a dagger. One particular dagger owned by Lawrence has an interesting history. In 1917, he was in Jidda for talks with Sharif Husain – head of the Arab nationalists – when he made his way illegally to Mecca. There he ordered a dagger with a gold hilt and sheath, probably supplying his own gold sovereigns to be melted down. "I did it because I wanted to choose my own gold dagger ... (it was made) ... in the third little turning to the left off the main bazaar, by an old Najd goldsmith." Lawrence sold the dagger in 1923 for £125 to his friend Lionel Curtis, who presented it to All Souls College, Oxford, where it remains. He used the money to refurbish Clouds Hill, his Dorset home close to where he was killed riding his motorcycle on 19 May 1935.

RIGHT Portrait of T.E. Lawrence wearing the silver-gilt Meccan dagger presented to him by Sharif Nasir in 1917.

Balkan Ottoman bichaq, mid-19th century

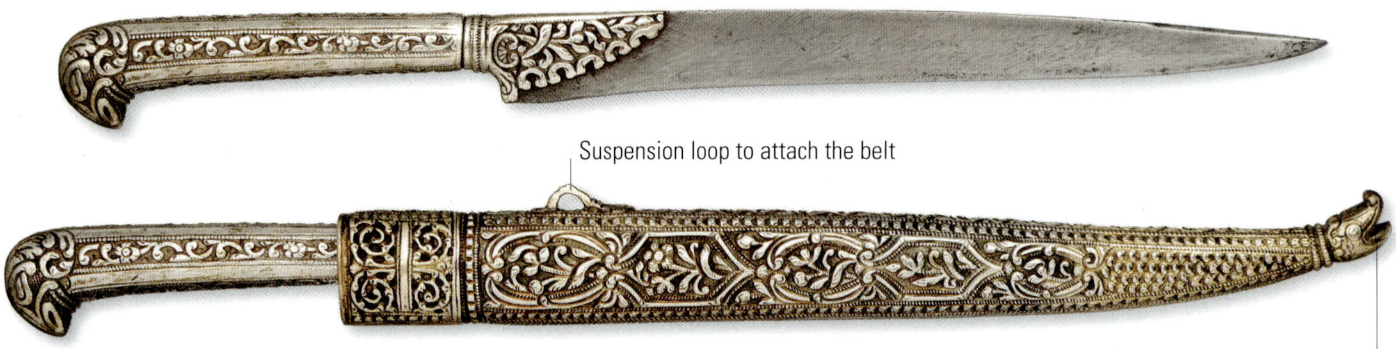

A silver-mounted Ottoman knife, or bichaq, from the Balkans. The scrolling foliate ornament covers the hilt as well as the sheath, whilst the pommel is in the form of a stylized animal's head, as is the finial of the sheath. The blade of the knife is thin and probably intended to function mostly as a utility knife.

DATE	mid-19th century
ORIGIN	TURKISH (BALKANS)
LENGTH	27cm (10.6in)

Saudi Arabian janbiyya/khanjar, mid-19th century

This silver-mounted Arabian janbiyya is from the Hijaz-Asir region. The double-edged blade is almost flat and has a simple chiselled device. The hilt and sheath are covered with silver, which is decorated with engraved decoration, granulation and filigree. Colloidal hard soldering is the process whereby tiny silver balls (granulation) or decorative silver wire (filigree) are applied decoratively to a silver ground with an organic compound. The work is then covered with silver salt and heated until the organic compound is driven off, and the salt turns to metal and fuses the decoration to the ground.

DATE	mid-19th century
ORIGIN	SAUDI ARABIAN
LENGTH	56cm (22in)

Omani janbiyya/khanjar, mid-19th century

The hilt of this Omani janbiyya, or dagger, is made from horn, probably from a rhinoceros, and was presumably believed to possess magical properties or to confer virility to its owner. Subsequent to the decline in the supply of rhinoceros horn, the giraffe horn and hoof became a popular material for use on grips. Now that conservation has become of great concern, the grips are usually made from plastic.

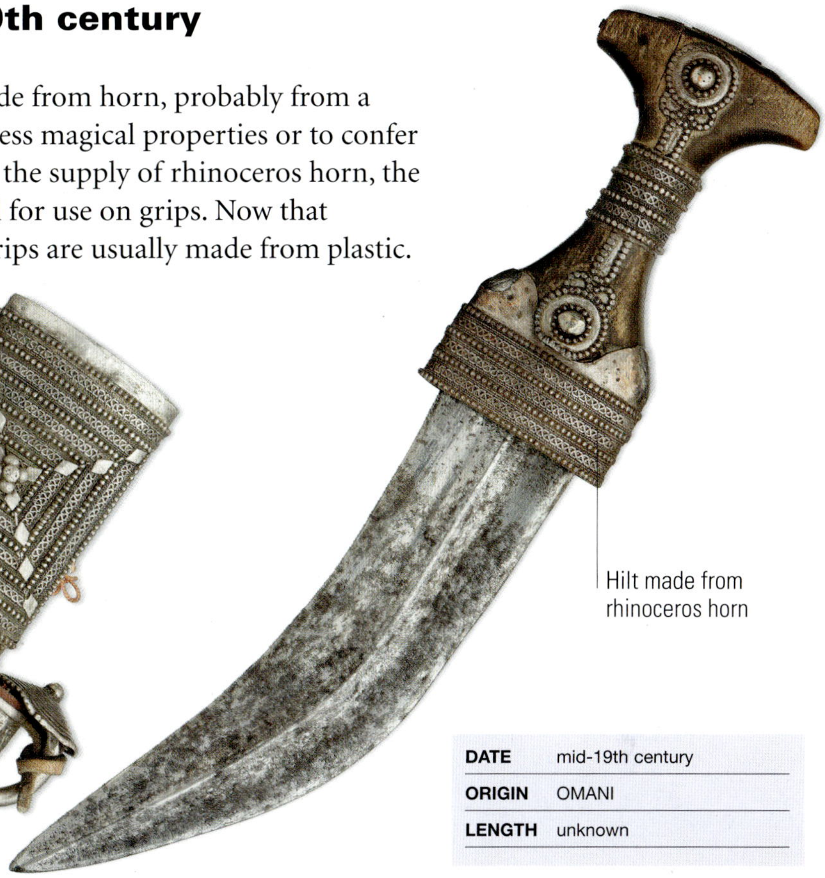

DATE	mid-19th century
ORIGIN	OMANI
LENGTH	unknown

Saudi Arabian janbiyya/khanjar, late 19th century

These janbiyyas with their distinctive long, curved blades are particularly associated with the conservative Wahabi sect of Sunni Muslims. The grip is made from horn, and reinforced with steel, copper and brass; the front has extensive silver ornamentation. The blade is noticeably thin and flat. The sheath, from a later date, is covered with multicoloured leatherwork.

DATE	late 19th century
ORIGIN	SAUDI ARABIAN
LENGTH	63cm (24.8in)

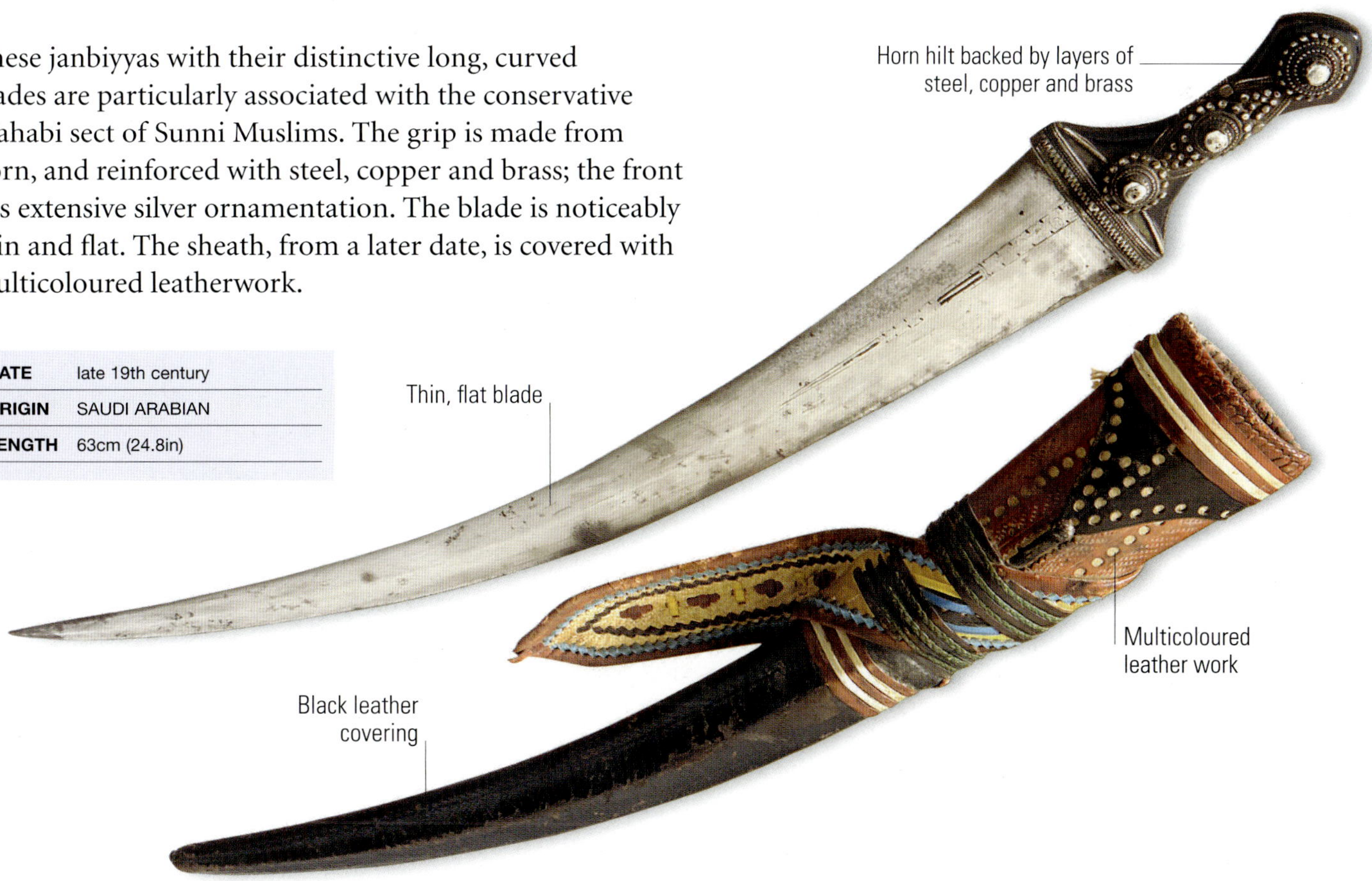

Yemeni khanjar and sheath, late 19th century

This is the classic form of Arabian khanjar and probably comes from Yemen. The horn is decorated with gold-foil imitations of the Venetian ducat (coin).The gold ducat was clearly held in esteem long after the Venetians ceased to be actively involved in trade in the area. The blades are burnished bright and the Indian-made sheath is fitted with a pierced silver chape.

DATE	late 19th century
ORIGIN	YEMENI
LENGTH	28cm (11in)

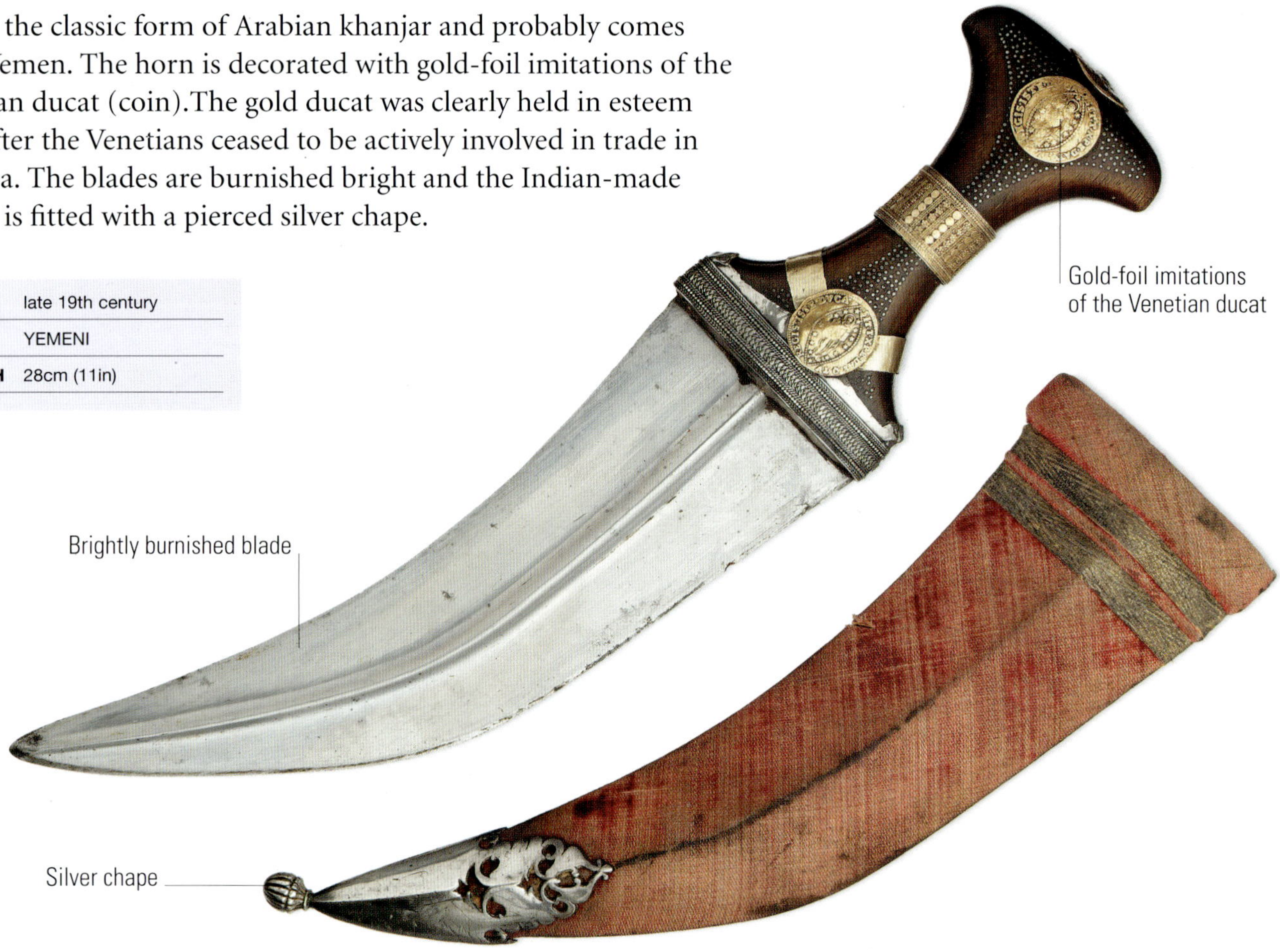

Gold-foil imitations of the Venetian ducat

Brightly burnished blade

Silver chape

Saudi Arabian janbiyya/khanjar, late 19th century

This massive dagger from Hijaz or Asir, western Saudi Arabia, is easily amongst the longest ever produced. The polished blade is stoutly reinforced by the raised central rib, and the hilt is secured by large and prominent silver-headed rivets. It seems likely that this weapon would also have been employed for various everyday purposes.

Large silver-headed rivets secure the grips

Stout reinforcing rib

Sheath covered in brown leather

DATE	late 19th century
ORIGIN	SAUDI ARABIAN
LENGTH	65cm (25.6in)

Persian khanjar, 19th century

DATE	19th century
ORIGIN	PERSIAN
LENGTH	41cm (16.1in)

The hilt of this 19th-century Persian khanjar is carved from a single section of walrus tusk and depicts a fashionably dressed couple carved in relief. The curved blade is T-section for half the length of the back edge, and is etched at the forte with an arabesque design. The blade is also etched with a pattern intended to imitate the watering of "Damascus" steel.

Omani janbiyya/khanjar, *c.*1900

DATE	c.1900
ORIGIN	OMANI
LENGTH	32cm (12.6in)

The silversmiths of Oman are renowned for their skills, particularly in the use of granulation. The back of the chape is embossed by the maker *'amal Abdullah Al-Beham* ("the work of Abdullah Al-Beham"), and the front of the sheath sports seven thick rings of silver. These are secured with twisted-silver wire, and the largest outside rings are used to fasten the sheath to a broad belt.

Saudi Arabian (probably Meccan) janbiyya/khanjar, *c.*1900

Both the hilt and the sheath are entirely covered with sheet silver on this dagger which probably comes from Mecca. The decorative silver ornaments applied to the hilt help provide a decent grip, whilst the sheath has engraved borders and an upturned finial, or *thum* (literally, "garlic bulb" in Arabic).

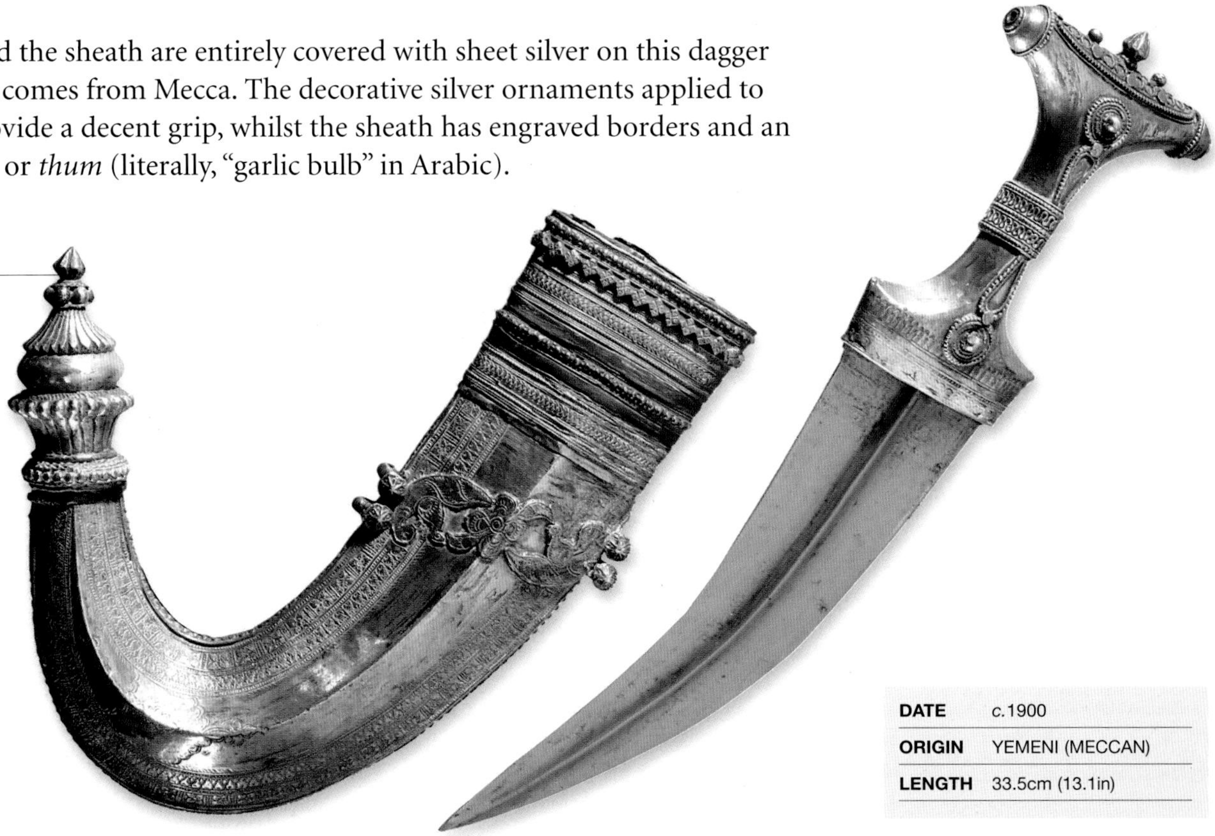

DATE	*c.*1900
ORIGIN	YEMENI (MECCAN)
LENGTH	33.5cm (13.1in)

Saudi Arabian janbiyya/khanjar, early 20th century

Few Arabian daggers are quite so distinctive as this example from Asir or Tehama in Saudi Arabia. The silver hilt and sheath display granulation as a decorative technique that also helps provide a firm grip. These elaborate daggers are still produced by Arab silversmiths for the tourist market today.

DATE	early 20th century
ORIGIN	SAUDI ARABIAN
LENGTH	46.5cm (18.3in)

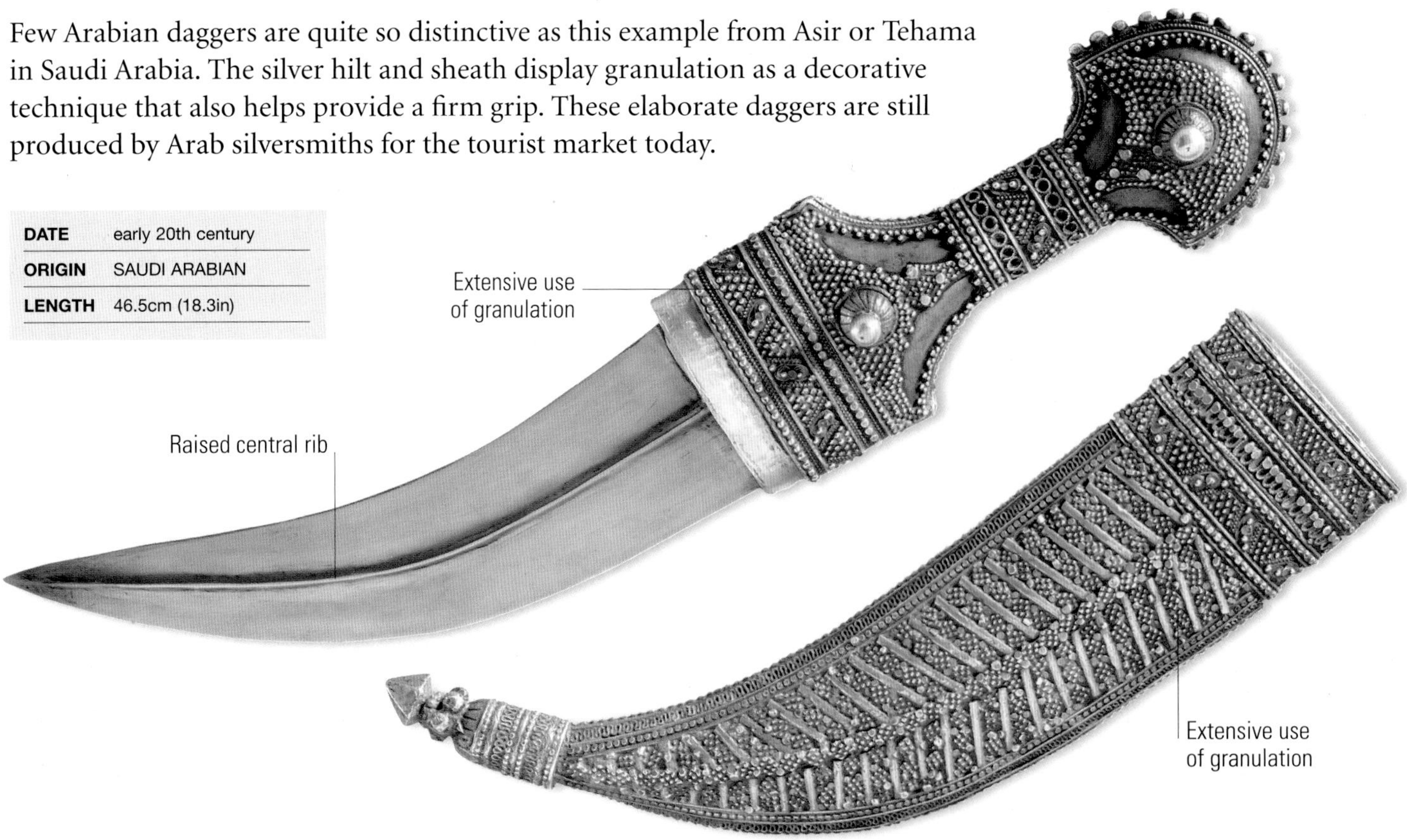

Omani janbiyya/khanjar, mid-20th century

Perhaps the most common dagger from the Arabian Peninsula, this example comes from Oman. The wooden hilt is faced with an undecorated sheet of silver, whilst the silver band at the bottom is embossed with foliage, and is designed to fit over the top of the sheath to prevent the ingress of sand and water.

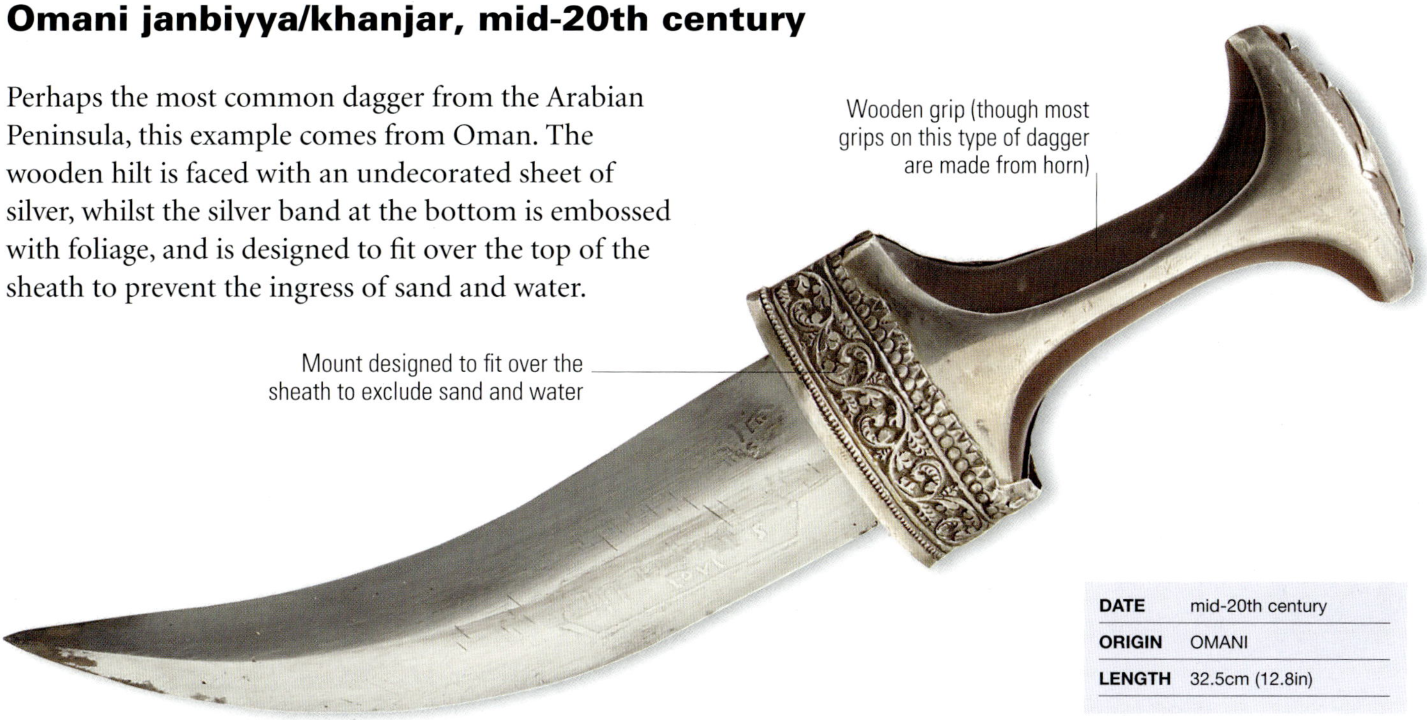

DATE	mid-20th century
ORIGIN	OMANI
LENGTH	32.5cm (12.8in)

Omani janbiyya/khanjar, *c.*1975

This late 20th-century Omani janbiyya is of poor quality. These types of daggers were produced not only for the tourist industry but also to fulfil a domestic Omani convention that the janbiyya (or khanjar) is an integral part of the national dress. It is unlikely that such a weapon would ever be required to see service.

DATE	*c.*1975
ORIGIN	OMANI
LENGTH	99cm (39in)

Indo-Persian khanjars

The expression "Indo-Persian" covers both the vast subcontinent of India itself and the lands occupied or ruled over by Persia when its empire was at its apogee. *Khanjar* is the general Arabic word for dagger.

Often, however, the term is used by collectors to describe a body of daggers with curved, double-edged blades from India, mostly with jade hilts, and from Persia, frequently with walrus-ivory or steel hilts.

Indian khanjar with Mughal hilt, late 17th century

The hilt is made from dark green nephrite (jade), the supply of which is supposed to have been exhausted before the end of the 17th century. The classic Mughal "pistol"-shaped hilt is carved with flowers and foliage in relief. The blade, which is probably of later date, is decorated with a repeated interlaced geometric pattern in gold koftgari.

DATE	late 17th century
ORIGIN	INDIAN
LENGTH	unknown

Indian khanjar, *c.*1700

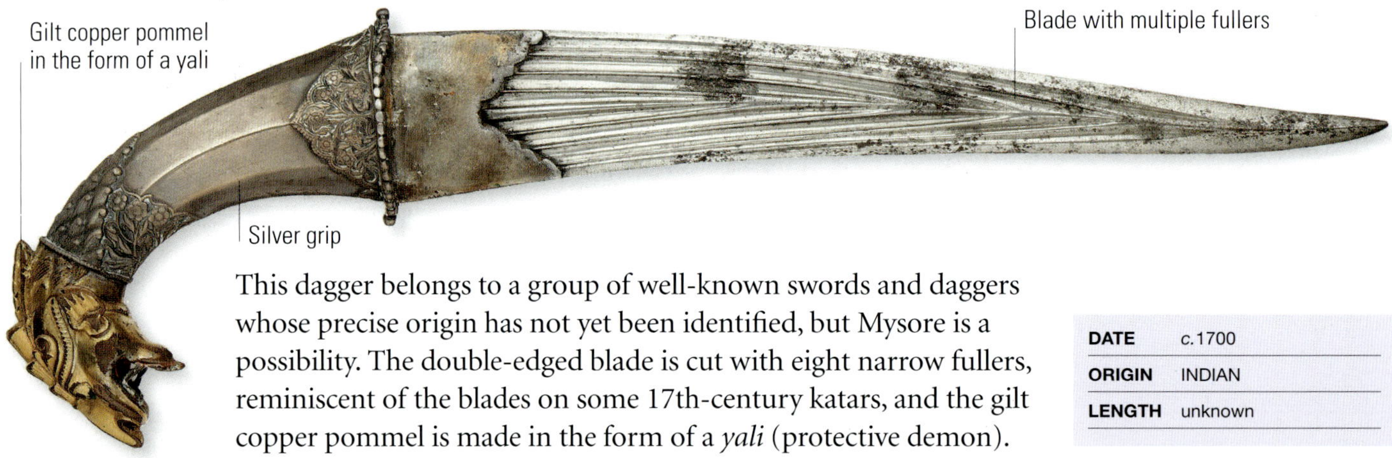

This dagger belongs to a group of well-known swords and daggers whose precise origin has not yet been identified, but Mysore is a possibility. The double-edged blade is cut with eight narrow fullers, reminiscent of the blades on some 17th-century katars, and the gilt copper pommel is made in the form of a *yali* (protective demon).

DATE	*c.*1700
ORIGIN	INDIAN
LENGTH	unknown

Indo-Persian khanjar and scabbard, early 19th century

A good-quality Persian dagger, the blade is of watered steel and is chiselled with the image of a lion attacking a gazelle (an allegorical scene). The ivory hilt is carved from a single piece of walrus tusk with figures and an inscription meaning "The shining blade of this amazing khanjar is so sharp it can split a thorn".

DATE	early 19th century
ORIGIN	INDO-PERSIAN
LENGTH	39.6cm (15.6in)

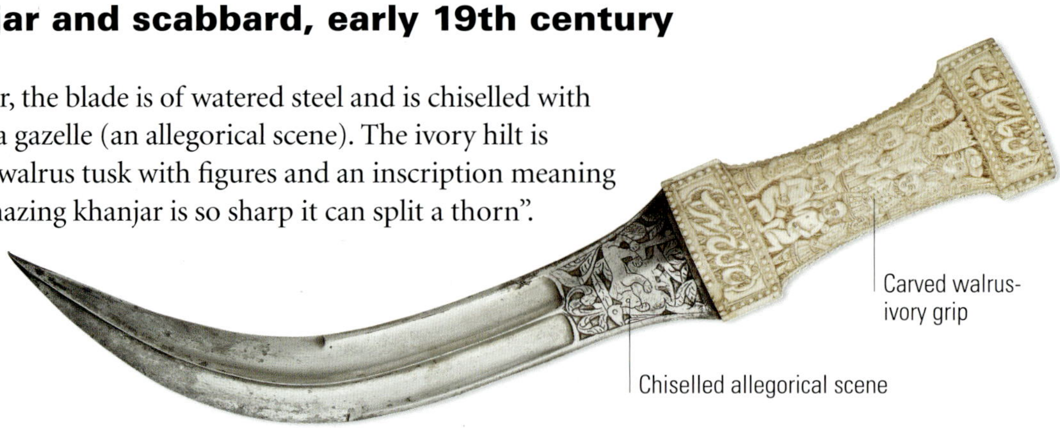

Indian khanjar, *c.*1900

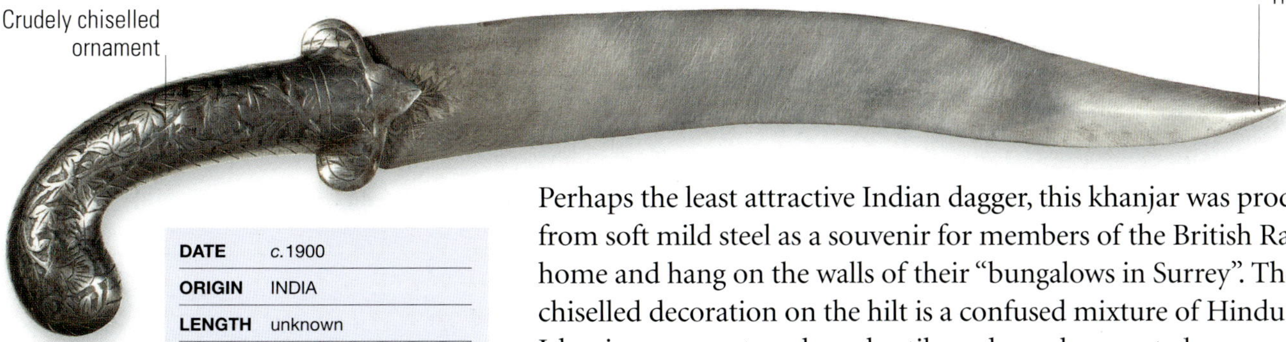

DATE	*c.*1900
ORIGIN	INDIA
LENGTH	unknown

Perhaps the least attractive Indian dagger, this khanjar was produced from soft mild steel as a souvenir for members of the British Raj to take home and hang on the walls of their "bungalows in Surrey". The chiselled decoration on the hilt is a confused mixture of Hindu and Islamic ornament, and was hastily and poorly executed.

Indo-Persian five-bladed khanjar, mid-19th century

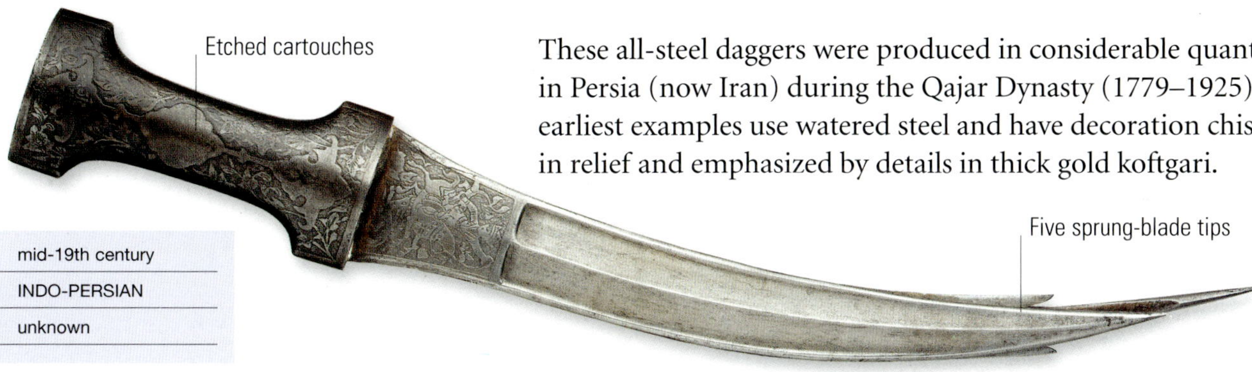

These all-steel daggers were produced in considerable quantities in Persia (now Iran) during the Qajar Dynasty (1779–1925). The earliest examples use watered steel and have decoration chiselled in relief and emphasized by details in thick gold koftgari.

DATE	mid-19th century
ORIGIN	INDO-PERSIAN
LENGTH	unknown

Indo-Persian five-bladed khanjar, mid-19th century

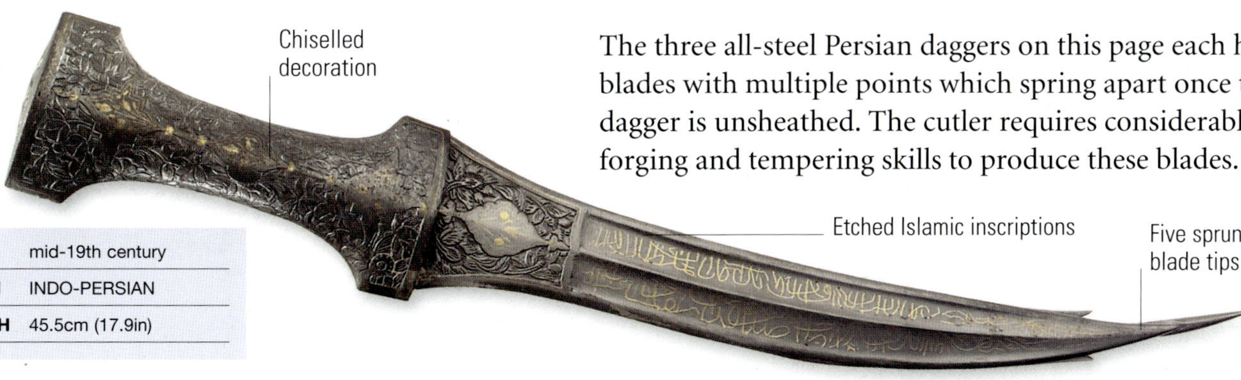

The three all-steel Persian daggers on this page each have blades with multiple points which spring apart once the dagger is unsheathed. The cutler requires considerable forging and tempering skills to produce these blades.

DATE	mid-19th century
ORIGIN	INDO-PERSIAN
LENGTH	45.5cm (17.9in)

Indo-Persian triple-bladed khanjar, late 19th century

DATE	late 19th century
ORIGIN	INDO-PERSIAN
LENGTH	49cm (19.3in)

The steel grip of this triple-bladed dagger is filled with a plaster-like substance which swells when moisture is absorbed. When this happens, the braised seam will begin to split open, as is the case here. Cartouches filled with Islamic inscriptions can clearly be seen decorating the hilt.

Indo-Persian kards

Kard is Farsi (the most widely spoken Persian language) and refers to a dagger with a straight, single-edged blade where the hilt is without a guard. Collectors apply the term to similar daggers from India and the Middle East. They may be fitted with delicately worked hilts of exotic materials, with blades of fine watered steel, but each will be of the same form as those made from more common materials.

Persian gold-inlaid kard, *c.*1800

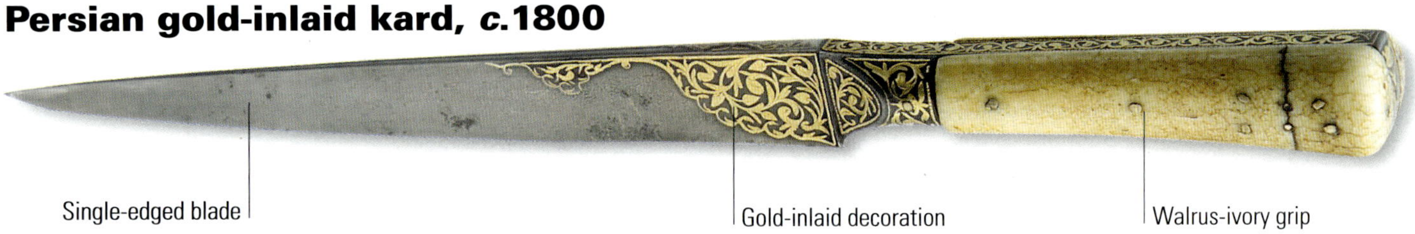

A classical Persian dagger of *c.*1800, this kard has a fine watered-steel single-edged blade which is decorated with gold-inlaid foliage in relief at the forte. This decoration continues around the grip strap. The grips are made from two pieces of walrus ivory. It seems ironic that these beautiful daggers were intended to be entirely covered by their sheath, with the exception of the last inch of the hilt.

DATE	*c.*1800
ORIGIN	PERSIAN
LENGTH	37.5cm (14.7in)

Uzbek kard with lapis lazuli hilt, *c.*1800

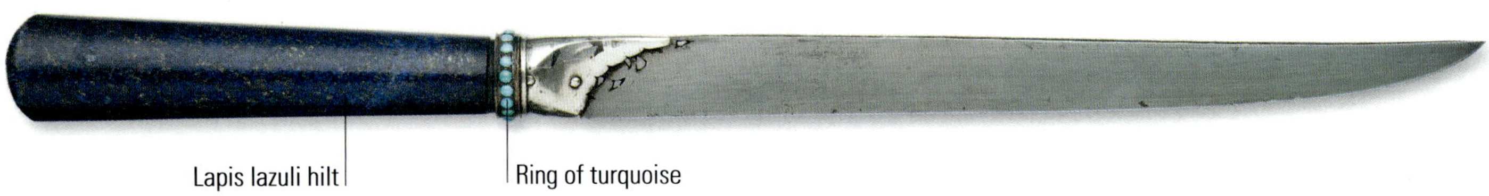

Lapis lazuli from Afghanistan is one of the most attractive stones with an intense blue colour. The ring at the base of the grip is decorated with polished turquoise, and this is almost a signature of production from Bukhara in Uzbekistan (formerly Turkestan). The small metal ferrule at the forte of the blade is also a feature of edged weapons from the Balkans.

DATE	*c.*1800
ORIGIN	UZBEK
LENGTH	34.7cm (13.6in)

Indian kard with stone handle, *c.*1800

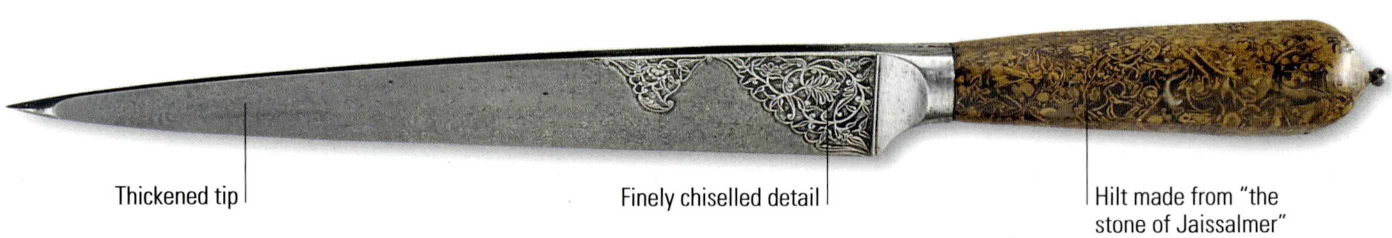

This high-quality Indian kard has a watered steel blade and is chiselled with foliage at the forte, while the tip is thickened to add strength at the point of impact. The hilt is made from "the stone of Jaissalmer", a yellow- and orange-coloured conglomerate which is highly attractive due to its clearly visible constituent parts.

DATE	*c.*1800
ORIGIN	INDIAN
LENGTH	44cm (17.3in)

Persian chiselled kard, *c.*1800

This kard is typical of high quality Persian work, the watered steel blade is nicely chiselled with arabesques at the forte, while the hilt is fitted with a two-piece walrus ivory grip. The blade looks slightly shorter than might be expected, possibly reduce in length by repeated sharpening during its working lifetime.

DATE	*c.*1800
ORIGIN	PERSIAN
LENGTH	38.5cm (15.2in)

Afghan "Khyber knife", early 19th century

"Khyber knife" is the term given by the British who fought on the northwest frontier of Afghanistan against various tribal groups who used this weapon, including the Mahsud, Pathans, Afridis and Waziris. The term is a slight misnomer because these weapons were used more as short swords than knives. Apart from the general shape, the defining feature is the very strong T-section blade.

DATE	early 19th century
ORIGIN	AFGHAN
LENGTH	58.6cm (23.1in)

Persian/Turkestan kard, early 19th century

DATE	early 19th century
ORIGIN	PERSIAN/TURKESTAN
LENGTH	40cm (15.7in)

This blade is of high-quality Damascus steel (wootz). The pattern has been revealed by polishing followed by treatment with one of dozens of "secret" processes or solutions, most of which involve a diluted form of acid. The two-piece grips were made from walrus ivory, identifiable by its "mutton fat" appearance.

Indo-Persian kard with green jade hilt, 18th century

DATE	18th century
ORIGIN	INDO-PERSIAN
LENGTH	37cm (14.6in)

The back edges of kard blades are slightly convex. This blade is made of crucible steel and shows a "watered" pattern which is an intrinsic property of the metal. The blade could have been made in either India or Persia, whilst the tapered jade hilt was probably made within the Ottoman Empire or in India.

Indian kard, early 19th century

Lahore is situated in the middle of the Punjab, and was an important centre of weapons production, particularly for the Sikhs. The unifying feature of Lahori arms production is the gold koftgari in geometric patterns, or a repeated foliate and floral motif often incorporating arabesques.

DATE	early 19th century
ORIGIN	INDIAN
LENGTH	unknown

Indian kard, early to mid-19th century

The shape of this fine-quality dagger from Rajasthan is testament to the care and skill of its maker. The recurved blade is made from finely watered wootz (crucible steel) and the grips are silver. The remaining mount (locket) of the sheath is decorated with gold koftgari. Rajasthan has a number of cities famed for the excellence of their swordsmiths and edged-weapons production.

DATE	early to mid-19th century
ORIGIN	INDIAN
LENGTH	31cm (12.2in)

Indian silver-mounted kard, early to mid-19th century

This silver-mounted Indian kard was probably made for a departing member of the Raj, and is quite an appropriate metaphor for the British who were soon to leave India. The lion looks both comic and bedraggled, a spent and forlorn force whose time has come. The blade is the work of a smith rather than a cutler, whilst the silver hilt and sheath have both been hastily fabricated.

DATE	early to mid-19th century
ORIGIN	INDIAN
LENGTH	unknown

Turkish kard, early to mid-19th century

DATE	early to mid-19th century
ORIGIN	TURKISH
LENGTH	26cm (10.2in)

This Turkish kard has been made with a jade hilt and the blade is of oriental Damascus steel (wootz). At the forte, next to the silver ferrule, it has been false-damascened with a gold inscription, typical of many kards and bichaqs produced in considerable quantities within the Ottoman Empire during the 19th century.

Afghan "Khyber knife", mid-19th century

DATE	mid-19th century
ORIGIN	AFGHAN
LENGTH	71cm (27.9in)

These short swords are always found with meticulously sharpened blades. Enormous strength was given to the blades by their T-section. The bolsters and grip straps were manufactured from steel or brass, and the grips, though normally of horn, were sometimes made from ivory or wood.

Afghan "Khyber knife", mid-19th century

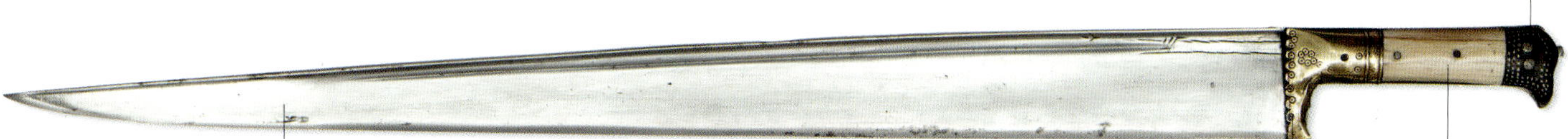

DATE	mid-19th century
ORIGIN	AFGHAN
LENGTH	72cm (28.3in)

The hilt of this "Khyber knife" is quite distinctive; there exists a matching smaller dagger which was probably carried through the same belt or sash. The grips are made from horn, though occasionally ivory was used, and the black buffalo-horn pommel is decorated with fine nail holes into which zinc foil has been pushed.

Turkish kard, *c.*1870

DATE	*c.*1870
ORIGIN	TURKISH
LENGTH	35cm (13.7in)

The hilt of this Ottoman Turkish dagger is made from polished sections of hard stone which have been inlaid with gold in a floral pattern. Frequently daggers with this type of hilt are found to incorporate cylindrical sections of the *munal* (mouthpiece) from a discarded *nargil* (water pipe), often with undecorated pommels.

Indo-Persian peshkabz

These daggers are common to Persia and northern India. They have single-edged blades which can be straight, curved or recurved. They are normally encountered with a T-section blade which imparts considerable strength. These daggers are found in a multitude of different qualities, from the refined and exotic court workshop productions to those produced by the Pathan tribal smiths in Afghanistan.

Indian peshkabz, mid-18th century

This Indian peshkabz is fitted with a blade of wootz steel which has been decorated with gold koftgari at the forte. The two-piece ivory grips show signs of cracking due to age. The slightly thickened cutting edge further reinforcing the strength of the blade can be clearly seen.

DATE	mid-18th century
ORIGIN	INDIAN
LENGTH	48cm (18.9in)

Persian peshkabz, *c.*1800

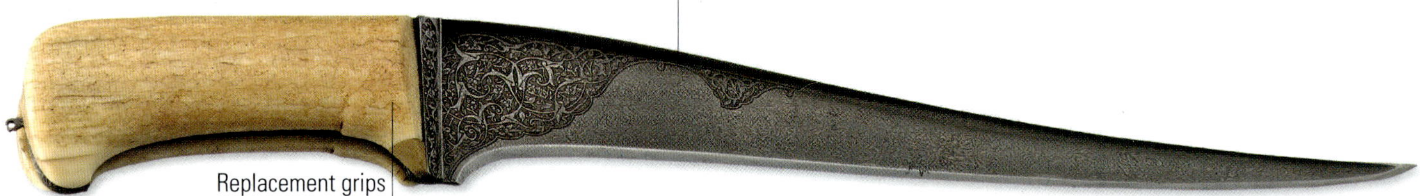

The recurve-shaped blade is made from finely watered steel, and the sides swell sharply outward before meeting the broad back edge. Chiselled arabesque decoration adorns the forte. The replacement two-piece walrus ivory grip overlaps the gripstrap; the original grip would have only reached the edge of the gripstrap.

DATE	*c.*1800
ORIGIN	PERSIAN
LENGTH	42cm (16.5in)

Indian peshkabz, early 19th century

The blade of this peshkabz is probably the most lethally efficient of any stabbing dagger ever devised. It derives its strength from the T-section which extends almost to the point. Such a blade would be perfect for penetrating the riveted links of a mail shirt. The ivory grips have been typically "pitted" to provide a firm hold.

DATE	early 19th century
ORIGIN	INDIAN
LENGTH	43cm (16.9in)

Rajasthani gold-inlaid peshkabz, early 19th century

DATE	early 19th century
ORIGIN	INDIAN (RAJASTHANI)
LENGTH	34.5cm (13.5in)

The button surmounting the pommel of this all-steel dagger from Rajasthan unscrews and the pommel hinges to reveal a hollow grip which could be used as a container. Similar but more elaborate examples contain small instruments, while legend has it that the space was used for more sinister purposes by would-be poisoners. The hilt is well chiselled in low relief with a repeated lotus flower pattern.

Indian peshkabz, early 19th century

DATE	early 19th century
ORIGIN	INDIAN
LENGTH	31.5cm (12.4in)

During the 18th and 19th centuries, Lucknow was famous for, amongst other crafts, its enamel work. The silver hilt and locket of this peshkabz are decorated with diagonal bands inhabited by assorted wild animals in multicoloured enamel. The predominant colours associated with Lucknow are blue and green.

Indian peshkabz with gilt copper hilt, *c.*1850

DATE	*c.*1850
ORIGIN	INDIAN
LENGTH	35.6cm (14.1in)

The hilt of this dagger is its most impressive part. It is made from gilt copper and is set with pastes of various colours. The overall effect is one of great richness, which has been achieved at limited expense. Such daggers were produced with matching sheaths and were made to satisfy the demand from well-off foreign buyers.

Indian knives, daggers and bayonets

The diversity of weapons found on the Indian subcontinent reflects the influences this area has absorbed from invading peoples throughout history. They include Persians, Greeks, Hindus and Muslims, with European influences later on. Apart from the excellence of their manufacture, it should be remembered that many weapons were invested with a spiritual or religious dimension by their owners.

Mysore bichwa, 18th century

This 18th-century dagger has evolved from earlier examples of the Vijayanagaran Empire (14th–16th centuries). A typical dagger from Mysore, the protruding eyeballs of the *yali* (demon) with their stepped, conical sockets are redolent of southern India. The looped bronze or brass hilt has a narrow integral grip.

DATE	18th century
ORIGIN	INDIAN (MYSORE)
LENGTH	32.5cm (12.8in)

Mysore socket bayonet (sangin) of Tipu Sultan, late 18th century

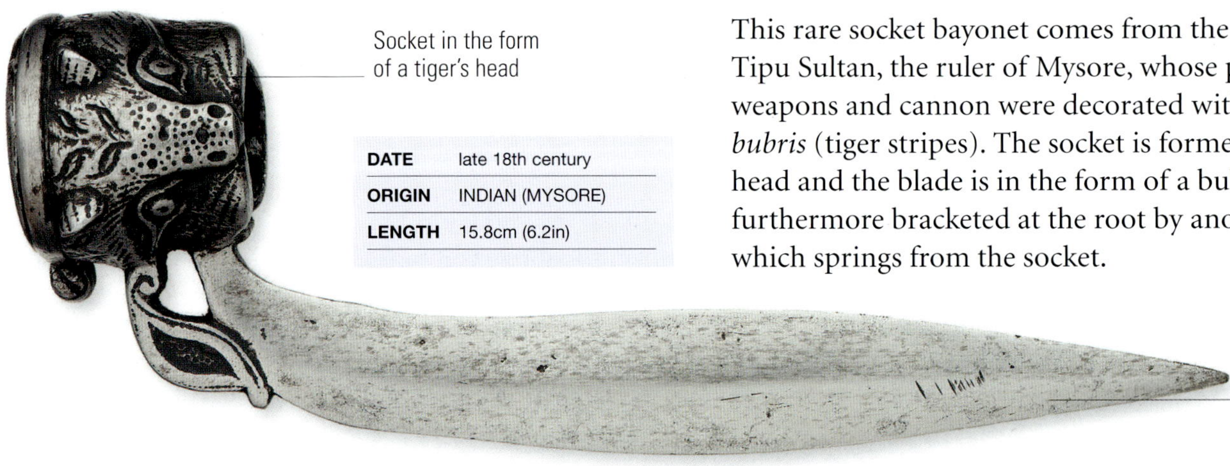

DATE	late 18th century
ORIGIN	INDIAN (MYSORE)
LENGTH	15.8cm (6.2in)

This rare socket bayonet comes from the armoury of Tipu Sultan, the ruler of Mysore, whose personal weapons and cannon were decorated with tigers and *bubris* (tiger stripes). The socket is formed as a tiger's head and the blade is in the form of a bubri which is furthermore bracketed at the root by another bubri which springs from the socket.

Indian plug bayonet signed by Anvar, late 18th century

The European plug bayonet design was later used as a model for hunting knives in France and Spain in the second half of the 18th century. This example is a southern Indian interpretation of one such hunting knife. The blade and cross piece are decorated with silver koftgari and signed *'amal Anvar* ("the work of Anvar").

DATE	late 18th century
ORIGIN	INDIAN
LENGTH	57cm (22.4in)

Indian bichwa with double blade, *c.*1800

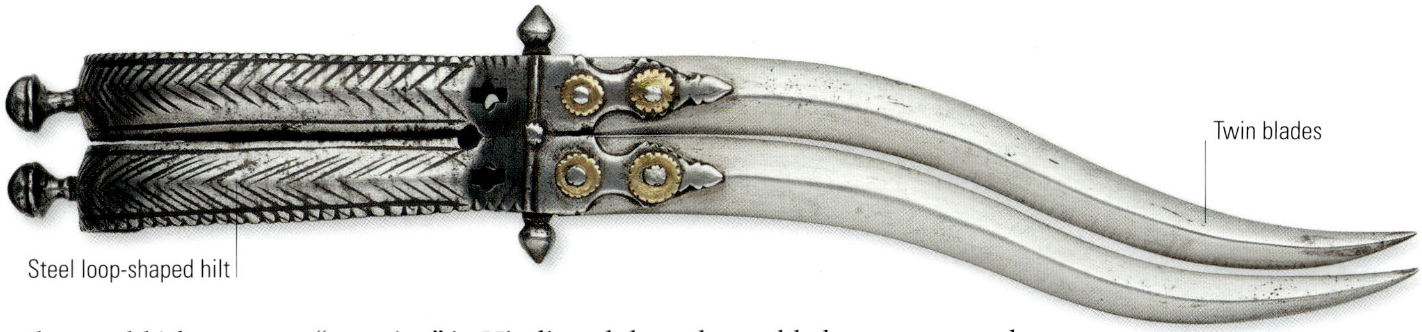

The word *bichwa* means "scorpion" in Hindi, and these dagger blades are supposed to have gained their name from their likeness to the tail of a scorpion or from their ability to "sting". The steel hilt is loop-shaped and the knuckle guards are cut with chevrons. There are bud-shaped finials to the pommel, and two buds protrude laterally as short quillons, or guards. This example is quite uncommon in having two blades and probably comes from Hyderabad. Being relatively easy to make, the bichwa has persisted into the 20th century as a decorative dagger.

DATE	*c.*1800
ORIGIN	INDIAN
LENGTH	32.8cm (12.9in)

Nepalese kukri, mid-19th century

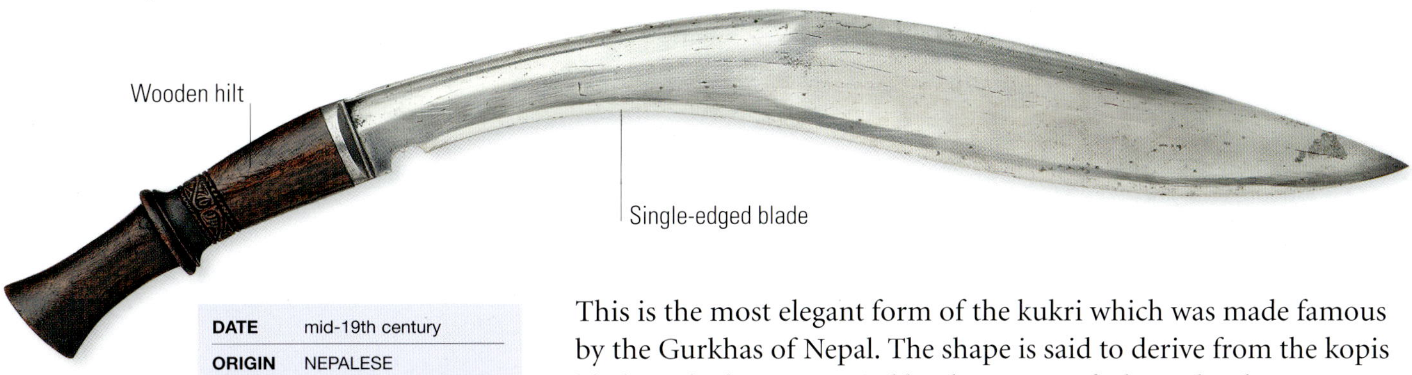

DATE	mid-19th century
ORIGIN	NEPALESE
LENGTH	unknown

This is the most elegant form of the kukri which was made famous by the Gurkhas of Nepal. The shape is said to derive from the kopis blades, which were carried by the troops of Alexander the Great into India in the 4th century BC.

Nepalese kukri, mid-19th century

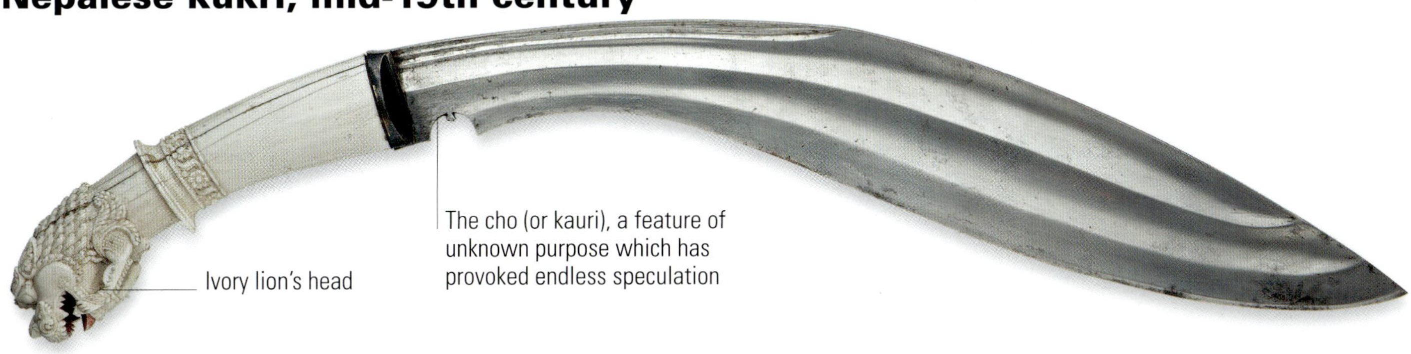

DATE	mid-19th century
ORIGIN	NEPALESE
LENGTH	40.6cm (16in)

The carving of a lion's-head pommel on the ivory grip of this kukri is a very unusual feature and denotes a high-status client. The blade too is a little unusual, and carving the channels and ridges into it in such a symmetrical and aesthetically pleasing manner requires a considerable degree of skill as well as artistry. The Gurkhas have earned a formidable reputation using this weapon for their fearlessness and bravery.

Mysore "knuckleduster" knife, early 19th century

This very exotic-looking Indian weapon from Mysore is a "knuckleduster" with two blades. The grip is made from brass and the steel blades protrude from yali heads. The manufacture is particularly well executed. Similar weapons, without blades, are used for a type of fighting during Dasara festivities and are called vajramustis.

DATE	early 19th century
ORIGIN	INDIAN (MYSORE)
LENGTH	32cm (12.6in)

Indian "tiger-claw" dagger, early 19th century

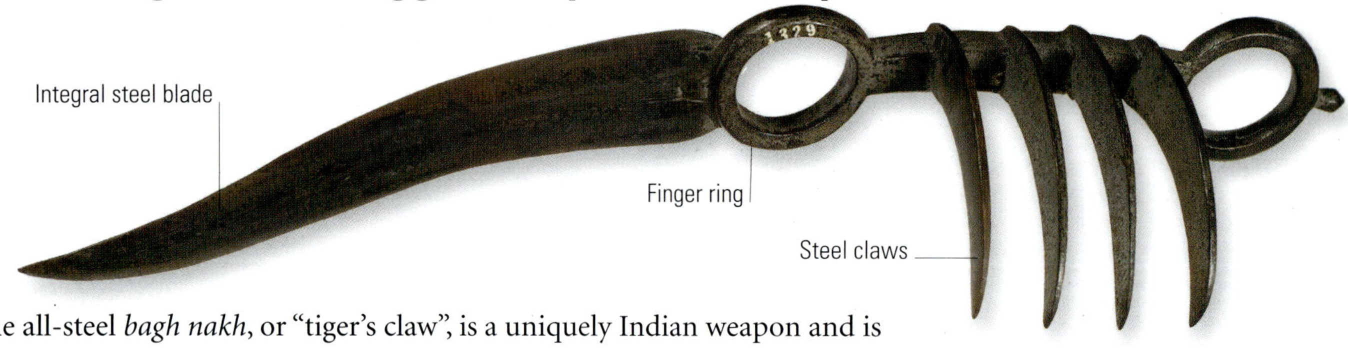

The all-steel *bagh nakh*, or "tiger's claw", is a uniquely Indian weapon and is designed for slashing. One was famously used in 1659 by Shivaji when he killed Afzal Khan; it had been concealed until the last moment within the palm of Shivaji's hand. The two rings are for the outside fingers, and the other fingers would lie on top of the steel claws.

DATE	early 19th century
ORIGIN	INDIAN
LENGTH	unknown

Coorg Tamil knife (pichangatti), mid-19th century

The *pichangatti* (the word means "hand knife") is a Tamil knife from Coorg. It has a broad, heavy, single-edged blade which turns up slightly at the tip. The hilts are often to be found made from silver, although brass and wood are also common. Most were made in the late 19th century and seem to have been used as utility knives or for chopping.

DATE	mid-19th century
ORIGIN	INDIAN (COORG)
LENGTH	unknown

Coorg Tamil knife (pichangatti), mid-19th century

DATE	mid-19th century
ORIGIN	INDIAN (COORG)
LENGTH	25.5cm (10in)

This pichangatti has a somewhat unusual silver hilt in the form of a parrot's head; the eyes are made from red stones. The Coorgs carry a chopper-like weapon called an ayda katti in a metal carrier called a todunga, and this is held in place by a belt. The correct position for the pichangatti is in the front of this belt. The sheath of this knife is bound with silver and from it, suspended from a chain, is a small kit of personal grooming tools for cleaning nails and ears.

Assam dagger (dha) with carved horn hilt, mid-19th century

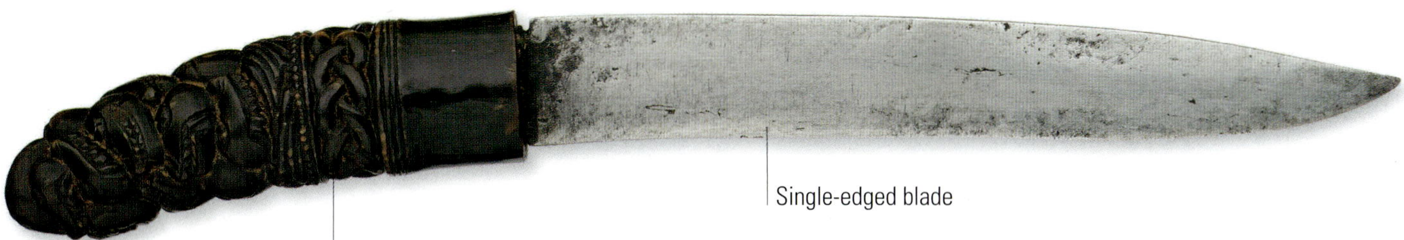

DATE	mid-19th century
ORIGIN	INDIAN (ASSAM)
LENGTH	23.6cm (9.3in)

This type of dagger, called a dha, is the classic Burmese form and is often found with a carved ivory hilt. The blades are slightly curved and single edged. This particular example has an unusual, carved buffalo-horn hilt, and is said to have come from Assam, close to Burma but sufficiently distant to have developed a somewhat unusual hilt. Formal Burmese dha hilts are carved with an assortment of demonic figures, sometimes in contorted poses.

Mysore bichwa, mid-19th century

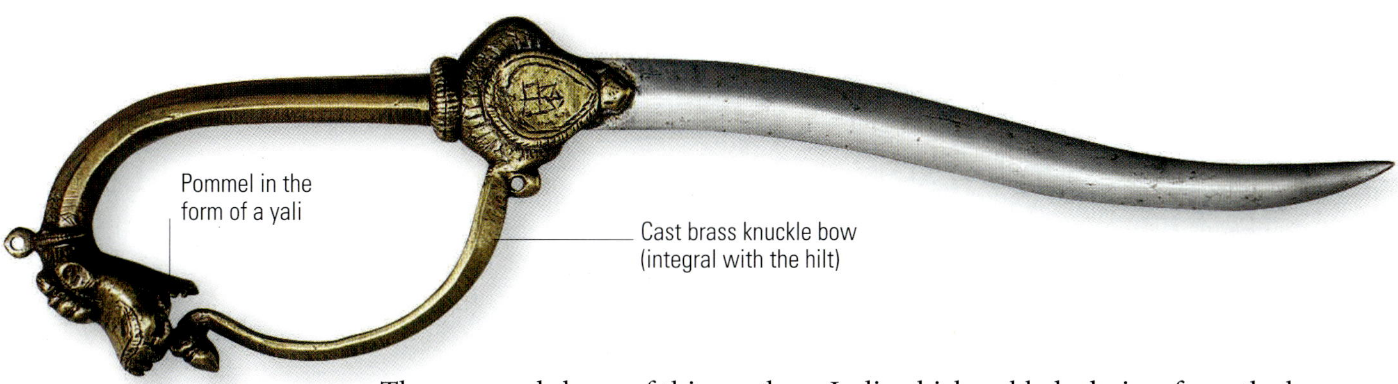

DATE	mid-19th century
ORIGIN	INDIAN (MYSORE)
LENGTH	unknown

The recurved shape of this southern Indian bichwa blade derives from the horn daggers made by the Dravidians (aboriginal inhabitants of India), who made their daggers from lengths of animal horns. The brass hilt has been cast in one piece and the pommel is in the form of a yali. The root of the hilt, however, is of such confused and debased design that it is likely to be of quite a late date.

Indian katars

The Indian katar is a punching dagger and, as such, the design is unique. It is an ancient Hindu weapon which was adopted by the Muslims. Usually made of all-steel construction, the hilt commonly consists of a pair of handlebars at right angles to the sides which extend upwards parallel with the user's arm. The triangular-shaped blade is normally cut with a number of fullers, although in the 16th and 17th centuries it became fashionable to fit katars with European blades which have parallel sides.

Indian katar, 17th century

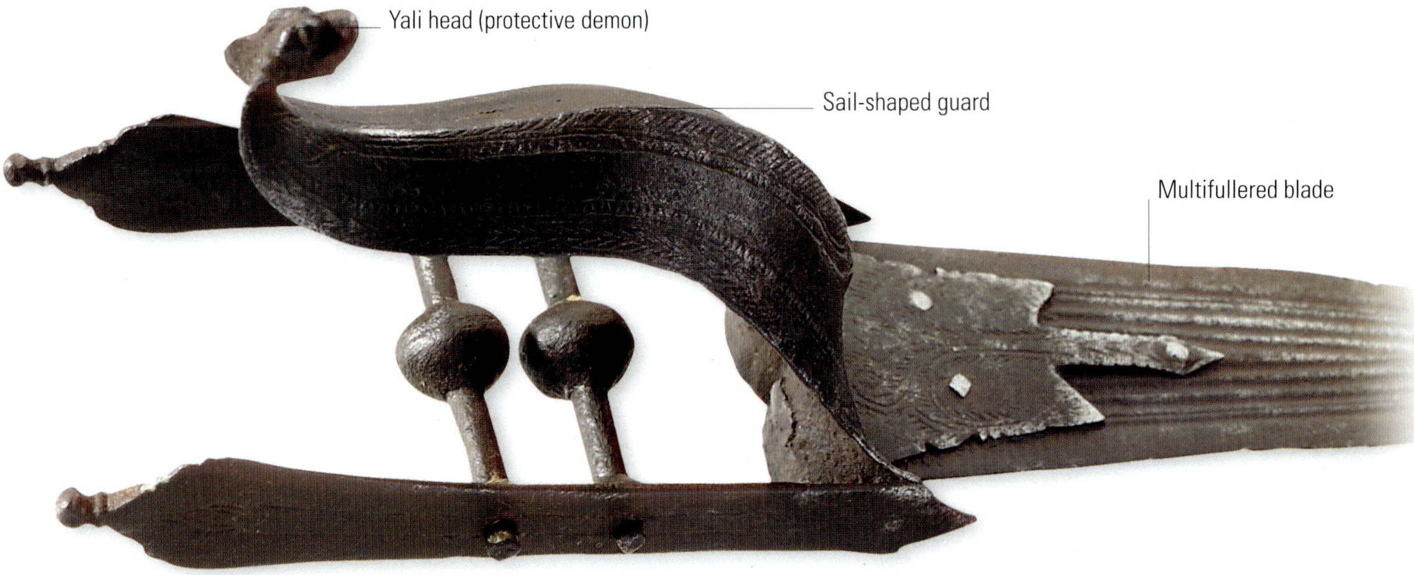

This form of katar, with its sail-shaped guard and multifullered blade, comes from the Vijayanagara Empire, which lasted until 1646 but whose power declined after a defeat in 1565. The twin-ball shapes inbetween the handlebars are hollow, and the sail-shaped guard that protects the back of the hand has a finial in the form of a yali.

DATE	17th century
ORIGIN	INDIAN
LENGTH	56.5cm (22.2in)

Northern Indian katar, late 18th century

The thickened tips of katar blades are often referred to as being "armour piercing". It is likely that only slender blades like this would stand a chance of performing that function. The twin handlebars are separated by a pair of confronting birds and the hilt retains traces of gold koftgari decoration. The fullers on the blade have been well cut.

DATE	late 18th century
ORIGIN	NORTHERN INDIAN
LENGTH	42.5cm (16.7in)

Rajasthani katar, 1800

DATE	1800
ORIGIN	INDIAN (RAJASTHANI)
LENGTH	30.5cm (12in)

This is a classic Rajasthani katar which has seen much use. The thickened point is clearly visible, and the irregular and "waisted" outline of the cutting edges are testament to the vigorous and persistent sharpening that it has undergone. The hilt is thickly covered with a conventional design of gold koftgari decoration.

Indian katar with scabbard, early 19th century

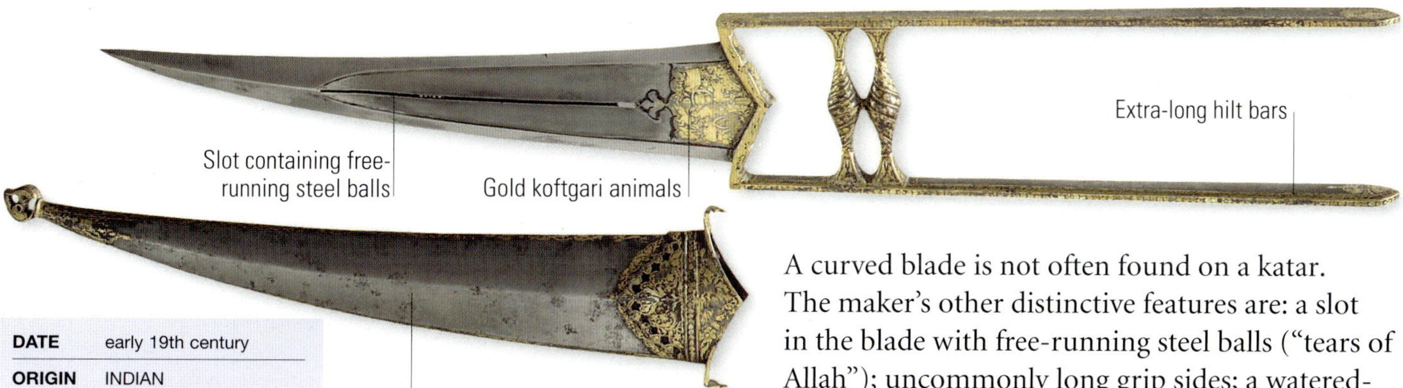

DATE	early 19th century
ORIGIN	INDIAN
LENGTH	61.5cm (24.2in)

A curved blade is not often found on a katar. The maker's other distinctive features are: a slot in the blade with free-running steel balls ("tears of Allah"); uncommonly long grip sides; a watered-steel sheath; and gold koftgari animal decoration more normally associated with the 17th century.

Rajasthani katar with elephant's head, dated 1849

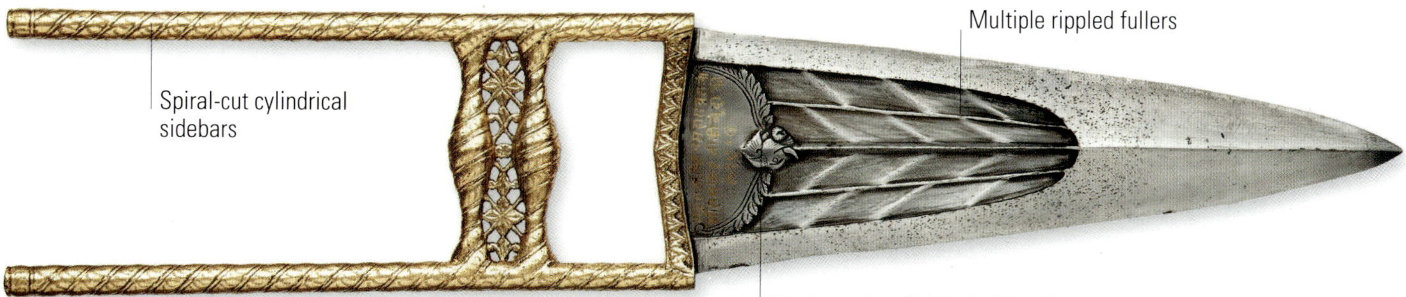

DATE	1849
ORIGIN	INDIAN (RAJASTHANI)
LENGTH	40.4cm (15.9in)

This katar belongs to a distinctive group of katars produced at Bundi in Rajasthan during the 18th and 19th centuries. This example is dated 1907, Vikrama era (AD1849), and belonged to the Maharajah of Bundi. Hand-forged, beautifully finished and with a hilt covered with gold foil, it was exhibited at the Great Exhibition of 1851 in Crystal Palace, London.

Indian katar, mid-19th century

Produced well into an era when such weapons had almost become redundant, this katar is nevertheless of reasonable quality. The hilt is decorated with gold koftgari, and the steel sheath is pierced with a pattern including pairs of confronting parrots within foliage, all of which is enhanced by further gold koftgari decoration. The extremes of both heat and moisture encountered in India would have rendered steel a most unsuitable material for a dagger sheath.

DATE	mid-19th century
ORIGIN	INDIAN
LENGTH	40.5cm (15.9in)

Indian katar with two percussion pistols, 18th to mid-19th century

In order to embrace "modern technology", a good-quality 18th-century Indian katar has been refurbished during the middle of the 19th century. A pair of percussion pistols has been added to the hilt sides, and the whole hilt has been covered with silver-gilt koftgari. The resulting ungainly weapon provides a strange foil for the beautifully carved Mughal iris flowers at the root of the blade.

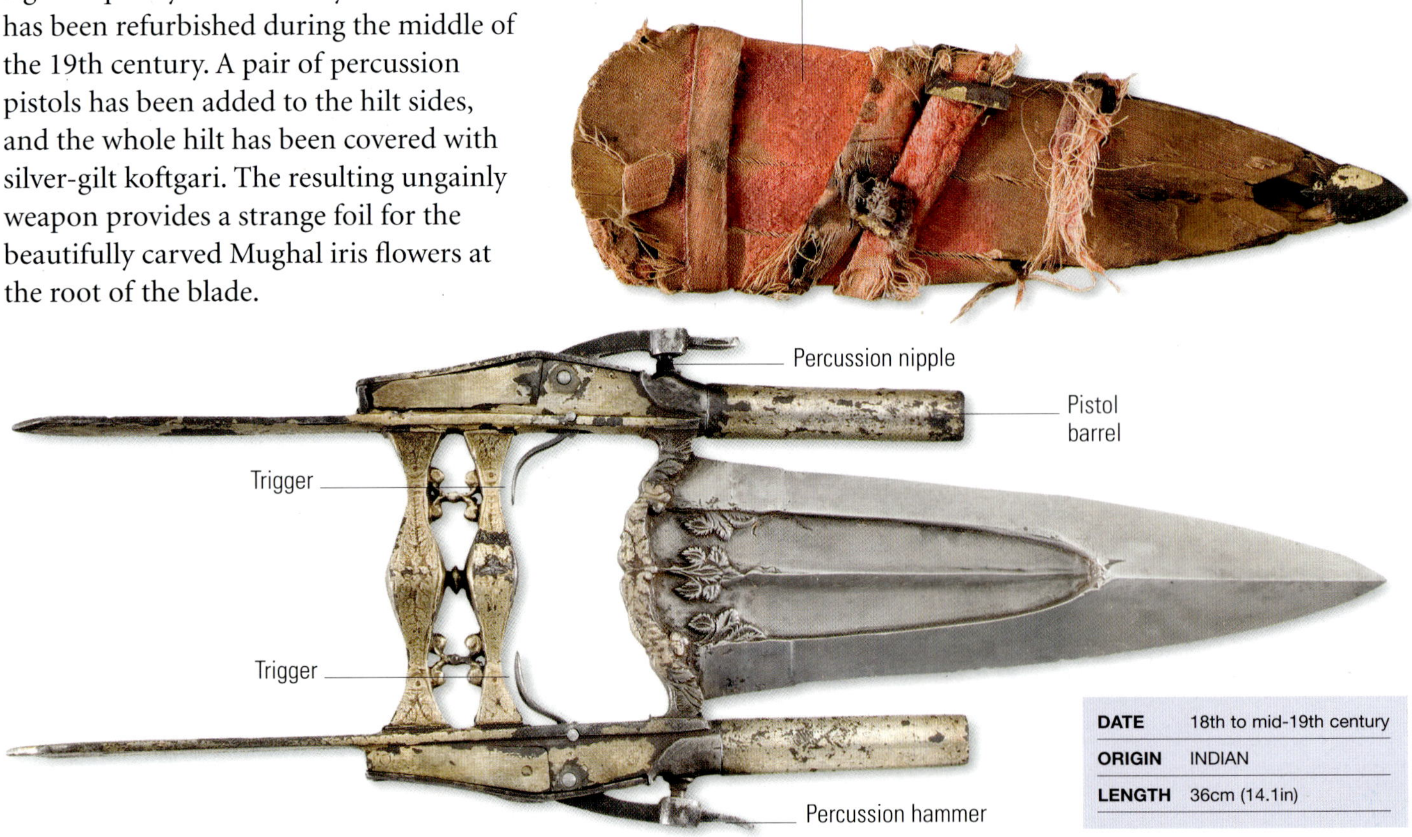

DATE	18th to mid-19th century
ORIGIN	INDIAN
LENGTH	36cm (14.1in)

Indian scissors katar, late 19th century

DATE	late 19th century
ORIGIN	INDIAN
LENGTH	41cm (16.1in)

The scissors katar is mechanical and when the twin handlebars are squeezed tightly, the main hollow blades hinge open to reveal a shorter blade within. These were contrived for a European market, and however impractical, they appealed to the same sentiments as those invoked by Q's special weapons for James Bond.

Indian scissors katar, late 19th century

DATE	late 19th century
ORIGIN	INDIAN
LENGTH	36cm (14.2in)

This is another example of the scissors katar. A very similar example was given to the Prince of Wales during his tour of India in 1875–76 by the Raja of Mandi (in the Punjab). They are normally decorated with silver koftgari and their survival rate in the west, and in Britain in particular, seems to have been quite high.

Indian scissors katar, late 19th century

DATE	late 19th century
ORIGIN	INDIAN
LENGTH	40cm (15.7in)

Evidence that the design is fatally flawed is provided by the fact that the blades cannot be made to open once the katar has been thrust into a body, and if the katar were to be used with the blades in the open position the force on the outer blades would have to be absorbed by the hinge pins at the root of the blades.

Indian chilanums and khanjarlis

The chilanum is an all-steel dagger with a recurved double-edged blade. The blade shape probably developed from the Dravidian horn dagger which was made from a longitudinal section along an animal horn. Examples occur from the early 16th century in Vijayanagara, and were used by Hindus (Marathan) and Muslims (Deccani) alike. The dagger evolves in easily recognizable stages into the khanjarli, whose defining characteristic is the large, lunette-shaped pommel normally made of ivory.

Vijayanagaran chilanum, *c.*1600

This all-steel dagger represents the earliest form of chilanum in this group and the design can be seen in miniature paintings dating from the 16th century. It is made from a single piece of steel, and the grip and pommel button are both lathe-turned. Miniature paintings from the various Indian courts are an invaluable source of information for the student of Indian weapons. Although the artistic conventions result in images quite different from their European counterparts, details have been rendered with astonishing fidelity.

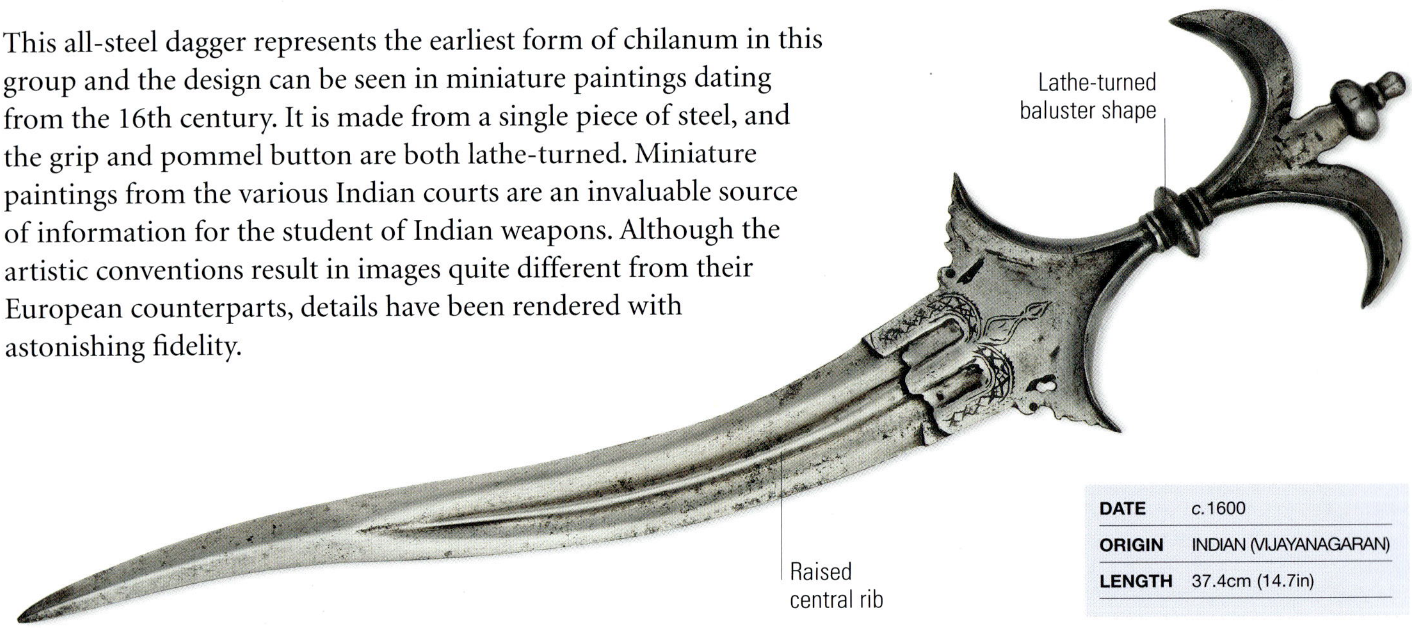

DATE	*c.*1600
ORIGIN	INDIAN (VIJAYANAGARAN)
LENGTH	37.4cm (14.7in)

Deccani chilanum with spiral decoration, early 17th century

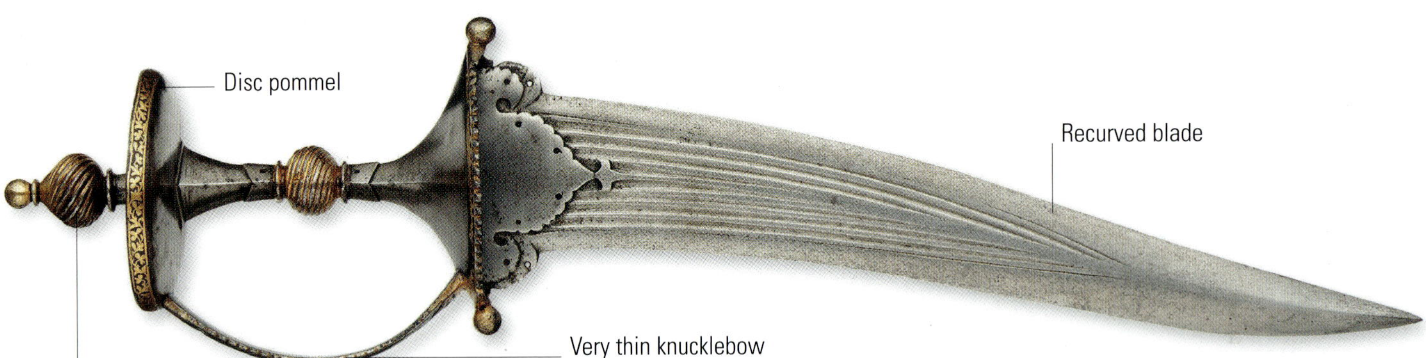

A group of chilanums of identical design made of polished steel exist in Bikaner in Rajasthan. Probably originating in the Deccan, they are distinguished by their circular pommels, whorled buttons, and by their slender knucklebows which appear to be almost an afterthought. This example is unusual in having gold-damascened (koftgari) ornament; those in Bikaner are perfectly plain. It is not certain whether the decoration is contemporary or from a later period.

DATE	early 17th century
ORIGIN	INDIAN (DECCANI)
LENGTH	42cm (16.5in)

Indian Mughal dagger with knucklebow, *c.*1625

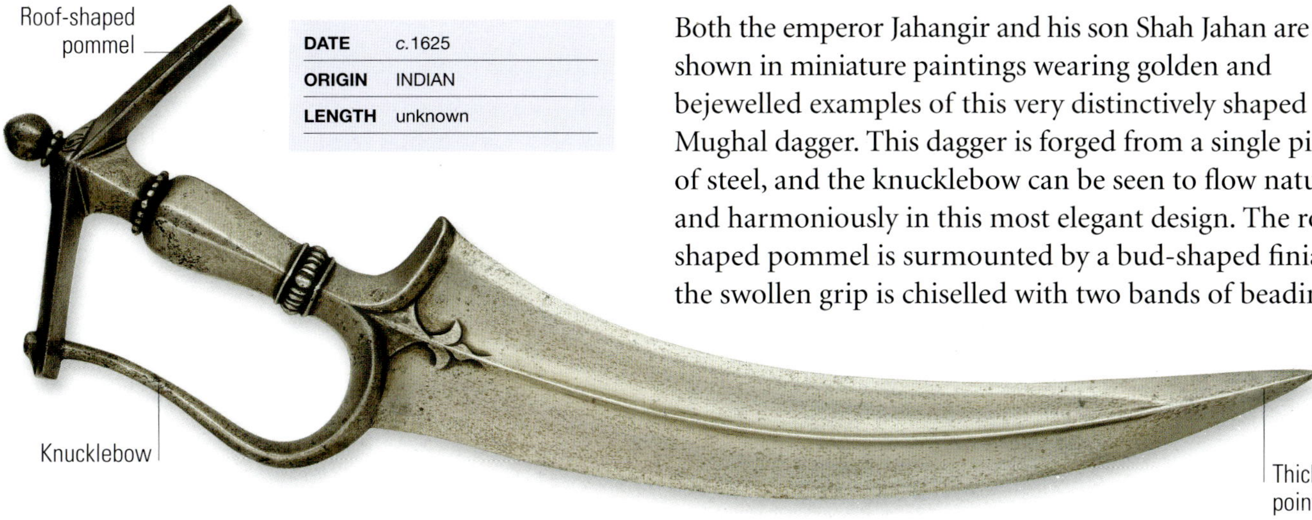

DATE	*c.*1625
ORIGIN	INDIAN
LENGTH	unknown

Both the emperor Jahangir and his son Shah Jahan are shown in miniature paintings wearing golden and bejewelled examples of this very distinctively shaped Mughal dagger. This dagger is forged from a single piece of steel, and the knucklebow can be seen to flow naturally and harmoniously in this most elegant design. The roof-shaped pommel is surmounted by a bud-shaped finial and the swollen grip is chiselled with two bands of beading.

Deccani chilanum, mid-17th century

DATE	mid-17th century
ORIGIN	INDIAN (DECCANI)
LENGTH	39cm (15.4in)

Representing a classic and fully accomplished all-steel chilanum, the hilt of this dagger sits easily on the blade. The multifullered blade is reminiscent of katar blades from the same period. The pierced silhouette at the base of the hilt is a representation of a protective force.

Indian khanjarli, *c.*1700

Traditionally associated with Orissa and the Hindus of Vizianagram, khanjarli daggers probably come from a much wider area. Their defining design feature is the large lunette-shaped ivory pommel, the ivory grips, and the recurved blade which betrays their common ancestry with the chilanum. This example has a slender knucklebow.

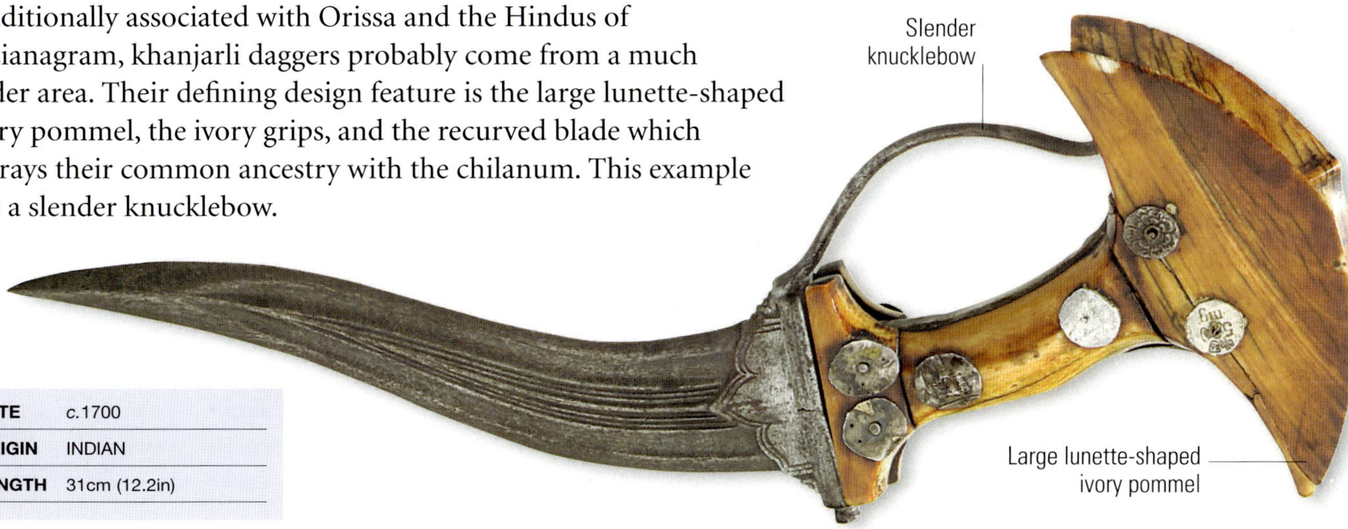

DATE	*c.*1700
ORIGIN	INDIAN
LENGTH	31cm (12.2in)

The Indonesian kris

The pre-eminent Hindu dagger from Indonesia is the kris. Examples from the 14th-century Majepahit Empire are not uncommon, and their lineage probably goes back to the Bronze Age Dong-Son era. The smith would use iron from more than one source, one of which traditionally came from meteoric ore which had a high nickel content. The resulting blade patterns and carved hilts are highly regarded.

Sumatran kris, *c.*1800

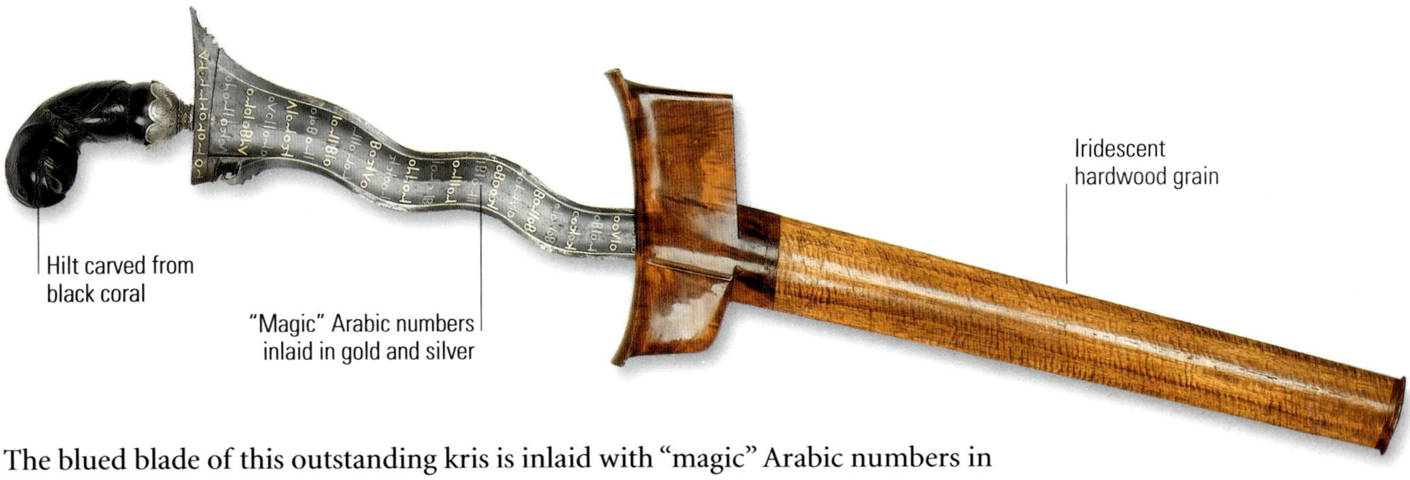

The blued blade of this outstanding kris is inlaid with "magic" Arabic numbers in alternate gold and silver bands. The hilt is carved from black coral in the form of a stylized parrot. The hardwood sheath has an iridescent grain. So heavily is the kris invested with legend that some believed a kris thirsty for blood had the power to leave its sleeping owner, kill someone, clean itself and return to its sheath.

DATE	c.1800
ORIGIN	SUMATRAN
LENGTH	49.5cm (19.5in)

Javanese kris, mid-19th century

The carved wooden hilt of this kris is intended to represent the god Raksha (or Raksasa), who is usually depicted with a long flowing coiffure. He is enveloped in foliage and his presence wards off evil spirits. The *pendok* (metal sheath covering) is made from nickel and chased with foliage. The armorial device engraved on the pendok was most likely introduced into Indonesia by the Dutch colonial power.

DATE	mid-19th century
ORIGIN	JAVANESE
LENGTH	35cm (13.8in)

Malayan kris, mid-19th century

This is a fairly typical Malayan kris, although it has been fitted with a wooden hilt from Sumatra in the form of a stylized Garuda – a divinity that takes the shape of a mighty bird. The silver mounts of Malayan krises have often been made by ethnic Chinese artisans, and these examples are engraved with a design of trailing foliage.

DATE	mid-19th century
ORIGIN	MALAYAN
LENGTH	30.4cm (12in)

Maduran kris, mid-19th century

The ivory hilt of this kris is typical of those carved on the island of Madura. The top of the blade exhibits the *pamor*, or watered pattern, created by the smith who forged iron of differing composition. The silver *pendok* (stem cover) is elaborately embossed with a Bonaspatti mask, the face of a popular Hindu divinity.

DATE	mid-19th century
ORIGIN	MADURAN
LENGTH	41.9cm (16.5in)

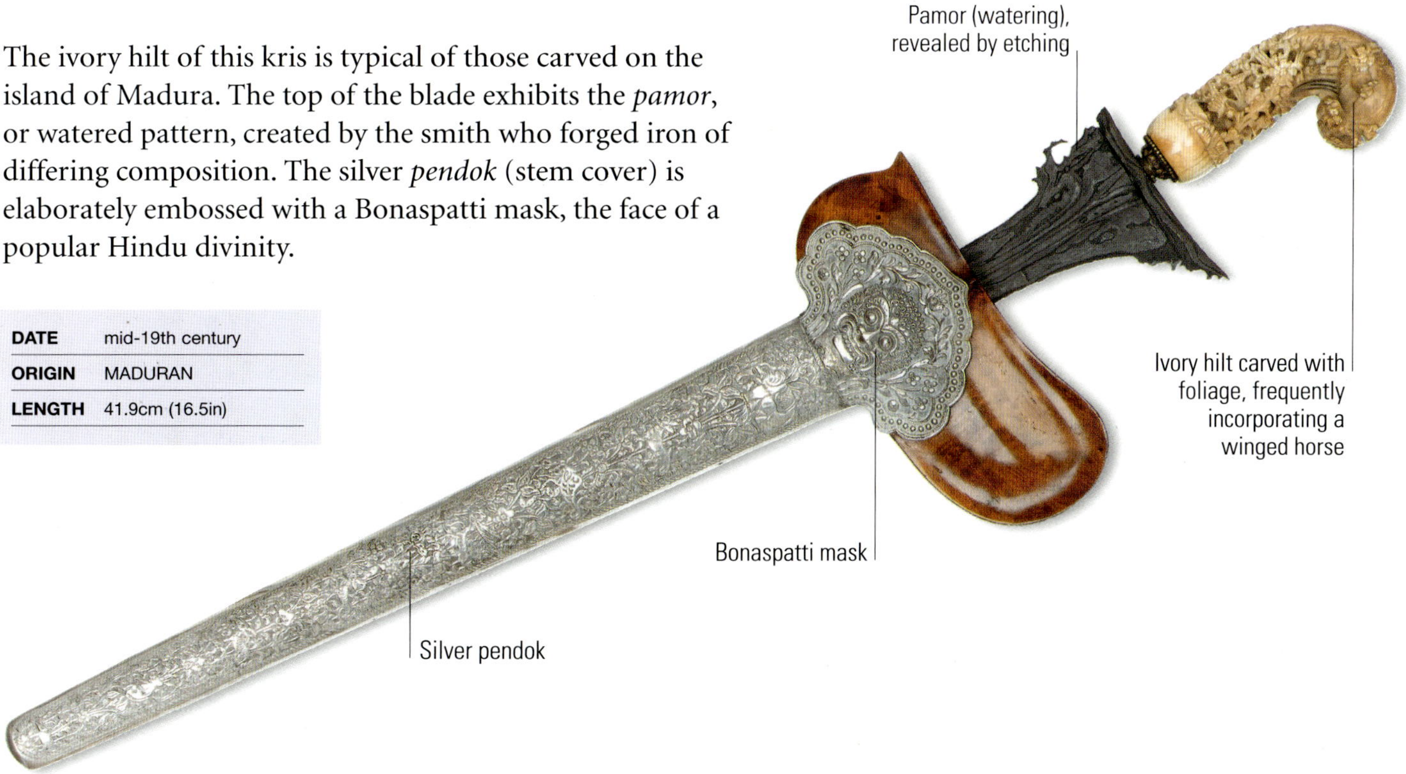

Malayan bade-bade, mid-19th century

The bade-bade is the classic Malayan knife. It has a slightly curved, slender blade sharpened on the inside edge. The hilt is carved from a whale's tooth, the sheath from hard wood and the top from ivory. Although mainly a cutting implement, the bade-bade could be used as a dagger.

DATE	mid-19th century
ORIGIN	MALAYAN
LENGTH	22.8cm (9in)

Malayan kris, mid-19th century

Malaya is rich in exotic timber, and very fine-grained woods have been chosen to manufacture this kris. The blades of such krises are often cleaned with lime juice, which relies on its citric acid content to etch the blade. They are then wiped with sandalwood oil for protection.

DATE	mid-19th century
ORIGIN	MALAYAN
LENGTH	33cm (13in)

Malayan kris, 19th to 20th century

No Malaysian or Indonesian would wish to own a kris that might not be propitious for good health, good fortune, wealth or good luck. Consequently, the *lok* (waves) of the blade are each counted by a would-be purchaser. An odd number is considered auspicious to some, an even number to others. The blade of this Malay kris is 19th-century in origin but the hilt and sheath are 20th-century.

DATE	19th to 20th century
ORIGIN	MALAYAN
LENGTH	unknown

Javanese kris, *c.*1900

This is an example of the classic Javanese kris. The *pamor* (or pattern) of the blade is created by a smith working with two different steels, one of which usually contains nickel. When the blade has been polished, it is covered with an acidic coating (often lime juice) which etches the steels differentially, thus producing the visible colours. The *gambar* (top of the sheath) is carved from an exotic wood with the random patterns of "doreng" grain. The hilt is the classic Yogyakarta (Java) form, possibly the most commonly encountered.

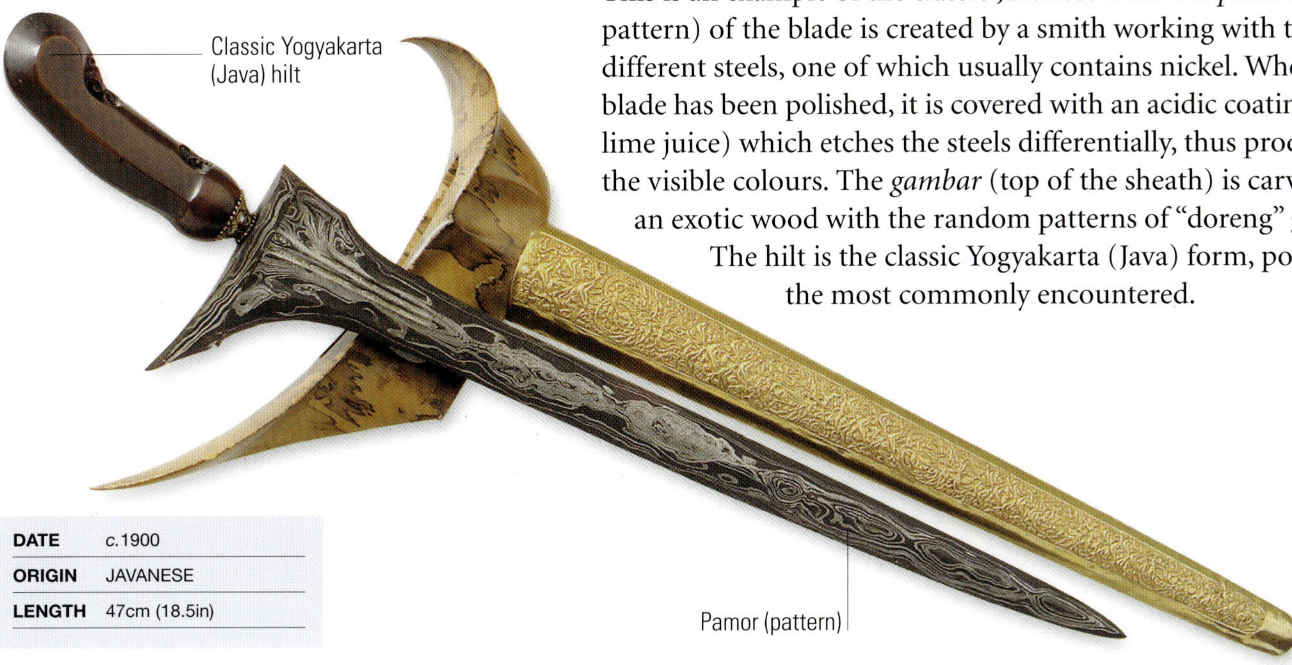

DATE	*c.*1900
ORIGIN	JAVANESE
LENGTH	47cm (18.5in)

The kris stand

Traditionally, the kris was kept on a wooden board, which was often carved and sometimes painted. Only a very few antique sculptural kris stands of the type shown here are known. However, when Bali became popular as a tourist destination in the1960s, a market developed for these extraordinary objects and production was revived. Skilfully carved from a single piece of wood, they are mostly in the form of brightly painted Hindu divinities. Typical figures include Ganesh (the elephant god), Hanuman (the monkey god) and Wayang figures (shadow puppets). Each figure is ostensibly designed for a kris to be held in the hand. The degree of skill used in the manufacture of some of the stands is very great indeed. The krises which the stands support also continue to be made and some are highly sought-after; the most exquisite specimens are very valuable.

RIGHT The stand on the right holds an "executioner's kris". The victim was tied to a chair and the long, slender blade thrust downwards into the heart.

Japanese daggers

The Japanese blade and its fittings represent the highest artistic achievement of the bladesmith anywhere in the world. They are regarded with the same reverence others hold for a great painting and its frame. Blades may be recognized as productions by different schools or individual smiths, and each will vary slightly in detail. Any comprehensive approach requires some understanding of Japanese and the swords and daggers themselves. To fully appreciate a blade's qualities, it must be held in the hand.

Japanese yoroi toshi, *c.*1400

The blade of this yoroi toshi dagger is intended to pierce armour so is quite thin in width, broad across the back edge and almost straight. The tang (*nakago*) is pierced with a hole (*mekugi-ana*) to receive a bamboo peg which secures the hilt. The remains of an earlier such hole shows the blade was originally longer.

DATE	*c.*1400
ORIGIN	JAPANESE
LENGTH	30.6cm (12in)

Japanese aikuchi, 1625 and later

The aikuchi is simply a Japanese dagger mounted without a guard (*tsuba*) to protect the hand. This dagger is almost certainly unique: the blade was made in Solingen (Germany) and is dated 1625. The rest was made later. It has been re-used by a Japanese smith and mounted for the Sanga family who used the *hoshi mon*.

DATE	1625 and later
ORIGIN	JAPANESE
LENGTH	48.7cm (19.2in)

Japanese tanto, late Edo, *c.*1840

The attractive copper-alloy (*shakudo*) mounts of this tanto are decorated in relief with gold and are typical of the late Goto School. Warriors form a perennially favourite motif, and those here are worked in high relief against a granular ground (*nanako*) made with a punch that produces a tiny hemisphere.

DATE	late Edo, *c.*1840
ORIGIN	JAPANESE
LENGTH	39cm (15.3in)

Japanese ken, late Edo, *c.*1850

DATE	late Edo, *c.*1850
ORIGIN	JAPANESE
LENGTH	30.8cm (12.1in)

The straight double-edged sword or dagger is called a ken, and is the weapon carried by some Buddhist divinities. It originated in China from whence the sword (and Buddhism) was introduced into Japan during the 7th and 8th centuries. Consequently many such ken were made for temple presentation.

Japanese tanto, late Edo, *c.*1860

DATE	late Edo, *c.*1860
ORIGIN	JAPANESE
LENGTH	43.3cm (17in)

The hilt (*tsuka*) of this tanto is bound with silk tape, although sometimes string, leather or even baleen was used. The grip is covered with ray skin (*same*) and fitted with two small ornaments (*menuki*) before being bound. The menuki provide a more secure grip. The sheath is fitted with an end mount (*kojiri*) intended to protect the sheath, but in practice it is merely a vehicle for further ornamentation.

Japanese aikuchi, late Edo, *c.*1860

In this example of a Japanese aikuchi, the mounts (*koshirae*) are made from brass (*sentoku*), while the hilt (*tsuka*) and sheath (*saya*) are beautifully lacquered. This particular dagger was made in the second half of the 19th century during the late Edo period. The *kogai* (skewer) was carried in a slot in the scabbard.

DATE	late Edo, *c.*1860
ORIGIN	JAPANESE
LENGTH	33.5cm (13.1in)

Japanese tanto, Meiji, *c.*1870

This blade is contained within a plain wooden hilt and sheath, usually made of magnolia wood, known as a *shirasaya*. It is entirely devoid of any fittings, and even the *habaki* has been replaced by a wooden equivalent made as an integral part of the hilt. The shirasaya is intended to protect the blade and to provide a suitable method of storage; it is not intended to be used. This blade has a carved decoration called *horimono*.

DATE	Meiji, *c.*1870
ORIGIN	JAPANESE
LENGTH	32cm (12.6in)

Japanese tanto, Meiji, blade date 1877

The beautifully lacquered, curved and segmented sheath of this tanto dagger probably betrays the maker's intention to sell it to a foreign (*namban*) buyer. The blade is dated 1877, and although some very fine blades were produced at this time the majority were intended for foreign consumption. The European "aesthetic movement" of the late 19th century was partly informed by Japanese art, and both Europe and the United States evinced a seemingly boundless appetite for Japanese art and artefacts.

DATE	Meiji, blade date 1877
ORIGIN	JAPANESE
LENGTH	41cm (16.1in)

Japanese dagger, early 19th century

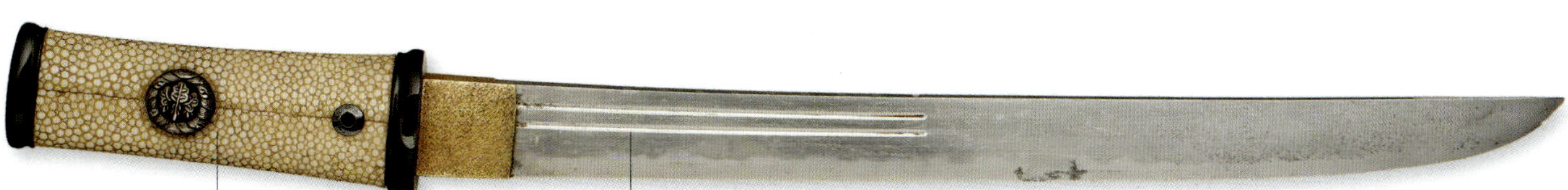

A blade which has been formed with no ridges on either side has a shape called *hira zukuri*. This particular example has been cut with a pair of short shallow grooves called *hi*. The mounting is tasteful and of good quality. The sheath is covered with lacquer which provides a very durable finish; it is made from the ground-up wing cases of various beetles.

DATE	early 19th century
ORIGIN	JAPANESE
LENGTH	43cm (16.9in)

Glossary

Aikuchi Type of Japanese dagger with a handle but no guard.

Antennae dagger Dagger with a pommel that is shaped into a pair of curved arms.

Bagh nakh The Indian "tiger claw". A crossbar pierced for the fingers fits over the knuckles; curved blades are attached and hidden inside the palm.

Ballock (kidney) dagger A medieval form of dagger with a hilt shaped like the male genitalia.

Baluster-turning Method of decorating metalwork, commonly used in the 17th century to decorate stiletto hilts and ricassos.

Baselard Type of dagger or shortsword with a hilt shaped like a capital "I".

Bayonet Dagger or fighting knife designed to be fitted onto the end of a firearm to convert it to a stabbing weapon for close-combat.

Bhuj Indian weapon comprised of a stout, single-edged cutting blade attached to an axe haft. Also called a "gandasa".

Bichwa Short Indian dagger with a long, narrow looped grip to which is attached a narrow undulating blade.

Blarka ngirdi Style of southeast Asian pattern-welding, producing a blade with the distinctive "palm-leaf" design.

Bowie knife Large fighting knife said to have been invented *c.*1827.

Butt The end of the handle of an edged weapon, having no pommel.

Byknife Small utility knife made as a matching companion to a sword or dagger, held in a small sleeve built into the scabbard of the larger weapon.

Chape Metal mount fixed over the tip of a scabbard.

Chilanum Indian dagger with a slightly curved blade and a hilt incorporating a pommel section with broad narrow arms.

Choil Unsharpened, rounded cut-out section of the blade on some knives, separating the sharp edge from the ricasso, or cut into the ricasso itself.

Cinquedea Type of civilian dagger or shortsword popular in Italy during the late 15th and 16th centuries.

Coutiaus a pointe "Stabbing knife" – a medieval term used to describe a narrow, stiff-bladed dagger designed specifically for stabbing with the point.

Coutiaus a tailler "Cutting knife" – a medieval term used to describe a wider bladed dagger, often single-edged.

Cross guard Shaped bar of metal between the blade and the top of the handle, mounted at right angles to them and designed to protect the hand.

Cross-hilt Hilt incorporating a simple cross guard. Also called "cruciform" hilt.

Cultellus Medieval Latin for "dagger".

Damascening The process of inlaying soft metal into a hard metal to produce intricate patterns.

Dirk Word used to refer to various types of dagger. Mostly commonly used in reference to the long dirks carried by the clansmen of the Scottish Highlands.

Dudgeon dagger Late Anglo-Scottish ballock knife of the 17th century, the handle of which was carved from a single piece of box-tree root or "dudgeon".

Ear dagger Form of dagger that probably originated in Spain in the 14th century. Characterized by the two large disks that make up the pommel section.

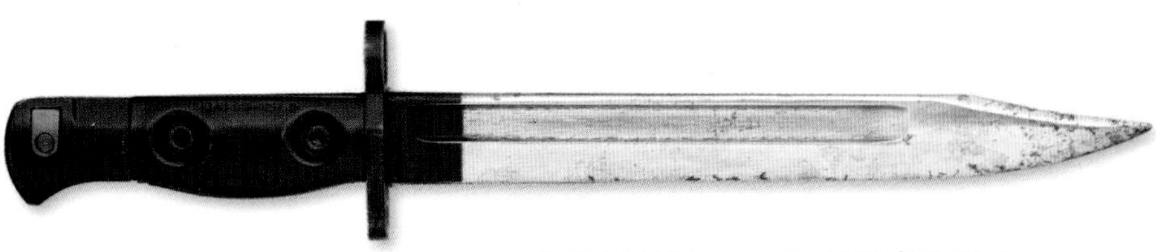

ABOVE British L1A3 bayonet for L1A1 SLR, 1957.

Ersatz bayonet Emergency bayonet, often rudimentary, made to fit a rifle for which it was not originally intended.

Escutcheon Small shield-shaped plate mounted on an object, usually to display the coat of arms or device of the owner.

Falchion Short, and usually curved, wide-bladed cutting sword popular in Europe during the Medieval and Renaissance Periods.

Ferrule A metal ring or short tube that is employed to join two shafts together, or to cover a join.

Fire-gilding A decorative technique for covering iron, steel, copper, silver or bronze with a thin layer of gold.

Foible The upper, weaker half of a sword blade.

Forte The lower, stronger half of a sword blade.

Frog stud A small metal button or knob mounted onto a scabbard for fastening it securely into the "frog", a tab of leather mounted to a belt.

Fuller Groove cut or hammered into a blade to reduce its weight without weakening it.

Ganja The narrow guard of the South-east Asian kris.

Gladius The famous shortsword of the Roman legionary, with a hilt of carved wood and a stout double-edged blade.

Granulation A form of decoration wherein a surface is ornamented with tiny closely-set beads or spheres.

Grip The handle of a weapon, usually made of wood and often covered with textile or leather, or bound with wire.

Guard The hilt structure of bars and/or plates that protects the wearer's hand.

Hilt The area of a dagger, knife or sword that is held in the hand, usually comprising a pommel, a handle and some kind of guard for the hand.

Holbein dagger Type of dagger popular in Germany and Switzerland in the mid-16th century, having a wide double-edged blade and a wooden hilt shaped like a capital letter "I".

Jambiya Arabic for "dagger".

Kard Persian for "knife".

Katana Japanese longsword, larger than the wakizashi (short sword) but smaller than the tachi (two-handed sword).

Katar Form of push dagger common in India. Also called a "jamdhar".

Katzbalger Type of shortsword used by German mercenaries in the 16th century.

Khanjar Arabic for "dagger".

Khanjarli Type of Indian dagger with a strongly recurved blade and a wide half-moon-shaped pommel.

Knucklebow A curved bar on the hilt of some edged weapons that protects the fingers.

Koftgari Indo-Persian term for false or counterfeit damascening.

Knurling Method of decoration involving a series of small beads, knobs, ridges or hatch-marks.

Kogai The Japanese byknife.

Koshi-gatana "Waist-sword", a long Japanese dagger or shortsword with no guard, worn with the *tachi* (two-handed sword).

Kris A distinctive type of Southeast Asian dagger of asymmetrical design, with a pattern-welded, often wavy blade.

Kukri Wide-bladed axe-like knife, the signature weapon of the Gurkha people of Nepal.

Landsknecht dagger A modern term referring to three distinct types of 16th-century European dagger: the "katzbalger" shortsword; a rondel dagger variation with a drooping guard; or an early type of ring-hilted dagger.

Locket Metal mount fitted over the throat of a scabbard to protect it.

Main gauche Mid-17th-century Spanish and southern Italian parrying dagger.

Mokume-gane "Wood-grain metal", a Japanese form of pattern-welding.

Navaja Type of folding fighting knife that originated on the Iberian peninsula in the 18th century.

Parry A defensive movement and the primary function of the parrying dagger.

BELOW Dutch bayonet, Beaumont-Vitali rifle, Model 1871/88, 1888.

Peshkabz Type of Indo-Persian dagger with a straight or recurved blade of T-section.

Pipe-back blade Type of blade found on 18th- and 19th-century military bayonets and swords, where the unsharpened back of the blade is given a rounded or tubular cross-section.

Plug bayonet The earliest form of bayonet – a dagger, usually with a double-edged blade, fitted with a handle that tapers down to a very narrow end.

Pommel A metal weight, often spherical, ovoid, or wheel-shaped, fixed to the end of a sword or dagger to counter-balance the blade.

Pugio Short wide leaf-bladed dagger of the ancient Romans.

Push dagger Dagger having a grip set at a right angle to the blade, so that the weapon is held in the fist with the blade projecting along the line of the arm.

Quillon Post-medieval term referring to one of the arms of the cross guard of a sword or dagger.

Rapier Type of predominantly thrusting sword worn in everyday life in 16th- and 17th-century Europe.

Ricasso The unsharpened area of a blade immediately above the hilt.

Rondel A medieval term denoting any circular plate used to protect a part of the body.

Saw-back blade A blade, the back of which is toothed like a saw though otherwise unsharpened.

Scabbard A sheath, usually made of metal, leather or wood, inside which the blade of an edged weapon is placed.

Scramasax (seax, sax) One of the primary edged weapons used by most north and west Europeans during the Early Medieval Period. Made in a wide range of sizes, from extremely long sword types (*langseax*) to very short ones (*handseax*).

Sgian dubh (skean dhu) Small knife worn with formal Scottish Highland dress from the 19th-century onwards.

Shell guard A small rounded plate of metal incorporated into the guard of some types of sword and dagger to give additional protection to the hand.

Side-ring A small ring of metal mounted on the outside of the cross guard of most 16th- and early 17th-century parrying daggers.

Socket bayonet A bayonet generally with no hilt, just a narrow tube or socket of metal, onto which is attached the narrow, often triangular section blade by means of a short curved arm.

Stiletto (stylet) Small stabbing dagger dating from the end of the 16th century.

Sword bayonet Very long type of bayonet having a sword hilt and wide cutting blade.

Tang Unsharpened end of the blade, over which fits the hilt or handle.

Tang button The end of the tang that is hammered (peened) over the top of the pommel, adding stability and strength. Some tang buttons are screwed into the pommel and attached to the tang.

Tanto Japanese dagger with diamond-sectioned blade.

Telek The northwest African arm dagger. Also called a "gosma".

Trumbash The sickle-knife of the Mangbetu people of the Congo.

Tsuba The guard, usually round or oval and beautifully decorated, of most Japanese daggers and swords.

Volute A spiral or circular motif often found in 16th-century weapons.

Ukiran The carved handle of the kris.

Yataghan Turkish or Eastern European short sword with a recurved blade.

Yoroi doshi Specially-thickened armour-piercing Japanese dagger or tanto.

Further information

BIBLIOGRAPHY

Anglo, Sydney, *The Martial Arts of Renaissance Europe* (Yale, London, 2000).

Annis, P.G.W., *Naval Swords. British and American Naval Edged Weapons 1660–1815* (Arms and Armour Press, London, 1970).

Blair, Claude, *European and American Arms* (Batsford, London, 1962).

Burton, Richard F., *The Book of the Sword* (Chatto and Windus, London, 1884).

Castle, Egerton, *Schools and Masters of Fence, from the Middle Ages to the End of the Eighteenth Century* (G. Bell, London, 1910).

Coe, Michael D.; Connolly, Peter; Harding, Anthony; Harris and others, *Swords and Hilt Weapons* (Multimedia Books Ltd., London, 1989).

Dolinek, Vladimir and Durdik, Jan, *The Encyclopedia of European Historical Weapons* (Hamlyn, London, 1993).

Elgood, Robert, *Hindu Weapons and Ritual: Arms and Armour from India 1400–1865* (Eburon, Delft, 2005).

Elgood, Robert ed., *Islamic Arms and Armour* (Scolar, London, 1979).

Evangelista, Nick, *The Encyclopedia of the Sword* (Greenwood Press, London, 1995).

Foulkes, Charles and Hopkinson, E. C., *Sword, Lance and Bayonet* (Arms and Armour Press, London, 1967).

Frey, Edward, *The Kris: Mystical Weapon of the Malay World (Images of Asia)* (Oxford University Press, New York, Dec 1989).

Gardner, G.B., *Keris and Other Malay Weapons* (Progressive Publishing, Singapore, 1936).

Gilkerson, William, *Boarders Away: With Steel-Edged Weapons and Polearms 1626–1826* (Andrew Mowbray Publishers, Lincoln RI, 1991).

Gyngell, D.S.H., *Armourer's Marks* (Cambridge University Press, New York, 1963).

Hayward, J.F., *Swords and Daggers* (H.M.S.O., London, 1964).

Holmes, Richard ed., *Weapon: A Visual History of Arms and Armour* (Dorling Kindersley, London, 2008).

Johnson, Thomas M., and Bradach, Wilfrid, *Third Reich Edged Weapons Accouterments* (Johnson Reference Book, Fredericksburg, 1978).

Kulinsky, A.N., *European Edged Weapons* (Atlant, St Petersburg, 2003).

Neumann, George C., *Swords and Blades of the American Revolution* (Rebel Publishing Co., Inc., Texarkana TX, 1991).

Oakeshott, R. Ewart, *European Weapons and Armour* (Lutterworth, London, 1980).

Peterson, Harold L., *American Knives: The First History and Collector's Guide* (Charles Scribner, New York, 1958).

Peterson, Harold Leslie, *Daggers and Fighting Knives of the Western World* (Dover, Mineola, 1968).

Reid, William, *Arms Through the Ages* (Harper & Row, London, 1976).

Robinson, H. Russell, *Japanese Arms and Armour* (Crown, New York, 1969).

Stone, George Cameron, *A Glossary of the Construction, Decoration and Use of Arms and Armor in all Countries and in all Times* (Southworth Press, Portland, 1961).

Thompson, Leroy, *Commando Dagger: The Complete Illustrated History of the Fairbairn-Sykes Fighting Knife* (Paladin Press, Boulder, 1985).

Thompson, Logan, *Daggers and Bayonets* (Paladin Press, Boulder, 1999).

Tirri, Anthony C., *Islamic Weapons, Maghrib to Moghul* (Indigo, USA, 2003).

Turnbull, Stephen, *Samurai – The World of the Warrior* (Osprey, London, 2006).

Van Zonneveld, Albert G., *Traditional Weapons of the Indonesian Archipelago* (C. Zwartenkot, Amsterdam, 2002).

Various authors, *Swords and Hilt Weapons* (Weidenfield and Nicolson, London, 1989).

Veleanu, Mircea, *Antique Swords and Daggers* (Schiffer Publishing, 2007).

Wagner, Eduard, *Cut and Thrust Weapons* (Spring Books, London, 1967).

Wallace, John, *Scottish Swords and Dirks, An Illustrated Reference Guide to Scottish Edged Weapons* (Arms and Armour Press, London, 1970).

Wilkinson, Frederick, *Swords and Daggers, An Illustrated Reference Guide for Collectors* (Arms and Armour Press, London, 1985).

Wilkinson, Frederick, *Swords and Daggers* (Ward Lock and Co., Ltd, London,1967).

Wilkinson-Latham, John, *British Cut and Thrust Weapons* (David and Charles Publishers, Newton Abbott, 1971).

Wilkinson-Latham, R.J., *Pictorial History of Swords and Bayonets* (Ian Allan, London, 1973).

Withers, Harvey, *British Military Swords 1786–1912. The Regulation Patterns. An Illustrated Price Guide for Collectors* (Studio Jupiter Military Publishing, Sutton Coldfield, 2003).

Withers, Harvey, *World Swords 1400–1945. An Illustrated Price Guide for Collectors* (Studio Jupiter Military Publishing, Sutton Coldfield, 2006).

ABOVE South Italian main-gauche dagger, *c.*1650.

MUSEUMS LIST

UNITED KINGDOM

The British Museum
Great Russell Street
London
WC1B 3DG
www.britishmuseum.co.uk

ABOVE British bayonet for Jacob's double-barrelled rifle, *c.*1859.

The Royal Armouries, Leeds
Armouries Drive, Leeds
West Yorkshire
LS10 1LT
www.royalarmouries.org

National Army Museum
Royal Hospital Road
Chelsea, London
SW3 4HT
www.nam.ac.uk

The Wallace Collection
Hertford House
Manchester Square
London W1U 3BN
www.wallacecollection.org

National Museum of Scotland
Chambers Street
Edinburgh, EH1 1JF
www.nms.ac.uk

National War Museum
Edinburgh Castle
EH1 2NG
www.nms.ac.uk

Victoria and Albert Museum
Cromwell Road
London
SW7 2RL
www.vam.ac.uk

Windsor Castle
Berkshire
SL4 1NJ
www.royalcollection.org.uk

Fitzwilliam Museum
Trumpington Street
Cambridge
CB2 1RB
www.fitzmuseum.cam.ac.uk

AUSTRIA
Historisches Museum der Stadt, Vienna
Wien Museum Karlsplatz
1040 Vienna, Karlsplatz 8
www.wienmuseum.at

Landeszenghaus, Graz
Abteilung Landeszeughaus
Herrengassse16
A-8010, Graz
www.museum-joanneum.at

Waffensammlung, Vienna
A-1010 Wien
Maria Theresien-Platz
www.khm.at

BELGIUM
Porte de Hal, Brussels
Boulevard du Midi 150
1060 Saint-Gilles
www.kmkg-mrah.be

DENMARK
Tojhusmet, Copenhagen
Tøjhusgade 3
1220 København
www.thm.dk

FRANCE
Musée de l'Armée, Paris
Hôtel National des Invalides
129 Rue de Grenelle
75007 Paris
www.invalides.org

Musée du Louvre, Paris
34, Rue du Louvre
75001 Paris
www.louvre.fr

FINLAND
National Museum of Finland
Mannerheimintie 34
00100 Helsinki
www.nba.fi/en/nmf

GERMANY
Historisches Museum, Dresden
Zwinger, Semperbau
D-01067 Dresden
www.skd.museum

Museum für Deutsche Geschicte, Berlin
Unter den Linden 2
10117, Berlin
www.dhm.de

Württembergisches Landesmuseum
Schiller Platz 6
70173, Stuttgart
www.landesmuseum-stuttgart.de

ITALY
Museo Nazionale, Florence
Via della Ninna 5
50122, Firenze
www.polomuseale.firenze.it

Stibbert Collection, Florence
Via Frederick Stibbert 26
50134, Firenze
www.museostibbert.it

NETHERLANDS
Dutch Army Museum
Korte Geer 1
Delft
www.legermuseum.nl

NORWAY
Universitetets Oldsaksamling
Frederiks Gate 2
Oslo 0164
www.ukm.uio.no

POLAND
Wawel Armoury, Cracow
31-001 Kraków
Wawel 5
wawel.krakow.pl

SPAIN
Armoury, Palacio Réal de Madrid, Madrid
Calle Bailén
28071 Madrid
www.patrimonionacional.es

SWEDEN
Statens Historiska Museum
Narvavägen 13–17
114 84 Stockholm
www.historiska.se

SWITZERLAND
Historischemuseum, Basel
Steinenberg 4
CH–4051 Basel
www.hmb.ch

Schweizerisches Landesmuseum
Museumstrasse 2
8021 Zurich
www.musee-suisse.ch

UNITED STATES
Metropolitan Museum of Art
1000 Fifth Avenue
New York, NY
10028-0198
www.metmuseum.org

Smithsonian Institution
Several locations at
PO Box 37012
SI Building Room 153
MRC 010
Washington, D.C.
20013-7012
www.si.edu

Allentown Art Museum
31 N. 5th Street
Allentown
PA 18101
www.allentownartmuseum.org

Brooklyn Museum
200 Eastern Parkway
Brooklyn
New York, NY
11238-6052
www.brooklynmuseum.org

Cleveland Museum of Art
11150 East Boulevard
Cleveland
OH 44106
www.clevelandart.org

Worcester Art Museum
55 Salisbury Street
Worcester
MA 01609
www.worcesterart.org

RUSSIA
Hermitage Museum
34 Dvortsovaya
Naberezhnaya
St Petersburg
190000
www.hermitagemuseum.org

Index

ABOVE 17th-century Indian khanjar with decorated blade and Mughal hilt.

ABOVE Czech VZ/24 knife bayonet, *c.*1926.

BELOW Japanese aikuchi dagger. The blade is dated 1625, the rest was made later.

Picture credits

The publisher would like to thank the following for kindly supplying photos for this book: AKG: 7t, 12l, r, 15t, 17t, 18t, 19t, 20t, 21bl, 22tl, 23t, b, 24bl, 31tr, 32r, l, 33tr, 36b, 38r, 39br, 40t, 41b, 53br, t, 54br, 55tr, 57t, 60t, 62tr, 63t, 64b, 73t, 79br, 81tr, 90bl, tr, 93t, b, , 96tl, 97b, 116b, m, 117t, 146b, 173b; Alamy: 11br, 30b, 39t, 14t, 69t, 80tl, 85tr; Ancient Art & Architecture: 19b; Barrett, Jonathan: 113ml, mr; Berman Museum of World History, Alabama: 77b, 8mt, 57b, 59m, 65b, 69b, 102br, 103tr, 105bmr, 119t, 150m, 152b, 158b, 162mb, mt, 164b, t, 165b, t, 166bb, bt, 167m, t, 170m, 188t, 190m, 195t, 196m, t, 201m, 202b, 203t, 213t, 225t, 234m, 244b, 245br; Bridgeman Art Library: 6b, 13tr, b, 14b, 15b, 16t, 18b, 21t, 22tr, 26b, 29bl, 30mt, 34b, 35tr, 38l, 42b, 43t, 47t, 51ml, 59b, 61br, 67br, 72bl, 74tr, 80br, 87tr, 88b, 105tm, 115t, 116t, 117b, m, 118t, 120t, m, b, 121t, 124b, 127b, 143b, 155b, 217b; Bruun-rasmussen: 11tl Corbis: 58tl, tr, 65t, 71t, 79tr, 92t, 119b, 167b, 200b; Ernest, PJ: 98t, 208b; Furrer, Richard 98b; Getty Images: 68b, 70b, 187b; Hermann Historica Auctioneers, Munich: 7b, 10t, 21br, 22b, 25b, 33bb, 35b, 42mr, 43b, 46t, 50b, 51r, 56t, 81bl, 83t, mt, 85b, 86b, 87 m, tb, bb, 89tr, 89bl, 91tl, tm, 92br, 94t, 95br, 96bm, 105mlt, mrt, tl, 106b, m, 107b, 109m, t, 111bb, bt, tl, tr, 115b, m, 118m, 121m, 122t, 131m, 132b, t, 134b, 135b, m, 136t, 139mt, tt, 148m, 149m, 157b, m, 162b, t, 163m, t, 165m, 182b, m, 183m, 192t, 193m, 211b, 214b, m, 215b, m, t, 216b, t, 217t, 218b, 219b, 220b, 221t, b, 222b, t, 223b, t, 225b, mb, 226b, t, 227mb, t, 228b, m, 229b, mt, t, 230m, t, 231mt, t, 232t, 236b, t, 237m, t, 238b, t, 239b, m, 241b, 245t, 246b, 247b, 248b, t, 249t; Kenney, DX: 121b; photos.com: 45tr; Picture Desk: 75tl, Stephens, Frederick: 199t, 201t, b; Royal Athena Galleries: 111mb, mt, 114b, m, t, 118b; Topfoto: 10bb, tb, 15mr, 16b, 20b, 24t, 27r, 37b, 48b, 49bl, 66t, 73br, 76b, 77t, 78tt, mt, 82tl, 95t; Wallis and Wallis Auction Gallery: 74bl, 75tr, 103tl, 112tb, tt, 151m, t, 152m, 153b, m, t, 154b, m, t, 155t, 182tt, 183b, t, 185bb, 210b, m, t, 211t, 242b, t, 243b, t, 244m, t, 245 bl; Werner Forman Picture Library: 46b. All other images from the Royal Armouries, Leeds in England. All artwork by Peters & Zabransky Ltd.

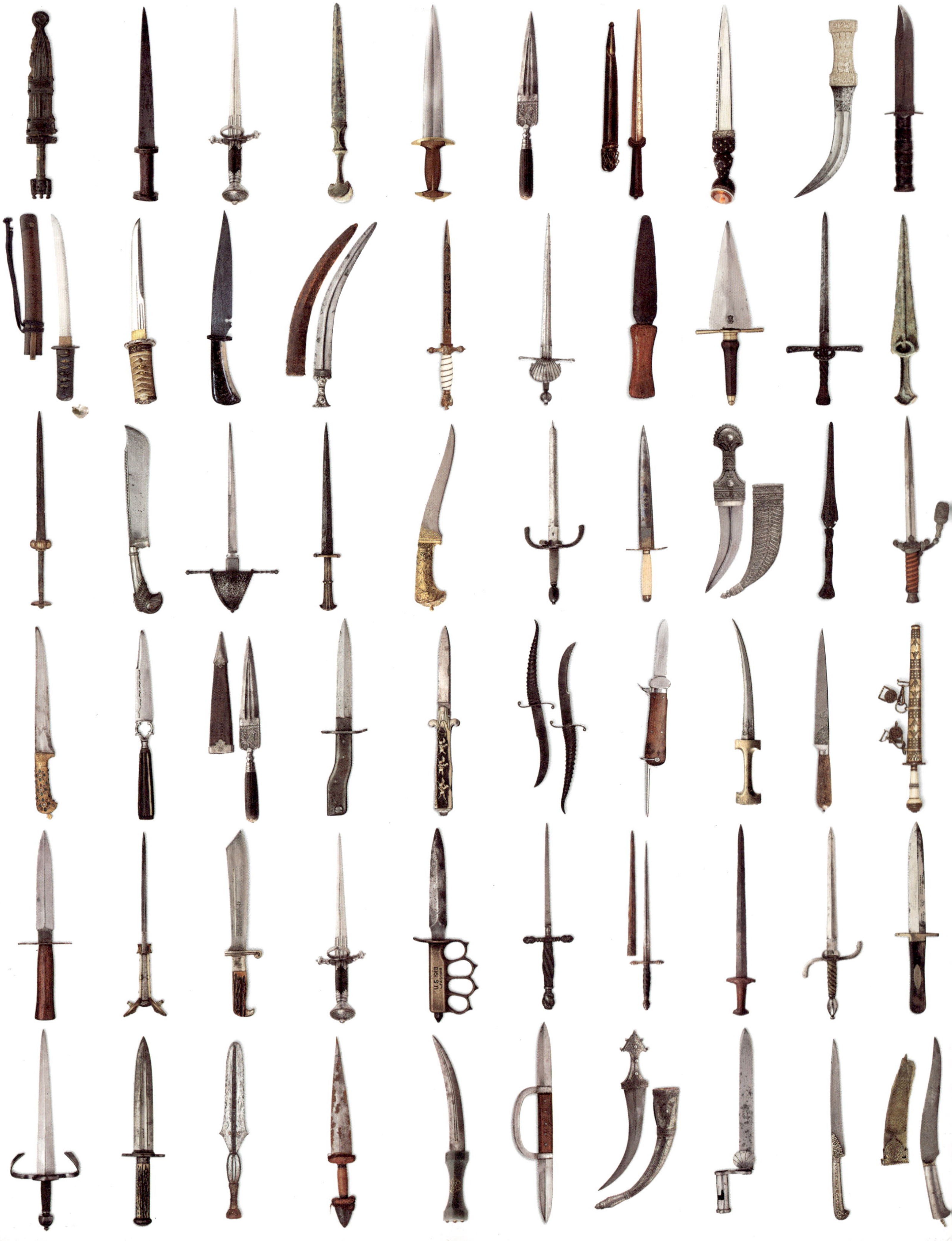
U.S. 1918
L.F.&C-1918

BRILLIANT!

ALAN C. McLEAN

HEINEMANN NEW WAVE READERS

Football! Tony Brill loves it. He plays football for Hampton Juniors every week. He's a good player and he scores lots of goals.

His favourite football team is United. His favourite football player is Steve Rice, the United striker. Tony's got a poster of Steve Rice on his wall.

He's got a video of Steve Rice's greatest goals. He watches it almost every day. Every time Tony watches it, he says 'Brilliant!'

'Brilliant!' is Tony's nickname. That's what the other players in the team call him. Tony scores a goal and they all shout, 'Brilliant, Tony!'

One Sunday Tony is playing for Hampton Juniors. A man in a black raincoat is standing on the touchline. He's writing in a little book.

Tony plays well and scores two goals. After the game, the man in the black raincoat comes up to him. 'My name is Frank Waters,' he says. 'Do you want to play for United?'

'United?' says Tony. 'Oh yes! United are my favourite team.'

'Then come to the United ground next Wednesday. Come and play in a trial match.'

Tony plays well in the trial. He meets the United Manager. Tony signs for United. He can't believe it. He's a United player at last!

At last Tony meets Steve Rice. Steve smiles and shakes Tony's hand. 'Welcome to United, kid,' he says.

Tony wants to be a better player. Steve helps him. He shows him how to head, how to shoot, and how to beat players.

‘Have you got a nickname, kid?’ Steve asks.

‘The other boys at Hampton Juniors call me “Brilliant”. My name’s Brill, you see.’

Steve laughs. ‘Okay,’ he says. ‘We can call you “Brilliant” too.’

After a year with United, Tony is playing in the second team. He plays well and scores a lot of goals.

Steve plays in United’s first team. He’s their top goalscorer.

It is May 15th. United are playing a very important game. They are playing Atletico in the Europa Cup. Atletico are a good team. They score one goal, then they score another. With five minutes left, the score is Atletico 2, United 0.

Then Steve Rice gets the ball. He beats two men and shoots. It's a goal!

'Great goal, Steve,' says Tony.

'2-1 isn't a bad score away from home,'says Steve. 'We can beat them next week at home. We only need one goal.'

The day before the second game, Tony sees a newspaper headline: UNITED STAR IN CAR CRASH. It's Steve. He's injured and he can't play again this year!

The phone rings. It's Frank Waters. 'You're playing against Atletico tomorrow, Tony,' he says.

Tony is afraid. 'I can't play. I'm not good enough. I'm not ready to take Steve's place.'

'Why don't you talk to Steve?' says Frank. 'He wants you to play.'

'Come on, Brilliant,' says Steve. 'This is your big chance.'

'I can't, Steve. I'm not good enough to play in the Europa Cup.'

'Rubbish. Of course you're good enough. But watch Moreno. He's going to mark you. He's a good player, but you can beat him. Look. This is how to do it...'

'The score is 0 - 0 here. United only need one goal to win tonight. But Atletico are defending well.
'The ball comes to young Tony Brill. But Moreno beats him. Moreno is playing really well tonight. Brill's nickname is "Brilliant", but he's not brilliant tonight.
MAY 22nd, ENGLAND

'Only two minutes left now. Still United can't score a goal. And once again the ball comes to Tony Brill.
'Moreno is with him, but this time Brill turns inside and beats him. He beats another man and shoots. Goal! A brilliant goal. It's 1-0 to United!'

The game finishes. The United fans are cheering. They shout Tony's nickname: BRILL-IANT! BRILL-IANT!

'Well done, Tony,' says Frank. 'Great goal! You're a real United player now.'

Tony is excited. He is very happy. But then he remembers Steve in hospital. How does he feel? What is he thinking?

Frank gives Tony a piece of paper. 'This is for you,' he says. 'It's from Steve. Read it.'

There are only two words on the piece of paper: BRILLIANT, TONY!

Heinemann English Language Teaching
A division of Heinemann Publishers (Oxford) Ltd
Halley Court, Jordan Hill, Oxford, OX2 8EJ

OXFORD MADRID ATHENS
PARIS FLORENCE PRAGUE SÃO PAULO CHICAGO
MELBOURNE AUCKLAND SINGAPORE TOKYO
GABORONE JOHANNESBURG PORTSMOUTH (NH)
IBADAN

ISBN 0 435 27702 2

This reader is also available on cassette
ISBN 0 435 27832 0

First published 1991

Designed by Threefold Design
Illustrations by Kevin Faerber

Typeset by Threefold Design
Printed and bound in Spain by Printeksa

Heinemann New Wave Readers
Series Editor: Alan C. McLean
Level 1

Star Picture *by John Escott*
The Bookshop Trick *by John Escott*
Brilliant! *by Alan C.McLean*
Fire! *by Karen E. Spiller*

94 95 96 10 9 8 7 6 5 4 3